STEPHEN LIVES!

STEPHEN LIVES!

His Life, Suicide, and Afterlife

Anne Puryear

New Paradigm Press
Scottsdale, Arizona

TO HERB
The love of my life-
times

Stephen Lives!
published by New Paradigm Press
Scottsdale, AZ

APRIL 1993

Cover design by Richard Firmage, Salt Lake City, Utah
Composition by Pat Merrill, Scottsdale, Arizona
Manufactured in the United States of America

Library of Congress Cataloging-in-Publication Data

Puryear, Anne. 1938 –
  p. cm.
"April 1993."
Includes bibliographical references.
ISBN 0–9634964–3–3 : $14.95
Stephen lives! / [Anne Puryear].
  1. Dennis, Stephen Christopher, 1958-1974 (Spirit) 2. Dennis, Stephen Chris-
topher, 1958-1974. 3. Puryear, Anne, 1938–   . 4. Suicide victims—United
States—Biography. 5. Mothers—United States—Biography.   6. Teenagers—
United States—Suicidal behavior—Case studies. 7. Spirit writings. I. Title.
BF1311.D43P87 1993
133.9'01'3—dc20   93–10232
                                                             CIP

DEDICATION

To:

My husband, Herb . . .
Your love has been a gift above all treasures.
I love you, sweetheart.

My children, Bob, Andrea, and Deborah . . .
I am grateful to God for letting me be your mother.
"I'll love you forever, I'll like you for always."

My grandchildren, Melissa, Robbie, Vanessa, and Krystalyn . . .
I love being your grandmother. I adore each of you.

My mother . . .
In whom I am well pleased. You have been
the very best mother for me. I love you.

My beloved son, Stephen . . .
You graced my life with love for fifteen years. You are
as special and dear to me in spirit as you were in life.

And . . .
To all the young lives cut short by suicide
because of pain none of you knew how to cope with.

ACKNOWLEDGMENTS

It would take another book to fully acknowledge my appreciation to all the people in my lifetime who have helped me in my growth and understanding.

My husband Herb is the author of many successful books of his own, including his latest book *Why Jesus Taught Reincarnation*. He is the most brilliant man I have ever met and is a delight to live with because of his good-nature and great sense of humor. He has encouraged, praised, and helped me, never faltering in his belief in me and my work. He is my dearest love and soul mate.

My children, Bob, my special first-born, Andrea, my dearest first daughter, and Deborah, my precious youngest, make this journey that has sometimes been uphill, worthwhile. I am proud of them for the fine and loving souls they have become.

Mother welcomed my birth singing, "Joy to the world, my daughter's come. . . ." This was the kind of love and adoration lavished on me all the days of my life. For that foundation of unconditional love, and for protecting me from having my spirit broken, I am forever thankful.

My sister Alwayne, an outstanding professional artist, painted a portrait of Stephen that lifts my spirit each time I walk into my office. Her understanding and tenderness toward me have been what being a sister is all about.

My brother Dean, who is a really nice person, somehow survived childhood with me and deserves great credit for the restraint he used in not pulverizing me as I so deserved.

My father joined Stephen in the spirit plane several years ago. He was kind and caring and loved us. Thank you, Daddy.

Reverend Dennis Linehan is not only our Administrative Director, but a once-in-a-lifetime friend to me. He has made it possible for Herb and me to get books written and published within months of each other. Without his help and support, it would have been impossible. No one works harder, with more caring and a better spirit. His "past life" playfulness and helpfulness is a delight. I love you, Dennis.

Elizabeth Linehan, a pharmacist and Dennis's better half, does the best presentations on the Edgar Cayce formulas I've ever heard. She deserves equal credit for enabling Dennis to do the work he loves. Bless you, Elizabeth.

Reverend Bill Roberts is not only a dear friend, but one of the funniest men I have ever known. Despite his busy schedule, he helped edit and proofread my manuscript, night after night, making invaluable suggestions and corrections. He has been there when I most needed an understanding friend. He also tries to keep us organized, which is no small task. He heals us all with his humor. I love you, Bill.

Virginia Ryder is my soul sister and treasured friend. She loaned or shared her condo on Oahu, Hawaii with us for a month every summer for almost ten years, so we could write and play. She has listened to, fussed at, encouraged, loved, and supported me as only a true friend would. I am blessed to have her in my life. She knows how much I love and appreciate her.

Dear, dear Peg Linehan, who thought she "retired" to Arizona, has been a lifesaver for us and for Logos. Bright and well-organized like her son Dennis, she has brought order to the chaos of our lives and offices. What did we ever do without her? You are a jewel, and I love you, Peg.

Don Wilson, Director of the Logos New York and Connecticut Group, Delta Captain, friend and fellow seeker has aided and encouraged us every step of the way. He has walked the pathway with us many times. I gratefully acknowledge his incredible spirit, his goodness, and all he has done to take this work forward.

John and Stephanie Schroeder moved to Phoenix to work with us, then moved back to California to work with us. You two are wonderful! (Oops—you *four*. I forgot Sylvia and Murray!) Who could ask for better friends and more dedication and love. The world is truly a better place because of friends like you.

Helen Mae Alexander Dimit gave us our start. She loved me and believed in me. Her book on angels touched so many of our lives, and she now rests in their everlasting arms.

Joanne enabled us to have a place to teach and work and we are grateful to her. Darlene and Cindy have been dear friends who helped make our work and our lives so much easier and more fun by their caring and support. Pat Harrison, in acts of faith and friendship enabled a work to be done that otherwise might not have had an opportunity to touch the lives of so many people.

Ray and Lou Dunn Diekemper, helped us from the beginning and are lights in Lubbock, Texas, with all their good work and Lou's "Odyssey Bookstore." David Stipes, my buddy, shares from his heart and listens from his heart. Ed Drach has been a very helpful and loving friend to us. Daphne Starr Bush of Starbright Travel, our friend and travel agent, does an incredible job handling our complicated travel arrangements and has organized and journeyed with us on eight Logos tours out of the country. Pat Hughes has been a wonderful help and good friend to us. Pat Suemoto, who directs the Logos Group on Oahu, Hawaii, is an angel, as is her sister Susan O'Hata.

Bob McIver was our dedicated and hard-working first staff member and is the reason we survived. Lucy Getgen Wornson helped us every step of the way and has been a good friend. We appreciate the hard work that two wonderful souls, Elizabeth and Joe Chevola, did to get us started. Marcia and Don Harrison are two very caring people. They know what their friendship and help has meant to us. Dr. Bill Risley is an excellent chiropracter, healer, and friend. Kelsey Sears makes our trips to Hawaii delightful with her enthusiasm and loving spirit. Dr. Terri Baltes does the same with her healing adjustments and loving care of us. Cec and Al Storer helped us get a roof over our heads and under that roof our work began.

I am thankful for the loving help and support of so many people. I acknowledge and thank each of the following: John Story, Brad Roberts, Richard Gerber, M.D., Bill and Jean Tiller, Connie Weber, Jeff Kirpach, John Walsh, Chrystal and Richard Otto, Harry and Dorothy Calkin, Bill Puryear, Betsy Haggerty, Kay Gee, Marie Kleyn, Col. Rich Cronquist, Susan and Bob Moffitt, Lois Monarrez, Gerry Bonheimer, Mary Best, John Bomhardt, June Berrington, Debby and Roger Cason, Cynthia Griffiths, Jo-Anne van der Vat-Chromy, Manec von der Lugt, Diane Ladd, Dorothy Drew, Grace White, Margann Gallwas, Dr. Hollis King, Tootsie Lyman, Frank and Audre Tribbe, Dean Marshall, Dr. Marilyn McGirr, Angelo Roca, Grace Fogg, Jaine Smith, Karina Singer, Fran & RL Day, Betsy Haggerty, Arlene Haven, Jeanne and Lloyd Marlowe, Joseph Gilmour, Dennis Gilmour, Regina Marshall, Jo Addah Watson, Patricia Mindorff, Patricia Perkins, and Dr. Tom Librande.

To our staff at Logos and the dedicated co-workers, volunteers, supporters, and friends, near and far, who make it all possible. Words cannot express my appreciation and love for your friendship, support, and caring. Stars belong in the crowns of all of you. I could mention hundreds of you by name and extoll your virtues for pages. You know who you are—put your name here, or I will: _____. Thank you and bless you.

Ruth Montgomery's book, *Search For The Truth,* woke me from a deep sleep and forever changed the course of my life. I treasure her friendship and I thank her for the courage to be a true herald for this new age. She has been a beacon in the dark for thousands of us.

Tony Robbins's *Personal Power* audio tapes, videos, and seminar were the most empowering and helpful tools in my personal growth. I use the techniques every day of my life. Yes! Yes! Yes! Tony!

The Gary Smalley *Hidden Keys to Loving Relationships* Seminars were fantastic in helping me to understand men—and women—and *me.*

During three summers, the librarians at the Waianae Public Library on the island of Oahu, Hawaii spent hours helping me find books on suicide and life after death, then ordered them from every library on the island. They never complained when I would check out ten or twenty at a time. Thank you for helping me in my search.

How can I *not* acknowledge my right arm and companion these last years, my now ancient and much-used Apple Macintosh Plus computer? I named her Hope and her companion, the printer, Glory. What did people do in the "olden" days without computers? Whoever invented her . . . bless you.

I am deeply grateful to those who helped get this book birthed and who encouraged me each step of the way. Pat Merrill, my book midwife, who has edited, produced final camera-ready copy, and made invaluable suggestions about this manuscript, I thank beyond measure. That you are reading this book is to her perseverance, patience, and caring. Bless you, dear Pat. And special thanks to Will, Pat's husband, who helps me in such good spirit with my computer woes.

Edgar Cayce's life readings numbered almost 15,000 and the legacy he left the world is unparalleled. He died in 1945. I regretted never having met him. Then one day, he introduced himself to me in a most unusual way and began to talk to me much like Stephen did. We began a friendship that has spanned dimensions. His work remains a constant source of inspiration to me. He has truly been, these last years, a companion in spirit. What's more, he tells me he communicates, and tries to communicate, with many others who will listen.

Morton Blumenthal, who received more Cayce readings than any other person, believed in a spiritual university, as do we. He has helped our work beyond measure from his realm.

Arthur Ford, Yogananda, Joseph Smith, Teresa, Efnron, and others, from their dimension, have much to share with those who will attune and ask for help. I believe it is our birthright to communicate with our Creator, and the spirit plane helpers, guides, and angels He sends. They wait for us to ask, and as we pause to listen, will aid us with the answers to what we seek. I am thankful for their guidance and help.

I mourn with all of you who have had a loved one die. Those who have experienced the death of a child in any way, and especially those who have had a child die of suicide, know a pain few can imagine. This book is a labor of love, a gift from Stephen and me to *you*.

Anne Puryear

Table of Contents

Life is eternal
and love is immortal
and death is only
a horizon
and a horizon is nothing
save the limit
of our sight.

– Author unknown

In My Darkest Hour

Do not stand at my grave and weep;
I am not here. I do not sleep.
I am a thousand winds that blow.
I am the diamond glints of snow.
I am the sunlight on ripened grain.
I am the gentle autumn's rain.
When you awaken in the morning's hush,
I am the swift uplifting rush
Of quiet birds in circled flight;
I am the stars that shine at night.
Do not stand at my grave and cry.
I am not there. I did not die.
— Indian prayer in memory of a tribe member

This is a book about the life, suicide, and afterlife of my son, Stephen. He took his own life when he was fifteen years, three months, and fifteen days old, because he felt it hurt more to live than to die.

This is a book about death and separation, but it is also about survival. It is a story about our lives and Stephen's life and all the things that each of us—his mother, brother, sisters, father and stepfathers, friends and acquaintances—did that led up to the irreversible decision he made. But most of all, I pray it is a story of hope, because it is also a story of my communications with him and of his work in his present state of consciousness.

I believe our loved ones who die continue on after death no matter how their physical lives end. I believe they have messages they want to bring to us about their survival and their continuing love. There are many

1

stories about the survival of those who die as adults but very few concerning *children*. So far, I have found none that pertain to children who commit suicide.

I have written this book as honestly and fully as I could without "sugar coating." It was not easy to write or research because of the pain and sadness it brought up. It bares my soul in my search for the answers to the questions which always haunt the survivors of suicide: *Why?* Why did he do it? Why hadn't I seen signs that he was suicidal? Why did I, his mother, do those things incorrectly that caused him to take his own life? Why? Why?. . . The never-ending whys.

I have learned to ask other, better questions now, such as: What can I learn from this? What gift is there in this? How can I grow from this experience? How can I best help others from my pain? In this process, I have learned some of the greatest lessons in my life, and I have grown in ways I would not have otherwise.

Part of the book was *dictated* to me by Stephen from the plane in which he now resides, often referred to as "the other side." Stephen says it's not "the other side" at all. He explains that those in that dimension may occupy the same space with us, their souls are simply vibrating at a different rate than our physical bodies. I don't know that dimension well yet, but I am learning about it with the help of Stephen and others who have gone ahead of me.

Stephen asked me to help him write this book in the hope that, by sharing our story, other children who may be lonely and confused might know where to turn to find some option besides suicide. He asked me to share our growth and life together with all possible honesty—the mistakes, the strengths, what we overcame, and what we failed to overcome. By the sharing of our story, other parents and young people may see their own errors and correct them before it is too late. His prayer is that young people will see that suicide solves absolutely no problems; instead, it leaves in its wake unbearable pain and sadness—on both sides—that is rarely completely healed. Stephen wants young people to understand that there is always another option—a better way—than to take one's own life. In choosing suicide, a young life filled with promise, that could have made a difference in the world, is destroyed. Loved ones are left with "what might have been" to carry the guilt to their own graves.

You may think, and perhaps rightly so after reading this book, "No wonder Stephen killed himself." Or you may think, "Things like that or worse happened in our family, and our child didn't kill himself. We were very lucky." On the other hand, it may help you see more clearly the things that often do irreparable damage to our sensitive children. And perhaps it will help you to make changes in your own life—and theirs—so that your child doesn't become one of the heartbreaking statistics, and you do not become a survivor of suicide.

Webster's New Twentieth Century Dictionary Unabridged lists *suicide* as, "noun, Fr., from L., *sui* of oneself, and *-cidium,* a slaying, from *caedere,* to slay. The act of killing oneself intentionally; in law, the act of self destruction by a person sound in mind and capable of measuring his moral responsibility."

Survive comes from two Latin words: *super,* meaning over, and *vivere,* meaning to live. When someone you love commits suicide, slays himself, you must go on and start over to live again.

In the United States, a suicide attempt is made every two and one-half minutes with a successful attempt made every twenty-six minutes. Over the last twenty years, the incidence of suicide by those between the ages of ten and twenty-four has increased by 136 percent. According to some statistics it is as high as 150 percent. Suicide has been confirmed as the second cause of death among this ten to twenty-four age group, yet many experts suspect it is actually the first cause. Statistics increase with the consideration of unreported and covered-up suicides, as well as so-called "accidental deaths" such as car accidents involving only one young driver.

Over 6,000 young people commit suicide each year, and 500,000 others attempt to do so. According to top child psychiatrists, evidence of suicidal behavior and suicide in children who are five to ten years old is common. Though statistics vary, the numbers are consistently revised upward each year. Many suicides in this age group are presented to doctors as accidents, as children vary their attempts to kill themselves, masking the intent.

Over 400,000 American youngsters suffer yearly from a newly recognized childhood illness: depression. This is felt by many suicidologists to be one of the reasons for the increase in childhood suicide. Another factor to consider is that teenage obesity has increased by 40 percent in the last two decades. Researchers state that 4.5 million youths between the ages of twelve and seventeen are more than 20 percent overweight. This often leads to teasing and rejection by peers, isolation, depression, and life-long problems with self-confidence and self-esteem. These are among the signs to watch for in teenage suicide.

Again statistics vary, but there is an increase in the rate of divorce of 50 to 70 percent after the suicide of a child. Some experts feel these numbers may be even higher. The loss of a child is devastating. The deterioration of the relationship and the ending of a marriage, as a result of that loss, creates additional grief that most couples cannot bear.

I was working on this book while in Hawaii, on the island of Oahu. I picked up a copy of the *Honolulu Star Bulletin* and read this article, from Associated Press:

TASK FORCE WARNS:
PREPARE FOR 1990s TEEN SUICIDE RISE

Washington, D.C.–In a report released yesterday, public health officials, under a task force appointed by the Secretary of Health and Human Services, have held a series of national conferences on youth suicide and state that public health officials must prepare now to meet an expected upswing in youth suicides in the late 1990s and recommends educating more people about the warning signs.

Perhaps your child or a relative or a friend has already taken his or her own life and you want to understand why. You may feel you are to blame or responsible in some way. It is never just one thing that causes a young person to take this final step but rather a series of actions and reactions accumulating over the years. One or more events may trigger the final act, but there is always more than that. You may need to understand your role in the event, but you also need to release blame or fault or guilt and get on with your life. Ultimately, the person who takes his or her life is the one who must take the greater responsibility for what he or she has done, no matter what the age.

The death of a partner, husband, or wife is usually heartbreaking, traumatic, and overwhelming. The death of a parent is very difficult for most of us. The death of family members or friends can leave a tremendous void.

But if your child dies, it is all these things and more. It is as if someone has reached into your chest and squeezed your heart over and over again and the resulting pain is almost beyond your endurance. It feels as if a part of your body has been severed and will never heal or grow back. Eventually, the pain eases, and you do learn to survive without that part—to compensate, to function.

If your child commits suicide, your pain and agony is doubled. Besides all the pain associated with the loss of a loved one, you also agonize over how you failed in your role as nurturer, as parent. Your child would rather die than live, would rather leave you than stay with you. Your child didn't give you a chance to help or even let you say good-bye. He has left forever—gone where you can't see or talk to him—and he has taken all your joy with him.

Who but *you* can possibly be to blame? This child was *your* responsibility. While your attention was elsewhere, he died. You failed to notice something was wrong. You failed to stop him. You failed to be there for him when he needed you. *You* killed him. You might as well have taken a knife and pushed it through his heart. He is dead and someone is to blame; and while you can direct your anger to all of the people around that did this to him, eventually, in your darkest hour, there is no one left to blame but yourself. *You* killed this one you said you loved. He is dead and gone forever, and there is nothing you can do to change that. There is no way you can ever tell him you are sorry or even that you understand. There is no way to find out how he is or even if there's a place *where* he is. You may even begin to hate God. How could a loving, just God let this happen?

This is the kind of thinking we do in that confused state in which we find ourselves. It is in that state we often remain, and in which we begin to die emotionally and break down physically. I was there. I remember.

I have begun to heal at last. I believe you can too. We can heal by sharing our grief and fear and by remembering the times of joy. We can heal by talking about our child and not hiding the facts of his death. We can heal by acknowledging our influencing role in our child's death, then forgiving ourselves and getting on with our lives. We can heal most by knowing that though the physical body is not present, the soul whom we love continues, often in our presence, in his or her life and love for us.

Stephen made a choice to end his physical life. I believe it was an incorrect choice. He also believes it was an incorrect choice. But the act was irreversible. A lifetime of regrets, guilt, and questioning cannot change the finality of it.

I was his mother for the fifteen years that he graced my life. I loved him with all my heart and soul. My love and caring were not enough. In one moment, he stripped the world of his youth, vitality and promise. With that act, my life and the lives of my three children would never be the same.

But in my darkest hour, a marvelous thing began to happen. I was given a gift beyond imagining. I could feel his presence and hear his voice—not only I but others. There would be an electric, thick energy that filled the room when Stephen entered, and my heartbeat would speed up. Sometimes I could hardly breathe and my whole body and brain reacted. It was the way you feel when you see someone you really love that you haven't seen for awhile. It was somewhat the way I always felt when Stephen was alive and walked into a room. The feeling of Stephen's presence was so powerful that without thinking I would say,

"Stephen. Stephen, you're here!" I couldn't see him or touch him, but I could feel his presence.

Shortly after these feelings began, I would hear a voice inside my head, talking to me. He would say, "Hi, Mom. It's me, Steve." The sentences and expressions were phrased exactly like Stephen talked. The information he gave me was often verifiable. Even though I was at first filled with doubt and thought it must be my imagination, his words were so comforting and the information he wanted to share so fascinating, that I soon relaxed and just listened. Then I began to dialogue with him.

I spoke to him out loud; he usually spoke to me telepathically. Occasionally, he spoke out loud so clearly that I turned in the direction of the voice. On those occasions when someone else was in the room as he spoke "aloud," not inside my head but from somewhere in the room, they usually could not hear him. However, there were several friends who could hear him just as I did. Sometimes they wrote down what they heard and shared it with all of us. When he finished, he would say good-bye, and the feeling of his presence left the room.

I am thankful to be able to hear him and to communicate with him from the spirit realm. But I wish he were here beside me so I could give him a hug and fix him his favorite meal and check his homework as I once did. I would much prefer to see his loving smile and blue eyes and watch his face light up with laughter as he leaned forward to talk to me. I miss hearing his barbell bump against the floor in his room as he did his workouts to keep in shape. I miss seeing the man he would have become and having the house filled with the sound of his children.

What I have with him now will have to do until we are together in the same dimension again one day. I don't hurry toward that time; it will come in good measure. Though there isn't a day I don't miss him after all these years, I find myself feeling stronger as the healing continues.

As he shared information, month after month, about his new life and provided clearer advice about my own, I too began to live again.

❦

CHAPTER ONE

... And Stephen Was Born

"I'll lend you for a little time a child of mine," he said,
"For you to love the while he lives, and mourn for when he's dead.
It may be six or seven years, or twenty-two or three;
But will you, till I call him back, take care of him for me?
He'll bring his charms to gladden you, and should his stay be brief,
You'll have his lovely memories as solace for your grief.
I cannot promise he will stay, since all from earth return;
But there are lessons taught down there I want this child to learn.
I've looked the wide world over in my search for teachers true,
And from the throngs that crowd life's lanes, I have selected you.
Now will you give him all your love, nor think the labor vain,
Nor hate Me when I come to call to take him back again?"
                                  – Edgar A. Guest

    I had never seen a dead body before. It was the winter of 1953. I was fifteen. Our family had returned to my hometown of Danville, Kentucky for my grandmother's funeral. We had driven from Cincinnati, Ohio where we had moved just months before. We had lived with my dad's mother, or she with us, all my life. When my dad was offered a job in Ohio, she had remained in Danville to live with my aunt. Now her home, the home of my childhood, was filled with grieving relatives from all over the state. It frightened me to think of seeing a dead person, especially someone I knew, like Granny, but it also made me sad.

    Without telling anyone, I walked the six blocks to the funeral home, alone, in case I cried. My grandmother's casket was open for viewing. She had on heavier makeup than she ever wore, bright red rouge on her cheeks, and her hands were folded over her favorite maroon dress. As I

7

looked at her, I couldn't breathe, my knees buckled, and I thought I was going to throw up.

I ran back to the house, crying all the way, and vowing I would never ever look at another dead body again. I was shaking all over. I felt sick at my stomach. That wasn't my grandmother—that was someone I didn't even know. She looked stiff and frozen like some wax doll. People dying was a terrible thing.

One of my aunts had yelled at me earlier in the day for running and laughing in the house, when I was just happy to be back home. "Don't you have any respect for the dead?" she barked. The whole thing was depressing and confusing.

I remembered that I was six when my grandfather, Granny's husband, died. Everyone was crying, and we had to be quiet. I didn't know what dead meant then, but day after day when Poppy didn't come home from the railroad where he was an engineer and pick me up and hug me, I began to realize that dead meant gone forever. We didn't go to his funeral because it wasn't considered good for children to see people who were dead. Remember them like they were when alive, they told us. When we visited the graveyard where he was buried, Granny would say Poppy was in the ground where they put him when he died. That was awful to think about. I vowed that death and dead people were not going to be part of *my* life ever again.

Once back in Cincinnati, I put Danville, my childhood memories, and death out of my mind. I soon developed a friendship destined to become my first serious romance with the boy whose locker stood next to mine. His name was Bill; he was president of the honor society, a popular junior, blonde, and full of life. I was flattered. He could have any girl he wanted—and often did, the rumor was—and yet he wanted *me,* a lowly sophomore.

My father lost his job that year, and we moved to Chattanooga, Tennessee where my mother had once lived. He went to work for a friend. I really felt uprooted. Torn from the arms of my boyfriend, and thrust into a boring town with a school I didn't like, I felt miserable.

Bill and I wrote daily at first. I had his class ring and we were going steady, professing our undying love to each other. At Thanksgiving, he came for a visit for several days. When he returned, his letters became infrequent. Our romance was cooling. I was lonely at first but soon began to go to church activities and to make some friends. I was getting on with my life. I was too young to go steady anyway. But in a few weeks, I realized I might be pregnant. I called to tell Bill.

Pregnant! In 1955, abortions were out of the question—they were illegal, and those done were performed in some dirty room by questionable "doctors." Besides, we had no money to even consider that.

Bill honorably drove to Tennessee to marry me. I didn't want to marry him even though I thought I loved him, and I doubt that he wanted to marry me. We were married in March by a justice of the peace, across the Tennessee border in Georgia.

We went home to tell my mother, and I saw her cry for the first time in my life. We drove away that night, back to Cincinnati, to begin married life. After Bill fell asleep in the motel that evening—our wedding night—I sat by the window and cried and cried. I didn't want to be away from my family. I wanted my mother. I didn't know anything about babies. I had only baby-sat a few times. This is not what I had planned for my life. I wanted to finish school and go to college.

On the evening of August 9, I began to have terrible cramps. I didn't even know what labor was. After a period of excruciating pain, we drove down to the hospital. The next morning, I gave birth to a beautiful baby boy. I was sedated the whole time. I woke up and I was a mother. This was to be Stephen's older brother, William Robert or "Bobby" as we would call him until he got older. The moment I saw him, I loved him. I had never even thought of what having a baby entailed. I was amazed the first time his diaper needed changing, but I learned very quickly how to do that and everything else.

As the years went by, Bill and I didn't fare so well. We separated a couple of times and then got back together because of Bobby. We didn't argue much. We cared about each other. But we were growing up very rapidly in different directions. We were careful now to avoid a pregnancy. Nevertheless, after one of our separations and reunions, I became pregnant again.

Different from the first one, this was a very difficult pregnancy. Almost at once, I began to have morning sickness which lasted all day and all night. I would nibble on anything to keep from being so nauseated, but it would start up again almost immediately. My doctor prescribed a different medication every week. Nothing worked. I hadn't been sick at all when I was pregnant before. I had never felt this bad in my life. I gained fifty pounds. I looked like a butter ball; I felt like a blimp. My doctor tried all the new drugs until, in exasperation, he said it must be in my mind, whatever that meant. He never explained. I was expected to just stop being sick.

I called to schedule my seven-month checkup, still sick day and night. The nurse said my doctor had suffered a heart attack. They referred me to another physician. The new doctor examined me very roughly, and when I cried out in pain, he became impatient with me, telling me I would just have to tolerate it. I was in agony by the time he was through and was having severe cramps, much like labor. He told me that I had a condition which he called, "excessive water around the womb" and that it was no wonder I had been sick all the time. He prescribed something that worked and my nausea ended. For the next twenty-four hours, however, the pain was unbearable from the exam; but, I was afraid to call him and get him irritated again. The pain finally stopped, and I was never sick again.

There was no one to talk to about my fears or questions. My first doctor was ill and the new doctor didn't want to be bothered. Because of that, my fears accelerated, and I began to think I was going to die during delivery. I was sure I wouldn't live, nor would my baby live. Frightened and confused, I began to prepare for my death.

I cried in my room at night while Bill was in school and Bobby was asleep. I missed my family and wrote letters to them telling them how much I loved them. I asked them to take care of Bobby and remind him how much his mother loved him, after I died. I sealed the letters and put them where they would be found when I was gone.

I would tiptoe into Bobby's room and watch him sleep, his thumb in his mouth, his curled finger resting on his little upturned nose. He always perspired and his golden hair would be damp. Little drops of moisture would be on his nose, winter or summer. I would touch him and tell him how much I loved him. I loved him so much that the thought of not being around to raise him was so painful I could hardly bear it.

My time was running out—my second child was due around December 6 and I had to make each moment with Bobby count. I hadn't shared my fears with anyone, neither with my family in Tennessee nor with Bill. It was my own deep and painful secret to spare them the pain until it was time.

My mother had told me about her own mother's death. Her father had told her that at the graveside, as they were lowering her mother into the ground, my mother, then only two years old, cried out, "Don't let them put my mommy in that dark hole!" I cried every time I thought about that story. Mother couldn't remember anything about her mother. There remained only some pieces of an unfinished quilt her mother had been working on just before she died. That's how it would be with Bobby, except for the notes I was leaving.

On December 2, I hoisted my swollen body behind the wheel of our 1956 Chevy and went shopping for the last Christmas presents for Bobby and Bill. They could open them when I was gone. Exhausted after shopping and fixing dinner, I put Bobby to bed and lay down to sleep. I was twenty, Bill was twenty-one, and Bobby was three years and four months old.

I had never read a book on childbirth. The few older women with whom I tried to discuss it would say something like, "Honey, it's all just natural and God will handle it just like he has for thousands of years." I therefore went into the delivery room that night in deep labor with the same lack of knowledge I had the first time.

On the frantic drive to the hospital before midnight, Bobby was in the back seat of the car. Bill was trying to make all the traffic lights. Between contractions, I reached for Bobby's hand and told him how much I loved him. Since I had had no guidance about breathing and relaxation, I held my breath when I should have been exhaling, unwittingly adding to my pain.

At the hospital, a nurse took me upstairs by wheelchair to the labor room. Fathers were not allowed past the first floor. I waved good-bye to Bill as he filled out the admittance forms, Bobby hugging his leg. Would Bobby remember how much I loved him when I was gone? I forced myself not to cry in front of them or the nurse.

In the labor room, the nurse had me undress, put on a white gown, and lie on the bed. She raised the rails and locked them, then shaved me, gave me a shot in the hip, and left. No one explained anything nor did I ask. I lost consciousness and thought, "This must be what death is like." I saw only darkness, and everything became a point of light. The points sounded a "ping" to communicate with other points. I didn't know this language, but they continued to move and touch each other, and I continued to hear their "pings." I felt very left out even though I knew I was one of them.

When I opened my eyes, I was in a large room. Three women whom I didn't recognize were lying in beds in different corners of the room. I guessed we were all dead and in heaven or somewhere. A nurse was taking my blood pressure and said I had a very rough labor and delivery. "You have a boy," she added. Still partly sedated, I asked, "What kind?" She laughed, and Bill was there smiling as I slipped back into my "ping" world.

When I woke up a few hours later, I remembered it was December 3, 1958, and I had given birth to another son. Shortly thereafter, they brought him in. He was sweet-looking, his face a soft dusty pink color. I unwrapped him and everything was perfect. He was bound with a cloth around the middle, just like Bobby had been. His eyes were blue and he had light brown hair. He wasn't beautiful like Bobby had been, but he was cute and very quiet and peaceful. My response to this one was so different—I felt terribly guilty. How would I ever love this little child like I loved Bobby? I told myself I would take care of him and that he would never know how I felt, but I just didn't feel the love toward him as I had felt with his brother.

They let me feed him a bottle which he drained to the bottom. My doctor didn't believe in breast-feeding and I never questioned that. Bobby had always sucked on his bottle and fallen asleep, then repeated that until the bottle was, at best, half-empty. This little one, with his chubby pink cheeks, didn't hesitate to drain the bottle to the last drop. Then he opened his blue eyes and looked at me. He was actually *very* sweet. As I was thinking this, the nurse came and took him back to the nursery until his next feeding. I pleaded to keep him a little longer. She said feeding time was over.

After several days, during which this quiet 7 pound, 15-1/2 ounce baby boy drank every bottle and wanted more, I discovered he was developing his own little personality.

After four days, they let me go home. I could finally see and talk to Bobby. There were no phones in our rooms, and we weren't allowed out of bed. I had missed him so. My mother had come from Tennessee to be with him and to help with the new baby for a week or more. Only weeks later when I found the notes I had written did I realize that I was supposed to be dead.

Bobby was delighted with his little brother. He touched and kissed him constantly. He held him carefully and tenderly and was his constant companion and shadow. Bobby would even stand quietly for long periods to watch his new brother sleep in his bassinet.

Now, all my mothering instincts came out. Christmas music was on the air, holiday specials were on the black and white TV, the tree was up, lights were sparkling, and everyone was filled with love. While I wasn't expecting it, I began to love this little baby just as I loved Bobby. The same. How amazing. I didn't think there was enough love in me for two.

We decided to name him Christopher Stephen. At the last moment, I changed it to Stephen Christopher after my dad, Stephen. I wanted to please him and it did. He always had a soft spot for "little Stephen" as my family would call him the rest of his life. Later, I discovered that Stephen meant "crowned with glory" and Christopher, "the Christ bearer." I always loved his names.

My mother bonded with Stephen instantly. She fed him and held him and got up with him at night. She took care of me and then devoted the rest of her time to this quiet little newborn and to Bobby. She included Bobby in Stephen's bathing and feeding. Bobby would prop his chin in his hand and watch her change him and have a one-way conversation with him for hours on end.

Thus began a love affair with the two boys that lasted for many years. I intuitively knew how important it was not to neglect the older child, though I had never read any books about that. I saw to it that Bobby was included in everything and had no reason ever to feel left out or jealous. The wonder of it all was that I had given birth to the two most perfect and beautiful children in the world—the same feeling most parents have, I learned much later.

Bill and I put our differences aside and devoted ourselves to the boys. I no longer worked outside of the home and was a full-time mother and wife. I loved it. I would sit and watch Bobby play for hours and talk to his imaginary playmates. I watched Stephen sleep, and both Bobby and I would hold and cuddle him the moment he woke up.

Our apartment had two bedrooms and was on the first floor. Bobby slept in the bottom of a bunk bed set and Stephen in his crib in the room they shared. They had a wooden chest filled with every toy they could ever want, all bought by two sets of doting grandparents for their first two grandchildren. Bill's father bought them clothes of all kinds, and we frequently dressed them alike. It was wonderful to be home with them all day. We had to be careful with our money, but we could just make it.

Bill was a kind and hard-working person. Both of the boys looked like him, I thought. Besides his full-time job and night school, he played golf most weekends. He loved playing with the boys when he was home and genuinely enjoyed them. We rarely argued or discussed our relationship. Our lives revolved around the children.

When Stephen was eight months old, we moved from that apartment into a four-family building. We had our own washer and dryer and shared a basement. There was a big yard where the boys could have a swing set and be outside more. As boxes and furniture were moved in, I picked Stephen up again and again from his crib, and hugged and kissed him. He had on a pale blue footed sleeper, and he looked like an angel with his little golden hair framing his face. He rarely ever cried, and when I kissed him under his neck on his "sweet spot" he would chuckle and smile.

Bobby ran in and out around the boxes and stopped to hug and kiss us both. He made Stephen laugh out loud. I remembered a quote from Bern Williams: "You can almost hear the voices of angels in the laughter of little children." At four, Bobby was filled with total enthusiasm and joy for life. He raced his bike up and down the sidewalk, so utterly charming that the new neighbors all stopped and talked to him. He became instant friends with everyone.

Stephen was quieter. He had a special quality that made you want to touch him, squeeze him, love him. Everyone around him commented that they couldn't keep their hands off him. For years we heard, "I could raise that one like my own," and, "I have never felt a child who *feels* so good."

Bill's parents lived in a mobile home near where his dad worked for the Air Force. Bill's mother needed a wheelchair, crippled since his birth with severe rheumatoid arthritis. The boys sat and climbed all over her lap and she never minded. If they hurt her with their play, she never complained. She stuffed them with cookies and candy, living for their visits. Bill's dad was an alcoholic but he didn't let his drinking disrupt his work. On weekends he indulged himself but never when he was keeping the boys. The boys adored them both.

During Stephen's first year, one of his eyes would not stop running due to a clogged tear duct. The doctor said it could be corrected. He wrapped Stephen in a sheet so he couldn't move, then ran a needle into the duct to clear it. I couldn't watch. Stephen never cried and the doctor praised him for being such a good boy, telling us how remarkable he was to tolerate the pain. At about eighteen months, he developed some respiratory problems; and, for several years, especially during winter, I sat in the bathroom with him, while the shower ran to make steam so he could breathe easier.

He began to walk at about eleven months and tried to dress himself. He put on strange hats and outfits with his brother's help. Then he had Bobby strap his toy guns and holster around his waist, over his diaper, and he climbed into Bobby's boots. We all laughed at our silly little clown, and he loved showing off. Bobby always said adoringly, "Isn't he the cutest thing in the world?"

If Stephen wanted a toy, Bobby gave it to him; if Bobby wanted one of Stephen's toys, he did the same. They loved each other, never fought or argued, nor were they jealous of each other. They were so tender and caring and considerate of each other's needs, it was a joy to watch. I filled our photo albums with their pictures. Where one was, the other was.

Even though our relationship revolved around the boys, it continued to deteriorate. When Stephen was still less than a year old, Bill and I separated for the last time. Amid tears and much sadness at things we couldn't reconcile, he moved back home with his parents, and I kept the apartment and the children. He visited the boys regularly and sometimes kept them overnight or for weekends. I didn't have a car, so Bill loaned me his when I needed to shop.

Our separation meant that I had to go back to work and to find a roommate to make ends meet. A blonde, single girl who enjoyed the night life, and wasn't home most evenings, moved into my bedroom. I shared the boy's room, sleeping on the bottom bunk, since Bobby now preferred the top one. Stephen's crib was across the room and we were crowded in together. Each night, we all crawled into my bottom bunk and said our prayers. I read to them and told them stories. Bill paid twenty-five dollars each week in child support which covered their baby-sitter, and I earned the rest to meet our needs.

The blonde moved out and a new roommate moved in who was quiet and had little of a social life. I found a job that paid better than secretarial work, but my hours were 3:30 until 11:30 p.m. We desperately needed more money to survive. I paid my neighbor to keep the boys until my new roommate got home at 5:30 p.m., then I paid the roommate to keep them until I got home. I could now be with the boys most of the day, work at night, and support us fairly well.

This arrangement didn't last long. I discovered that the neighbor baby-sitting the boys would prepare meals and feed herself and her four children in front of my boys, before my roommate got home; she wouldn't feed the boys anything, telling them they could eat later. Bobby told me how hungry he got while they were eating. I spoke to my neighbor, asking if she could postpone dinner half an hour until the boys were gone, or if she would let me pay her to feed them. But she insisted on doing it her way.

I stopped taking the children there and changed jobs. I hired a woman to care for the boys in our apartment during the day, and I was now home in the evenings with them. It was easier; still, I missed them so much during the day. I kept them up late at night to be with them and agonized over missing so much of their growth.

Within a few months, Bobby began to pick on Stephen for no apparent reason. At first I chalked it up to his age, but the situation grew worse. From adoring Stephen, he was now always irritated at him and wouldn't share with him. I discovered that the new baby-sitter held and played with Stephen but pushed Bobby away. She did not give Bobby any attention and made him give Stephen anything he was playing with, whether he wanted to or not. I also discovered that her husband often came over while I was gone, and both boys were being neglected. I noticed that items were missing from the house. I fired her.

Then there was a succession of baby-sitters, and it was a difficult time. I had no choice but to work. I worried about the children, yet when I got home from a long day and a lengthy bus ride back and forth, I was often exhausted. As much as I wanted them to stay up late, sometimes I was relieved when they went to bed early.

Despite the difficulties, the boys seemed to be fairly well-adjusted. Their dad saw them frequently, along with a nice woman to whom he was engaged. I had met a professor from a southern university, and he had proposed marriage. He drove up every month to see me; and, after awhile, we were engaged. He didn't really care for the children. Sometimes when Stephen or Bobby were affectionate with him, he couldn't hide his irritation and turned away from them. At first I thought he would change, but his only interest was in me. I realized I could never marry him. One weekend when he was getting ready to drive home, I hugged him good-bye and sensed I would never see him again. I never did. I broke off the engagement, though he continued to call and write for months afterward, promising me he would be a good father to the boys. I had no intention of letting them be mistreated by him in any way. If I remarried, I wanted someone who did more than tolerate them, someone who would love them like I did.

Bobby and Stephen played out-of-doors on their swing set, watched "Howdy Doody" on television, and were full of energy. We delighted in our time together on weekends. I was their playmate too.

Bobby was the more physically beautiful child. His halo of golden curls made him look almost like a girl, his eyes were huge blue spheres, and he manipulated everyone with his charm. Stephen looked much like him with straight blonde hair, exactly the same eyes—but was quieter, more peaceful. I dressed them alike in red pants and shirts, matching knee socks, and shiny black leather shoes. They made quite a pair with Bobby a good head or more taller, often tucking Stephen under his arm to hug him.

Bobby was never quite so loving or gentle with Stephen after the baby-sitter incident. There was a slight cutting edge, a possessiveness with his toys, an impatience that I thought he would outgrow. I was very specific in instructing each baby-sitter that the treatment must be equal and fair for them both; I expected it to heal in time, but it never fully did.

Stephen's quiet acceptance of any situation endeared him to us all. He expressed few needs, he was content to ride behind his big brother on the tricycle, and would hand over his toys to Bobby or any neighborhood child who wanted to play with them. He went to sleep when he was put to bed, woke up with a smile and hugs and kisses. Everyone who knew the boys commented on how well-behaved and happy they were, how beautiful Bobby was, and how they loved to hug Stephen.

We had lived by ourselves for almost two years. I had gone to an employment agency to find a better-paying job that would allow me more time with the children. They hired me for their own staff instead. They were the biggest agency in the country, they said, certainly in Ohio. There were thirty-five men and women on the staff in Cincinnati alone. I got a draw and a commission. I was twenty-one, still very naive, and certainly not as self-confident and worldly-wise as most of the counselors were. The man who hired me felt I had some special quality that could make me successful at the work. Within six weeks, I was sixth in the organization in placing people in jobs, and had won numerous gift incentives for finding job openings. I was making more money than I'd ever seen in my life.

This job, taken to allow me more time with my sons, took me away from them even more. I was more exhausted and had little energy left over to attend to the needs of two growing boys. We needed the money, and I tried to juggle baby-sitters, spend time with them, and meet their needs and mine. I enrolled in a business college to develop shorthand skills, attending daily during my lunch hour, so I could prepare for another job where I might have more time with them.

My manager tried to get me to quit school and devote more time to my job. He said I had an uncanny natural ability to know which people to place in what jobs and almost a sixth sense in finding job openings before companies even listed them. It was true, I did *know,* without knowing how I knew. It was strange but was very helpful. I was exhausted from the long hours, but I let his flattery keep me there another month.

Desperate to be with my sons more and sensing their need to have me, I quit the employment agency and got a job at a small family-run business near where I lived. I was their girl-Friday, secretary, and receptionist. The bus ride was only ten minutes. Though the salary was much lower, I would finally be home several more hours each day. I could be closer to being a real mother, at least in my own mind. My new boss was president of the company as well as a minister in some church that believed in the *Book of Mormon.* I wasn't interested in the least in their church, and they did not pressure me to attend or to believe as they did. We developed a genial working relationship. They were solicitous about my children and gave me time off to be with them when necessary. Life settled into a peaceful, loving routine.

That summer, the company hired a young engineer named Richard. He was a member of their church, single, and four years older than I. He was tall and thin, and I did not personally find him very attractive. In December, the company had a family Christmas party and I brought the boys with me. Richard sat with me, played with the children all evening, hoisted them on his shoulders, and generally saw to it that their evening was enjoyable. Stephen laughed and played with him; Bobby sought Richard out when he couldn't find him.

I was impressed. What a kind man he was with children. While he was carrying Bobby on his arm, and Stephen was sitting with legs around his neck, they said they were thirsty. I asked Richard if he would get them a Coke before we left. He answered, "Cokes aren't good for you, but I *will* get them ginger ale." I didn't particularly agree that one was any better than another, but I thought it very nice that he cared that much.

Richard and I were together almost daily, after the party. He played with the boys, took us to the "company church," The Reorganized Church of Jesus Christ of Latter Day Saints, and began to move into our

lives. Most of our dates revolved around the church. He was a priest—
a type of lay minister—whom they believed was called by God. He and
his family had been members of this church all their lives. The people at
church were warm, welcomed us in every way, and invited us into their
homes. The services were interesting and sometimes inspiring. The boys
loved Sunday School since they had never attended one regularly before.
I had missed being part of any type of religious activity since my
childhood attendance in the Baptist Church and the Church of Christ.

It felt good to belong to something, to be with people who cared, to
be taken care of. Richard played sports with the boys, talked to them
about the Bible, and spent as much time with them as with me. I was tired
of living alone and providing so much of their care myself. It was a relief
to have such help. Richard truly seemed to care about us, and he began
to plan all our activities.

When he proposed, we set a February date for a church wedding. We
had known each other for a number of months, but since we hadn't dated
very long at all, I was concerned that the wedding was so soon. However,
I felt thankful to have found such a caring father for the boys, convinced
myself I was in love with him, and began to think he was actually an
attractive man after all.

We adapted to Richard's schedule. He spent all his spare time with us,
returning to his apartment at night after the boys had said their prayers
and were tucked into bed. They would rush to meet him after work, we
ate dinner together, and he played with them all evening. I had never seen
the boys happier. I began to relax. Richard and I did not sleep together
because of his religious beliefs. We planned for our wedding.

In late January 1961, a month after we had met, we drove to visit my
family in Tennessee so they could meet Richard and get to know him. My
parents and sister adored the boys and were glad I had met someone who
would also be a good full-time father to them.

Richard became very upset during the visit. He said my family didn't
discipline the boys and let them get by with anything. He was jealous of
my mother, irritated by my sister, and he became very strict and
controlling with the boys. We went outside to the car to talk and had a
terrible argument. I told him the boys had spent parts of summers with
my parents, loved them dearly, and no one could be more loving and kind
than my family were to them. They were the only grandchildren; if they
spoiled them a little the few times they saw them, it didn't matter because
the boys behaved well and it wouldn't hurt them.

He was furious. Seeing this side of him, being unable to reason with
him, his coldness and anger making a mask of his face, I decided to call
the wedding off. The trip was ruined, and we returned home. I was so

insecure and confused that by the time we got home, Richard had convinced me the argument in Tennessee was my fault. We ironed things out or, more accurately, swept them under the rug. The wedding was back on. I continued to defend my parents to Richard, and Richard to my parents. They did not like him, warning me about marrying him. He never acted so badly again after we got back, but I began to notice how much he tried to control everything we did, how bossy and domineering he was becoming. I tried to talk to him about it, but he defended his actions. Nevertheless, I was beginning seriously to question the coming marriage.

A few days after our trip, snow covering the ground, we attended, as usual, the weekly Wednesday night prayer service at the church. After the service, people were milling around talking to each other in the upper sanctuary. Stephen had turned two in December and could talk in short sentences. People stopped to visit with him as they went by. He had on a little navy blue suit, white shirt, and red bow tie; Bobby was dressed the same. I thought Richard had Stephen's hand; he thought I did. The next thing we heard was a woman screaming hysterically. Stephen had started down the steps to the first floor and evidently had lost his footing. He slipped through the metal rails, falling a story and a half onto the concrete floor below.

I ran to the top of the stairs and, looking down, could see his little body, left leg bent to the side, lying below on the grey concrete floor. Richard and I ran down the stairs to where people were already gathered around him. Someone was yelling to the others not to touch him or move him in case his back was broken. Someone else was calling an ambulance.

There was nothing I could do. I bent to touch him and was afraid to kiss or hold him because everyone was screaming not to touch him. I hurt so badly and was so frightened, that it was almost like watching a movie. I pleaded with God in my mind for Him to save Stephen. I was fully aware of everyone standing around, their attention and eyes on me. It all felt unreal. I didn't act as I felt, I acted as I thought I should. I cried, but actually, I hurt so badly that forcing tears out wasn't real. I wanted to scream and plead for help. I felt like an actor in a dream.

It seemed like forever, but an ambulance finally arrived. The attendants carefully loaded Stephen into the back. I was the only person they allowed in the ambulance with them, and I had to sit in the front. I could only look back through a glass window and see Stephen being tended by a man in white clothes. I wanted to shout to the driver to drive the ambulance faster. I remained quiet, but it seemed as if they were driving unusually slowly. During the half hour it took to get to the hospital, I couldn't be sure whether Stephen was dead or alive. He didn't move.

When we pulled up to the emergency door at the hospital, they brought him out on the stretcher. His eyes were open but his head had been strapped down so that he couldn't move. I talked to him all the way into the emergency room and touched him. He didn't cry but occasionally moaned. I loved him so. "Please, God, don't let him die." I silently implored. I promised God anything if only he would let Stephen be okay. I made a hundred pacts with God during those long hours.

The admitting nurse asked for his history and if he had been exposed to any contagious diseases recently. I told her that several of his playmates had mumps and his brother had just gotten over them. She said, "Then we can't admit him." My jaw dropped. I couldn't believe she had said that. Here was a two-year-old boy who had just fallen down flights of stairs on his head. He might be dying, yet she wouldn't admit him. The ambulance attendant said, "We'll take him to the contagious ward at Children's Hospital," and they quickly put him back into the ambulance. It wasn't too far away, and when they unloaded him this time, he was admitted.

Richard and two of the ministers at the church arrived shortly afterward. I told them the doctors had taken Stephen into an examining room and wouldn't let me go with them. One of the ministers asked the admitting clerk if they could go in and do laying-on-of-hands for Stephen. They explained that they were members of a church that believed in this type of healing. They then let us all into the room. I could see Stephen now and touch and comfort him.

He cried when he saw me. I would always bless the ministers for getting us in. They anointed Stephen's head with oil that had been blessed, laid their hands on him, and prayed for him. I prayed too, but I kept my eyes open, and Stephen never took his eyes off me. He was frightened and in pain.

The doctors made us leave after only a few minutes. We waited for hours and were not allowed to see him. Finally, a doctor came out to us. He said they would have to keep Stephen in the hospital for several days. The X-rays showed a fracture from the top of his head down the left side. There was no bleeding or swelling, and he would probably be alright, but he had to be watched constantly. He had no broken bones and was in very little pain now. They had given him something to help him sleep. He said it was a miracle he wasn't dead or wasn't hurt worse. A miracle! "Thank you, God," I said to myself over and over.

We were allowed to see Stephen and to go with him to the contagious ward where he would spend the next several days. The ministers left to tell the people at church who were still there praying for him and who were taking care of Bobby. I knew the healing and prayers had worked.

I was so thankful to them, to God, and to everyone. I cried and held Stephen's chubby little hand as he lay on the bed.

The contagious ward was a shock to us. There were dozens of beds lined up against the walls and a double row in the middle, with two beds touching head to head. Plastic oxygen tents were over many of the children. Some were crying and screaming, others making no movement, with tubes coming out from their bodies, and clear or blood-filled glass bottles hanging around their cribs.

Stephen was rolled to the end of the room and carefully placed in a crib. The rails were snapped in place. He cried again, though he was getting drowsy from the medication. I touched him and talked to him until he fell asleep. I was not allowed to stay in the room or in any room near by. I was told that even if I stayed at the hospital, I couldn't see him until the next day. They sent us home, telling us they would call if there was any problem. His eyes had pleaded with me to stay before he fell asleep. He looked so little and so frightened.

I couldn't stand to leave him, asleep or not, but Richard finally insisted we leave and we did. I thanked God over and over again that he was alright. My heart ached at the last glimpse of him, alone in the crib. What would he do if he woke up and I wasn't there? Would someone pick him up and hold him?

We returned for Bobby, and I slept with him all that night, holding him close to me. Richard went back to his apartment. I prayed again and again that Stephen wouldn't wake up and be frightened. He had never been without one of us who loved him at night. I prayed that he would be okay. I prayed that he wouldn't have brain damage. I slept very little.

The next morning, we were allowed to see Stephen as soon as we arrived. A nurse was feeding him. He had been able to feed himself for months, but she was carefully spoon-feeding him every bite. He wasn't stopping her. He grinned when he saw us and held his arms up. The nurse said he was doing so well that they would let us take him home. He would need to be observed, and we were to call them if there was any problem. The left side of his face was considerably swollen, but they assured us it was causing no pain and would soon be back to normal. Once again, they remarked that it was a miracle Stephen had survived. I *knew* it was a miracle.

His jaw seemed especially swollen, both to the left and underneath, where there was no fracture, but he seemed to be doing fine. It was only weeks later, looking at pictures taken back then, that we realized he had had the mumps. It was so obvious, and we would have realized it then if we hadn't been so worried about his fall.

His accident endeared him to the church members even more. They felt God had spared him for some special reason. Richard was especially caring and helpful. Stephen's accident had pushed away my remaining doubts about him and the marriage.

Our wedding was scheduled for the middle of February. My roommate found herself another apartment so Richard could move in after the wedding. The whole church prepared for the event. Richard's parents came from Pennsylvania, my parents from Tennessee. Stephen was adorable at the ceremony and many photos were taken of people holding and loving him. Bobby was attentive and solicitous with him. They were dressed alike in their little blue pants, grey jackets, and red ties.

There would be no danger of Stephen slipping through the guard rails again, nor of any child having the same accident. We donated the insurance money we received to have a solid side added to the rail, which should have been done years before.

My mother and dad took the boys to Tennessee after the ceremony to keep them while we went on our honeymoon. Stephen and Bobby loved their Nanny and Poppy and were excited about going, so I had no worries about leaving them. No one loved them more than they did, I thought, except me.

On the honeymoon, faces of Richard surfaced that I had never before seen. We fought continuously. He wanted to skip meals to save money; I was hungry. He brought along a grill to cook in the room. I reminded him there was a "No Cooking" sign in every room where we stayed. I worried that if the management smelled food, we would be kicked out. Nevertheless, we cooked every breakfast and some dinners in the rooms where we stayed.

Richard refused to tell me where we were going on the honeymoon, nor did he give me any hints. It turned out to be Niagara Falls. Since I didn't know, I didn't bring snow boots or any of the right clothing. I got so cold climbing a snow-covered mountain where we stopped to hike on the way that I cried from the pain. Richard was irritated and angry at me, because I couldn't make it to the top. But with snow in my shoes, my feet were freezing.

On the way back home, late at night, he stopped the car at a gas station on top of a mountain. He said we were going to sleep there overnight until the station opened. I asked if we didn't have enough gas to make it to a motel. He said we probably did, but to think of what we would save in a motel bill—at least thirty dollars. I almost froze. Richard slept in the back, I in front. We had no blankets, just our coats. With the cold, the steering wheel, and the narrow seats in his '53 Ford, I couldn't sleep all night.

The honeymoon was a disaster. I came home five pounds heavier from the stress. I was disillusioned, insecure, and irritable. I hardly recognized the man I had married. There was a cruel streak in him and a lack of compassion and understanding that I had never seen before.

We picked up the boys in Tennessee, and the honeymoon fiasco was buried for the time being. On the entire trip back to Cincinnati, Richard corrected and disciplined the children, yelling at Stephen and Bobby over the slightest little thing. He refused to stop to let them go to the bathroom or to get a drink until he found the "right place" which was sometimes over an hour after they expressed a need. The boys cried, "Mommy, we have to potty. We can't hold it." I begged Richard to please stop. He said they were sissies. I had never seen him like that. Or had I? The signs had been there—with the cola versus ginger ale, and the horrible visit to my family among other things—from the beginning. In the clouds of my own insecurity and preparation for the marriage, I hadn't allowed myself to see them clearly.

I continued working for the next year. We had several good baby-sitters, but Richard kept saying I needed to quit and stay home with the boys as soon as we could afford it. I couldn't wait. I had missed them so much, being away from them all day, and was so glad he wanted me to be a full-time mother. I would have endured anything to stay home with them.

Richard soon began to insist that he needed to adopt the boys. I was reluctant. I didn't think it was a good idea. Their father, Bill, saw them some weekends. He loved them and they loved him. He had remarried and they liked his new wife. Richard then began an all-out campaign to adopt them. He insisted, "Children shouldn't have but one father, it will confuse them. The boys will grow up disturbed if they have to have two fathers. What will people think if they have a different last name from mine? It will do them harm in school, when all of their friends have the same name as their father and they do not. I want them to be mine. They can still see Bill, but they will have my name." These were among the dozens of statements he reiterated daily. He also talked to the boys about this, and they, not knowing what it all meant, said they wanted him to adopt them and be their daddy.

He convinced me that I should ask Bill about it. I was sure that Bill wouldn't agree and that would end it. Whether I was too convincing with Bill or whether he wanted the best for them and felt this was the right thing to do, I will never know, but he agreed.

We began the adoption proceedings with the stipulation that Bill could see the children whenever he wished. He continued to do so, though Richard often made it difficult by scheduling other things for them.

The adoption was soon final. Now they could use Richard's last name at school and church, almost as if there had never been another father, another marriage. I had joined his church in the meantime. The church members had been very uncomfortable with my divorce, so this made them happy too. I was not at ease with their attitudes nor Richard's but tried to convince myself that Richard really loved the boys and wanted what was best for them.

Richard and I fought daily about the discipline of the children. At first, he would storm out of the house if I confronted him or stood up for them. When he came back, he would be cold, withdrawn, and wouldn't discuss anything until I apologized. It was impossible to resolve anything that way. I would finally apologize because I couldn't bear his silence. As weeks passed, he would no longer leave but would stay and fight. The boys were asleep most of these times and I never realized how often they must have awakened and been fearful but never said a word. How frightened they must have been! We were fighting about them, and about most everything else too. It's foolish to think children don't hear and aren't aware of what's going on, but I actually fooled myself that they didn't hear.

Richard sent out feelers for a new job and, shortly after, was offered one in Washington, D.C. We drove there without the children to check it out. I loved the whole area—it was the most exciting place I had ever been. A dusting of snow covered the ground and the monuments glistened in the moonlight when we arrived.

Richard thought the job was ideal, the salary was bigger, and he felt it would be perfect for the boys. Things had a chance to get better here, away from Cincinnati, Bill and everything else, he assured me. This would be a new start. Stephen and Bobby could visit Bill and stay in touch, and we could get about our lives, he said. Maybe, I thought, it *would* help. Maybe everything would get better.

It didn't happen that way. Bill never called or wrote the boys. I wrote to his mother and sent photos and a letter every Christmas. I learned later that he thought it was better to get out of their lives.

Richard was pleased that the boys didn't see their father—he was their father now, he would say. Whenever I mentioned Bill and showed the boys pictures of him, Richard became annoyed and reprimanded me for not letting them get on with their lives. I was encouraged to destroy most of the photos of the children with Bill. In order to end the constant badgering, I finally did so, reluctantly.

Soon Bill was rarely ever mentioned. It did seem to be true; the boys mostly forgot about him and got caught up in their own lives. Bobby asked me about him occasionally, but Stephen, barely three-and-a-half, soon forgot or seemed to forget his first father. He acted like he loved Richard as much as he had Bill.

Our life in the Springfield, Virginia suburb of Washington, D.C. again revolved around the church. It was not too far from us, and the members were loving and supportive just as in Cincinnati. We did not mention that Richard was the boy's stepfather, although some people knew. He wanted everyone to think they were his children. This was stressful for me; I wanted to be more honest. Few people at church were divorced, and divorce was frowned upon unless adultery was the cause, which was not the cause of mine. So we lived a lie with some, and were honest with others.

I loved staying home with the boys. We had such fun together. Richard insisted they needed a dog, so we had several dogs over the years, with me taking care of them. It was much like having another child, I felt. The dogs had puppies and both boys spent hours playing with them. They cried when the puppies were given away or sold, which happened with every litter and with almost every animal they loved. Either Richard got rid of them, or I would be so tired of caring for them, that I did.

Behind closed doors, unknown to the church people, our life was one of constant fighting, mostly concerning the children. Richard sometimes got so angry at me that he would slam his fist through the wall. In several homes, we had to patch the walls before moving. In my pain, I threw a plastic radio and several other things at him, always missing. He berated me for destroying property. My aim was never good, but I didn't want to hit him anyway. I wanted him to stop being so mean to us. Only a voice louder than his or actions stronger than his would end the current fight.

We attended church on Sundays, Wednesdays, and whenever the doors were open, smiling, dressed in our Sunday-best, holding Stephen's and Bobby's hands. No one knew how bad it was. I was embarrassed to tell anyone.

I kept thinking that our situation would get better. The boys were fine, or so I fooled myself into thinking. It seemed as if the stress of it all was affecting only me.

One evening as I lay on the bed, drained from the latest shouting match, having run out of tears and feeling like giving up, something very strange happened. I didn't feel any more pain, neither in my body nor in my mind. It was as if I were floating about a foot above my body. I couldn't speak or feel any physical sensations. It was wonderful. I didn't hurt anymore. I had been in such mental and physical pain for so long, I had forgotten how it was to feel good. This unique experience lasted about five minutes. Then it was as though I floated back down into my body. I tried to tell Richard what had happened and how I had stopped hurting for those minutes. He told me I was imagining things.

The situation and our relationship continued to crumble, yet Richard wanted a baby. I sometimes thought he might mellow out with a child of his own and stop his over-disciplining of the boys. With each month that passed, he put more restrictions on them and criticized them more. They loved him but waited and watched, as did I, for his next angry outburst. I tried for months to get pregnant and nothing happened.

Richard suggested that I go to the doctor to see what was wrong with me. I did, but the doctor suggested that Richard come in since I already had two successful pregnancies. Richard refused, saying there was nothing wrong with *him*. So I prepared temperature charts, everything, but still no pregnancy.

Finally, the doctor convinced Richard that he should have a sperm count test. Reluctantly, he did, and the doctor called to say that Richard had no sperm—absolutely none. I remember crying. I knew how much he wanted a baby, and I wanted to give him one.

At Richard's insistence, the doctor referred him to an infertility specialist in Philadelphia where he could be tested to see if there were some blockages to sperm production or release. After the various tests and exams, we went home to wait for the results. The doctor called. Nothing could be done. Richard had been born sterile; he had never produced sperm. Since we could never have children, I thought having Bobby and Stephen would mean even more to him, but he became worse with them. I finally suggested that he might be taking out on them his anger at being unable to biologically father a child. He was enraged by my remark. We could not talk about it. I hated for him to hurt so badly, and I hated the pain he caused the boys.

In 1962, television programs reported on the dire plight of foster child care in Washington, D.C. Hundreds of children, sometimes two to a bunk bed, twenty-five and more to a room, were being housed in the city. The daily needs of these children were barely being met, and no one had time to give them the attention and love they needed. Bobby, Stephen, and I watched these specials and the pleas for foster families. The boys promised they would take care of a child if we brought one into our home.

My heart too went out to these children. Surely, since I discovered I could love two boys instead of one, there might be room to love another child—at least for awhile until someone else was found to love them.

Richard and I talked about taking in one of these children. He agreed, in part, because families were paid each month enough money to cover their food, so this wouldn't cost us anything. Their clothing and medical care was also taken care of. This combination of advantages suited him fine. He even calculated that we might make some money doing it. I had my doubts about that. We would need to spend every cent we received to make the child's life the best we could.

In August, 1962, after extensive interviews with the family, the social worker brought not one but *two* children. She drove over with a little boy who had been taken by court order from his sixteen-year-old mother, and a little girl, fifteen months old, taken out of another foster home because of neglect.

Two! I hadn't counted on two, but the boys, Stephen at four-and-a-half and Bobby seven, pitched in to help. Even Richard shared the load lovingly. The little girl's name was Andrea. When the boys helped change her, they both pointed to her little bottom, covered with fluid-filled blisters from lying unchanged for days. They gently helped put salve on her. They both adored her from the moment they saw her.

Stephen wasn't in school yet, and he and Andrea became buddies. She held him around the waist, on the back of his tricycle, as he pedaled down the sidewalk. He helped bathe her and put her to bed. He held one hand, Bobby the other, and tried to help her learn to walk. She responded to their love immediately and blossomed. She began to walk and talk and smile and became an important part of our lives.

The courts removed the small boy from our home days later. His parents had gotten a temporary court order to have him returned. I cried for two days for this child whose head was already flattened from never being picked up. He was going back with a family that simply didn't know how to care for him properly. This gave me my first clue to the pain and heartache of being a foster parent. We never saw him again. I tried to prepare myself to lose Andrea.

Stephen and Andrea played together for hours. He taught her words and would grin and laugh when she said "pintoot" for pencil and "Ruuubeee" very loud in calling the name of Richard's mother, Ruby. He was her protector and guardian. He knew that she might have to leave anytime, that we could keep her only for awhile. It didn't stop him from totally loving her. She became his sister, his playmate, and friend. He was much like a proud father to her.

I got Andrea dolls and little girl toys. It was fun to have a daughter to shop for and the boys had mostly "boy" toys. Stephen and Bobby would play "house" with her and be daddies for her dolls. Richard was sarcastic to the boys about playing with dolls. Bobby got by with playing with G.I. Joe dolls because they were male, but Richard still made snide remarks about them.

Stephen had a natural inclination to want to cuddle animals and even Andrea's dolls, but he was reluctant to do so with his dad around. Several times I found him sleeping with his arms around his metal robot. It was cold and hard. This was ridiculous. I went to the toy store and bought him Beany and Cecil dolls. Cecil was a dragon and Beany was his friend. Beany was a *boy* and that was acceptable. Richard teased him, but Stephen was able to endure it and slept with Beany for years. When I went into his room to tuck him in at night after he was asleep and bent to kiss him, Beany was always snuggled under his arm and covered up with his blanket.

Each year, we expected to lose Andrea and tried to prepare for it. But one can never fully prepare to lose a child so loved. She remained with us for five years before we were able to adopt her. She became the first foster child able to be adopted by foster parents in the District of Columbia, they told us. We fought long and hard for her; her mother was dead and the father wasn't in the picture. I think the way the boys loved her helped stack the deck in our favor with the social workers.

Stephen fell in the bathtub during this time and split his chin open. Richard took him for stitches while Bobby, Andrea, and I waited anxiously at home. Stephen cried more when he saw the tub turn red with his blood than from the pain. Richard said he endured the stitches fairly well, and he soon healed. He would always carry a small white scar under his chin from that mishap.

When Stephen was about four or five, he loved to watch the garbage men empty the trash each week. If asked what he wanted to be when he grew up, Stephen answered, "A garbage man." I had responded, "A garbage man, Stephen? Why do you want to be a garbage man?" "Because they're so nice to me," he answered. This should have been a clue about how he was feeling in the family. I discovered that he went outside and talked to them, and they looked for him and waved. He considered them his special friends. None of the rest of us, I believe, were ever aware of them or of all the good work they did—only Stephen saw this.

He often played with or brought home the kids no one else liked or ones who were dirty and obviously neglected. The few times I suggested that he ought not spend so much time with "so and so," he would reply, "But, Mom, I like him and he doesn't have any friends." He lived the kindness that we were only teaching. Stephen possessed a pure acceptance of people just as they were. He didn't experience that at home.

It was a rare day that Richard didn't find fault with something he or Bobby did. Because of this, I began a very destructive pattern. I have no one but myself to blame for such stupidity. I began disciplining the children before Richard walked through the door, because I knew that my yelling and punishment wouldn't be as severe as his. Often, I discovered, if I was yelling at them or punishing them, he would leave them alone. It was my foolish way of trying to make things easier on them. It seemed like nothing I did made things better. I felt helpless, confused, and frustrated as the situation in our home continued to deteriorate.

❦

CHAPTER TWO

Broken Spirits

Sing to the Lord a new song. (Psalms 96:1)

Take no thought for what ye shall put on. (Matthew 6:25)

What makes one instrument sacred and another secular? Is an organ really more holy than a guitar? What if there were no pipe organs in heaven, and angels played guitars, drums and tambourines? What if God danced instead of walked? What if angels told jokes and Saint Peter laughed a lot? What if finger painting was required and Heaven's board meetings were held on a merry-go-round?

Let them hear music blasting from the sanctuary and dare to believe that God is not turned off by jeans. If you dress up so much on the outside, don't you tend to dress up on the inside too and bring to God a presentable self—instead of the real you.

          – Found among Stephen's writings

Early in 1963, we bought a four-bedroom house with a delightful yard for the children. It had a small ankle-deep, manmade pond in the backyard with a bridge across it. Bobby and Stephen loved to wade in the pond with Andrea and pretend to fish. They swam and played all kinds of imaginary games, sitting on the bridge, dangling their feet over the edge.

Andrea had her own room and the boys shared a room with bunk beds. They attended a school within walking distance and made lots of friends. Active in the church, we often had new families over for meals and were part of a large fellowship of friends there. The children were an active part of it all.

There was a housing development in downtown Washington, D.C. where welfare mothers and children lived. I organized a group of women at the church to go there twice a week. We taught classes on arts and crafts, took the families on field trips, and volunteered at the community day care center held at a nearby church. Stephen went with me each time, since he wasn't yet in school. Andrea stayed with a neighbor. The women and children were without so many of the things we all took for granted: books, decent furniture, and clothing. Often, they did not even have enough food to eat.

We enlisted the help of the church people to donate these items and to distribute them. Stephen would go through his toys and clothes and give away many things he really loved because, he said, "They don't have *anything,* and I have *everything.*" He rode with us to the zoo and other places about town, as we took the children on field trips. He was shocked when the little black children yelled, "Cop!" upon seeing a policeman and ducked down in the back seat in fear. Policemen meant something entirely different to him. He was saddened even at five and six by this and by what he saw in the homes of these people. He said that when he grew up, he was going to get them good furniture and nice clothes and lots of food and toys. He continued to worry about them after we returned home.

At mealtimes for months, when it was Stephen's turn to pray, he bowed his little blond head, folded his hands in front of his plate, scrunched his eyes shut, and solemnly began, "Dear God, bless everyone who doesn't have everything we have. Bless everyone who doesn't have a bathtub and help them to get bathtubs." We never knew how he came to be worried about the bathtubs. The people with whom we were working *did,* at least, have bathtubs. We grinned to ourselves every time he prayed this prayer until he must have felt it was answered and began to pray for other things.

He entered first grade at six and fell in love with school. He knew Andrea missed him at home, and he brought her his drawings and special papers, trying to teach her what he was learning. He made friends so easily—the house was always filled with his various playmates. He seemed to be especially aware of the good qualities in his friends and was rarely critical of them. I doubt that he was ever aware of how different he was in this respect from the rest of his playmates. The others constantly fought among themselves and were always angry at each other for some imagined thing or another. If his friends fought among themselves, he tried to help them make up. Stephen was our little peacemaker, and I often thought of the Scripture, "Blessed are the peacemakers . . . ," whenever I watched him play.

Stephen was delightful to raise. He brought such joy into my life, into all of our lives. He was so affectionate and loving, and he was very kind and considerate of everyone and everything.

He loved "Superman" on television and heroes with swords and capes who always won over the "bad guys." I made him a Superman cape, and he "flew" around the yard rescuing the cat, the dog, and other imaginary victims. On his sixth birthday, I surprised him with a black cape inset with a large golden eagle covering the back. It had taken hours for me to design and sew this gift. I bought him a gladiator sword and helmet to wear with it. These were his prized possessions for years. With sword extended and cape flying, he spent hours preparing his "army" to fight to save the world.

He needed little attention. He played alone quietly for hours. He also played days on end with his friends. They played cowboys and Indians and all the wonderful games of the imagination in which children of that age excel. His years were filled with celebrations of birthdays, Halloweens, Christmases, and Easters.

I loved buying presents for him, because he appreciated them so much. I loved doing things for him because he didn't expect them. It was a rare day that he didn't come up to me several times, unasked, to give me a hug and kiss and say, "I love you, Mom." How could one *not* respond to a child like that?

He often called me outside to show me something, saying, "You've gotta see this, Mom," as he leaned down and pointed to a ladybug crawling up his metal robot or to the cat sleeping peacefully against the dog's belly. He always saw things we didn't notice, and they became special to him and to us when he pointed them out.

We had a blonde Pekingese dog named Pudgie that followed Stephen's little white rabbit around and ate up all of its droppings, then had diarrhea for days. Stephen raced to pick up the little pellets before the dog reached them. He was gentle and considerate with all the animals, and they too responded in kind. We often found him asleep on the couch, with Pudgie asleep beside him, four paws in the air, belly exposed. As an amateur photographer, I took countless delightful shots.

I loved him so much that, when my mother visited, she said, "When Stephen walks into a room, you light up." When he did sometimes have to be corrected, it hurt me more than it did him, I think. He took his punishment very well if it was from me. It usually consisted of a whack on the bottom, being sent to his room, or being talked to about the consequences of his behavior.

I also adored the other children. It wasn't that Stephen got all the attention and love. His brother and sister needed far more attention than he did. Bobby was often going through some crisis with friends or at school. Andrea just needed more physical attention as the youngest. Stephen seemed to have far fewer needs and wants than either his brother or his sister, or his friends. He seemed to live what the Apostle said, "I have learned, in whatever state I am, therewith to be content." (RSV Phil. 4:11) Despite all the criticism from Richard, Stephen remained loving and caring with him.

Richard spent a lot of time with him and with Bobby, but there was always a cutting edge in his manner with them. Games that should have been fun were filled with biting criticism that stressed winning, not joy in the playing. The children and I began to get nervous several hours before Richard was due home, because we knew the criticism and the fault-finding would soon begin. And mealtimes were when Richard vented his anger the most.

Bobby began to rebel. Stephen gained weight and began to look a little chunky. I gained back to my pregnancy weight. There were so many rules. We loved mayonnaise, for instance; but Richard liked only mustard, so we were not allowed to put anything except mustard on hamburgers. Only two pieces of ice were allowed in a glass. If he saw more, they were removed and thrown away. We had to eat every bite on our plates, no matter how full we were. He usually served the children, so they couldn't put smaller helpings on their own plates.

If the boys cried, Richard told them not to be sissies, to be men. He told me I hadn't had enough discipline when I was a child, and he was going to correct that. He was thirty-three at this time; I was twenty-nine.

Richard and I battled almost daily—I tried to get him to ease up on the children, while he told me we all needed more discipline. It seemed none of us could do anything right. He drove us crazy. One minute he told us how much he loved us, and in the next breath he berated us for some wrongdoing. If Bobby and Stephen were playing with building blocks, he had a better way. Whatever any of us did, *his* way was better. We either changed quickly to his way, or he withdrew from us emotionally until we complied.

A crazy thing began to happen to me. I began to feel that I was alive only to please Richard, and if I didn't, then any happiness I might have from doing things my way was wrong. It was very subtle at first; I wasn't even aware of it. I had both this compulsion to try to please him and this rebellion against his control. I felt as though I was losing my mind. Sometimes I fantasized about hanging myself over the bedroom door with a note pinned to my chest stating, "Look what you did to me!" I knew that was crazy thinking, and I never told anyone about it. When things got unbearable, it worked as a mental escape that restored my sanity.

My mother had told me that life with my grandmother living with us was sometimes so unbearable for her, she would think of killing herself. But when she thought of us children, it was no longer an option. That's how I felt. I couldn't leave my children or hurt my children that way. Lots of women I knew said that they sometimes wished they were dead or felt like killing themselves. We all understood that it was just talk. No one ever did it, no matter how bad things were.

The children reacted to Richard's excessive control and discipline in more subtle ways. They knew that whatever they did, he would change or destroy it if he didn't like it, so they began to hide things from him and to lie to him. They were completely intimidated when he was around. They desperately wanted his approval and attention, and Bobby began to get it in less than desirable ways.

I didn't let myself realize at the time just how bad the home situation was becoming and how traumatizing it was to the children. I kept thinking that Richard would mellow, that we would stop fighting. I felt that somehow, whatever I was doing wrong, I could correct it so he wouldn't be so angry all the time.

I began to do anything to keep the peace. Unless something was of earth-shaking importance, I tried not to fight with him—I let him do it his way. We all tried to get him to love us, to gain his approval. We agreed with him, we complimented him, we tried to meet his every wish. Nothing worked. Something was always wrong. If he came home and the children had picked up all their toys, the house was immaculate, a home-cooked meal was on the table, the children and I dressed up, and we greeted him with hugs and kisses—praying for a peaceful evening—he said, "Did you boys read your Bible today? I bet your mother didn't work on the budget. You didn't, did you?" When we answered, "No," he began his lengthy lectures about why we shouldn't neglect the Scriptures and how we had to get our priorities straight.

Stephen, Bobby, and Andrea loved church and Sunday school, partly because Richard was always on good behavior there and we didn't fight. We were the model family for two hours or more. We continued to attend on Sunday mornings and almost any time the church doors were open. If the children woke up on a Sunday and didn't feel well, they got a lecture from Richard about how important it was to go to church. They needed to make an effort or God would be disappointed in them. So they would get dressed and go to please their dad, unless they were very, very sick. I tried to talk to Richard, telling him to let them rest and let me stay home with them. He insisted that they could rest when church was over. Church changed from a joyful experience to one the children and I frequently resented.

Every weekend, Richard had the boys sit with their *Stewardship Books* and write down how they were going to spend their allowances. Bobby got twenty-five cents and was required to tithe three cents and save ten cents. Stephen got a dime and was required to put a penny into the church plate and to save a few cents. I told Richard they would grow to resent not being allowed to make their own decisions. Bobby was always complaining about the restrictions. Stephen was so young, he just did what his dad told him to do. I tried to explain to them how Richard's parents had required him to tithe and save his money when he was their age and that was why he continued this with them. The end result was that the boys never had enough money left to buy anything they wanted. I tried to support Richard in this endeavor, but after a few months, I sneaked money to them when they went to the store.

Stephen and I continued to spend time at the housing project every week, working with the families. They loved him and he loved them. He let the smelly old lady with the pale face, ragged clothes, and stringy gray hair hug him whenever she wanted. He was as friendly and loving with the unwashed, runny-nosed little children as with his many well-dressed and clean friends in our neighborhood. With the turmoil in our life, this volunteer work was a blessing to Stephen and me. We enjoyed our time there. When we returned home, we gathered toys, clothes, food, and books to take for the next visit.

I was more worried and concerned about Bobby during this time than about Stephen. Stephen seemed to be doing fine. No matter what Richard said or did, Stephen would sit on his lap and talk to him, seemingly without anger and resentment. He seemed to love his dad no matter what. Bobby was hurting, difficult to control, in constant scraps with his brother and his sister, and the neighborhood children. He was in so much pain and needed so much attention daily. He decided what games would be played; he was the leader. Where he had no control over his own life, he exerted that tiny bit of control with friends in school and with his brother and sister. His grades remained good, but his discipline problems increased. Bobby was so loving and tender, but he was suffering beyond endurance.

I tried not to go against Richard, but he was so angry and unfair to the children that despite my vow to keep the peace at almost any cost, I had to help protect them from his emotional and physical abuse. Our home now became a war zone with the fighting between Richard and myself. I didn't think I could ask for help from the church. I didn't want to ruin Richard's reputation. In all honesty, I didn't want to burst the bubble of our "ideal" family either. Besides, Richard didn't think we needed help; he thought *I* needed help. I wondered many times what *was* wrong with me. The children must have felt it was *them*.

The children were getting older and bigger. Stephen was now seven. We needed a larger house. We found one in Rockville, Maryland, on the other side of town. It had a large backyard where Richard could have the garden he wanted, and he could walk to his job as a mechanical engineer only a few blocks away. For a while, our attention was taken up by the move and fixing up the new house. Soon, every Saturday morning, Richard woke us up so that I could cook breakfast and we could all get out and weed the garden. It was hot and humid as only the Washington area can be in the heat of summer. No matter how early we got up, after several hours, the children would be exhausted and complaining. I was irritable and dripping with sweat. Richard reminded us how healthy it was to grow our own food, how we should appreciate having a garden, and how good the discipline was for the children. I calculated that with the time and money we spent on everything, a tomato cost over four dollars. He did not find that amusing. The children were proud of the gourds and the pumpkins they grew themselves, but the stress wasn't worth it to any of us.

Richard bought a poodle so that we could mate it with the Pekingese to make some money selling the pups. There was dog poop all over the yard which the children and I could never keep clean. For me, it was like having two more children only worse. We got rabbits, guinea pigs, cats, and various animals for the children, because Richard felt they needed to be raised with the responsibility of taking care of animals. The children really did love them and, in theory, this was a fine idea. In actuality, it was messy, hard work that was difficult to keep up with. I had to clean the pens and handle most of the feeding and care. If I complained, Richard said the children should be taking care of those things. I couldn't force the children to do what I myself hated to do. I began to feel more like one of the children than a wife and mother.

If I took a stand with him and refused to do what he said, which I sometimes had the courage to do, he withdrew for days. He had nothing to do with me and totally ignored the children, which devastated them and me. When I gave in, he was friendly again. I loved him and I hated him. I was fearful of him, yet afraid to leave him. Two years before, he had blackened my eye in anger, holding me down on the bed. My eye turned purple, black, and yellow. I lied when anyone commented, saying I had hit it on the edge of the sink. However, as low as I was sinking in losing all respect for myself and any self-confidence I had, I did stick up for myself on this. I told him that if he ever hit me again, I would leave him and never come back. He ridiculed me, saying it was my fault and I deserved it. Never again, though he threatened, did he ever hit me. Why I couldn't be stronger about all the other things, I didn't know.

We drove to Missouri several times to visit Richard's parents. On one of the first trips there, when Stephen was only three or four, we stopped at a motel for the night. There was a swimming pool where we all played in the water. Richard told the boys to stand on the side and jump in the deeper water. He told them he would catch them when they went under and pull them up since neither could swim. Bobby did fine, but Stephen was terrified and wouldn't jump. I told him it was okay, he didn't have to jump, but Richard shamed him until he finally jumped. Though he got through it, his eyes were filled with panic and he shook all over. We argued about it the rest of the evening. Stephen so wanted to please Richard in spite of his fears. Years later, he became a fine swimmer. Richard constantly reminded me that he had said he would make men out of those boys and toughen them up—and that it had worked.

As the boys got older, other visits to Missouri were equally unpleasant. If the boys played outside so they didn't mess up their grandparent's trailer home, making little rock piles in the gravel, they were reprimanded immediately by Richard's mother for disturbing the yard. They weren't allowed to dig; they were allowed only to sit and play games. Whatever their ages during a particular visit, they could constrain their energy only for so long. Being there for several days was very difficult for them and for us all. Richard's mother genuinely loved Stephen. She tolerated Bobby, but simply could not stop finding fault with either of them. They seldom had a moment's peace.

They sent the boys one dollar each Christmas and birthday, and in the card, told them how to spend it. They had enough Gulf Oil stock to paper their walls; still, they wrote, "Don't spend this. Put it in your savings." Their other grandparents sent train sets or other glorious, fun toys, on an income that barely covered their own needs. The comparison was painful. I complained to Richard, saying it wasn't that I didn't think it nice of them to remember, but that it was about as cheap as you could get. He must have said something to them because they sent five dollars from then on, but with the same instructions to save it.

I felt thankful for any happy times—there were some; I tried to make it through the awful times—there were so many. I tried to find the joy missing in my marriage in the children.

Sometimes a warning bell would sound within me, and I knew I needed to get the children away from Richard, and to make a better life for myself. But I kept waiting and hoping against hope that things would improve. In spite of it all, I thought I loved him, yet there was some kind of sick feeling that I couldn't live without him. I was convinced, in my limited awareness of God, that *He* would never forgive me for another marriage failure. These things outweighed my personal pain and anguish. It made me wonder sometimes if Richard was perhaps justified in his strict discipline with the children and me. Perhaps somehow I was wrong and just too rebellious to give in to him. My thinking became warped. I did everything I could to please him and to keep him from getting mad. When it didn't work, I fought him but never seemed able to make any progress toward change.

Stephen and Andrea walked to school together. They played together after school. Bobby was most often with his friends, but he loved playing games with Stephen, especially Monopoly and Parcheesi. They wanted me to play too. I was so worn out from the work and fighting, I often put them off and promised to play with them later. Even then, I wished I could have forced myself to have enough energy to spend a playful hour with them.

Stephen gave me some presents during this time that touched my heart. He and Bob had gone to the dime store to shop for my birthday. Stephen insisted that he would find just the perfect earrings and necklace for me. He picked out blue ceramic clip-on earrings that I wore for years along with a blue glass necklace which I wore with everything.

I sewed a lot to save money, though I was never very good at it. Stephen went to the store and picked out a green plastic sewing box. He then personally selected all of the supplies to fill it. There were about ten thimbles, thread in every color, needles, buttons, elastic, needle threaders—everything imaginable. He had saved his allowance for months to surprise me that Christmas. He couldn't stop grinning as I opened each wrapped item. He was so pleased every time I used it, and I always praised him for his thoughtfulness.

He also had his other moments. "Mom!" Bobby screamed one afternoon after school. "Mom, come here quick and spank Stephen!" Stephen was about seven, dressed in his blue jeans and T-shirt, standing silently beside the staircase. I asked what had happened. "Stephen, tell Mom what you called me. Tell her," Bob commanded.

Stephen remained silent. "Stephen, what did you call him?" I asked. He looked at me without even a smile and answered, "I called him a 'shit ass.'"

"See, Mom, I told you. That's disgusting. Aren't you going to spank him?" Bob demanded to know. Stephen wasn't smirking or smiling, and I thought to ask him, "Do you know what 'shit ass' means, Stephen?"

"No, but that's what my friends call each other," he explained.

I laughed out loud. I tried to explain to Bob by that Stephen didn't even know what it meant. Bobby just didn't believe that. He wanted me to spank him. I couldn't—it was too funny. I tried to explain to Stephen what it meant, which wasn't that easy to do. I warned him that he mustn't say it again or call anyone that. I could never again think about it without laughing.

Stephen loved sports. He and Bobby joined the basketball, baseball, and football teams in junior high school. Richard encouraged and supported their efforts in sports. He played with them and instructed them. He was quite proud of their successes, but he tried to get them to practice more, to excel. It took some of the sheer fun out of it for them.

At the first basketball game we attended, where Stephen was just learning to play, he and his teammates dove onto the ball to secure it instead of passing it. The game turned into one more like football than basketball. We cheered him on. Sometimes we laughed so hard at these developing athletes that we had to hide our faces so they wouldn't see. They were too busy trying to find the ball to notice anyway.

Later, both boys won trophies from the recreation department as part of winning basketball teams. Stephen was so proud when he went up to receive his trophy. He kept it displayed in the living room for years, then moved it to his own room. Bobby was always the more natural athlete. Stephen, however, always tried as hard as he could but hated to knock anyone down or to hurt them to win. He did not like to hurt anyone, and he did not like to *be* hurt.

• • •

Richard decided he wanted to adopt a baby. Andrea's adoption was complete; we would never again have to worry about losing her. He talked and talked about adopting a newborn baby to raise, saying he had never had that opportunity like I had. The boys caused Richard no end of irritation. He was almost as impatient with Andrea, and I seriously doubted the advisability of adding another child, so I kept putting off doing what he wanted.

His rules were driving us crazy. He allowed the children only two inches of water in the tub when bathing because he considered more than that to be a waste of water. He measured their water with a ruler and drained it down to that level if it was above his imposed limit. We were not allowed to buy anything on Sundays because that was the Sabbath. If we skipped church for any reason, whether due to sickness or just not wanting to go, Richard either hid the Sunday paper so we couldn't read it or took it to church with him. If we didn't go to Wednesday services, we couldn't watch television while he was gone or even when he returned home.

If the children left lights on accidentally, Richard removed the bulbs from their sockets and could only be redeemed through money paid from their allowances. If they were out of money, their rooms remained dark until they earned some.

If certain rules weren't followed, the guilty child would have to stand in the corner, facing the wall, and tell the wall about what he or she had done. Richard made them say, "Wall, I will not leave my clothes lying around. Wall, I lied about brushing my teeth. Wall, I didn't weed the garden today." I thought it was the most humiliating thing one could do to a child. I begged Richard to stop. In the beginning, I pleaded with him quietly in our room where the children couldn't hear. Later, I began shouting at him to stop, telling the children to go to their rooms and not to do what he said.

The children were confused. Two messages, totally different, were coming from their parents. Wanting to listen to me but fearful of their dad's wrath, they would continue talking to the wall or doing whatever Richard had commanded them to do. When Richard felt they had done as he asked long enough—sometimes ten or twenty times, sometimes for an hour—he sent them to bed. He and I would then fight until the early hours of the morning over the incidents. The children were kept awake by the fighting, I'm sure.

Richard found a tool missing and no one admitted using it. It was a school night, but he kept the children up, and ordered them to march up and down the two flights of stairs at the entry of our house. From living room to basement, up and down—again and again—until someone admitted their evil deed. I begged him to stop, and the children cried and cried from exhaustion. Another fight between us continued into the night after the children were finally allowed to go to bed.

Still, the children loved Richard and tried to gain his approval, as did I. In the mornings after he had left for work, I tried to explain to the children how he had been raised and hurt as a child. He had a neurotic mother who blamed him for her ill health and a father too much a Caspar Milquetoast to stand up for him. Richard was trying to be like Thom, a military friend of his whom he admired, who disciplined *his* children this way. I told the children that Richard loved them and couldn't help the way he was. Bobby said "I hate his guts." Andrea simply stared at me. Stephen said, "I know Dad doesn't mean to hurt us."

I had to lie about and hide things I purchased for us. The children wanted clothes like their friends. Richard decided upon the kinds and brands we were allowed to have. Bobby longed for a Nehru jacket when they became the fad. All his friends had one. By the time he was allowed to purchase a cheap one on sale, they had been out of style for months.

Richard continued to talk about a baby. He wanted a newborn, he said, that was *his* to raise from infancy. I tried to believe, in my optimistic moments, that deep down he really loved children and would change with a baby to call his own. I finally convinced myself this was true and agreed to apply to adopt a child. The thought of a new baby also appealed to me. I loved children, and though I was overwhelmed by the family situation and the arguing, I rationalized that it would be fun to have a baby.

We applied through the Child Welfare Division of the welfare department in Washington, D.C. where we had adopted Andrea. In 1965 there were hundreds of children waiting to be adopted. With military and transient government personnel moving in and out all of the time, the institutions were filled with children of all ages needing homes. Very shortly after, this would change as the pill and abortion came more into use.

We applied for a girl or a boy of any nationality, but specified that it be a very young baby. The same case worker who had helped us adopt Andrea came out to interview us. The rules were somewhat more strict for this type of adoption. She interviewed Richard and me together, then separately, and interviewed all three children. I coached the children to say only good things yet be as honest as possible. That was actually an impossible task.

A few days later, the social worker called, saying she didn't know how she could possibly recommend us to adopt a baby. She explained that when she interviewed Richard alone, she realized how strict, unbending, and dogmatic he was. I was so easy-going that she wondered how in the world we ever got along. Didn't we fight? Wasn't there great difficulty in our different ways of dealing with children? The children seemed fearful of him, yet seemed to love him, she noted. They loved me, she said, but they felt I wasn't able to protect them from their father. Richard would have been furious if he had known what she had said, so I lied. I told her we were certainly different but how good Richard's ways were for the children, and for me, who had lacked discipline as a child. Actually, I neither believed that nor was it true. I had been loved as a child and didn't feel any lack of discipline.

I must have lied convincingly, pleading Richard's case well. I felt in my heart that this was my only hope of saving my marriage and my children. To mellow Richard out, to give him a baby to love so he wouldn't hurt the children so much, seemed to be the answer. I must have convinced her and caused her to doubt what she had heard and felt. Or perhaps the children were so desperately in need of homes that she rationalized ours would be better than if left in their existing situations. I will never know for sure, but shortly thereafter, she gave us the okay to adopt a child when one became available.

We were all so excited. Stephen, Bobby, and Andrea helped get a room ready, though we didn't know what sex the baby would be or when one would come to us. Even Richard relaxed a little and things were somewhat peaceful for awhile. It was much like being pregnant. We knew we were going to have a baby but weren't sure of the exact delivery date.

On February 27, 1966, we received a call from our social worker. She said a baby girl had been born on the February 22, and we could come down in two days to see her. If we approved, she could come home with us. We all rushed out to get diapers, clothes, and last minute items for a girl. We fixed her crib with new sheets and blankets. Stephen placed toys in the crib. Bobby and Andrea rearranged the room. We were as excited as if I were about to give birth.

All three children had just had chicken pox and were confined to the house. We couldn't take them with us when we went to the welfare department to see the little girl. They waited at home with a friend until we got back. The doctor said there was no danger of the baby getting chicken pox, so they eagerly awaited our arrival home, when they could see and hold her.

At the welfare department in Washington, D.C., we were ushered into a room to wait. Our social worker was a lovely middle-aged woman whose kindness and smile were so genuinely warm that you couldn't help but like her. She walked in carrying a very tiny bundle wrapped in a pink blanket with blue satin trim. She removed the corner of the blanket to let us see the baby. We both fell in love with her on the spot. She was so very tiny—only six pounds, twelve ounces at birth and slightly smaller now. She had the tiniest little face and head, dark hair, blue-grey eyes, and hands so small they could barely reach around our fingers. I would have fought an army if they had tried to take her away, such was the immediate love I felt for her. I thought she was beautiful beyond description.

When we arrived home and Stephen and Bobby saw her, they passed her from one to the other. They said over and over how cute she was, how beautiful, how adorable. Andrea was allowed to hold her too. She was nearly five and held her lovingly, like a mother. The boys were, from that time on, her protectors, her warriors, her adoring big brothers. We searched for a name, finally coming up with Deborah, although she would always be called Debbie.

Stephen held her as she slept. He bent his head to kiss the tip of her nose and did anything to wake her up so she would look at him. She would grin at him the moment she saw him and laugh out loud. He could always get her to make noises and cute expressions. As she got older, he played outside in the snow with her, pulling her up and down the sidewalk on the small hill in front of our home—Debbie never tiring, Stephen never complaining.

He would rush home from school to watch her sleep, to play with her, to feed her, to cuddle her. He adored her. Bobby did the same, even teaching her to climb trees. She was racing down the hill in his bike basket, when most babies would be lying in their playpens. It was a love affair with their little sister throughout their childhood that never ended. They included Andrea in everything they did, and the four of them played together by the hour.

Once, I was preparing a talk to give at church, right after Debbie was born, and found a poem that I read over and over again. It reminded me of the great and awesome responsibility of raising these precious children. This had been a time of such peace in our home that I wanted to believe we were finally doing things right with the children. Perhaps they could overcome the earlier damage done to them.

> *I took a piece of plastic clay*
> *And idly fashioned it one day,*
> *And as my fingers pressed it, still*
> *It bent and yielded to my will.*
>
> *I came again, when days were past,*
> *The bit of clay was hard at last,*
> *The form I gave it, still it bore,*
> *But I could change that form no more.*
>
> *Then I took a piece of living clay*
> *And gently formed it, day by day*
> *And molded with my power and art,*
> *A young child's soft and yielding heart.*
>
> *I came again when years were gone,*
> *It was a man I looked upon.*
> *He still that early impress bore,*
> *And I could change it, nevermore.*
>
> – "The Sculptor," author unknown

For a while, things continued peacefully. Richard loved this child of *his*. He carried her everywhere and attended to her every need from the moment he got home from work. His whole countenance changed when he saw her. He thought she was the smartest, cutest, most perfect baby born. She brought out the very finest and best in him. She had him wrapped around her little finger from the moment he laid eyes on her. Debbie could sass him as she got older, and he would laugh, whereas the boys would have been slapped or punished. Instead of resenting her and what she could get by with, the boys loved seeing this kinder side of him and how gentle and lovable he could be. But this was not to last.

Before Debbie was a year old, Richard had reverted to his old patterns with all of us. Finally, in desperation, after being up night after night fighting with him, I stuffed our dirty and clean clothes into suitcases, dressed the children, and we caught a plane to Chattanooga. I was going home to my family. I didn't care what the church people thought. I didn't care anymore. I knew if I didn't get the children away, he would destroy the three older ones and me. Either that or I would kill him or myself. The situation had become intolerable.

My mother and father encouraged us to come and welcomed us with open arms. Our many visits over the years never endeared Richard to them; they couldn't stand him. They always felt he was the most cruel man with children they had ever seen. My mother and sister always asked why I stayed and continued to put up with his treatment. I was more honest with them this time, and didn't try to defend him.

While we were there, and I was taking a nap in the upstairs loft of my sister's house next door, Stephen climbed the stairs and came into the room crying. I was half asleep and suffering terribly from allergies, no doubt intensified by the stress of all that had happened. I could hardly breathe or see out of my swollen eyes. I hadn't slept in days and was tormented about what to do. Instead of asking Stephen what was wrong and trying to help him, I told him to lie down and be quiet. I dozed off and on for awhile, each time being awakened by his whimpering and calling my name. I finally told him to run downstairs and let me sleep, something I would never have said to him under normal circumstances. He must have gone downstairs. Before long, my sister came up and told me something was very wrong with Stephen; he was in terrible pain, holding his ear and crying.

I jumped up and ran downstairs. He was sitting on the couch, hand over his ear, with his head bent against his shoulder. His shirt was soaked and tears were running down his face. He could hardly talk, he was in such pain. We rushed him to the doctor where we learned he had a severe ear infection. The pain must have been unbearable for him. The doctor prescribed medication that would stop the pain and infection, but we would have to watch for days to be sure his hearing wasn't affected.

The guilt I felt was overwhelming. I read to him, I held him, I did everything I could to make up for being so self-centered. I apologized over and over. I must be the worst mother alive, I thought. My child was sick and needed me, and I was too concerned about myself even to care.

We stayed a week. I was beginning to realize I couldn't live with my parents, no matter how caring they were. There wasn't enough room for five more people. I didn't know what to do. I didn't want a divorce. I wanted some peace. I wanted the children to be treated tenderly. I wanted Richard to love us and not hurt us.

Richard called at the end of the week. He didn't call to tell me he loved and missed me; he called to remind me that Stephen was due to be baptized on a certain date. I asked him if he wanted us home. His only reply was, "I want to know if you are going to have Stephen baptized as you have told everyone you would, or if you're going to make a fool of us all."

I was foolish enough to let him intimidate me and convince me to bring Stephen back for the baptism. We went home. Stephen was baptized. The church people never knew I had left.

This was the wrong decision. Richard became even worse with all of us from then on. He did cruel things to hurt the children emotionally. They were frightened of the dark and wanted to leave their doors open; he insisted upon closing them firmly. When the children cried, he told them they were babies. I begged him to let them leave the door open a crack. I remembered being afraid of the dark as a child too. He would not allow it. They sobbed in fear behind the doors, and I opened them a crack, but he slammed them shut and pushed me away. I would sneak and open the doors again when he went in another room. He berated me for hours as they lay frightened in their beds.

One night, one of the children had left a shovel out on the lawn. It snowed and the shovel was now buried where Richard couldn't find it. He woke the children and got them up. It was eleven o'clock and they had school the next day. He grilled them about who had left it out and where it was. Hour after hour, he lectured them about this terrible thing one of them had done. He said if the guilty one would admit to it, they could all go to bed.

At about 2:00 a.m., they were so exhausted that Stephen said he had done it. Richard asked him where he had left the shovel. He didn't remember. It was obvious he hadn't been the one and didn't have any idea where it was. The lecture continued with browbeating and accusing. I pleaded with and hollered at Richard to let them go to bed. Finally, he did. By then, whoever did it was too terrified to admit it. Perhaps they didn't even know or remember. They were expected to get up early the next morning for school.

Every day, one of us was accused of something by Richard. On the weekends when he was home, it was a living hell. By Saturday night, we were all emotional wrecks. I didn't know what to do. Richard reminded me often that I had my one chance from God with a wrecked marriage. This was my last chance, so I'd better straighten up. I began to buy into that. What was wrong with me?

Sundays were disgusting now—it was so phony, the way we dressed up, pretending to be the perfect family. At the end of the service, I was irritable and distraught. We often argued for the rest of the day.

We got an old piano for the family. The evening before had been one of the terrible times where Richard over-disciplined the children, and I intervened, and then he and I quarreled long into the night. The next afternoon after school, the children and I talked about what had happened. I tried to bring them some hope that it would get better. I reminded them of how much I loved them and that God loved them even more. I assured them that God was trying to help us. We were all exhausted from the previous night and laid around our family room, resting and talking.

Stephen then sat at the piano and began picking out a tune. I sat beside him to watch him play. I couldn't read music, nor sing very well, but we began to compose a song together. We wrote several verses, both of us adding lines and words. Stephen picked out the notes as I hummed my version of what I thought sounded good with the words. It went like this:

Cast your burdens on the Lord,
And He will give you peace.
Let Him gather all your cares and woes
His loving arms beneath.

Let him know you trust and love him.
Never doubt His loving care,
When the days are dark and gloomy,
You will always find him there.

Let no doubts and torments hold you.
Put your trust and faith in Him,
And He will lift and bless you,
Through golden days and dim.

Oh, praise be to my Savior.
For His patience, love, and care.
I will always trust and seek Him,
For He said He would be there.

Thank you, God, and thank you, Jesus,
For a place to turn and rest,

When the burdens of the world
Weigh too hard upon my breast.

We were very proud of our creation. We played and sang our song when we were sad and when we were happy. We repeated it so often that Andrea and Debbie began to learn the words and sing along with us. We never sang it in front of Richard.

When Stephen was almost nine, he woke up every morning and told me about his dreams. An amazing number of these were about Jesus. In these dreams, Jesus talked with him, showed him around heaven, and answered his questions. Jesus visited him in this manner almost every night for months. Every morning when he woke up, he was so excited, his little face beaming with joy, as I sat on his bed and listened to him relate his experiences.

It never entered my mind to record the dreams he told me; I have regretted that a thousand times. The tales he told, the messages from Jesus, and his utter childlike enthusiasm in relating them should have been permanently recorded. Sometimes Richard listened to the dreams too and was deeply touched by them. There was no denying that these were joyful experiences for Stephen.

When Stephen was nine and Bob was twelve, they were tested in school and both of them ranked in the upper 5 percent of their age group, nationwide. The school would not reveal their IQ scores to us. I never understood why. Much later, I saw Stephen's score. It was 157.

Both boys were excellent readers. They checked out scores of books from the library. Their teachers treated them very well because they were such good students. Even though Bobby was having some disciplinary problems, he was so charming that he got by with a lot of it. Stephen underachieved somewhat. He was so sociable and easy-going that he didn't always push himself to make A's. He came home with report cards of A's, B's, and, occasionally, some C's.

From eight to ten, Stephen seemed happy. He made lots of friends and he had a special buddy, Ralph. They were together constantly. Ralph was a darling Catholic-Italian boy who lived next door. They rode bikes and played sports together. Ralph had to go to church classes on Saturday and would tell Stephen what he was taught by the priests. One time, Stephen came home and said that Ralph told him the priests warned them that the devil would punish kids in hell with fire if they were bad. It scared him. I imagine it scared Ralph even more. I told him that was *their* belief, but we didn't believe that way. I assured him it wasn't true. Ralph also told him that if they put their hands in their pants and touched themselves, they would be punished by the devil. But I told Stephen that touching himself was very natural, not harmful, and that no one would punish him.

When Stephen was about eight months old, I had made up a song for him that I sang when rocking him to sleep. He was so sweet and lovable, that I found myself composing that short verse without any awareness of doing it. As he got older, and I tucked him in bed, he would remind me to sing it to him several times before I left the room. Even when he was nine and ten, he often asked me sing it to him when I kissed him goodnight. I would lie beside him, stroke his hair, and sing it quietly over and over against his cheek. It went: "And bless my little Stephen, help him always be tender, kind and loving, Lord, and always near to Thee."

Stephen began to think he was fat when he was about eleven. He was only slightly chunky. He was so clean cut and good-looking that mothers who saw him often commented, "I hope my daughter has a boyfriend just like him." Kids would sometimes tease him about being fat and it would hurt him. He was already gaining height while many of his friends were still very short and kiddish-looking. He was beginning to show glimpses of the man he would be.

He had blonde hair, streaked with a darker golden blonde. His eyes were a clear blue that changed with the sky or the colors he wore. His eyelashes were black, and though not long, framed his striking blue eyes. His eyes were the feature you noticed most. His eyebrows were dark and thick. Kindness and love, mixed with a little mischief, seemed to radiate from his glance. His teeth were straight with one front tooth slightly rough from a time he had dived too deeply into the shallow end of a swimming pool and hit bottom. Little freckles dotted the ridge of his nose and were sprinkled under his eyes. His shoulders were becoming broad. I thought he was built like a football player.

During this time, the school called me in for a conference with all of his teachers. He was making mostly A's and B's. They said that he should be making A's in everything and wasn't applying himself. I asked if he was a problem in class. They all assured me that he wasn't. They all enjoyed him very much and wished the other students were as nice and well-behaved, they said. But, they tried to convince me, with *his* mind, (they still hadn't told us his IQ) he should be earning much better grades. I questioned, "Isn't he happy and well-adjusted?" "Oh, yes," they agreed. I told them I wasn't going to force him to do better just for grades, that he was a happy, peaceful child. They were obviously frustrated with me. They said, "This child is remarkably bright. You should encourage him to do far better."

Later, they wrote to tell me it was no wonder Stephen didn't do better since he wasn't encouraged at home. I was irritated at them because

Stephen was so utterly happy at school and he had more than enough pressures at home. I wanted him to enjoy school and without added stress there. I didn't feel the grades were as important as the fact that he was learning and content in school. They didn't agree. They continued to be on him to do better. I encouraged him to do his best but to enjoy school. But after this, Richard pressured Stephen constantly about his grades.

Stephen continued the same, near the top of the class but not *the* top. I thought that was fine. I had previously allowed him to be skipped from first to third grade at the recommendations of his teachers. I also did it because my mother hadn't allowed me to skip, and I had always regretted that decision. She felt I would be out of my age group which wouldn't be good for me socially, so I endured the boredom. I didn't want Stephen to feel that way. He was always taller for his age, and he fit right in with those a year older and kept his grades up. If he missed his classmates, he never mentioned it. He quickly made new friends.

Within months after the conference with the school, he had slipped somewhat in his testing, but still ranked in the upper 5 percent of the country. Later, he dropped down to the top 10 percent. He still tested, at 9.7 or more out of a possible 10 on most of his subjects. He was expressive in his writing, read far past his grade level, devoured books and comics, and loved television. The slip in ranking seemed of little concern.

However, both Stephen and Bobby began to do worse in school. Their grades dropped, Bobby's more than Stephen's. Notes such as, "Stephen does not pay attention, poor written assignments and bad days in class," began to come home frequently. I tried to help them with homework and encourage them, but things were getting so bad for me that sometimes I would lie around all day, just barely taking care of Debbie. I could hardly walk up the stairs I was so weary. When the children did get home, I frantically had them help me straighten up the house and get dinner ready, knowing that Richard would get angry if these things weren't done.

I realized I needed help, that we all needed help. Had I read anything on psychology, or if there had been information on co-dependence and self-esteem, I might have known how to handle things better. I rarely read anything except religious books because Richard felt I had missed so much of the history and information about the church that I needed to catch up to where he was in that knowledge.

Fearful and desperate, I took a chance and called a counselor whose name I found in the *Yellow Pages*. He wanted to see both of us. When I related this to Richard, he ranted and raved. He said the money would be wasted and that he didn't need help, I did. So I told him I would go myself, alone. But he then insisted I couldn't go alone, because I would only tell my side. Therefore, we went together for counseling, first to one, then to another. Each counselor, when pointing out something Richard might change or see more clearly, was met with denial and anger. He wouldn't go back to that particular counselor, and I'd be forced to find another. Finally, one very tender and loving woman said, "Richard, you want a master/slave relationship and you want your wife and children to be your slaves." Richard became violently angry, saying I'd never had any discipline and neither did the children, and he was going to see to it that we had it.

He wouldn't go back, so I sneaked out alone for another session. The counselor asked me if I was going to put up with that kind of treatment. I, also into denial, told her that he was a good man and that he really loved us. I explained to her that he didn't mean to hurt us and couldn't help how he was. I began to tell her all the things I did wrong, trying to take the blame. I asked her what I could do, what I could change so Richard wasn't so angry all the time, so fault-finding with us. She said, "The only solution I can see is to leave him." I wasn't ready to hear that. I found yet another counselor.

I was given the same advice. Most asked why I tolerated living as we did and why I didn't leave. They did not feel Richard was willing to make any changes. No one suggested bringing the children in, nor did I think of counseling for them at that time. I had never heard of children getting counseling. There was so much I didn't know. Nothing helped. I wanted a counselor to tell me it was me, give me some quick solution to change things, and be healed.

Things became even worse after the counseling, so I suggested we see one of our ministers since Richard hated all the previous counselors I had picked, and the church counseling would be free. He refused, saying we didn't need to drag in the church. However, in another act of courage, I secretly went to see one of our ministers. He was kind and loving, did not suggest separation, and tried to help me see what I was doing wrong so I could correct it. He asked to see Richard, and since the secret was out, Richard had little choice. We both went in for several sessions which turned into yelling matches. On our last visit the minister said, "I don't usually recommend this, but I don't see how you two can possibly stay married. I suggest a divorce." That was unheard of in the church. I should have felt justified, happy, and vindicated, but I simply never went back. I didn't want a divorce. I prayed daily that I could change enough to help heal our relationship. I prayed for God to give me another chance and that we wouldn't divorce. I prayed that Richard would be kinder and love us.

Bobby, reaching his teenage years and hurting so badly, took out all his aggression on Stephen. I realized this displacement of anger was a fairly normal response to the sick situation in the family. Richard took his anger out on us, I took mine out on the children, Bobby took his out on Stephen. How much further it would go soon became clearer.

One day, I found Bobby's two gerbils dead in their cage. Stephen had killed them after Bobby had been particularly mean to him. Bobby was furious and rightly so. He demanded that I punish Stephen. I tried to tell him that he had pushed Stephen beyond his limits with his constant picking on him. He only saw that as taking Stephen's side. Bobby was stretched beyond his own limits with Richard's cruel disciplines and fault-finding. I was on him all the time for hurting Stephen or Andrea. He must have felt totally unsupported despite my love for him.

Stephen cried and apologized again and again. He loved animals. To have killed the gerbils was like murder to him. He wept and said he was sorry over and over. I held him and comforted him. Thoughts kept coming through my mind that something was very wrong here. I knew that what Stephen had done was a warning to me. I must stop the damage Richard was doing to the children before something even worse happened. But as time passed, I did not take any action. Stephen never again hurt a living thing.

Both Stephen and Bobby began to bite their fingernails down to the cuticle, which I should have noted with more concern. They battled all the time. It seemed that Bobby deliberately tormented Stephen. I tried to intervene to protect Stephen. I tried to reason with Bobby, but it made him more angry. I couldn't punish Stephen because Bobby usually started the fights and made Stephen's life miserable. While I understood his pain, I couldn't let him constantly hurt his brother. Now, standing on the battlegrounds, were Richard and me, Bobby and Richard, Bobby and Stephen, and Bobby and me. Stephen seemed to survive with his usual good disposition, but he became more quiet and subdued. Andrea began to have difficulties in school. She too developed some aggressive behavior with teachers and classmates, though, like Stephen, she was pretty easy-going at home.

From the time Stephen was seven years old and every year until he reached thirteen, we attended church camps in Pennsylvania. Stephen and Bobby loved this break in the summer schedule. The people who attended were like family and really cared about the children. They were in classes most of the day for the whole week. It was a wonderful breather for them. They made crafts of all kinds and proudly displayed them. Richard, as usual, was always on his best behavior with the church people and it was a blessed week of relief each year.

We bought a Starcraft pop-up camper that slept all of us. We camped once or twice a month during those years. We first had a tent, but after a while, that proved too difficult with four children. Besides, we couldn't get all our supplies into the small, aging 1956 Ford that Richard kept to save money. It was a lot of work to load, unload, clean up, and wash out the camper, but it provided almost the only truly happy times we ever had. Richard showed the older children how to make a fire, and even though he nagged and fussed at them, it didn't have the cutting edge it did at home. He played games with them and taught them to tie special rope knots. We were, for those brief days, the perfect American family we only pretended to be the rest of the year.

We were never allowed to sleep late even when we camped. Richard got us up early and built a campfire. We all cooked breakfast, and he did more than his part at these times. No matter how cold or rainy or snowy, we camped. Stephen and Bobby ran free, rarely fought, and were like they used to be before I married Richard. I clung to every moment of this time. No cost was too great to get us ready for the next camping trip. Stephen collected rocks and found bugs and brought them over for Debbie to see. Andrea found mud and water to play in and thoroughly amused herself for hours. Bobby climbed trees, built fires, forts, and tree houses. After a few days, I would almost forget how life was at home.

Then the weekend would be over. Even in the car going home, Richard began his criticisms. He instructed us as to what he wanted done at home and what we had done wrong at camp. He would not stop for drinks or food, saying we had eaten enough junk that weekend. We began again the living hell we would endure until the next trip.

When the children had a holiday or a week off from school, we were still required to get up as early as Richard did for work. He said since he had to go to earn a living, we should be up doing chores too. He woke us all up, and I fixed breakfast while he instructed the children on their responsibilities for the day. Sometimes we sneaked back into bed after he left. Other times, we laid around and then frantically tried to get everything done before he got home. What went on when he left for work was always our secret.

Even in those years, I knew Richard fancied himself a great father. He wanted them to grow up to amount to something, he said. He felt if he could control their lives, they couldn't possibly go wrong as adults. It had exactly the opposite effect. His punishments were so severe for the smallest infraction that when they did something that really justified some action, he had nothing left with which to punish them. The punishments became harder and longer and more humiliating.

During these years, I told Stephen and Bobby that if they ever felt like smoking, not to sneak around and hide. They could come to me and smoke in front of me. I said I didn't think it was good for their health, but

I didn't want them to feel they had to lie about it. My mother had said the same thing to my brother, sister, and me—about smoking and drinking—and none of us did either one. The fun of secretiveness was taken away, and it didn't appeal to us. I felt this approach had been good and wanted to use it with my children. Richard forbade them to smoke, saying he didn't care what I said, that he wouldn't allow it. In defiance, Bobby began to smoke as soon as he could buy or beg cigarettes.

We discussed sex; I told the boys it was perfectly normal to masturbate and that it was nothing to feel guilty about. I explained that it was a good feeling and that when they were older and found partners to love, the feelings would be even better. Until then, I assured them, it was normal, healthy, and pleasurable. Richard was incensed when he found out. He told them they should never masturbate because it was wrong. Rather, they should discipline themselves to engage in sports and take showers to forget about it. As for sex before marriage, that was a sin. They must wait until they were married.

The children had good, healthy diets; but, if we went out, I allowed them to buy candy or a soda if they wanted it. I felt they would more naturally turn to good food if junk food were occasionally allowed and not made into such a "forbidden fruit." Richard never allowed them to buy a soft drink in front of him. He lectured them on the evils of sugar and candy, making them feel so guilty when they wanted something that they stopped asking.

They began to sneak and eat forbidden foods behind his back. If we went to a fair, they were allowed only one thing. There was always a restriction placed on any desires they had for food, movies, books, or anything *they* wanted.

We were a family in crisis. I fooled myself that despite all that was happening behind closed doors, we were like most families, and it wasn't that bad. I even told the minister that things were better—not just better, but fine. He accepted that. Overall, it seemed that most of the church people, loving and caring as they were, didn't really want to hear that anything wasn't perfect. Any scandals were hushed up, no one discussed anything negative. There was an unrealistic emphasis on outward appearances for "show" which was very easy for me to buy into. How dare I burst the bubble, to say that one of their "called by God, ordained ministers" was a tyrant? That one of their "chosen" was sadistic and cruel to his family and made life a living hell for his wife and children?

To add to the stress, my doctor discovered two lumps in my breast during a routine examination. She said she was sure the lumps were cancerous and sent me for a mammogram. She would inform me of the results in several weeks when she came back from out-of-town.

On the way home, I bargained with God. I asked him to please let me live to see my children grown and not let them be raised by Richard. I promised Him the rest of my life in service and that I would change, do anything, be better, nicer, kinder. I pleaded with him to let me live. I cried and I prayed.

When I looked in the mirror the next morning and remembered the doctor's dire prediction, I began to cry again. As clear as if someone were standing by my side speaking to me, a voice said, "Stop using the 'Five Day Deodorant' and the lumps will go away." There was no one in the room but me. I stopped using the deodorant. When I went in for the results of my tests, the doctor examined me again. The lumps were gone. She said the lumps showed clearly on the X-ray, and she couldn't understand how the lumps disappeared so quickly. I told her I had stopped using the deodorant. I was examined regularly for years and the lumps never returned. Years later, I read an article about the dangers of these long-lasting antiperspirants and it verified what I had "heard."

We had some friends from church about our same ages that we visited frequently. They had four sons about the ages of our four children. We received a call one morning informing us that the mother had died during the night in her sleep. She woke up choking and unable to breathe. Before her husband could get help, she was dead. The entire church mourned. It hit me especially hard. I could so relate to her. We were both about thirty. One day she was alive, having no idea she was going to die and leave her children; the next day she was dead and her children had no mother.

Our ministers were conducting the funeral service. After the childhood trauma of my grandmother's death, I had promised myself never to attend a funeral for anyone—ever—but I felt I *had* to attend. I did not have to see her dead body at least; the coffin would be closed. The husband and four boys would be there, and I felt I must go.

A group of us who were her friends were seated together. All of our husbands were at work. Our dead friend's husband and her children were in the front row, sobbing out loud. Tears were rolling down the faces of each child. It was heartbreaking. I knew it could be *me* in that casket, instead of her. Why did some mothers die and some live? Was it chance? It must be. What if I died now and left my children? Would they be sitting in the front row crying just like these four? All my friends were sobbing; the entire congregation was crying. Now I can understand that perhaps every mother there identified with our friend, just as I did. At that time, I just thought all funerals were this way. I began to cry and couldn't stop. The organist played the most heart-rending songs imaginable. The minister spoke words that were probably meant to be comforting but only added to the sorrow. I found myself sobbing out loud. I simply could not cry silently. None of us could.

When the service was over, I was emotionally drained. I swore I would never ever go to another funeral, no matter who it was for. I would never be around a dead body, much less look at one. Death was the saddest, most horrible, painful, and final thing in the world. For weeks, I woke up in the middle of the night, unable to get a full breath, feeling sure I was going to die in my sleep. For years afterward, when anyone died, I wrote notes to the family, called, took food, or visited. But I never went into a funeral home for a viewing or to a service or to a wake or a memorial service.

The children and I were sick a lot. Among other ailments, we had strep throat six or seven times a year. Only later, from Louise Hay's book, *You Can Heal Your Life,* did I learn that sore throats often have as their psychological basis the "holding in of angry words, feeling unable to express the self." All of us, with the exception of Richard, were treated frequently for infections of all kinds, which also psychologically relate to anger, irritation, and annoyance. We were a sick group, mentally *and* physically.

My sister and her three year old son, who was Debbie's age, came to live with us in 1969. It was healing for me despite the stress another two bodies added. She was my ally. She asked me why I continually told Richard I was sorry. I hadn't noticed, but I did, sometimes a dozen times a night. She refused to eat things she didn't like; Richard didn't intimidate her so much. He was on slightly better behavior when she was there. She was going through some difficult emotional problems, but she was like a breath of fresh air.

My sister thought Richard was cruel and overbearing. I began to let myself see that more and more clearly. She commented that I rushed to punish the children before he did, that I didn't stand up to him, and on and on. It was all true. I knew it but had pretended it wasn't so. To hear it from someone else who lives right there with you was something else. In her honesty and caring, she helped me face some painful truths, and a new spirit of self-worth and independence began to emerge from within me.

Stephen loved my sister and her son Tom. He played with Tom and Debbie whenever he was home. I watched Tom while my sister worked. My four, plus another child, were sometimes an overload. Even so, I was glad to have her there, no matter how hard it was. I hated to see her leave after their stay of a few months, but Richard wanted them gone, and I made it happen as he wanted. I was frightened when she left, because I felt so utterly alone.

Often when the children were all outside playing, I buried my head into my pillow and screamed and pleaded with God to help me, to tell me what to do to heal my marriage. Sometimes I thought I was going crazy. Other times, I fantasized about killing Richard or about him being in a car wreck. I had great compassion for women, men, or children who killed an abusive parent or spouse, or for those abused ones who killed themselves. But for the grace of God, I could be in jail for murder, or dead myself, the pain and anger were so great.

When Bob was fifteen, he ran away. The pressures had been building up and now he was gone. I was brokenhearted. We called everywhere— his friends, homes for runaways, police, hospitals. I was in agony. I loved him so. Stephen and Andrea tried to comfort me. I pictured Bob dead in some alley. Race riots were everywhere during this time. I prepared myself for the news of his death.

The police found him seven days later in Texas and sent him home. Richard knocked him around when he got back as I cried out for him to stop. I held Bob and talked to him and told him how much I loved him. He promised he would not run away again and settled down for awhile; but, most evenings for him and his dad, the house was a battlefield. He stayed out more and more. Richard put more and more restrictions on him; Bob broke them every time. Life was a war of their wills—the teenager no longer willing to be browbeaten and abused, the father jealous and resentful of his budding manhood and independence.

I reminded Richard he no longer had any effective way to punish Bob. He had used up all his punishments on unimportant little things for years. Bob was not about to endure the humiliations and criticisms any longer. Richard could always intimidate him, but Bob developed many and various ways to get back at him. To the outsider, we had a rebellious child who wouldn't listen to his loving father. Inwardly, Bob was fighting for his life.

There was another minister at church that Bob liked and had talked with a few times. I called and asked him to counsel with Bob further, and I explained what Bob had really been going through with his dad. For weeks, he counseled with Bob. But too much time had passed before this counsel, and Bob continued to rebel, though now, at least, he had a sympathetic ear. The minister called me with deep concern about how Bob had been treated, and he made a real effort to continue helping him. He suggested to Richard, for starters, that Bob should be allowed to decorate his room the way *he* wanted it, not the way Richard wanted. Richard would not allow that.

It was not possible to heal things between Bob and Richard. Something different had to be done. I sent Bob to my family in Tennessee. My mother loved him and went out of her way to help, but he was so rebellious by then that it was too difficult for the family. Before Bob came back home, I called the minister that had been counseling him. His name was Tom, and he was married and the father of four children. I told him what was happening with Bob and that I thought it was Richard and I who really needed his help. He was caring and said he would do all he could.

It was soon evident that even though I tried to do everything Tom suggested to heal the marriage, the counseling didn't help. As a lay minister, he simply wasn't sufficiently trained to know how to help us, though he tried. After several months we stopped seeing him. There didn't seem to be any place or anyone left from whom to seek further help. I still prayed daily but seemed to get no answers.

Bob's pain increased and so did his rebellion when he returned home. I loved him so much that I ached for the torment he was going through. Stephen stayed in the background and was almost no trouble, doing fairly well in school. He was always there to love and hug me when it all became too much. I tried not to talk about Richard in front of the children, but sometimes I did since there was no one else with whom to share.

What could I do now? I hadn't worked in ten years and had lost so much confidence in myself. My children were suffering badly. Stephen and Andrea were staying out of sight in the downstairs family room as much as possible to avoid their dad and our arguing and fighting. Debbie, barely five, never feared anything. Feisty as always, she ran in and out in the thick of the battle. Richard would grin and take her to the downstairs family room for Stephen and Andrea to watch while we finished another skirmish. Bob was most often at a friend's house or out somewhere. So I just gave up for a while. I continued with volunteer work at the church. I was active in women's work, giving talks and helping with programming. Once a week, I volunteered as a "grey lady" at Walter Reed Army Hospital on the orthopedic ward while Debbie was in kindergarten. These activities helped me escape for awhile.

Stephen and his friends kept busy with sports, Cub Scouts, trumpet lessons, and bike riding. I went to his school for all the PTA meetings and his music concerts. When he played the trumpet in the performances, I cried. He wasn't awfully good at it, but he loved playing and practicing. For the several years he had played, Debbie and Andrea sat at his feet, or crawled around and played in his room while he practiced. He never complained about their noise and interruptions, and they thought he was every bit as good as his heroes Al Hirt or Herb Alpert and the Tijuana Brass.

Stephen even agreed to participate in a children's talent show at the church. He stood up boldly in front of scores of people, music stand in front of him, and he blew his heart out on his trumpet, playing *When the Saints Come Marching In*. He was applauded with great enthusiasm, for effort alone if not for musical ability. Tears ran down my face, I felt such love for him.

We took our camper on a trip to Algonquin Park in Canada the summer of 1971. Stephen was twelve-and-a-half. Some friends met us there with their son and his friend. These boys and Bob, all several years older than Stephen, were going to hike and camp overnight by themselves. Stephen didn't have a back pack. He wanted to go so badly that Richard made him a makeshift one. It was bigger than Santa Claus's pack, and he trudged off with them, barely able to stand upright. The straps were already cutting into his shoulders before he left. I knew he couldn't possibly make it up and down the mountain trails, and he would feel so bad when he had to turn around and come back. Richard insisted it would make a man of him and he would be fine. But I knew how discouraged he would be.

He returned home six hours later, totally downhearted, feeling a failure because he couldn't keep up with the boys and carry the weight of the pack. I knew I couldn't keep him protected forever, but I felt somehow I had let him down terribly.

He bought a microscope at a rummage sale and sat for hours looking at weeds, hair, and anything else that could be placed under it. He was inquisitive and read constantly to find answers to questions we couldn't answer. He built snow forts when the winter drifts made tents up to our roof, and he loved sledding down the hill in front of the house or in any fields he could find.

While I still tried to fool myself that what was happening in our family was no worse than most, every day it seemed we were losing ground. The children began having more and more difficulties—not sleeping well, experiencing problems in school, fighting with each other. They were beginning to lose their childhood enthusiasm and joy. I felt I was losing my mind.

I didn't know what to do. My family said leave him, my minister said leave him, but in my heart I kept feeling there must be a way to make things better. When Richard and I fought, as the adrenaline rushed through my body, I realized I wasn't losing my mind, that he was sadistic and disturbed. Still, I couldn't get the inner strength to leave, having failed at this marriage, and be in disgrace with the church and God.

I tried to be thankful for all my blessings. I tried to become better, I prayed to become better. I worked at keeping Richard from doing serious harm to the children. I prayed day and night for my marriage to be healed, for my children to be healed. My prayers went unanswered. I felt God had deserted me.

During these dark days, just before Christmas of 1971, I did something that made them even darker. Money had been missing from the house and, of course, no one would admit that they had taken it. Stephen had admitted previously that he had taken some money, and Richard punished him severely for it. I could hardly stand the pain he suffered. There was still a question that he actually took it. He might have taken the punishment for someone else.

Now there was a can of money missing. I was sure I remembered putting it in a certain place, and now it was gone. Things had been particularly stressful for days, and I was tense, irritable, and distraught. I went down to Stephen's room and asked him about it. Richard followed me and said, "We've got to do something about this. He's got a problem. I'll handle this. When I get through with him, he won't steal anything again." I asked Stephen if he had taken the money, but he swore he hadn't. I asked him again and again. He became more frantic in his denial. He must be lying, and I knew Richard would really hurt him if he admitted it.

Something snapped in me. I began to slap Stephen. I hit him on the arms and on the face. I went crazy. I had never done such a thing to him. It wasn't that I was hitting him so hard, though the blows weren't light, but that I was hitting him at all. He cried and I screamed at him. In the back of my mind, I thought that this wouldn't hurt him as bad as Richard would if he hit him. That was no excuse. Stephen was crying and pleading with me to stop. Finally I did, and walked out of the room, shaking and crying.

What had I done? I had beaten my little son, my beloved Stephen. Richard went upstairs, assuring me Stephen had deserved the punishment for stealing. I stayed downstairs on the couch in the family room crying, feeling as bad as I ever had in my life, wanting to die for what I'd done.

I couldn't believe Stephen would steal like that. It wasn't like him, it just wasn't like him. He knew I would give him money whenever he needed it. I felt sick at my stomach. I started to vaguely remember something. I walked into another room and found the can of money. I had put it in a special place so I would be able to find it.

I ran back into Stephen's room. He was lying on the bed, still sobbing. I told him I had found the money, that I was wrong, and how sorry I was. I held him, stroking his damp hair and patting his back as I cried and apologized. I promised I would never hit him again. I told him I loved him and promised him this hell we lived in was going to end. I apologized again and again. My heart ached for what I had done to this tender soul. My son, my son.

In bed that night, I prayed for forgiveness, and I prayed for Stephen. He had just turned thirteen, and I had done him a terrible injustice. I would have to live with that for the rest of my life. I had never done more than slap him on the arm or leg or whack his bottom. My mother had said that a slap in the face was too humiliating ever to do to a child. I had never been slapped in the face, nor had my children, by me. I held him and apologized a hundred times in the months to come for what I had done. He always said, "It's OK, Mom. I understand. I love you." "Oh, I love you too, Stephen. I love you too. More than you will ever know," I would tell him.

After this episode, something snapped. No longer did I put up with Richard's fault-finding and meanness. I began to fight him every step of the way and *not* back down. We battled daily. Richard was not going to change, and I was not going to tolerate the status quo. I became a worthy opponent verbally, though I knew I was no match for him physically. I felt better and better about myself. Each day I became stronger.

Finally, if ever there was the living of the phrase, "let go and let God," I did just that. I didn't pray for God to save my marriage, and I didn't pray for my marriage to end. I prayed daily, from my heart and soul, for God to show me what He wanted me to do and to give me the strength to do it.

A deep inner knowing began to fill me with more peace than I had felt in years. I knew that God did not expect me to live like this much longer. I knew that my prayers were going to be answered.

CHAPTER THREE

The Voice From Nowhere

If God doesn't fizz, how come I feel all these bubbles?

May the Holy Spirit zap you!

If you're ready to fly there's always someone who wants to stand on your wings.

— Found among Stephen's writings

A trip to the grocery store is rarely a life-changing experience. But for me, on the afternoon of January 10, 1972, it was.

I welcomed the opportunity to get out of the house for a few moments of quiet and peace. I even drove to Giant Food, a grocery further from the house, because they carried clothes, books, and items that were not in most food stores then. All I really needed was milk and bread. I was disappointed when I discovered that I had forgotten my checkbook and had very little money with me. Shopping for something—anything— was sometimes therapeutic, and I needed that with all the turmoil.

I walked by the book section and was drawn to a small paperback with a blue cover. As I was reading the title on the front, *Search For The Truth,* by Ruth Montgomery, a loud voice right behind me said, "Buy that book!"

I turned around to see who had made such a suggestion. There was no one there! No one! There was no one behind me nor anywhere near me. In fact, I was the only person in the entire department. I even looked in back of the bookshelves to see if a person was hiding, thinking perhaps someone was playing a joke. No one was there. My heart began to race. Something unusual had happened. I didn't even know the word "paranormal" at the time; but, had I, it would have been appropriate to describe my experience.

I bought the book, the need for milk and bread forgotten, climbed into the car and headed for home. I was still shaken by the voice, wondering what it meant. I reasoned that if a voice out of nowhere tells me to read a book, at least I'd consider reading it. I didn't tell Richard about the voice. He would have thought I was crazy—crazier than he already thought I was. I couldn't wait to read the book. I felt as if something wonderful were about to happen, but I had no idea what.

The book was fascinating. I read it from cover to cover. It was incredible yet made such good sense. Ruth Montgomery, the author, a former political writer during several presidential administrations, told of her experiences with her guides and helpers from the spirit plane. People who had died spoke to her. They dictated books from the "other side." Everyone, she said, had such guides. Her guides told her that people lived after they died. They just discarded their physical bodies. They worked and learned in the spirit plane. They were able to communicate with us on this physical plane.

The book read like sacred scripture to me. It filled in all the pieces I had always thought were missing. It spoke to my soul, my heart, my mind.

I felt like I'd been asleep most of my life and had just awakened. I was so excited I couldn't sleep or eat. Feeling brave, I even tried to mention it to Richard, but he said he didn't believe it was true. I knew better. I wanted to share the book and the truths in it with everyone. What it contained could change people's lives because no one ever had to fear death. People who died could still communicate if we learned how to listen. A few of them were even assigned as guides, for periods of time, to help those of us who were still living. How wonderful!

Ruth Montgomery wrote that a man named Edgar Cayce had been able to lie down, go to sleep, and travel into the spirit realm. He then began speaking and bringing information from that realm. It was dramatically clear that it was accurate information that was completely unknown to him when he was awake. These "life readings," as they were called, had brought help and healing to many people. Ruth Montgomery had written other books, and I was eager to read them.

The next morning, after a sleepless night, I arose early and sat in the living room alone in the blue reclining chair. I often sat there to relax and think when all the children were asleep or at school. I looked at the wall. Something moved! There were pictures on the wall, moving pictures! Some were of people I knew; some were of me. We were doing all kinds of things, like in a movie. Somehow, I knew these things I saw were yet to happen—I was seeing the future. I was amazed and blinked my eyes. I discovered I could still see the pictures with my eyes closed.

A battlefield with soldiers appeared, as if I were viewing it from a hill. Men in armor with swords and spears were fighting each other. It reminded me of Roman soldiers from a movie, but a movie I hadn't seen. I could see the maneuvers in a 360 degree circle from atop a hill, yet I was watching from my chair. How was that possible? I closed my eyes and the battle continued; I opened them and these scenes from the past remained. I watched for a long time. No one seemed to be winning, though men were falling down and dying in battle. Then the "movie" stopped.

I was amazed. But as if that weren't enough, a voice began to speak to me, then another voice, then another. There were three distinct voices. They identified themselves as my guides. I couldn't see them, but I could hear them just as if they were speaking out loud, only the voices were inside my head. I wondered if I were going crazy. The voices assured me I wasn't crazy at all, just finally able to hear them. They told me they had once been alive in physical bodies but were now assigned as my guides and had been waiting to communicate with me, when I was ready to listen. They said that they were assigned to me for the next few years, would never interfere with my free will, and that I could stop their voices at anytime just by asking. They further said they didn't have all the answers, but if I asked them things they didn't know, they would try to find the answers from those with more wisdom and in turn share those answers with me.

They suggested that the next day at 2:00 p.m., before the children came home from school, I sit at my typewriter. They would talk to me, and I could type what they said so I wouldn't forget it. It didn't dawn on me to say no. They told me they could see the pathway only somewhat more clearly in all directions than I could. Further, one told me that I had been meditating all my life, not even realizing it, when I would sit and be silent and quiet my mind. Another said, and the other two agreed, that I should never be afraid because my prayers had created a Christ-like light of protection around me. They said I should always pray before receiving guidance, and I would always have that protection. If anything ever came through with which I was uncomfortable, I could challenge it until I felt at ease with the information. If I still felt doubtful, I could refuse to listen or accept it. In that way, I would not be misled or fooled. I didn't tell anyone of the experiences—people would have thought I had lost my mind even if "they" said I hadn't.

Shortly before 2:00 p.m. the next day, according to the instructions I had been given, I pulled out my manual typewriter, set it on the dining room table, and placed a clean sheet of typing paper through the roller. I was a fast typist and this was an easy mode of expression for me. I was somewhat embarrassed—this seemed silly. Perhaps I had imagined the voices. I hadn't heard them since, so maybe I would sit there and nothing would happen. I began to pray. Promptly at 2:00 p.m., one of the voices began to speak. I looked around to see its source. It seemed to be coming into my head from outside to the left but, again, I was hearing it *inside* my head. Then another voice spoke from behind me, and another to my right.

They told me to breathe deeply and relax, not to be fearful, and always to begin with a prayer. I repeated the prayer they gave me, "I ask for the very highest spiritual guidance to come through. I ask to be protected by the white Christ light and to be a clear, pure channel of truth. May all things I receive be helpful and hopeful." They also instructed me to wait until I saw a white cross before I began. That would be the sign to me from Spirit that only the highest and purest guidance would come.

Then they began to instruct me. "Listen, so your own thoughts won't intrude, and type what you hear," they began. Often I stopped typing and questioned them. They instructed me like a child just learning to write or read. Sometimes they gave me one letter at a time until I got it correct and then a word at a time when my thoughts wandered. They explained that they were communicating with me at a soul level, telepathically, putting their words into my thoughts. Their thoughts could come in and overshadow my own if I would allow them to.

I discovered years later when using biofeedback equipment, that the act of "listening" would alter my consciousness to an alpha or theta brain wave pattern. At the time, I knew only that when they said, "Listen," something happened and then I heard them clearly. I often described it as "clicking down" to hear. The information given to me ranged through many subjects such as how the world was created, information about life after death, the work I was to do, and about my children. There was also information about other lifetimes, other incarnations. They spoke about a God of love, about Jesus, about wars and man's inhumanity to man. True to their promise, when I questioned something that came through, they carefully explained and let me ask as many questions as I desired. Nothing was ever given that didn't make sense. When they didn't know an answer, they told me they would try to find out before our next session, and they usually did. The guidance continued for an hour.

When I asked them who they were, they asked me just to use their initials, J and M and G. One said he had been a writer and that I would know his name. It was not important who he was, instead I needed to concentrate on receiving the information he had to share. Another said

I wouldn't know who he was but others might, and he didn't want to detract from the guidance. The other said I didn't know him but had known him in another place at another time.

The pictures on the wall continued, but by now I knew I was seeing them inside my head, without my physical eyes, and I could turn them on and off. They were not always significant things; but, they were evidential in that I saw them before they happened. All the while, as I continued to listen, the ability to communicate with my guides became stronger and clearer.

I begged Richard to read the Ruth Montgomery book, but he wasn't interested in it. I talked to Stephen and the children about some of what was happening. I didn't want them in trouble with their dad until I saw where all this was leading.

There was no adult with whom I could really talk. For two weeks, all these wonderful things were happening and no one even knew about them. I had no idea there were dozens of books and hundreds of people who knew about and had experienced similar kinds of things.

At church the next Sunday, Tom, the minister who had counseled with us, gave the sermon and afterward, stopped and talked with me for awhile. He commented on how different I looked and acted. He asked what was happening to me. Were Richard and I doing better? I decided to take a chance and hint at what was occurring. He seemed interested, and I found myself telling him even more of what had happened. He told me it sounded fascinating and wanted to read Ruth Montgomery's book. I had a copy with me and gave it to him. He promised to let me know what he thought.

The following Sunday at church, Tom said he had read the book and he had no doubt it was true. He felt, as I did, that it filled in much that was missing in Scripture. He bought several copies and gave them to friends; I bought thirty more copies and gave them to everyone. Some of my friends were enthralled and excited, others said it was the work of the devil. Tom was teaching a youth class of older teens and he began to share the book with them—they loved it.

One of the other ministers to whom I had given a book seriously feared that I was being misled by the devil. His doubt planted some doubt in me. That night, and after everyone else was in bed, I sat on the couch and prayed. I asked God to give me a sign that this was from Him and not the devil. In all sincerity, I asked Him to take my life if I were following the wrong pathway and it could do anyone any harm. I meant it with all my heart and soul.

Within moments, across the room, there appeared a sphere of white light in front of the wall, about eight or ten feet away. It was a glowing, brilliant light. I started to sit up; but, I couldn't move. Though I was propped on the arm of the couch, with my head tilted to the left side, I could see the form as if I were sitting up straight. Try as I might, I could move no part of my body. A peaceful feeling came over me. This being of light did not communicate with words or even thoughts, but I felt totally at peace and at one with it. It stayed almost fifteen minutes and then disappeared. I could move my body again and I sat up. I questioned in my mind what had happened. I could not deny this incredible peace I felt. I knew that God was answering my prayers.

Only a few minutes later, the being of light appeared again! As before, I could not move, but this time I was sitting up. It stayed about ten minutes before disappearing. More of His healing and peace and love and light filled my whole body. When He left, I knew that Jesus had been with me. At first, I was reluctant to tell others it was Jesus. I thought myself unworthy to say that He had appeared to me. I would refer to Him only as a "being of light." Years later, when He spoke and appeared to me again, He confirmed that He had come that night as I prayed, I finally acknowledged the truth publicly. My prayers had been answered—first with Ruth Montgomery's courageous book, secondly, with the appearance of the Master himself.

From that night on, everything became much clearer. Deep within me was a knowing of what I must do with my children, my personal life, and my spiritual life. I would have to leave Richard despite still caring for him. He couldn't or wouldn't change this lifetime. I knew I was unable to be strong enough to handle him, nor need I live in such misery. I could see that my children were already damaged and would continue to be until I got them away from his influence. Most of all, I knew that what I had received and continued to receive was not the work of the devil but a gift from God. With a certainty, I was aware of some mission or work I had to do, but I had no idea of exactly what. I wanted Stephen and the children to be part of that. I needed to prepare myself first.

Where before there had been fear and indecisiveness about the relationship, now there was confidence and determination to do what was for the highest good for all of us. Where there had been timidity and lack of self-love, I was filled with power from on high and the return of the deep inner strength I had lost these last years.

The answers to my questions fell into place. They were not easy but they were clear. My guides confirmed this the next morning and explained what I was feeling and the correctness of my planning. They said my life was going to change completely. I welcomed it with open arms. Never before had I felt so alive. When I told one of our ministers of the spiritual experience, he actually said, "I could understand this happening to you if you were a man, one of the priesthood, but you're a *woman.*" I knew then that my life with the church I had so loved was ending.

My guides directed me to Spiritual Frontiers Fellowship, an organization begun by the late Arthur Ford who became one of Ruth Montgomery's spirit plane guides. I began to attend their meetings. In this organization ministers and people from all faiths explored the esoteric and metaphysical teachings, yet were encouraged to remain in their churches, helping to expand the consciousness within their own organizations. Since I had shared my experiences with our minister, Tom, I also told him about the meetings. He wanted to go. I explained that I was leaving Richard. He agreed that it was for the best, and said he would help us both in every way he could. He also said he had realized months before that there was little chance that Richard and I could work things out, but he hadn't wanted to discourage me further.

Tom began to attend the weekly meetings at Spiritual Frontiers with me. We learned about the spirit world, the teachings of many of the world's great religions, about colored energy patterns around people which were called auras, about reincarnation, life after death, and all types of psychic phenomena. We eagerly soaked up this new information. I felt like I had been waiting a lifetime to hear it all.

As our search and friendship continued, Tom began to confide in me, telling me of the great difficulties he had been experiencing for years in his own marriage. He had tried to leave several times, once for another woman. When he told his wife, Sue, that he wanted a divorce, she took a knife and threatened to kill herself. Later, each time his determination to leave became apparent to her, she would get pregnant. He loved his children and couldn't bring himself to leave them. He said he had never been in love with her. He was stationed in Alaska in the military where there were very few women available. He met her, talked her into having sex, and she got pregnant the first time they were together. He hadn't wanted to get married but it became a necessity.

Their relationship had been very difficult, he continued. He had run around with other women. Once when she found out, she had stormed into the place where the woman worked, to confront her. From then on, he became very careful. They had settled into a lifestyle, with their four children, in which he had been faithful since being called to the ministry, but he was very unhappy.

We commiserated with each other. He was two years younger than I. I didn't find him very attractive, but we were drawn together by our common interest in the whole metaphysical and spiritual field because it added to our beliefs in the Scriptures. He seemed to have a trust and complete faith in these teachings from the beginning, having had experiences of his own to confirm much of what we were learning.

I asked Richard for a divorce. I had been sleeping on the downstairs couch for weeks. I told him the children needed to stay in their schools since it was mid-semester. I asked to keep the house so that the children could continue in their schools. He refused to move and told me to get a court order and even then the police would have to drag him out. I pleaded with him to think about the children. I told him I would get a job and pay the bills and mortgage, and when it came time to sell the house, we could split the proceeds. He would not bend. He told me he was going out of town for three weeks on business and if I wanted a divorce, the children and I would have to move out.

I went to an attorney. She said not to move or he might sue me for desertion and try to get the children. She explained about getting a court order. I couldn't bring myself to have the police come in and bodily remove Richard in front of the children. I thought that would really traumatize them.

Tom counseled with me about Richard and the divorce. As the weeks went by, and he studied and learned, he knew he could no longer continue with his loveless marriage. Yet, because of his wife's past reactions, he had some real apprehension about telling her. He would decide one day to go forth with it, then back down, then try again to figure how to break the news. I understood because it had taken me eleven years to have the courage to leave Richard.

My guides worked with me daily, helping me become clearer and sharing so much knowledge with me. I studied, read, and prayed, always asking what God would have me do. I knew that when Richard returned, if he again refused to move, I would have to move out with the children. We couldn't continue in the house with him. I began to look for a job.

Tom made preparations for his own separation. His wife reacted exactly as she had in times past. She screamed, yelled, carried on, and threatened to kill not only herself but everyone around. He talked with his children to help them understand. This time he said he knew he would never go back.

When Richard returned, he was adamant about not moving out. "You want the divorce, you move out." I had no choice. It was a very difficult time for the children. None of them complained about the divorce or encouraged me to stay. Despite it all, they cared for their dad but were happy at the new me who really wouldn't put up with his treatment of them any longer. They didn't mind living *without* him in the house, but they didn't want to move. Stephen and Andrea didn't want to leave their school and friends. It was a time of tears and pain and happiness all mixed together. There were no apartment buildings within miles of their school and the suburb where we lived. I could not afford to rent a house like ours in the neighborhood.

Besides being a minister, Tom was the warehousing manager of a large company and needed a secretary. His present secretary was leaving to have a baby. He offered to have me work for him for awhile. I grabbed this temporary lifeline. Finally, this brought some hope for the next step.

Tom had confided to a minister friend about all the things that were happening, what he was studying and learning, his divorce plans, our friendship. The minister, feeling that my guidance and experiences were leading me astray, and Tom with me, made a judgment that we were sinning against God and he reported it to the church. Tom tried to explain to them that he felt that God was directing him every step of the way. They were convinced of just the opposite, and plans were made for "silencing" him, an action akin to excommunication in the Catholic church.

Ministers came forward to talk to us, relating "visions" they were having of the devil causing all this. Prayer groups met to pray for us, and we were shunned by all. No one spoke to us, and even those who had read the book and heard my testimony at church, pulled away from us with all the pressure. Richard was the wounded husband, I was the evil wife. Never mind the hell the children and I had lived in for eleven years. No one cared. In their minds I was following the devil. The one minister, besides Tom, that we had seen for counseling, had been transferred to another state, so I had no support.

In all fairness, only a handful knew the difficulties Richard and I had been going through for all these years. I wanted to be honest about Richard; but, at the same time, tried to keep from disrupting the church people by revealing too much and hurting Richard's ministry and reputation. I knew I was leaving this church and Richard had belonged to it all his life. What good would it do to tell the truth and destroy him?

We ended up with some of the members thinking I was leaving Richard for Tom, and others believing I was being misled by evil forces. None of it could have been further from the truth. Even Richard knew I was not leaving him for another man, but he enjoyed seeing me be made the scapegoat. After all, he didn't want the divorce and felt I deserved whatever was being said. I had stepped beyond the allowable parameters of our church dogma with divorce, a belief in the "occult" and an unwillingness to repent. After my experience with Jesus, I knew He was directing my life, so I withstood the pain much better than I might have otherwise.

I found a two-story townhouse miles away but halfway between my new job location and the children's old neighborhood. It was all I could afford. It had three bedrooms, a living room and kitchen with not much yard. It was in a nice complex which would have to do until we could move to bigger quarters.

Moving from a five-bedroom, three-bath house with a huge yard, where each child had a private room, was a difficult shift. Bobby and Stephen bunked together in the master bedroom as their need for space was greater. It was extremely difficult on them. With Stephen at thirteen-and-a-half and Bob at seventeen, both needed their own space desperately. There was just enough difference in their ages that their interests and schedules didn't mesh well together. Debbie and Andrea slept on bunk beds in the smallest room with barely space for one chest. School would soon be out for the summer and we could survive.

I cried the night we moved out. I still cared for Richard. I had prayed for so many years for things to work out and they hadn't. I had thought I would spend the rest of my life with him. As I was leaving and unable to stop crying, he shouted, "This was *your* idea, not mine!" Sobbing, I could only reply, "You were destroying the children and me. You never gave us any peace." "I still don't know how you can leave now when the dogs are ready to breed," Richard snapped.

I stopped crying and laughed. Despite my care of the poodle and the Pekingese, I had told him again and again that I didn't want to have dogs and breed them for the money. He obviously had never once heard me, just as he had not heard much I ever said. His last remark put everything into perspective. I was better from then on. I never cried as much about us again; but it was months before I totally stopped missing him.

Bobby hated having Stephen in his room and Stephen didn't like it all that much either. They fought all the time and Stephen was his scapegoat. Stephen did his part to stir things up too. They argued and yelled at each other most days.

Despite that, I felt as though we had been let out of prison. No one criticized me or yelled at me. No one yelled at the children but *me*. No one said degrading and humiliating things to them or to me. We were finally safe and free.

But it was almost too late. Things didn't change that much for Bobby. He was difficult to communicate with and always rebellious. While I understood, I felt helpless as he went through such pain and unhappiness.

Stephen was at loose ends. His friends were miles away, and he was alone with the girls much of the time. He wasn't old enough to drive and, besides, my Rambler station wagon wasn't working well, only shifting into forward gear. I couldn't back it up, and I didn't have enough money to fix it. I was working every day while Stephen watched Andrea and Debbie after school.

My mother offered to keep the children part of the summer which was a great blessing for them and for me. After they left for Tennessee, I called and wrote them frequently. They were having a good time.

While they were gone, I communicated with my guides in the evenings when possible. They directed me to places where I could learn more, including Virginia Beach, Virginia. They explained that some of what I had read in Ruth Montgomery's book, and much of what they were sharing with me, could be found and verified at the Edgar Cayce organization, called the A.R.E., the Association for Research and Enlightenment. I knew from further reading that Edgar Cayce was a psychic and a mystic. He had studied and experimented with hypnosis, and in a deep hypnotic or sleep state, gave "readings" about people's past lives, medical conditions, and all sorts of information. He was a very spiritual man who read his Bible every day until he died in 1945. Cayce's work was being studied and researched at this association in Virginia.

Tom and I took time off from work and drove there. We knocked on the door of an old frame building. It housed the library in those days before the new buildings were constructed. A woman invited us into the bookstore. I told her what had been happening to me and that my guides had sent me there. I asked where I could get a "reading" like Edgar Cayce gave. She said that they didn't refer anyone for readings and that I had to go within. I told her I didn't know how to go within, not realizing, of course, that I did. She suggested certain books to buy and conferences to attend. We couldn't stay for the conferences, and I left very, very disappointed.

Here I was in Virginia Beach. My guides had directed me to the Edgar Cayce work and now that door seemed closed. The book I had read, *Search for the Truth*, said that Edgar Cayce and people like him could lie down, go to sleep, and tune in to the soul records of individuals. The seeker could ask questions and receive guidance from these "channels" such as Edgar Cayce. Yet the woman at the Cayce association had said no one gave such readings at the very place which was promulgating his work. She seemed even to disapprove of such a practice. I didn't understand, it didn't make sense. Cayce's own readings said hundreds should be giving readings just like he gave. At the request of those working with him, he named three who could work as he did. Yet his own organization wouldn't even refer inquirers, desperate for help , to other "channels" who worked as he did. I pondered it all, anxious to hear why my guides had misled me. I would ask them the next time I contacted them in my meditations.

In the following weeks, I read several books about Edgar Cayce and learned more about him and his work. My guides informed me that they hadn't misled me, that Mr. Cayce's prayer had been, indeed his guidance had been, that *hundreds* would be trained to follow in his footsteps, going perhaps far beyond what he had done and even giving guidance about the future and the past. They directed me to Edgar Cayce's readings about this:

Question: Give the names of three individuals who might be associated with The Cayce Institute of Psychic Research for the purpose of giving psychic readings for Physical, Mental and Spiritual diagnoses and readings of a similar nature, as have been given by Edgar Cayce in the psychic state.
Answer: Edwin Roth, Linden Makaja, Ross Weaver.

Question: In order to develop the Cayce Institute it might be necessary from time to time to have additional psychic readers. How should the governing board of the Institute proceed to get in touch with such people as may be required.
Answer: The developing of the psychic forces . . . will develop those now being brought in the earth and physical plane. Be not afraid, for the developing of many will be the guiding force in hundreds that will give assistance to the people. It will be developed then in the work itself. Choose those. (Reading 254-4)

Question: Should a program be started for developing assistants to Edgar Cayce?
Answer: This should; . . . it should take the form of that as of the giving of the future; yet this must be approached with prayer and fasting. . . . Not as man counts fasting—doing without food; but one that would abase himself that the creative force might be made manifest. (Reading 254-46)

This was very specific; why weren't they doing that, I questioned. The guides gave me a long discourse about the situation at the foundation, how the decision had been made not to research psychics, how hundreds came just like me seeking help like Cayce gave, and also went away disappointed. They said they had been unable to put me in touch with someone there at that specific time who believed these particular readings to be true, and who could help. Instead, I was to read all I could of what was written about Mr. Cayce and to know that he was a very spiritual man who was still continuing his work from the other side.

They said I could do what he did. Do what *he* did? I didn't think so. I could see auras like he did, the colors around people, and pictures or symbols around the aura; but I could not lie down, fall asleep, and answer questions about things of which I had no waking knowledge. They assured me that one day I would.

After the Virginia Beach door was closed, the guides directed me to get a reading from a psychic in Rossville, Georgia named Doc Anderson. They directed me to several books that had been written about him. After I read them, they said it would be interesting and helpful to hear what Anderson would share with me because he was a very good psychic. We decided to go there. Rossville was just across the border from Chattanooga, so on the way, we could stop by to see my family and my children who were still visiting them.

The place where Anderson gave readings was an old white farm house with chickens in the yard, fences in disrepair, and the house in need of paint both inside and out. We discovered he didn't live there, only gave readings there. No one could make an appointment. All received the same first come, first served treatment. Old and young, black and white, rich and poor were lined up that day. The line moved slowly.

A man waiting behind us showed us a newspaper article about himself. Doc Anderson had found oil in his fields that had gone dry. Anderson had gone to the oil fields where he put his hands out in front of his body as he walked the fields and prayed. Blood began to ooze from his hands when they were over oil. Photographers had captured this phenomenon in full detail and he showed me the photographs in the newspaper of the stigmata, as it was called, on Doc Anderson's hands. When the man drilled where Anderson said, oil was found and his fortune was restored. He donated a percentage of these riches to Anderson's favorite charity. He had nothing but good to say about how accurate he was and how he had helped him and hundreds of others.

Amazing! I had never dreamed of such a thing. Imagine this! Here was a successful oil man, with several articles to prove this psychic's credibility, waiting behind us in line. On the walls were statements, testimonials, and clippings from books, magazines, and articles about Doc Anderson's work and successes. Even with all these testimonials, we were still so new in the field that while we believed, we were also very cautious. We still clung to some of the dogmatism of our old church. We felt safer going in together.

When our turn came, we were ushered into a small room with a large chair designed like a throne. In that chair was a huge, dark-haired man, filling it totally. He smiled, welcomed us, told us how much the session cost, and we paid him. Then, without even asking our names or anything about us, he proceeded to tell us how many children we each had. Item by item he predicted things for each of us. Then, surprisingly, he said something was holding up our marriage, but we would be married in fifteen months. (We hadn't talked about marriage, but he ended up being only one month off.) He asked for our birth dates and, in his head, worked the calculations for our astrology, wrote them down, and told us more about ourselves.

Before I could ask a question about my experiences, he told me that I should be sitting where he was, doing what he was doing. I thought that highly unlikely and said, "Me?" He looked me straight in the eye and said, "Yes. *You.*" He then told me I would be very wealthy one day and would use the money to help a lot of people. All of his other predictions came true; I'm waiting on this one! He told us dozens of things which we either knew to be true or later saw come to pass. We were very favorably impressed to say the least.

We didn't tape record the session but discussed it in detail the whole trip back to Washington, D.C. We were amazed and shocked that someone, without knowing us, could *know* us so fully. The guides had been right—it was a good and helpful experience. For months, Anderson's predictions occurred just as he had said. We did not always find this to be so true with some of the other psychics to whom we went after that.

The summer passed with us being very much without friends, since none of the church people would associate with us. This was sad because both of us had been sociable, highly visible, and so loving toward so many of these people. Rumors about us continued, but we had no chance to dispute them. It hurt to be lied about and to be so misunderstood. If only these people would read the books we were discovering and see the truth and beauty in these teachings. They weren't *new*, but *old* truths that had been hidden by churches and dogma. We had time to read scores of books about the psychic field. We visited lots of spiritualist churches and organizations and talked with many people.

Some of the things we discovered seemed highly irregular and fake. Some of the people we visited seemed simply misguided, and others seemed intentionally deceitful. But in between disappointments, we came across some truly attuned souls who gave us evidential guidance far beyond our own knowledge. These good experiences added new impetus to our search.

We were directed by the guides to go to a church on 16th Street. We arrived one evening for a service, and tentatively walked in the front door of a huge white mansion. In the dark it might be easily mistaken, we thought, for a haunted house. The lights were dimmed and strange things hung on the walls of the entry and room where the service was being held.

One large picture in particular, with snakes wrapped around a head, drew our attention. We began to wonder why we had been directed here. These things were still new and sometimes uncomfortable for us.

The service started, led by a middle-aged, dark-haired woman who closed her eyes and began speaking of some very interesting things about life and death. Her voice sounded different from when she earlier spoke to welcome us. It sounded like another person. When she finished, she introduced several other people; they gave "messages" or predictions to people in the audience. It was interesting, and a little spooky, but it seemed quite genuine.

After the service, we talked with the woman, Reverend Diane Nagorka, and her husband Henry, both directors of the National School of Spiritual Science. They seemed very sincere and well-educated. Henry had been a diplomat overseas. They had formed this church and school to teach parapsychology, religion, philosophy, psychology, metaphysics, and much more. They had a two-year and a four-year school which culminated in certification and ordination, like a seminary or a university. Diane also gave individual readings. We decided to schedule two the following week to see what they were like.

We arrived, still timid and hesitant in our exploration. Tom went first, alone. I was next. Diane closed her eyes while sitting in a chair. She prayed, and began to speak. What she said had a ring of truth, some of it very evidential. Her guidance about my future work was almost identical to that of my guides and of Doc Anderson. I liked Diane and felt an instant trust. Afterward, we discussed her school and decided to enroll and learn all we could.

Tom was being "defrocked" in our old church. He would no longer be permitted to be one of their ministers. Not that we attended there anymore. I had left before a decision was made to kick me out. We were essentially, at that time, searching souls, with only our children, a few friends from work, and no clear idea about what we were to do next, except for the information from our guides, and our own intuitive feelings.

Classes were to begin in September. In the meantime, we attended their services and began to understand Spiritual Science teachings. We also investigated other organizations. It seemed a place was being opened for us to "belong" again. My guides confirmed our decision to participate and to graduate from the school. This was a next step, they said. They encouraged us not to be limited by just these teachings, but to explore further in many directions.

People at the school accepted us fully. We explained about our background and the church situation. There was only friendship and unconditional love. No judgment! They understood. Many of them had experienced very similar things in their own churches, relationships, and lives when they had the courage to change and grow.

School, for the children as well as ourselves, would begin soon. We picked the children up from Tennessee. Summer eased out as fall began.

Stephen had discovered and loved karate, so Tom and I enrolled with him in a weekly karate class. Our instructor, a man dressed in a white karate gi and black belt, was a hard taskmaster. Before we began our instruction, we had to do a series of warm-ups, jumping jacks, push-ups, and other aerobics to get us ready. I hardly made it through ten push-ups, while many of the men in the class could do a hundred or more. I was out of my league. Stephen not only kept up—he loved out-doing us. He did the exercises and practiced the kicks for hours on end. We bought him a white gi and a matching white belt. It became his uniform. He always wore it before and after school and on weekends.

As I prepared dinner in the kitchen at night, Stephen would come up beside me, do his karate yell, and practice high kicks so I could watch him. He became quite good at it and bought books on karate, read Chinese philosophy, watched every "Kung Fu" program on television, was devoted to Bruce Lee, and practiced to get his next color belt. He taught all the children the karate kicks. The house was alive with their yells, kicks in the air, and makeshift karate outfits.

Stephen loved the outfit so much that I bought him a short bathrobe in the same style, which he wore anytime he didn't have on his gi. How we escaped getting any photos of him in the gi is beyond any of our knowing. We just did not take many photos in those years.

I had always been the family photographer, recording the children's growth from birth, with literally hundreds of pictures only a family would appreciate. After the divorce, I lost my enthusiasm for this record keeping. I had believed that Richard and I would be married forever. When things didn't work out, I was left with albums of photos capturing a time period that was still raw and painful. The future was uncertain; the present too shaky to chronicle.

Stephen would watch football with Tom and his children in the living room when they visited. At first, he had been astonished when Tom jumped up from his chair, hit the ceiling with his hand and screamed out loud when his favorite football team made a touchdown. After the initial weeks of this behavior, he just smiled when Tom screamed, and tried to act as interested as they were. He grew to love the Redskins but didn't try to mimic Tom's behavior at touchdowns.

My divorce was now final, but Tom's wife would not give him a divorce. In 1972, Maryland had a divorce law on the books that could keep a couple married for years if either contested it. Tom was impatient to be free and to have closure on his marriage. Virginia had an easier divorce law at the time: residency for a year in the state, then a divorce could be granted even if contested. He might never get his freedom if he continued to live in Maryland.

He decided to move to Virginia. Our relationship had evolved past friendship, so we agreed to move there together and share a large split level home in Alexandria. My children could live with us and there was room for his children to visit. It was a long drive back and forth to work each day. I explained to Stephen and the children why we would be moving there. They understood and were cooperative and good-natured about it.

The children loved the house. Everyone had a room again and there was a large family room where we could put a pool table. The yard was big and grassy with a tree they could climb. Schools were within walking distance. We settled in for the year.

One evening, a most unusual thing happened in this house. We came home from classes to find Stephen and the girls in the upstairs family room, watching television but obviously frightened. Stephen said that while we were gone, the billiard balls in the game room began to roll back and forth on the table, but no one was in the room. At first, he thought Bob was playing a joke to scare them, but he checked the whole house and found he wasn't home. The children stood on the stairs and watched the balls roll across the table, as if propelled by some invisible player. They then ran upstairs and turned on the television to wait until we got home. They continued to hear the balls careen back and forth for some time.

We had been sharing with them all the things we were learning and all of them were interested and not in the least frightened, but this was something we hadn't covered. The balls moved several more times during the next weeks until, finally, the children were getting spooked every night if we weren't there with them.

I began to read about such phenomena. Some experts felt there were spirit beings, those who were dead, who moved things to let you know they were there. Others said that a physical phenomenon such as this often occurred in families were there was a young person reaching puberty. Somehow, their energies created such happenings. I shared that with the children and we went down to the pool table and called on whatever forces were at play to *stop* because it was scaring everyone. We all prayed that whatever it was it would end. It never happened again from that moment on.

The problems with Tom's wife and children did not let up. Most of our time was devoted to trying to keep things on an even keel for his children when they were with us. The constant barrage of lies at home from their mother as she used the children as pawns was causing them many problems. We did everything possible to see that they had whatever they needed and to help in whatever way we could. We drove to get them every weekend and once during the week, despite the hour-long trip each way.

My children were out of the horrible mess in which they had lived and seemed to need less attention. All of our children played well together and were, if not close friends, fairly close playmates for the time they spent together.

My feelings at that time were that it was such heaven to be free and out from under the constant fighting and criticism that, no matter how bad Tom's situation was, we could handle it. My children would be fine. Richard couldn't hurt them anymore, and I could love them and try to make up for what they had gone through.

Tom and I didn't allow our children to play us against each other. All the things Richard found in me as faults, Tom loved. I would have done anything for him, I was so appreciative of this kind of treatment. It seemed a blessing for me and for the children.

We were working full time, going to school two nights a week and parts of some weekends. Stephen and the girls visited their dad every other weekend. At first, they seemed to handle visiting him fairly well. Within a short time they begged not to have to go, asking me to call him and say they were sick. I told them he couldn't hurt them anymore, but they found reasons, either separately or together, not to go. Richard got angry at me, thinking I was keeping them away. I couldn't tell him the truth since he would have taken it out on them on the weekends they saw him.

In my divorce settlement, I had custody of the children and we would split the proceeds on the house when it sold. Richard had visiting rights at my discretion. He paid one hundred dollars per child a month, which didn't hurt him with his salary, but he complained about it all the time to Stephen, now almost fourteen, and the girls when they visited. Richard couldn't get healed from all his childhood fears and lacks and he was totally alienating the only children he had.

Tom's divorce proceedings got worse. Sue went to court asking for a thousand dollars a month more than he made. The judge threw the request out, but she still would not consent to a divorce. Tom's growing impatience turned into determination. After her attorney tried to black-mail him several times, he flew to the Dominican Republic and got an uncontested divorce. His wife did not have the money to challenge it, and he was free. She never stopped harassing him, but the blackmail was over. The whole mess, however, severely traumatized all of us. It had been extremely difficult for my children as well as his.

Finally we decided we *would* get married and planned our wedding for November 1972. None of the children felt at home at the church of the National School of Spiritual Science. So we were married in our home in Alexandria with our teachers, the Nagorkas, presiding. The house was filled with our new friends and fellow students. All eight of our children were there. During the ceremony, I presented each of them with one of eight different flowers from my bouquet, to celebrate their individuality and specialness.

It made me sad that Stephen wasn't overjoyed about the wedding. He took off his jacket right after the ceremony and put on a bathrobe. We didn't get many wedding pictures of him. He had told me weeks before that Tom always made him feel inadequate, always contradicted him about things he said, and made him feel stupid. I told Stephen he would like Tom after he got to know him better. I should have realized that, by then, he had known him almost two years and had lived in the same house with him part of that time. I thought that Stephen probably felt some disloyalty to his father, living with us and me remarrying. Time would change things, I was convinced. After all, Tom adored his children and treated mine kindly and would grow to love mine like his own.

However, I began to observe that what Stephen said *was* true. While Tom was patient and loving with his own children, he wasn't as patient with mine. Almost 100 percent of the attention centered on his children, on their needs and wants, on what would make *them* happy. I thought that would change as we became a family and got to know and love each other, out from under the strain we had been experiencing.

A few months before the wedding, after a particularly difficult weekend at Richard's, Stephen had run away overnight. He loved the house and the extra room, but was having trouble making friends and adjusting to the new school. We came home from work to find a note that said he needed to get away and was going to sleep overnight in the woods. He said that life wasn't worth living, and he wanted to get away and think. I couldn't believe it. How could life not be worth living for him *now* when we were finally free and happy? No one kept him up at night, grilling him about anything. No one said cruel and mean things to him. I honestly thought that the past eleven years could be quickly healed and forgotten.

How could he spend the night in the woods when he was afraid of the dark and it was starting to rain? How could he tell us in his note not to look for him, that we wouldn't find him. We *would* find him. I was frantic. I insisted on going to the woods near us and bringing him home.

I was worried and scared. We drove to the woods and walked to the edge. It covered many acres and was dense and dark. I yelled Stephen's name at the top of my lungs. No answer. I didn't know if he could hear me. I screamed his name and pleaded with him to come home. He didn't answer and it was too dark to go back in the woods; we hadn't brought a flashlight, and besides, he could be anywhere. I had no idea he was so unhappy. I thought he was as happy as I was, as I thought we all were.

Tom finally said we should leave, that Stephen would come home in the morning. I wanted to stay and keep calling him, but I realized it was doing no good. I shouted out a few more times for him to please answer; but he didn't, and sobbing, I rode home and cried myself to sleep. My baby, alone in the dark woods at night in the rain. I woke up praying for him and trying to understand his hurt. In my mind, I replayed the last few months to try to understand what he was feeling.

The first thing that came to mind was that Stephen had recently come back from a camp sponsored by our former church. He was very depressed and discouraged. People had told him his mother was living in sin and they had him pray with them for us. They had tried to get him to start reading and preparing for the priesthood in case he was "called by God" when he got older. When he left for camp, he had no embarrassment about us; he was just accepting and loving. We had talked with him and shared with him the wonderful things we were learning. But, after camp, he came back detached, depressed, and confused by all the contradictory things he was hearing from his church.

He loved and trusted me and yet the ministers he'd been brought up to trust and listen to were telling him that what we were studying was of the devil and that we were living in sin. He was understandably confused. After a few weeks, he seemed his old self, but he never attended a camp or church activity again. I'm sure he missed all his friends from church and all the good he learned, but he couldn't handle their judgment about his loved ones. Did this make him run away? Was he ashamed of me? Of us?

Or perhaps it was the fact that several weeks before, he had asked not to have to go to his dad's, but I had insisted he go. Stephen came home from that visit and cried for two days, his confidence utterly shattered. His dad had been on him about not folding up his sleeping bag, about getting urine on the toilet, about his hair length, about almost everything he did. He declared, "I hate him! I hate him!" We talked a long time, and he stopped crying but he seldom went back after that no matter how much his dad tried to make him feel guilty. He said, "I love Dad but I don't like him. He makes me feel like shit." I told him I understood. I said the children were all Richard had, and I asked Stephen if he couldn't try to tell him what he had told me about how he felt. He couldn't. How could I expect *him* to do that when I hadn't been able to myself. Did I fail to support Stephen enough? Was this why he ran away?

Or was it the fact that he had talked to me one night while Tom was taking his children home and said, "Mom, you're different around Tom than the way you are with us." He explained what he felt. I told him I didn't realize it and I would try to do better. I told him about some of the stress with Tom's children and ex-wife that I felt. He seemed to understand, but he was hurting. Did my lack of sensitivity drive him away?

Could it have been that he was in a new school, hadn't made friends yet, and felt left out? He thought he was too fat, so he wore loose clothes and an overcoat to hide himself. He didn't realize how good-looking he truly was. He didn't see himself that way. He wasn't fat, but maybe I should have taken him to a doctor anyway to help him lose a few pounds. Did the pressure make him want to leave school and run away? What could I have done?

My mind continued to race. We were at school so many nights and weekends and worked so much to support two families. I thought we were spending enough time with him, but I could see that we weren't. Did he think I didn't love him, that I didn't care?

Stephen was the one who always entertained Tom's children, playing games with them by the hour. He took them outside, played football, and trekked through the woods with them. He made their visits so much easier for us and fun for them. Was the responsibility too much for him?

All night I thought about him, agonized about what I had done and what I could do when he came back. I thought about how things could be changed. I prayed for him and asked God to help him. Maybe he was dead and I'd never see him again. Maybe he had an accident in the woods and needed help. My imagination tormented me. Never once did I imagine him taking his own life. I would die if something happened to him, I loved him so. "Oh, Stephen, *know* how much I love you and come home," I prayed. I fell into a troubled sleep.

Morning came and no Stephen. I stayed home from work and agonized about him and about his feelings. I replayed the last eleven years over and over. He had needed me, and I hadn't been there for him. Just as I was ready to call the police, he sheepishly wandered in about noon. I ran to him and hugged and hugged him. I told him how worried I had been. I kissed him and hugged and squeezed him. I held him to me like he was a baby. He apologized again and again, saying he just couldn't take it anymore and needed some time to himself. I really did understand. We talked and talked. He promised he wouldn't do it again. He had something to eat, went to bed early, and was his old self when he got up, making jokes and laughing.

From then on, I took extra time to talk to him, to listen to him. I tried to see that his needs were met in every way I could think of. He wasn't as joyful or as smiling as he had been. I felt it must be partly his age, partly the stress, but I felt sure things would get better now.

But Bob was going through hell a few weeks later, and our attention was again taken off of Stephen and directed onto Bob. Bob had joined the Air Force at his uncle's suggestion. He was miserable. So he told someone at boot camp that he was going to run away and kill himself, and the entire fort was put on alert to find him.

They called us. I couldn't do anything because I was so far away. He was just barely eighteen. We had tried everything we could think of, and nothing seemed to help. He was rebellious, wouldn't take any suggestions from anyone, and his experimenting with drugs was making it worse.

In desperation, I called a general's wife whom I knew. She called her husband who knew the general in command at the fort where Bob was stationed. He personally sent out special troops to find Bob. They found him, called me, and sent him home with an honorable discharge. The general said he understood some of these very young kids away for the first time. He was so compassionate about Bob's well-being that I still carry a warm spot in my heart for him.

Bob came home. He had nowhere else to go, and besides, I wanted him home. It was more peaceful when he was gone, but I missed him so. I wanted my son living with *me* where he belonged for a time yet. I wanted to make up for all the years of hell before he moved out on his own. I loved him and wanted to help, but I couldn't undo those years of what Richard and I had done to him.

Bob turned the house upside down. He picked on Stephen, he wouldn't follow any rules, he made the children's lives miserable— except for Debbie who brought out the best in him. With her, he was gentle and loving just like when he was a very little boy. We couldn't handle him, and though Tom had counseled with him in the past, now it did no good at all. After a short time, he moved out on his own.

The year's lease on the house in Virginia was almost over, and we could now move back near our jobs and not have to travel back and forth so much. What a relief. Stephen had made some friends as had the girls, but there was no way we could stay—the driving was killing us. Besides, I rationalized, their friends were only months old, this would be our last move, and they could settle down and make new and lasting friends.

Though we had lived for more than nine years in our old house, this was our third move in less than two years. I hated moving, I was tired of moving, but this was the final one. We were even going to have a huge pool put in the back of the new house we were building, even though the swimming season was short in Maryland.

A couple we knew, good friends for several years, were each going through their own painful divorces. They had met and fallen in love and had moved in with us just before our wedding. Norris was a carpenter and classmate, Diane was Tom's former secretary. She brought her baby from her first marriage, Jennie, a beautiful black-haired darling that we all adored. Debbie had always begged for a baby, and for awhile, she would have a real live one to play with. The three of them moved into one of the downstairs rooms. They didn't have anywhere else to go. They would help us finish the upstairs of the new house when we moved and stay until they could afford their own place.

As the house was being built, we supervised it weekly. Each child had a room, the upstairs unfinished second floor would be Stephen's room and a classroom, which Norris and Diane would occupy until they moved. Stephen was to have his longed-for privacy to lift weights, practice karate, and play his music with no one to bother him. The girls were to be downstairs in separate rooms. Tom's children were to share all the rooms when they came to visit. We would finish the upstairs rooms at once with Norris's help. He would do the work in lieu of paying for room or board for the three of them.

We moved into the house at the end of November in 1973. On December 3, Stephen celebrated his fifteenth birthday there among the unopened boxes. We had a cake and gifts for him, including a blue padded weight bench with weights. No one can remember his other gifts, and no pictures were taken since we were so busy unpacking, working, and going to school. Our attention was focused on trying to fit four adults and four children—plus Tom's visiting four—into the finished three bedrooms downstairs.

The upstairs, unfinished and unheated, was not livable in the icy Maryland winter. Norris promised to finish it quickly, but weeks went by. His job was demanding, and he was busy with other things. He made little time to work on it as he had promised. His procrastination drove us crazy. Tom helped him whenever Norris made time, but only a partition was up, with no walls and only some insulation.

The overcrowded conditions, tolerable at first, became unbearable as the weeks went by.

CHAPTER FOUR

The Pains of Puberty

*We are in the monsoons and we must weather it out—the way of
wisdom is, instead of pining for calmer days, to learn to live wisely
and well in the midst of continuous strain.*

– Elton Trueblood

*If while you are a child, just one someone loves you uncritically,
then you will have love to give the rest of your life.*

– Flavia

Despite overcrowded conditions and the stress, the move to the new
house in upper Marlboro, Maryland was like a breath of fresh air, a gift
from heaven.

No more long drives. The children were enrolled in schools where
they could remain until graduation. New friends wouldn't have to be left
behind in another move. It was only a fifteen minute drive to pick up
Tom's children twice weekly. This was a brand new house no one had
lived in before with rooms planned for each child and a huge yard. It was
on a corner with a wooded hill in back that provided privacy, and there
was a vast woods across the bridge from our street.

Only a few neighbors had moved into the new houses. Streets were
finished and many houses almost completed, but few were occupied. No
yards were sodded or landscaped yet. There was someone occupying the
house directly across from us, but we hadn't met. One by one, families
began to move in during the next months; but, for those first months, we
saw very few people. The streets were lined with earth movers and
construction crews. Building materials were stacked along the road-
sides. Dust and mud were everywhere.

No matter what the weather—rain or snow—all of the children played football, running up and down the streets in wild abandon. They could make noise to their heart's content. They went to the woods, built forts, and climbed on the parked earth movers and construction equipment the crews left when quitting for the weekend. Outdoors was an adventure for them all. As the oldest now, Stephen was the shepherd, coach, and ringleader of all activities.

While the children had marvelous times in their outdoor sanctuary, inside living conditions continued to be far less than desirable. Norris, Diane, and the baby were sleeping on the living room floor in sleeping bags until the upstairs was finished. Stephen was sleeping in Debbie's bed in her new room, which held his chest of drawers and hers, and all of her toys. Because of this, her little seven year old body usually occupied the room during the day too. She slept in Andrea's room but played in Stephen's temporary room because of the lack of space elsewhere.

Tom and I occupied the master bedroom and bath. We suffered the least. We could retreat to our room and had a place for our things. Books were piled in high stacks around the room until the upstairs was finished and library shelves were installed. We planned to teach classes on the second floor when it was finished.

In the family room, connected by a bar to the kitchen, the children could watch television or play games. They could go outside through the sliding glass door. With the dirt yard still unsodded, it was difficult to keep any entrance free from dirt, as nine children, four adults, and a newly acquired dog tracked in and out countless times, day and night.

The living room was spacious but contained both living room and dining room furniture plus Norris and Diane's sleeping gear, the baby's playpen, and various clothes and necessities. The result inside the house was crazy-making. It was a cross between a war zone and a shelter for the homeless.

We picked Tom's children up after school twice a week; they also came on Friday nights until Sunday night. Those days were especially chaotic. The four of them slept on the floor, couches, or wherever there was room.

The kitchen was small and only six people could squeeze around the table, so we ate in shifts. Often there were thirteen of us for each meal. Stephen sometimes took a tray and ate in the lounge chair while watching television. He usually wore shorts, in summer or winter, and put his karate-style bathrobe on over them, letting it hang open. He fixed lunch meat and cheese sandwiches if he didn't want to wait for dinner, or he snacked on beef jerky.

I rarely commented on anything he or any of the children ate, although I wished they would have eaten healthier foods. After years of being forced to eat whether they were hungry or not, whether they liked a particular food or not, they deserved some personal freedom for awhile. Since Tom and his children were accustomed to a white bread and junk food diet, that's primarily what we ate from the time he and I got together.

Tom and I were both working full time, Norris and Diane also held full time jobs, and the children were at school during the day. We all descended on the house within several hours of each other every evening. Some work had been done on the upstairs, but there was not enough completed to allow anyone to stay up there in the freezing weather. The temperature fell to below zero and snow covered the ground. The children chose to remain indoors more now. Later, when the snow was melting or the ice thawing, the neighborhood became a mud puddle. All this contributed to the stress and tension for everyone.

Though Norris was genuinely busy at work, he got sidetracked with other activities after hours. The completion of the upstairs went very, very slowly. Norris knew how crowded and messy things were, and he could have used his time better to do what he had promised. He and Diane were paying no rent and yet the work wasn't being done. We became very exasperated with him.

Even the children were getting sarcastic about Norris not finishing the upstairs. They resented being crowded into two bedrooms when a vast full story above them lay unused. Sometimes they went up and played on the wooden floors but the cold drove them back downstairs. Stephen put his weight bench in the area where his room was to be one day, and worked out on weights until he couldn't stand the cold any longer. He tried to find moments of privacy up in his Arctic sanctuary whenever possible. When we told Norris that we were going to hire someone to finish, he worked hard for a short time to assuage his guilt. Then he dropped back into his procrastination.

Thirteen people, depending upon who was home, lived in these close quarters, often jailed in by snow and rain and cold. We all began to grate on each other's nerves. We knew we had to do something; it had gone on too long. Finally we told Norris that it was absolutely urgent that he spend the next weekend getting the second floor livable, no matter how many other things he had to do. We insisted that by Sunday night we would put in space heaters, move him, Diane and the baby up there, and Stephen into his own room. We wanted the rest of the insulation and the partitions up before Monday. The remainder of the work was to be completed in the next week. We thought if Norris knew he had to live upstairs, finished or not, he would hustle. We committed to help him day and night that weekend and the following week until it was done. He agreed under duress.

On Friday night, we began. Stephen helped put in insulation. He never complained, though his hair and clothes were filled with dust and fibers as were all of ours. We nailed, hammered, sawed, and glued. By Sunday night, there was plastic placed over the insulation to seal the drafts, and sheets hung on the partitions. Space heaters were connected in Norris and Diane's area and another in Stephen's room. They could move in and exist fairly comfortably until it was finished the following week. Norris now *had* to finish the upstairs. They couldn't live in these conditions for very long.

Stephen was delighted to have his own room. The upstairs had the shape of a large, high attic. The window at the end in his room allowed him to see the yard and hill in back. We lugged his chest, bed, and treasures up to his area. There was no door, but a sheet hung where the door would shortly be. He was excited, saying it felt like camping out. He was a great sport about it. I gave him a hug and realized he was now a head taller than I. I told him how proud I was of him and how hard I knew he had worked. He seemed pleased with the progress made and knew what a good job he had done helping all weekend. The space heater took the chill off the room, and while it was somewhat drafty, it was tolerable. He finally had a place of his own. He arranged, rearranged, and planned how to hang his posters and pictures when the paneling was up.

Norris and Diane weren't that comfortable, but we felt this was the incentive Norris needed to finish things quickly. Had we known that the completion would still drag on for months, we would not have felt so optimistic and relaxed that first evening.

Within a few days, the baby got a cold and Stephen got a sore throat. It was probably from the heater and drafts along with the constant change of temperature. We told them all to move back downstairs. With our help, Norris could swiftly finish, then move them all back upstairs. Diane and Stephen declined and confided individually that they hoped by staying there it would spur the completion. It didn't. All of them continued to suffer and to complain about the drafts. Stephen was just a sheet away from them, and there was no privacy. Stephen finally told me that he wasn't moving back down, no matter what. He was sure that with him there and no door or walls up, Norris had to finish the rooms.

I was very irritated by the whole thing. I didn't like Stephen up there in such an unfinished mess, cold and coughing. I did like the lack of clutter downstairs and having the girls settling down in their own rooms, but I worried about Stephen. Many times I tried to get him to move back into Debbie's room and let Norris and Diane remain there alone. He assured me he loved his privacy when they were gone, and again, he was sure if he stayed up there it would force Norris to finish.

Day after day, we tried to be understanding of Norris's procrastination, but sometimes we lost our patience. We constantly offered to help. We didn't know how to finish the work alone and mentioned hiring someone many times. Norris always apologized, worked a few hours, getting our hopes up, then became too busy to work for days at a time.

Little by little, we began to see some progress. Walls went up, paneling finally covered the insulation, and a door was hung to Stephen's room. Still, nothing was finished. The windows had no moulding around them. You could see outside through the cracks and feel the winter breeze. But it was so much better than before.

Stephen was always appreciative of every new thing done. He made his unfinished area into his private retreat. He borrowed our tape recorder and typewriter. We could hear him recording music and typing by the hour. Often the house would shake when he dropped the end of a bar bell or a weight. He continued to practice his karate, and we could hear the noise of his movements and the sounds so familiar to us for these last years.

He was making a few acquaintances at Largo High School, but it was very slow. He was fifteen and cliques had been formed from grade school that didn't allow penetration by a new kid. He had come in on the middle of a school term, making him even more of an outsider. The subjects were different, and he found himself behind the other students in some of his classes. The teachers were new to him, and because of the size of the classes—thirty-five and more—they didn't have much time to help a new student.

Stephen was given extra assignments to bring him up to the level of the class. He brought them home and worked diligently. He often woke up, saying he didn't want to go to school. I understood what he was going through. I remembered having had the same experience myself when I changed schools twice at his age. I told him if he'd just hang in there it would get better and he'd begin to fit in just as I had done. Some days I talked to him and encouraged him to go to school. I told him that he could always come home. Other days, I gave in to his plea to stay home. He had various complaints to confirm not feeling well enough to go. We both knew without saying that he wasn't sick. At times, I insisted firmly and not always lovingly that he go to school. Other days, I was compassionate and gave in to his needs. I tried to sense when he could handle going and when he couldn't.

I thought he would soon overcome feeling like an outsider, settle down in school, and enjoy it as he had before. We often drove him to school on our way to work, though it wasn't a long walk. The three of us sat together in the front seat. Tom drove, and I rested my hand on Stephen's knee, squeezed it, told him I loved him, and encouraged him to have a good day. He would sometimes give me a kiss, sometimes not, sometimes say he loved me too, sometimes not.

One cold and windy afternoon, we picked him up near the shopping mall after school. He had taken a short cut; we watched him walk to the car. His shoulders were stooped, his raincoat blowing in the breeze. I saw him in a different way. How lonely he looked. How very alone. I was aware for a brief moment that some of his spirit was gone.

As he came toward us, he slipped on the hill, righted himself, and came limping to the car. I was concerned that he was hurt, but he had only broken the heel off of his black ankle-high boots. I was relieved. Tom, always very compassionate about the frequent damage his children did to clothes and shoes, spoke harshly to Stephen. "Those kind of boots weren't made to walk down hills. You know better than that." I defended Stephen, and Stephen became very quiet. I told him I'd get the heel fixed. He didn't say anything. His feelings had been hurt at a time he was feeling most vulnerable. I had the heel repaired right away because he loved his boots. He never mentioned the incident again.

Afternoons after school, Stephen worked in his room on his weight bench, making lengthy schedules about the number of leg lifts, biceps exercises, push-ups, and conditioning exercises to do daily. We heard the weights bump as he diligently worked out, trying to discipline himself to his schedule. He wanted a body like Billy Jack or the Karate Kid. He thought his body was flabby and not strong enough. His hair hung across his face as perspiration dripped from his body after his workouts, but he was pleased to have completed what he had set for himself.

He still loved karate and wore his white gi most days. He wanted to enroll in a karate class but there wasn't one near us. We were looking into where he could go. He couldn't get a driver's permit yet, and with both of us at work it meant driving him back and forth a long distance for a class. We procrastinated about finding one to give us a breather since there were so many other obligations.

He was now about five feet, eleven inches tall. He didn't discuss his weight except to say he was "fat, fat, fat." I found a notation on his calendar that he weighed 183 pounds. I assured him that he wasn't fat. If he wanted to lose a couple of pounds—or even ten—to feel he looked better, fine. But he wasn't fat. I thought he was so good-looking that his worry about being fat seemed more funny than a concern. I remembered being obsessed with looking in the mirror when I was fifteen, thinking

I was fat and ugly, but in my rational moments knowing it wasn't true. I totally empathized with him. He'd get over it. I did. All kids go through that, I reasoned. He had a clean cut face and hair below his ears but not down his back like so many young men of the early 1970s. Our friends thought he was handsome and had a wonderful personality. Everyone we knew liked him.

When I was about thirteen and had developed and matured so quickly, with large breasts and baby fat, I was kidded at school. That was part of life. It hurt, but it had made me stronger and less judgmental about how people looked. My parents couldn't convince me that I wasn't fat and ugly. I was sure no boy would ever look at me. Remembering my feelings, I praised and encouraged Stephen about how good he looked, but that didn't do any good, either. I understood and thought he would get through these emotionally painful times as we all did.

He swore off food, then ate and berated himself. During one of his most unhappy times, complaining that he couldn't stop eating, I gave him two or three old diet pills I had used years before. He took them, with my warning that they weren't good for him, but probably wouldn't hurt for a day or two to help him get his appetite under control. He didn't like the way they made him feel, but he lost a pound or two. I was glad he didn't ask for any more or want to go to the doctor for a prescription. Our doctor believed in diet pills and would have prescribed them. At that time, I had never heard or read any warnings about the danger of such pills, but I intuitively felt they weren't good. Later, when the papers were filled with warnings about their harmful effects, I realized why I had felt as I did.

Every week when Tom's children came, Stephen played football with them and took them into the woods to build forts. They learned to tie knots, as he had, and build fires outdoors. They must have irritated him on many occasions, but he was always patient, played games with them by the hour, taught them his karate kicks, and shared the weightlifting knowledge he had. As their leader, we never saw him become angry with them or shout at them.

Stephen prepared many of his own lunches and breakfasts, becoming quite expert at fried eggs and sandwiches. Other than helping, he didn't attempt dinners. The sheer number of us was intimidating. Tacos or hamburgers for thirteen was a major undertaking. Cleanup, shared by all, was a madhouse with me "scraping" the floor with a spatula before mopping it.

Stephen seemed unaffected by the chaos. His disposition stayed the same—loving and easygoing. Our living conditions drove Bob crazy when he came to visit. It drove me crazy sometimes to live in it, but even at its worst, it was like living in heaven after those earlier years. The good seemed to outweigh the bad.

With Bob gone, Stephen organized activities or made the things happen that the kids requested. Most anything they all wanted to do, he had the energy to tackle. He was never overbearing or bossy with them. The weekends or holidays were his happiest times. Monday mornings after the weekends brought the pain of another week of school. My heart ached for him. He had always loved school, excelled, and had usually been somewhat of a teacher's pet in every grade. He had never before lacked for friends.

Now, here was a Stephen who said the teachers didn't care. They probably didn't, actually. It seemed they were so busy with all their own personal problems as well as overcrowded classes, that a new student entering in mid-semester disrupted their schedules. Stephen had never been critical of his teachers before, but he insisted over and over that no one wanted to listen to him or to help him. He felt that none of them cared at all. This was what hurt him most—that the teachers didn't care. Ordinarily, I would have gone in to see his teachers about him because Stephen's perceptions throughout the years had always been so accurate. He bent over backward to be fair. I knew what he felt was either absolutely true or that he at least felt it to be true. Either way, something needed to be done, but I wasn't sure exactly what. I continued to rationalize that it was just the normal settling-in. In time it would resolve itself. If it didn't soon, then I could do something. It seemed premature to defend him and to ask for help this early on when it had been only a few weeks. So much was happening in our lives with the home situation that I simply put off going to the school. Procrastination on all fronts became a slow cancer in our lives.

Stephen complained often that the kids at school wouldn't talk to him and ignored him. I suggested he pick out some who looked lonely and be friends with them, which seemed good motherly advice at the time. He said he had tried. I suggested he get involved in some activities. He said the clubs were already full or too far along in their projects for him to join. I told him many times that I had felt the same way when I changed schools and was away from my friends. I assured him that it would get better. I should have known that kids don't want to hear these platitudes. Who cares what Mom and Dad experienced in the "olden days?" He would nod and go up to his room.

When I came to pick him up after school one day, he was sitting on a bench talking to a boy about his age who overflowed the bench, weighing at least 300 pounds. A lower part of myself emerged. Stephen explained that the boy was very nice and they had had a good talk. I said,

"But Stephen, wouldn't it it be better if you found someone else to be friends with too? This boy couldn't even play sports or anything with you. He may not be the best person for you to hang around with." As I said it, I felt like a heel, but Stephen had been so unhappy recently. I was fearful that if he were to be friends with this poor soul, obviously an outcast because of his being so grossly overweight, it would make things even worse for Stephen. He said that no one else would even talk to the boy. I apologized. I was being judgmental and very wrong. Nevertheless, I had said some very unfair things which couldn't be unsaid, out of my worry about Stephen.

During the week, Tom mostly ignored Stephen, speaking to him occasionally but with no particular interest or genuine concern. I tried to talk with Stephen every day and ask him how things were going. Sometimes he expressed how he felt; usually he was not very happy. Other times he would just say, "Nothing," or "OK," or "Fine," or "It's alright, Mom." I was honestly relieved when he at least pretended things were alright since so much else was going on in our lives. It was a breather to *think* things were better. How I fooled myself!

We often came home to find him watching television in the family room and eating a sandwich because he had skipped lunch. At night, he worked on weights, practiced karate, or watched TV again. He still loved "Kung Fu" with David Carradine; and, as he had while living in Alexandria, yelled for me to watch certain things he enjoyed. He wanted me to share some of the oriental philosophy they were teaching. He mimicked the body postures his hero used to fight off the bad guys. Sometimes he joined us for dinner, sometimes he didn't.

Tom and I were still going to our own classes two nights a week, so Stephen watched the girls on those nights and saw that they were fed and put to bed. Some of our friends began to come over every Tuesday night for a meditation and a get-together where we discussed everything we were learning. It was usually the same six to twelve people. Occasionally, they brought a friend.

We invited Stephen to join us around the table in the living room, but he usually declined. However, he sat on the stairs leading up to his room and listened from there. At times when we took a break, he joined us, or he asked questions about what he had heard.

He had a cautious interest at first, then a growing interest, in the whole field of parapsychology. We told him more about what we were learning. Some things he thought kind of crazy, as did we. Other things stimulated question after question. Much of it was in conflict with his former church teachings which we discussed. There was less dogma, more openness, more acceptance in these new truths than we had experienced in our old churches. All of us were excited about the research in telepathy, dreams, psychic abilities, and paranormal experiences.

Stephen told us he tried to talk to his dad about it, but his dad ridiculed everything we were doing. This planted occasional doubt in him. We talked it over, trying to help him see different perspectives, sharing our personal feelings but letting him make up his own mind. He seemed enthusiastic and happy talking and hearing about everything. Then, on the rare occasions when he visited his dad, he came home depressed and confused. This was not always because of what he told his dad we were studying, but because, as he would say, his dad still made him, "Feel like shit."

He worked on biology papers, composed many stories, and did a lot of drawing, often having a wastebasket filled with discarded work and art. He sketched and traced bodies in different karate poses, placing them around his room. He listened to all the current popular songs of the year on his radio.

Despite all the stress, overcrowding, and confusion in the house, December brought the anticipation of Christmas and lifted all our spirits with renewed hope. We sneaked around, purchasing and wrapping our special gifts for each other, and hiding others so that their shapes would not give away our carefully planned surprises.

The whole family rushed out the weekend after Stephen's birthday, and with much discussion and care, selected the perfect tree from the hundreds on the lot. We carefully trimmed it to fit the stand and placed it in front of the expanse of windows in the living room. We unpacked the many boxes of trimmings and lights, decorated the tree with ornaments I had collected for years as well as ones we had acquired recently as a family and, of course, those the children had made. Tom was his most friendly, outgoing self, and he arranged the lights. The seven children and I added most of the ornaments, with Norris, Diane, and the baby helping. When we finished, there was the sense of pride that perhaps our tree was the most beautiful in all of Maryland. With eight children, even a few presents each made quite a pile under our tree.

Christmas was two weeks away. We had all the coming days to enjoy the tree and play the tapes and records of Christmas music. The mountain of presents under the tree grew. Stephen and the children would squeeze and shake them, trying to guess what was in each carefully wrapped package.

The days were filled with the children playing football outside except when the melting snow and rain halted their fun. When they had to stay inside, they baked Christmas cookies and cakes which they devoured almost as soon as they came out of the oven. If ever the happy family was in evidence, it was that December. Any worries, problems and fighting were put on hold. It was the time to love everyone and everything, to give thanks for this new life, this new chance we had to begin again.

I had bought eight small candleholders, one for each child the year before, and I placed a candle of a different color in each. There were paneled windows along the wall in the living room so I placed one candle in each of eight window panes. As we lit them, I told the children it was to celebrate how special each one of them was to us. Each child knew one of the candles to be his or her own, but we hadn't assigned anyone a particular color. The little candles glowed in a rainbow of colors.

Stephen and the other children listed all the things they wanted as gifts. We selected quite a few of these from each one's list. No expense was spared at Christmas. It was both Tom's and my own favorite time of the year. Christmas of 1973 was celebrated on the day before Christmas since Tom's ex-wife insisted she have the children every Christmas. The day of our Christmas began before dawn with the younger children waking up the older ones. The custom in Tom's German family was to get up, to eat a breakfast of grapefruit and fruit stollen baked by his mother, and then to open the presents. However, since his mother wasn't there, we skipped that custom, eating the stollen she had mailed to us, before, during and after the frantic gift opening.

Tom stood by the tree, selected a present, read the name of the person it was meant for and who it was from. The excited child ran up to get the present and everyone had to wait until the child opened it and thanked the giver, before another present was selected for the next child. It took forever. After the first half hour of opening, selecting, thanking, and squealing, five or six presents began to be opened simultaneously. Even at that, it was almost lunch time before the gift orgy was finished. The living room looked as if a tornado had whipped through it.

Stephen got lots of toys and presents that year, as did the others. One gift was a belt, which he opened, smiled, and thanked us for appreciatively, but I could tell he was a little disappointed. There was enough of the kid in him that games, toys, and fun things outweighed the more practical items. He helped the younger kids open gifts that were tied too tightly, and played with them with their games and toys the rest of the day.

He wore his karate-style, rust colored velour bathrobe that now came to just above his knees. Underneath the robe he wore shorts and a T-shirt, with his high-top Converse tennis shoes and socks. Neither he nor any of the children had combed their hair in anticipation of Christmas pictures.

Taking Christmas pictures reminded me of a silly thing that had happened several weeks before at school. We were being taught to develop our intuition in a weekly class and our teacher, Billie, giving me an intuitive message said, "Be sure to take plenty of pictures this Christmas. Things will never be the same and you will want to take more than the usual number of pictures." I didn't think that was very profound. Of course, things were never the same from one day to the next, much less from one Christmas to the other. Nevertheless, as I watched Stephen and the children open presents, I remembered this strange prediction and had the camera out, trying to remember to photograph everyone. Stephen kept avoiding the camera because he said he looked awful and asked me to wait until he combed his hair and got cleaned up.

Stephen gave us a *Jonathan Livingston Seagull* record album because he knew how much we had loved the book. It was a great gift; we were surprised and delighted, and Stephen was pleased.

It was a perfect day: laid-back, peaceful, and relaxed. Children found corners of the house where they stacked their gifts, going back to them again and again. Stephen took his presents upstairs to his room. Everyone played—alone, in small groups, and together. Bob wasn't able to come home that Christmas which was the only sad part of our day.

When it was time to take Tom's children home—it was now Christmas Eve—we loaded the car with their toys, to be taken to the safety of their own rooms. Later, it was a quiet and pleasant evening of talking, snacking and basking in the glow that would soon dim when the bills for the charges came in the next month. Our Christmases always put us thousands of dollars in debt. It seemed worth it during that special day, but not always afterward.

Stephen and the girls were out of school until January. They kept themselves occupied with reading, bicycling, and retreating into their own inner worlds. They did not have baby-sitters, but, instead, took care of each other. Stephen, fifteen, was in charge, and Andrea, twelve, was second in command. Debbie was almost eight. Stephen and Andrea had temperaments much alike and even looked alike. Both were more kind, loving, and quiet, more well-behaved than the child on each end. Bob needed attention and demanded attention, with one crisis after another. Debbie as the youngest and most "spoiled" in the opinion of several of the children, also demanded much attention, partly from age, partly from her personality. She had many demands and Stephen and Andrea either met them or ignored them, depending upon their frequency. When her demands were ignored, she was quick to tell us about it when we came home. Her threats of "I'm going to tell!" were frequent while we were gone, I'm sure.

Debbie was a fairly typical youngest child and during that time she expected the world to be at her beck and call. It usually was. She was bossy, charming, loving, and irritating, sometimes within the same five minutes. Stephen would bribe Andrea and her to scratch his back. He loved having his back scratched or rubbed. They got paid in coins for their efforts. I once heard him plead with Debbie to scratch his back after I had told him I was too busy right then. She wouldn't. He pleaded some more, upping the ante, but finally gave up. Sometimes she called him a "fat slob" when he didn't do what she wanted, knowing his constant worry about his weight. When I heard her, I reprimanded her and made her apologize. I told her how much it hurt him and I reminded her how it hurt her when people called her a midget because she was so short. Always being petite, she would never have a weight problem, but she went through a stage of being critical of others who were overweight.

Stephen's worries seemed rather normal along side Debbie's, Andrea's, and Bob's. Bob hated his too curly hair, Andrea thought nobody liked her. Added to that, my remembrances of my own insecurities, though twenty years in the past, made it seem that he was going through a childhood rite of passage.

Money was short after the holidays due to our Christmas gluttony, and in buying the house, fixing it up, and continuing the snail pace construction on the upstairs. The cost of supporting two families was astronomical. We bought food weekly that filled two or three baskets each trip to the store, and clothes for seven children that seemed to magically develop holes or be outgrown before the first washing. The pool would have to wait a year. We were not poor, but our cash flow was low.

Stephen needed new clothes to start the semester. He and I went shopping at Montgomery Ward one afternoon. I was tight and stingy with him. It had been a stressful week worrying about money. I bought him a few things he wanted, always commenting on or asking about the price.

My compassion about his clothing needs for his self-esteem were buried under my worry about paying the bills, especially since the Christmas mound had arrived in the mail. When he asked if he could get something and I refused because of the price, he didn't ask again. He seemed satisfied with the meager amount of things I got him, though the great difference between what he got and the clothes we had bought for all four of Tom's children the week before couldn't have gone unnoticed.

Money or not, Tom saw that his children got whatever they wanted. My children sometimes got what was left when the money ran out. I rationalized that his children didn't live with us, that he had left them, that their needs were greater, that their mother was so unfair to them . . . and on and on. I doubt that I shared this with Stephen, nor did it justify not meeting his needs at this critical time in his life.

Stephen was not happy when school began, but he talked about being really determined to make a new start with friends and teachers. He went back to school with renewed optimism. Almost immediately, the same pattern reappeared. He was ignored and left out and even the teachers had no time for him. Why I didn't go to the school cannot be excused by Tom's insisting that Stephen had to learn to handle his own problems, or by my feeling that perhaps I wasn't cutting the apron strings sufficiently and letting him grow up. The end result was the same—I didn't talk to his teachers and they didn't ask to talk to me when his grades dropped and his assignments weren't finished. I rationalized that it was because of Stephen's age, the moves, and the changes in schools. It would resolve itself in time.

As the weather got a little bit warmer, Stephen continued to wear his navy blue raincoat, even though some days it seemed he didn't need it. He felt it kept him from looking so fat. He seemed relaxed and happy on weekends, and while at home he was his old smiling and joking self. Every Monday his face changed, his shoulders sagged, as he forced himself to go to school, reluctantly putting his arms into his raincoat just before he left.

Months before in Alexandria, he had played football for a short period of time. I had taken Andrea and Debbie to see him at a practice session. I wished I had taken a camera. Stephen was wearing an orange and white jersey and helmet. He was one of the tallest and biggest kids. I was so proud of him. He didn't get knocked down too often. He wasn't an aggressive player. I wondered how he would last because, as little as I knew about football, I could see that he pulled back, not wanting to make the tackle he should have, and he did not let himself be tackled. Then I observed that many of the other boys his age did the same. There were some that got knocked down every play, but many, like Stephen, held back.

Within a week, Stephen came home to tell me that he wasn't on the football team any longer. He had gotten tackled and hurt; there was blood in his urine. The coach had the doctor examine him and, afterward, Stephen decided he probably shouldn't play football anymore. I knew he was okay. He knew he was okay. I understood. Who would want to be knocked down, grabbed, tackled, and hurt in the name of fun? I hugged him and said, "That's fine. If you ever want to play again, go ahead. If you don't, that's OK." He hugged me back and said, "Thanks, Mom." That ended his football career.

We talked about Stephen's friends a lot during February and in early March. He had a crush on a girlfriend from our former church, and we had a long discussion about it seated on the couch in the living room one evening. She had kept in telephone contact, and he saw her when his dad insisted on taking him to church. This was mostly a distant, unrequited love on Stephen's part. She was in love with someone else, which Stephen seemed to understand with little jealousy, but a bit of sadness. Now she thought she was pregnant. She couldn't tell her parents who were pillars of the church, and there was no one in whom to confide but Stephen. I doubt that she knew how much he cared for her. He told me he didn't know what to tell her and asked my advice. I suggested several things, places, and people. He asked me to talk to her. He assured her that I wouldn't tell her parents or anyone. When she and I finished talking, he hugged me and said, "Thanks, Mom. I knew you would understand and help her. I told her you would help."

We discussed many things that night: his worries, fears, hopes, his philosophies, karate, girls, life. Afterward, I felt so good. He had always talked with me about his feelings, but this time it was like two adults talking. I was pleased with his concern for his friends, his maturity in dealing with his thoughts and desires, and his confidence in me. Also, I was pleased that he was so affectionate. Most of his friends would not let their mothers hug them much less return the hug with a kiss and say, "I love you." I felt really proud of him. My young son was becoming a thoughtful and caring person—I had no worries about the man he would become. After all the difficulties with Bob, Stephen made me feel that perhaps I had some redeeming qualities as a mother.

He was becoming really handsome, I thought, losing the little boy chubbiness of body and face. His eyebrows were becoming darker and somewhat bushy, and his blue eyes radiated kindness and warmth—and mischief. Plainly and simply, I adored him. Perhaps he acted and looked like a thousand other boys his age. I saw him through the "mother glow" of love. To me he was very, very special, not only in looks, but in spirit.

On a Friday night late in February, Richard had already picked up the girls before Tom and I arrived home, exhausted from a long, hard week. We did not have Tom's children, and Norris, Diane, and the baby were somewhere else. The house was quiet—a most unusual occurrence.

Stephen was sitting in the lounge chair, watching the television, and eating. He had on his favorite blue slacks and navy blue, long-sleeved shirt, rolled up to the elbows, his bare feet hanging over the end of the foot rest of the chair. Tom and I decided to go to a movie to relax. I asked Tom about inviting Stephen to go with us, feeling guilty because I knew we didn't have a lot of time alone. He agreed but wasn't very enthusiastic about it. I knew he'd prefer that we go alone. I said I wanted to ask Stephen anyway, so he didn't have to be by himself. When I invited him, his eyes lit up. Then, hesitating a moment, he said he didn't want to go.

I tried to talk him into coming with us, but it was one of those conversations where the main communicating was being done non-verbally. I really wanted him to go and he knew it, but also I didn't want to disappoint Tom. I realized if we were to maintain our relationship with eight kids, we needed time alone. I knew that Stephen *knew* that and declined. My heart ached when I couldn't convince him. I knew he *needed* to come with us; I could feel his loneliness. I let *him* decide, and his decision was for *me*. He knew this, and I knew that he knew. The whole thing made me sad all evening.

With Stephen's growing maturity, he felt good enough about himself not to subject himself to further browbeating by Richard, so he seldom went to Richard's anymore. He said he hated being there because his dad was always finding fault with him. He would, however, sometimes go when Richard's new girlfriend had her fifteen-year-old daughter along. Then he would come home and say he had a wonderful time, and that he really liked the daughter. He hoped her mother and his dad would marry. Richard had a series of short relationships after we divorced, but none of them lasted long.

Stephen said that every time he didn't go with his dad, he felt guilty—guilty that he didn't want to be with him because he loved him but didn't *like* him, guilty that somehow he was hurting his dad each time he didn't go over. Richard would call him and amplify the guilt about his not coming, but Stephen generally stood firm and made excuses about other commitments. The times he gave in when he didn't want to, he would be in a deep depression for days after he came home.

The girls, not as strong, acquiesced most of the time, and even when I told them they could stay home, they often went anyway so their dad didn't get upset. While he did not treat Debbie as badly, even she made sarcastic comments about how he treated the other two.

Stephen had a maroon gym bag he carried back and forth to school. It became his security blanket, his purse, and perhaps his long-gone Beany doll. Everything went in it—books, socks, clothes, all the mysterious things a fifteen-year-old boy carries. Once in his room, I saw several new things from the drug store. I asked him where he got them. He said that he had bought them. I questioned if he had enough money, asking if he had just taken the items without paying for them. He denied it.

I questioned him about this because a year earlier, I had picked up an extension phone by accident, while he was talking, and heard his friend mention shoplifting. Curious, I listened further and heard Stephen say he had shoplifted the ring he was wearing. I confronted him and told him I had listened. He said he really hadn't stolen his ring, he had bought it, but all his friends were shoplifting and he felt left out, so he had bragged that he had done it too. He was always honest with me, so I had no reason to doubt him. He lied to Richard, but rarely to me. He knew I wouldn't punish him, so he was usually honest with me.

He also knew I had never snooped in his room or listened in on his conversations. My mother had honored my privacy, and I did the same with my children. I never went in his room or read his writings even when he wasn't home. Knowing that, he and the other children left personal things out and were usually honest with me. I respected the fact that sometimes they simply didn't want their mother to know everything. I honored this as a sign of their growing up. So, while there was a tiny seed of concern that maybe he had shoplifted the items, my past experiences with him overrode these suspicions and it was soon forgotten.

My heart would ache each time we drove him to school. He looked so lonely and vulnerable—his shoulders stooped, blue raincoat unbelted and flapping around his body as he walked slowly into the building for classes.

Every day without fail, when he got home in the afternoon before the girls arrived, he telephoned me at about 3:15 p.m., at work. When I answered, a familiar voice would always say, "Hi, Mom, it's me." Or sometimes, "Hi, Mom, it's me—Steve." He always called himself Steve, I always called him Stephen. He never said, "Don't call me Stephen," but he liked to refer to himself as Steve with everyone else. I would ask him about his day or he would ask me about something. If there was time, we visited awhile, and I played "mother" by phone. If we were very busy, the conversation was short—just Stephen checking in that he was OK and that I was there. I often dictated a few things for him to write down to have all the children do before I came home — things such as turning on the stove to cook the meat, or cleaning up their rooms, or emptying the trash. The conversations usually ended with, "Bye, honey. I love you." And he responded with, "Bye, Mom. I love you too." After Stephen's call, there were often others from each of the girls. Working for Tom as his assistant and secretary in a private office gave me freedom to talk to the children daily; I could keep in touch with them off and on until we went home at five o'clock.

The three of them got along reasonably well, with Debbie the most difficult to handle and discipline. They sometimes reported on each other when I got home. I scolded, laughed, disciplined, or smoothed things over, depending upon the situation.

I wasn't always consistent. For some things that probably needed correcting, I laughed and hugged them. For others, things seemingly minor to them I'm sure, I reprimanded them. I didn't like to punish them physically or emotionally—they had too many years of that. Mostly, I fussed at them or hugged them or talked to them. I was not a very consistent disciplinarian.

The mistakes that I made with them, which were many, were out of my absolute ignorance of child-rearing at the time. There was, no doubt, a kind of self-centeredness in being in school and working, consequently becoming overly tired. Nevertheless, everything I did was clouded by this incredible love and pride I had for each of them. They seemed to be exceptionally good kids—very, very special. We hugged and loved each other and talked, and I felt that nothing very bad could ever happen to us again now that we were away from the hell we had endured for so long.

When I realized I had done something to hurt them or had handled things poorly, I apologized, thinking that would make it better and believing it did. I guess I felt like one of them. I remembered my own childhood so clearly. Their childhood seemed so much richer and fuller than mine. They had all the material things I had always wanted. I had never lacked emotional support and love; and, I thought I was giving them what I had received and more plus all the material things. I had my work and my education, my life separate yet a part of theirs. I let them have a degree of freedom and free will to make some of their own decisions as they matured. I could joy in their accomplishments and they in mine. I didn't feel I had much trouble letting them break free of me to grow up. How much of this was true I will never know unless they write their own memories and accounts of me. However, I doubt that I was as good a mother as I aspired to be or thought I was, nor was I as bad as I could have been. Time, the great healer, may have dimmed my memories of my shortcomings and magnified the memories of my strengths.

Stephen continued to be ambivalent about school most mornings. One morning I found a note on our bedroom door, "I can't force myself to go in. Please let me stay home and sleep today." I let him sleep, not even going upstairs to talk to him. His note was so boldly written, so intense—not the words, but the inner feeling it gave me. He called me later at work, thanking me, and explaining how he felt.

One afternoon in early March, he came home from school carrying a yellow belt for his karate gi. He said his male biology teacher had let him demonstrate his karate in class. The teacher was a karate black belt so he could test Stephen and give him the next step up—a yellow belt. He was beaming with pride. He intensified his practice of the karate kicks, yellow belt tied firmly around his white gi, which was getting a little short in the legs due to his added height. The outfit was now a year-and-a-half old and despite numerous washings, looked somewhat dingy.

The dirty and much used white belt, which was never washed, was hung over the back of the door, having served its purpose. Stephen was preparing for all the next stages of colored belts, from brown to the coveted black. He loved karate and practiced, not to hurt anyone as he said, but to stay in good physical shape, able to defend himself, and to be strong. He continued to watch "Kung Fu," cheering the good guys winning over the bad with their soft words and martial art movements. I found the program fascinating myself. If only life were really like that, I thought. He had added Spiderman, whom he called "Spidey," to his list of personal heroes. He wanted to be like him too.

Stephen continued to check books out of the library on weightlifting, Chinese philosophy, karate and the martial arts. He read, practiced, and set up disciplines and sets of exercises to follow. He wanted a strong, powerful body just as did most of our friend's kids at that time. No one could have kept up such a regimen, but he tried and was hard on himself when he faltered. His heroes did not falter. They could jump tall buildings, take on half the Chinese army, and stop wild animals and criminals with a soft-spoken word and look in the eye.

Stephen had finally made a friend at school and invited him over to practice karate in his bedroom. While trying some kind of kick, the friend broke his finger. Stephen rushed to the neighbors' house across the street and they drove him to the emergency room. We were at work and Stephen called me, concerned, but feeling he had handled it pretty well. The neighbors had been very helpful. The boy was going to be fine. It was no big deal. Still, the boy's parents never allowed him to come back.

I had no idea of the depths of Stephen's loneliness and pain. When weekends came, he was his old self—playing with the kids, teaching and helping them with homework, cooking, watching TV, practicing his karate. He would be full of life and laughter, and I fooled myself into believing that things were getting better.

We often laughed about a time when Stephen had asked me to watch "Kung Fu" with him while we lived in Alexandria. He was dressed in his gi, taking in every word, asking me if the program wasn't "the greatest." I laid beside him on a bean bag chair. Bob and the other children were sprawled all over the family room. Halfway through the program, I let out a blood curdling scream and jumped up, ripping off my bathrobe. Stephen jumped to his feet to protect me from whatever unseen enemy had attacked me. A daddy long legs had crawled up to my stomach as I lay there. I had a terrible fear of bugs—a fear which the children laughingly played upon with rubber spiders and insects, hidden in various places to scare me.

After killing the spider and being sure I was alright, Stephen and the family joked and laughed about my piercing screams, and how everyone thought I was having an attack of some kind. Stephen would tease me during the rest of the program by tickling my arm or leg as if the creature had returned. I joined in the laughter.

Stephen and Bob loved practical jokes—it was always good clean fun, followed by belly laughs. Therefore, my reactions in front of the television were far better than all the tricks they could have planned. We shared many laughs among ourselves, about that experience and about the other people who had fallen for their tricks over the years. Stephen was always a particularly good-natured kid with a wonderful sense of humor.

Now that laughter and humor only surfaced on weekends, if then. The situation at school was wearing his gentle spirit down little by little. It was only in looking back that I became so painfully aware of that.

✽

CHAPTER FIVE

Rainy Days and Mondays

Ah, Christ, that it were possible
For one short hour to see
The souls we loved, that they might tell us
What and where they be.

 – Alfred Tennyson

Nurture strength of spirit to guide you in sudden misfortune.
 – Found among Stephen's writings

Monday afternoon, March 18, I came home from work and Stephen wasn't there. He hadn't called me at work as he usually did, and I had been so busy I hadn't called home.

I asked where he was. Andrea said he was over in the woods camping. Camping on a school night? The girls told me they had come home from school and found him packing his gym bag and getting a sleeping bag ready. When they questioned him, he told them he needed to get away and to tell me not to try to find him—he wanted to be alone. He was going across the bridge into the woods for the night and would be OK.

I recalled the events of that morning before we left for work. He had again not wanted to go to school. This time I had insisted he get up and get dressed. I told him things would be fine. A half hour went by and there was no noise from upstairs to indicate he was dressing. I was annoyed and knew something had to be done. He had been such a fine student and so sociable, it wasn't like him to continue feeling this way. I had also seen some items from the drugstore on his bed the day before and was pretty sure he hadn't bought them, but I hadn't taken or found time to talk with him. I was in a hurry getting dressed and felt agitated. I just didn't know how to handle the situation regarding this unhappiness in school. Quite unlike myself, I asked Tom to go to Stephen's room and tell him that I insisted he go to school. I also asked him to tell Stephen to leave his gym bag at home since I didn't want him taking any more things from the store.

This was out of character for me. I seldom asked Tom to talk to Stephen about *anything*. I normally handled my children and their problems and needs myself. I felt Tom had enough to do with his own four. Perhaps I also asked Tom to go to Stephen's room because Tom had told me he had a long talk with Stephen a few nights before. They had discussed life after death and reincarnation; and Stephen had asked many questions with great interest. He wanted to know more about all we were learning and studying. Maybe I was just tired and wanted someone to do my dirty work. I can't remember.

Tom came back down from Stephen's bedroom after a few minutes, saying he had talked to him and told him to leave his bag home from now on and that he was to get dressed for school. I asked him what Stephen had said. We were interrupted by one of the girls, and I didn't learn any more about their conversation.

When we were ready to leave, Stephen yelled downstairs to us that he'd walk to school and for us to go ahead. He had recently admitted to riding to school with us, then coming back home, skipping school. This had to stop. I told him we'd wait, that I wanted him to come along with us. When he slowly climbed into the car, I asked him to promise to stay in school until it was out. I assured him that when we got home that night we would talk and work things out. I decided I had put off talking with his teachers at school too long. It had been over three months and things weren't improving.

We were sandwiched in the front seat of the car, Tom driving. Stephen was on my right next to the door, and I sat in the middle. As usual, I squeezed his knee and thought how good he still felt, just like when he was little. His head was down and he didn't say anything. I told him he *must not* shoplift things, that if he needed something we would buy it for him or give him the money. When he climbed out of the car, I said we'd see him when we all got home. We would talk further then. He agreed. He walked toward the school without looking back, his shoulders slumped, blue raincoat blowing in the March breeze. I couldn't bear for him to hurt so much. This just wasn't like him. A few days before, he had even given the other kids all of his karate equipment and knives. He had loved his karate gear so much.

Now he was out. Darn it. I was irritated with him. He knew we were going to talk that afternoon. I had made special plans to be with him and here he had gone camping in the woods just as he had when we lived in Alexandria. I wasn't going to go after him. He wouldn't answer anyway. We wouldn't find him, just like last time. He would either come home tonight when it got dark or tomorrow. When he did, I would be tougher on him. Maybe I was babying him too much. I was definitely going to the school tomorrow and get all this straightened out. The school was falling down on its job too, and I would let his teachers know in no uncertain terms.

He didn't come home that night and though I was worried, I was more irritated. After all, he had done this before, and I had been beside myself with pain. He had come back the next morning and had promised he would never do it again. He knew how I agonized the night he ran away and slept in the woods months ago. He knew how devastated I was when Bob ran away. I couldn't believe he was this uncaring. It wasn't like him. I didn't go across the bridge to the woods to find him or call him. This had to stop.

After we went to bed that evening, I fell asleep but awoke in the middle of the night to the sound of rain beating down on the roof. I felt such overpowering sadness, I cried and cried. As much as I pretended not to worry, my son was outside by himself in the dark and pouring rain. It was March and still cold. Stephen must be cold, wet, and feeling scared and unloved. I wanted to go out in the dark to find him and bring him home and just hold him. I loved him so. If he would spend the night in the dark and cold and rain, things were pretty bad. When he came home tomorrow, I would talk to him and then go to the school right away. I swore it as I prayed for him and fell asleep again.

In the morning, I decided to stay home from work. I had been awake off and on all night. I wanted to be there the moment Stephen came home and talk with him. I couldn't go to the office, and worry until I heard from him. I waited and waited. It was noon and he still hadn't come home. I talked to Tom who said he was picking up his children after school. He would come home early and we'd go get Stephen or send the children to the woods to find him and tell him to come home. He could tell how upset I was and assured me that we would find Stephen.

Tom arrived home sometime after four o'clock that afternoon with the children. While they were getting a snack, we discussed going to find Stephen and what to do about how miserable he was in school. Someone knocked on the door. Andrea answered and brought two men in dark suits into the living room. They showed me their badges, asked me my name, and said they were there about Stephen. I wondered what in the world he had gotten himself into that the police or detectives or whomever they were, came to tell us about in person. Stephen had never been in trouble with the police, ever. The men asked us to sit down and motioned us to the couch. They pulled up two chairs and sat across from us. The children hovered in the doorways to the kitchen and entrance to see what was going on.

One man spoke quietly and said, "Your son is dead. We found him in the woods a little while ago."

I felt as if someone had hit me in the stomach with a sledge hammer. The pain was so intense that I gasped for breath. I couldn't exhale or breathe. Finally I asked, "What? *What*?" He said that two men gathering firewood in the woods across from us had found him, called them, and they had come and cut his body down. Stephen had hanged himself from a tree.

This couldn't be possible. There must be some mistake. I didn't cry. The pain was so bad in my stomach that I couldn't cry. I heard gasps from the children and cries, but my pain blocked out everything else. I needed to question the men, but I couldn't speak. I couldn't even seem to breathe.

Stephen had left a notebook, they told me, with messages to us. I could read it if I wanted, but they would have to take it for a few days. They handed it to me. As I read each page, it sounded so much like Stephen, I smiled and even laughed. Bless his heart, even just before he died, he had thought of us. He had written everyone of us some words of caring and comfort. He had even made some jokes about it all. It was so like him, yet the notes were also heartbreaking. Stephen was no longer alive, the words said. My body heard and felt the words, but my mind didn't register then fully. I think I expected Stephen to walk through the door at any moment and say, "Just a joke, Mom. Fooled you, didn't I?" much like he and Bob had done with their practical jokes which had often worked with me.

His body was just outside in an ambulance, they said, as they stood to leave. Did we want to identify it there? We would have to identify it there or in the morgue. His body? I had only seen one dead body in my life and it almost made me throw up. His body? My baby's body! Stephen had been hanging on a tree with a rope around his neck. How could I look at his precious body with a rope around his throat. How could I see him dead? I didn't want to see my baby dead. I couldn't bring myself to look at him. All my life I had stayed away from funerals and dead bodies. I couldn't stand to *think* of dead bodies. How could I possibly look at my own son's body?

I thought about the neighbors, none of whom we knew. I couldn't face going outside and seeing them watching Stephen and me and our family in our pain and grief as they pulled back the sheet to show us his body.

I couldn't think clearly. I was frightened. I was so sick. I think I felt if I didn't see him dead, he would still be alive.

I didn't know what to do. I wanted to see him, but I was frightened and in pain. I asked Tom to identify him. He went outside with one of the detectives and came back in the house with tears in his eyes. I repeatedly asked him in years to come if Stephen's eyes had popped out. I had read an account of someone who had hanged himself and was found with his eyes popped out. He assured me they weren't. To this day I don't know if they were or not. The men took his notebook with them. I wanted so much to keep it, but they wouldn't let me. They promised to return it later.

The ambulance pulled away, without sirens. The children were crying and heartbroken. I hugged Andrea and Debbie. Andrea sobbed and sobbed. She and Stephen were the closest of the four. Debbie had no real awareness that this meant Stephen wouldn't come back home again, ever.

I looked down at my lap after the men left. I was wearing a blue and red patterned flannel caftan. It was my favorite warm and comfortable outfit to lounge around in. I had made it to wear to relax in. I pulled it over my head and stuffed it deep into the garbage can. It had covered my body on the worst day of my entire life. I felt an overwhelming desire to bathe all over or to claw the skin from my body. I wanted to die myself.

People had to be called—my parents and sister, Richard, our ministers, whoever loved and knew Stephen. One call melted into another. Everyone cried. I cried.

Tom needed to take the children home. I didn't want to ride along, but I could not stand being alone now and neither could the children. We all got in the car to go with him. When we pulled up in front of his children's house, Tom's ex-wife was on the lawn. Tom walked over to her with his children to tell her about Stephen. She had never spoken to me since Tom and I had gotten together. She was rude to my children if they happened to be with him. She still tried to use his children for blackmail when she wanted something, and generally tried to make all our lives miserable.

She began to hug him and cried, spending about five minutes clinging to him. I tried to be understanding but was incensed. I was sitting alone in the car with my children, *my* son dead, and *she* is wanting comfort. She never came to the car to tell me how sorry she was about Stephen's death, but, as usual, only seemed to think of *her* needs. I felt she was at least partly responsible for Stephen's death with her calls, the stress we were always under as she tried to turn the children against us week after week, as well as the lies she had told the church about us. I shouldn't have been surprised. That moment was the worst. After that, she could never hurt me again, ever.

We drove home. I was alternately crying and silent, trying to comfort the girls, feeling waves of pain flow in and out of me like sharp razors. I put the girls to bed, held them, and tried to tell them Stephen was okay, for them not to be afraid. Then I fell across my bed and cried until I couldn't breathe or sit up, I was so weak. I would stop, blow my nose, and start again. My life was over, my son was dead. I wanted to die too. "Oh, Stephen, Stephen, I love you, I love you." I moaned the cry heard throughout the ages from parents who have lost a child. The pain was as searing as if a torch were being shoved into my heart and stomach.

When we heard Norris and Diane come in, Tom went to tell them what had happened; they went upstairs without bothering me. I cried and moaned and sobbed all night, trying to cover the sounds in my pillow, not realizing the girls were probably doing the same in their rooms. Tom held me as I rambled on and on about Stephen, how I should have gone to the woods to find him, how he must have been hurting more than I knew, how I wanted to die.

I blamed everyone. Richard had killed him with his fault-finding. Tom's ex-wife, Sue, had killed him with her lies. The judgmental people at church had driven him to this. Most of all, I had killed him. I didn't know he had hurt so much he would rather be dead. Tom held me, comforted me, and listened. I kept us awake all night, crying.

Just before daybreak, I fell into exhausted sleep for an hour. I awakened to the sun on my face. I looked around and felt so happy. I looked over at Tom sleeping. Then I remembered! Pain hit my heart and stomach and head, and I moaned in agony. I cried and cried and cried. Tom woke up and held me and tried to comfort me. I was immobilized. I could barely walk to the bathroom. I wanted to lie back down and sleep and never wake up. Stephen was dead—my beloved Stephen. My son, my beloved son. He had everything to live for; things couldn't have been that bad. They *must* have been that bad or he wouldn't have preferred dying to living.

I tried to remember his notes. If I remembered right, he had assured me he would communicate with me, saying to keep the channel open. His notes were hopeful, almost funny. He had said he was writing the last ones with the rope around his neck. I had told my mother that while he was hanging there dying he had continued to write. How long did it take him to strangle, hanging there? I learned later, of course, that he had written them with the rope around his neck before he jumped to his death, not as he was hanging. But for several days, I pictured him hanging, gradually suffocating as he grasped his pen to write his final words.

I called the number on the card the detectives had left. The police had Stephen's belongings, everything they had found on and around him when they cut his body down. I could come to the station and claim them the next day. They asked what I would like to have done with the body. It was in the morgue. I got off the phone, and discussed it with Tom.

Stephen had said in his notes to cremate him, he guessed. I couldn't bear to have his body burned, but I didn't want his precious body buried in the ground, alone. I had read only a few months before how few bodies of children were donated to the hospitals for research. Physicians in the article were expressing how important it was for them to have young cadavers to study to help save other children's lives. My naive picture of this at the time was that they would open his mouth, check his throat, eyes and ears, and examine his body, just like his doctor did for his checkups. I was so distraught, I falsely assumed that they would write what they found on a chart and then save his body forever in a drawer. Autopsy was just a word; it had no visual or intellectual meaning to me then. Feeling so unbearably sad and not thinking clearly, I decided that my act of love for Stephen and the children of the future would be to donate his body to science. In fact, I told myself, it could be Stephen's gift to the world too. It was too late to donate any of his organs. His body hadn't been found until some twenty hours or more after he died. Donating his body would be all that he and I could do to help others.

I called and told the police what I wanted to do, and they agreed they would make arrangements. When we arrived to pick up his belongings, they told us the name of a hospital where I had to go to sign papers for the donation of his body.

In the car, I cradled the plastic bag they gave us that held his things; his sleeping bag and clothes were in the back seat. A silver ring he wore was in the bag, along with his watch which wasn't running. His billfold contained only his social security card, but he had signed his name and I held that to my cheek and cried. The rope had been wound and placed in the bag. I unrolled it to see where it had been around his neck and realized he had been cut down, and, of course, they wouldn't send that part of the rope.

I removed the book in which he had written his final words. It began, "Give this book to my mom, please . . ."

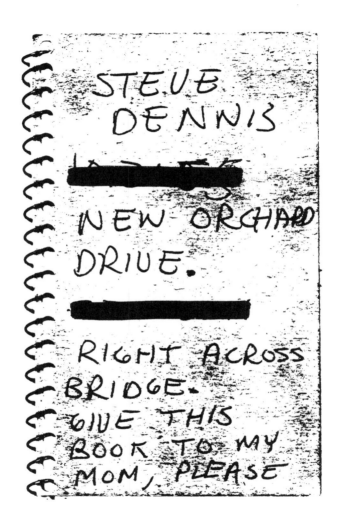

DEAR WORLD

BEING OF
UNSOUND
MIND + BODY,
I LEAVE MY
LAST WILL
AND TESTEMANT.
THE WORLD
IS IN BAD
SHAPE + I
DID NOTHING
TO HELP IT
CHANGE

AND THERE-
FORE AM
NOT FIT TO
LIVE IN IT !?
I LEAVE
FINAL INSTRUCT-
IONS TO MY
LOVED ONES

MOM — I'LL
BE IN TOUCH
(YOU NO WHAT I
MEAN) I LOVE
YOU

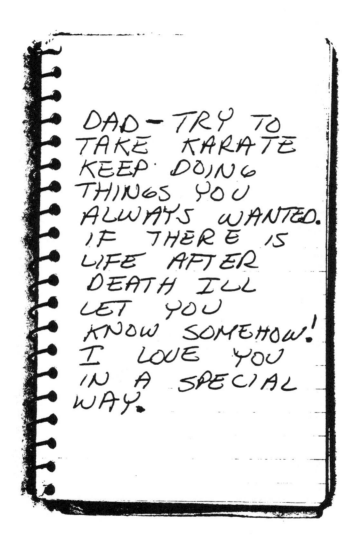

DAD - TRY TO
TAKE KARATE
KEEP DOING
THINGS YOU
ALWAYS WANTED.
IF THERE IS
LIFE AFTER
DEATH ILL
LET YOU
KNOW SOMEHOW!
I LOVE YOU
IN A SPECIAL
WAY.

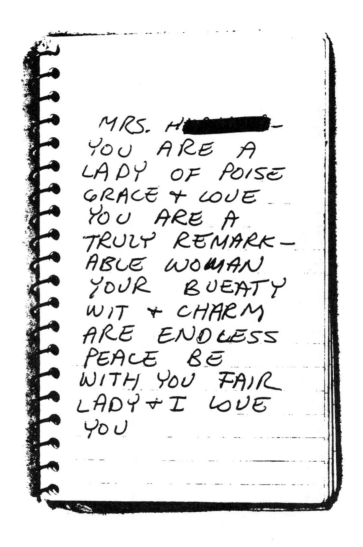

LYNN H██████

YOU ARE ONE
OF A KIND YOU
ARE BUITIFULLY
STUNNING, KIND &
GRACEFUL & I
FOUND MYSELF
IN LOVE WITH
YOU. IF WE
LIVED IN
MID EVEL DAYS
I WOULD BE
YOUR NIGHT AND
YOU A BUITIFUL
PRINCESS. LOVE
ALWAYS!

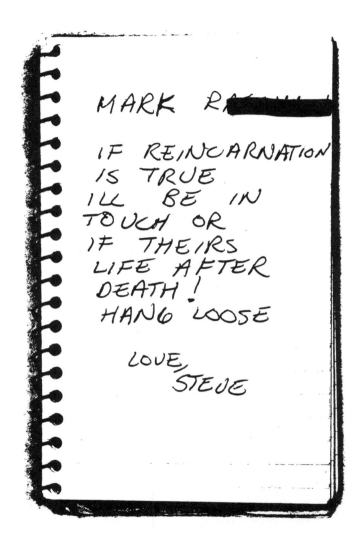

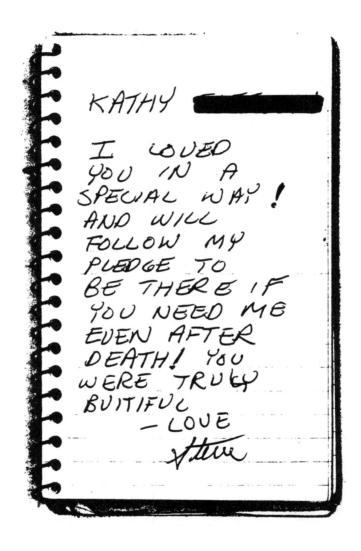

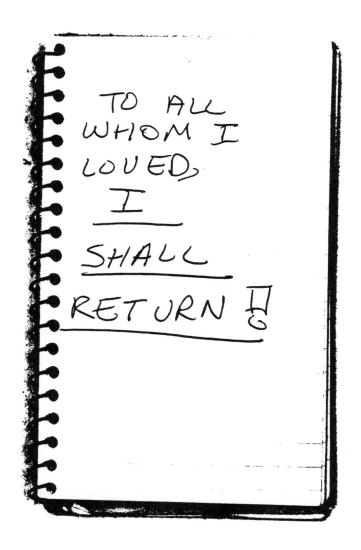

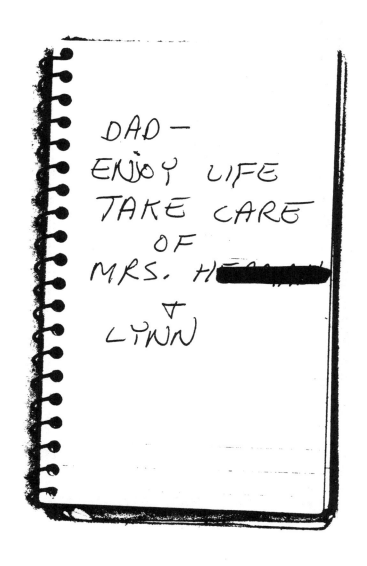

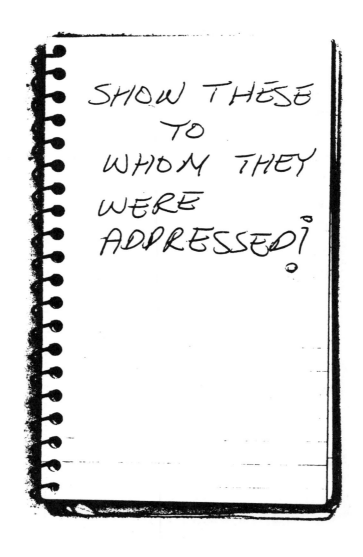

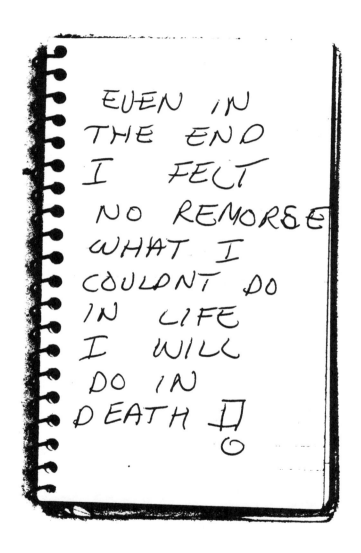

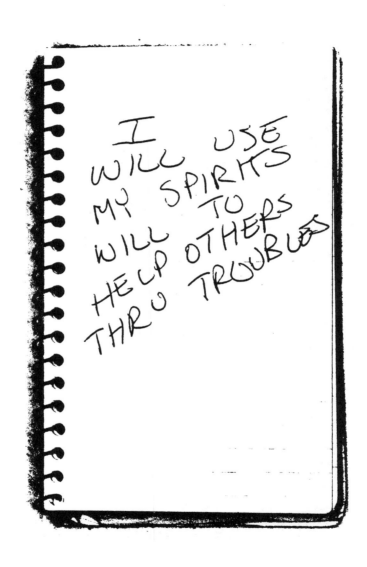

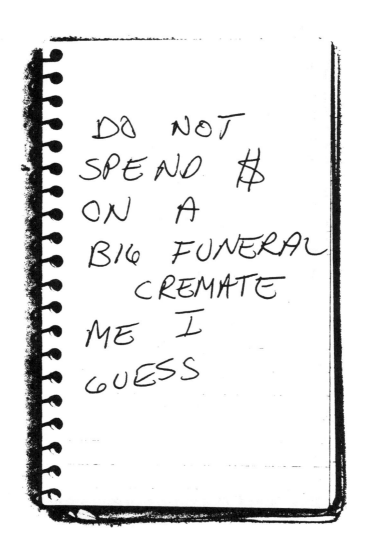

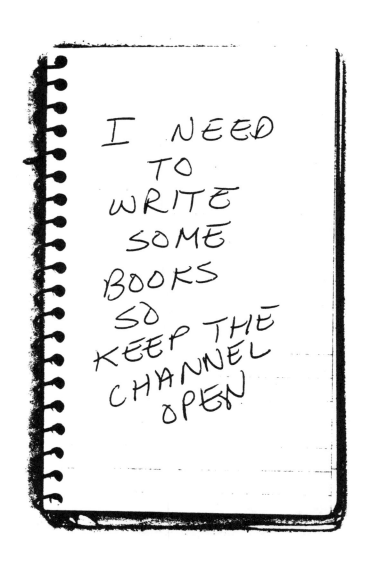

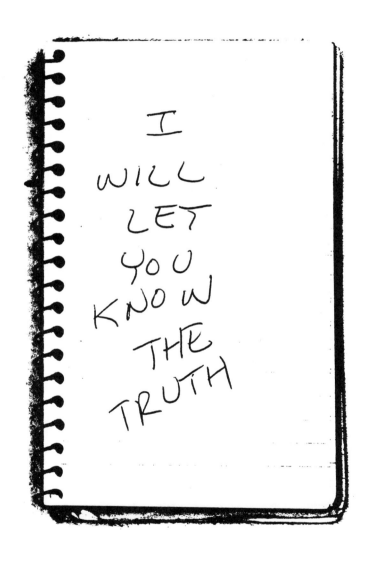

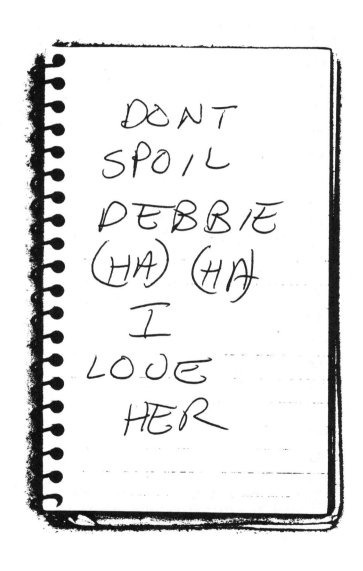

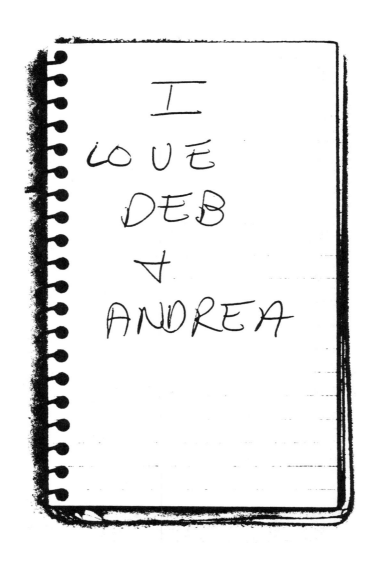

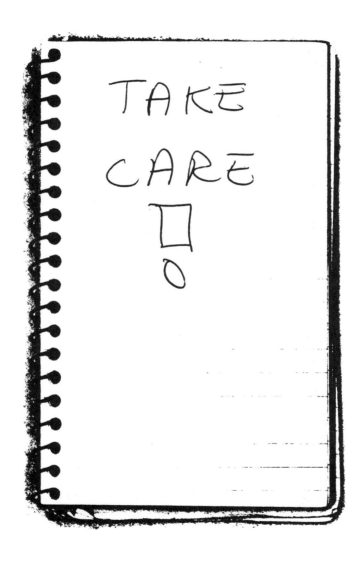

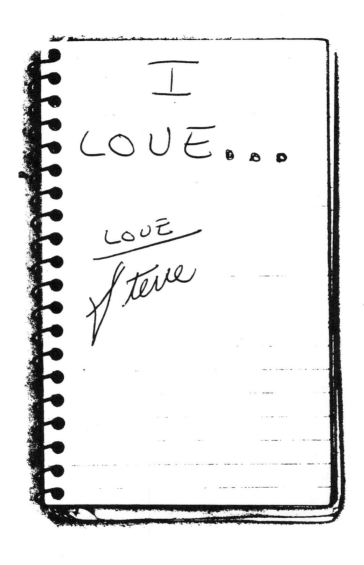

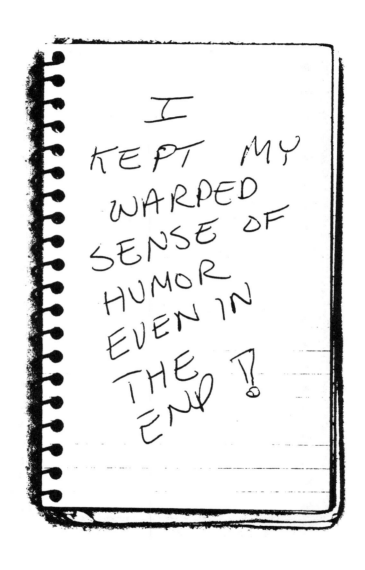

I
ALMOST
DIDNT
DO IT
BECAUSE
I
WANTED TO
LOVE
KATHY
&
LYNN

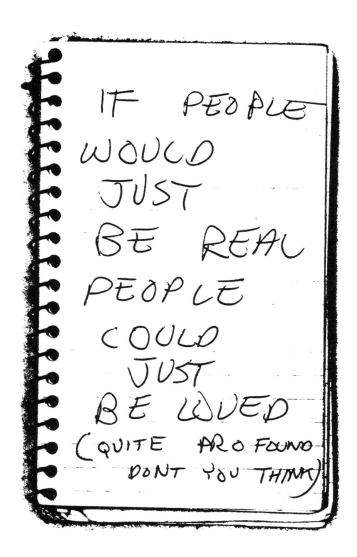

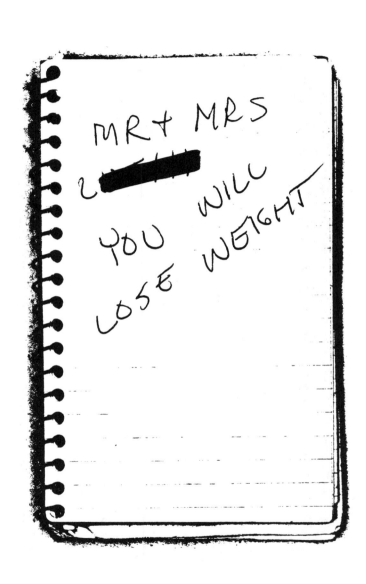

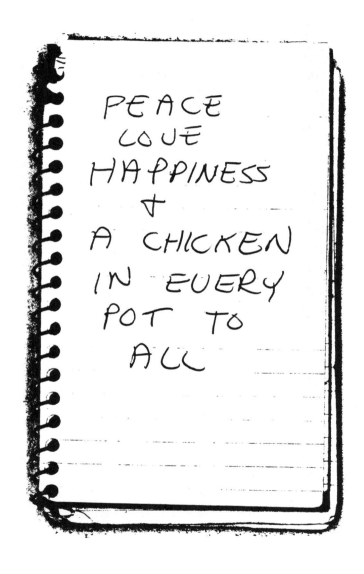

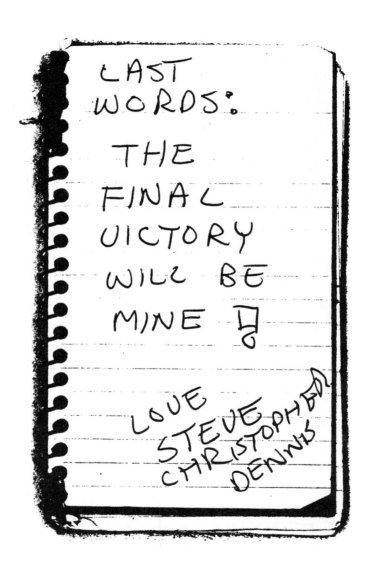

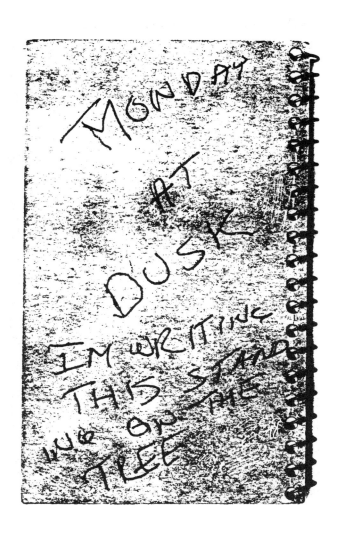

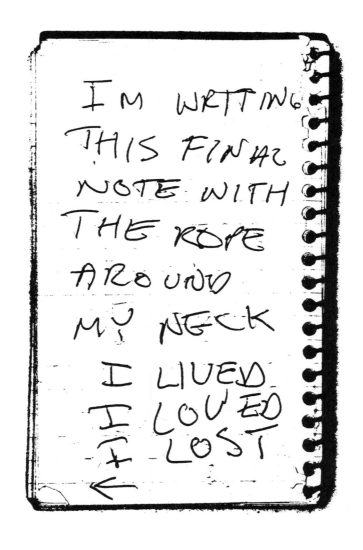

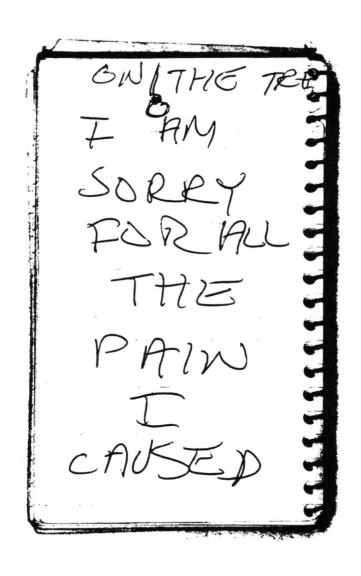

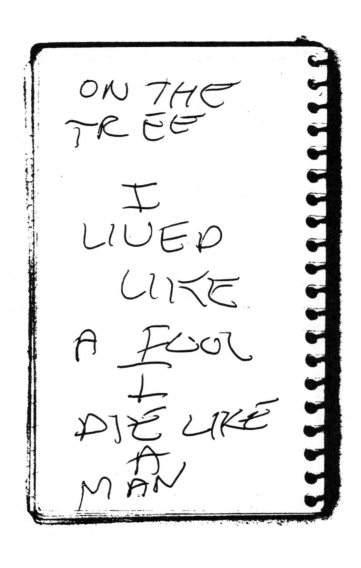

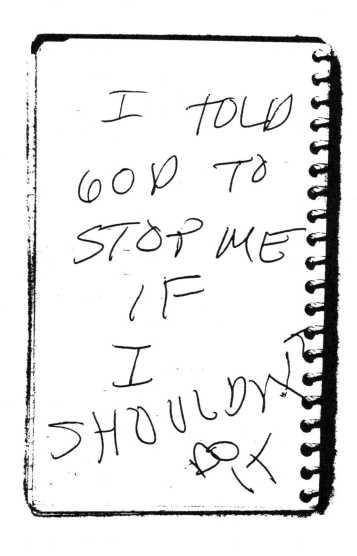

I had just read Bishop Pike's book, *The Other Side*—his son had killed himself too. From the other side, his son had then done a number of things, such as bending safety pins, and speaking to his father through "mediums," people who could talk to the dead. Here was a ray of hope.

If these people could speak from the "beyond," surely my beloved Stephen could get through, and I could talk to him even if he didn't have a body anymore. It encouraged me. Despite the incredible physical and emotional pain I felt, there was a glimmer of hope that we could at least talk to each other again. I hadn't gotten to say, "good-bye." I needed to find out about all the things he had been feeling and thinking that I hadn't known. I needed to tell him I loved him. I needed to hear his voice. In my prayers, I promised to "keep the channel open," as he requested.

I rode to the hospital to sign the forms with a mixture of pain and optimism. At the desk, an overly cheerful nurse gave me the papers to sign for release of his body to be used for research. Just as I was ready to write my name, I suddenly decided I wanted his body back! I didn't want to donate his precious body to anyplace, ever! I wanted to go find his body, pick him up and take him home, climb in bed with him, cover us up and protect him always.

I felt in a panic but tried to say calmly that I just wanted to see his body. My plan was to grab it and run away with it, but I didn't want the nurse to know that. She said, "You *can't* see the body, I'm sorry." I told her firmly, "I want to see his body for just a minute. *Right now*." My heart sank when she answered, "I'm very sorry but it isn't here. It's been moved to the Baltimore morgue. Then it will be taken to the teaching hospital."

I wanted to scream, to cry, to yell, to break down the doors and find him and to steal his body back. But I knew she was telling the truth. There was nothing I could do. If I called the morgue in Baltimore and told them they couldn't have his body after all, that I wanted it back, they would think I was a fool. What would I do with his body? I couldn't stand to bury it or burn it. I couldn't leave it in the house.

Again I rationalized that many children could be helped by doctors studying Stephen's body, which he could no longer use. I still had no idea what happened during a research autopsy and how a body was disposed of afterward. A part of me felt guilty that I had let them have it, while another part tried to remember it might help some child or maybe many children. No one told me until years later that I could have requested his ashes when they were finished working with him. No one even told me that the body would eventually be cremated. I didn't think of there being an ending to it at the time. Somehow it seemed the act of donating it would make it continue somewhere, always.

The rational part of my mind thought of the money wasted on funerals and embalming, on coffins and such nonsense. This would be so much cheaper and better, I convinced myself. The mother in me didn't want him under the ground rotting away or consumed by fire. This way the decision didn't have to be made, and this seemed the best of the other alternatives.

We decided on a memorial service instead of a funeral. Where would we hold it? Most of his friends were from the old church or neighborhood where he had spent so many years. He hadn't attended the church where Tom and I went, though they were willing to have it there. I talked to Richard and together we decided that for the good of all, and for Stephen, the old church might be the better place for his service, despite all that had happened. However, I told him that since Tom and I were to be ordained the next year, we wanted to conduct the service, and he could assist us. The ministers at the old church could not possibly conduct it with the love and caring we could. He reluctantly agreed and had one of the ministers call us to set it up.

The minister, a friend of Richard's from years past, and supposedly a friend of mine, said they would be glad to have the service in the church, but Tom and I could not possibly be in on conducting the service. I told him all three of us had talked and agreed that this might heal the chasm between all of us. Despite our new directions, we cared for the people at church and thought many of them cared for us. Stephen was, after all, *my* son, and as his mother and a ministerial candidate, no one could conduct it with more caring than I. He insisted the church would not allow it and that Richard did not want it. We never spoke again.

Richard decided to hold the service without us. We would have no input. I protested, to no avail. Richard said Stephen had been mentally ill, that I was trying to pretend he had been normal. I argued that he was depressed but certainly not mentally ill. Richard told me it was my fault he was dead, that if I hadn't left him, Stephen would be alive. He also told this to the girls at every opportunity.

This was *not* his child. He had done nothing but bring misery into his life—into all our lives. He had no right to pretend this great interest and love now. His church had treated Stephen like an outcast because of me. None of them had the right to conduct this last rite for him and pretend great concern about him. When he was living they didn't care, except to confuse him. Now he was dead and it was too late to be concerned. I was angry, hurt, and felt helpless. They had no right to do this without my approval. Richard had no right to do this, but there was nothing I could do to stop him. Richard made the girls attend with him.

We had no choice but to make other plans ourselves. We decided to have the memorial service in our home, instead of at our new church. We would invite only our close friends and those who loved Stephen. Richard was not invited. We would read the things Stephen wrote, express our love for him and celebrate both his short life and his death in the way we felt appropriate.

Tom and I went to the grocery store the day before his memorial service. It would be held on the afternoon of March 23. We asked that no flowers be sent for the service. When friends asked what they could do, we suggested they donate to some favorite organization in his name. As I walked through the grocery store, buying food and drink for after the service, the pain at his loss was so severe I could hardly walk. I held on to the grocery cart to help me remain upright. People were smiling and walking around as if nothing had happened. I wanted to scream, "Don't you *know*? *My son is dead!* Stop smiling! My child is dead! Stop acting happy! Stop smiling!" Why couldn't I just die right there and make it stop hurting? How could they be happy when I hurt so much?

We passed by the refrigerated cases containing flower arrangements. I needed to buy him some flowers in spite of what I had requested of others. There was a beautiful arrangement of pink roses with baby's breath and greenery. I reached for them and held them close.

The girls were at home and my mother was coming shortly. Our friend, Cathie, had stayed to clean up the house for us, so we drove back to help get things ready. Stephen had especially liked her and her husband and left a funny note to them about their weight. As we drove in, Cathie rushed up to us. She said, "While you were gone, I heard footsteps from up in Stephen's room, but when I went up no one was there. I came back down to finish dusting, and I heard them again. Then I heard a voice. It was Stephen. He said he wanted me to give a message to his mother."

She began to read what she had hurriedly written down. It was nice. It sounded like him, but how much did she want to comfort me? Maybe she wanted to hear a voice and think it was Stephen to make me feel better. I couldn't be sure. Though I was skeptical, I hoped it was true. This was a gift I could accept only years later.

I thanked her. She was visibly shaken and talked nervously. She said, "It's all true. No one dies. He's alive. Stephen is alive." I wished *I* could have been that positive. If all the things about life after death were true, why hadn't he spoken to *me*? I was his mother. I needed to hear his voice. Why not me? Jealousy, sadness and hope fought against each other. We told everyone what Cathie had experienced, but somehow it was neither very comforting nor could I be sure it was true. I went in my room and pleaded with Stephen to talk to *me* and I cried and pleaded some more. I didn't hear anything.

I took the roses and placed them on the mantel over the fireplace with a card that said, "In Memory of Stephen." On the day of the service, a minister friend crossed out *Memory* and wrote in *Awareness*. "In Awareness of Stephen."

Cards, telegrams, and letters arrived each day from people as they heard the news. Some came by to console us. Others tentatively hinted that Stephen must have been mentally ill. I was defensive. I knew he wasn't mentally ill, but I didn't have any other rational explanation as to why he killed himself.

Many were so uncomfortable about suicide that they didn't know what to say. Some stayed away because they didn't know how to act. I wanted to choke the ones who said, "God wanted Stephen to be with Him." Or the ones who assured me, "God saw pain and suffering in his future and called him home."

One dear person wrote, "We're with you in your grief. We love you. We're here if you need us." I knew she meant it. The mother of a friend sent a card that said, "The caged bird is free," which I found comforting. Another wrote in longhand a quote from John Donne, "No man is an island entire of itself. Every man is a piece of the continent, a part of the main. If a clod be washed away by the sea, Europe is the lesser, as well as if a promotone were or a manner of thy friends were. Any man's death diminishes me for I am involved in mankind. And, therefore, never send to know for whom the bell tolls. It tolls for thee." Our friend added a note of his own, "I'm sure that the future holds the answers to his questions. Anyone so sensitive is destined to glory in the next life."

Others sent consoling poems:

> *I do not know why sorrows come*
> *and burning teardrops fall;*
> *I only know God still is God*
> *And watches over all.*

> *I do not know why we must part*
> *From loved ones and from friend;*
> *I only know God's love lives on,*
> *and will live to the end!*

> *I cannot see with earthbound eyes*
> *the guilded courts above*
> *But by faith I know I'm kept*
> *within His boundless love!*

– John Gilbert

There is comfort in just knowing
there's a loving God who knows
why dark clouds obscure the sunshine
why a frost should blight a rose!

Why the beauty of a songbird
is oft prematurely stilled,
or why a loved one journeys on,
leaving voids that can't be filled!

May you today in simple faith
trust all your "why's" to Him,
and know someday He'll make it plain
when clouds of sorrow dim.
                    – "Someday He'll Make It Plain," author unknown

These would comfort me for a few moments. One of the most helpful and delightful letters was from a woman in our old church who had known and loved Stephen. She reminded me how Stephen and I had sat at church with her family one Sunday, and he had proposed to her daughter. He was about nine, she was about sixteen. He asked her to wait and marry him when he grew up. I remembered the whole sequence which lifted my spirits. It was as if someone had given me a special gift, because it enabled me to remember something that I would have forgotten and might never have recalled again. Such memories were like precious jewels.

Another friend, Joanne, to whom one of Stephen's notes was directed, wrote, "How can a person take another's pain away? I can only say I share your sorrow. You must remember that he was God's child also. He was young in years, but years mean nothing as far as Stephen was concerned. He was a truly beautiful soul. He has touched the lives of all who knew him. None of us will ever be the same from this time on. Each of us has learned a new awareness of life. We all pain with you and we all struggle to understand what is not always easy—death. But he's not dead and that's your joy. To know, when the raw pain is over and the channels are open, you may communicate at will. Stephen will be with you always and God is with you. He feels your pain. Look to him for the relief you need and the knowledge that death is not the end, only the beginning. Peace to you and all my love."

Several people wrote poems or feelings they had about his life and death and that was comforting. Others brought uplifting messages they felt were from the other side about what was happening to him. These, even though I doubted their authenticity, were helpful, and for a brief moment, healing to my heart. I showed Stephen's notes to all our friends. They cried, laughed, and smiled along with us.

I prayed that someone from the old church, from anywhere, would send me photos they had taken of Stephen. No one ever did. That would have been such a gift. Since then, whenever anyone dies, I try to find photos I have taken of the person and send them to the remaining family members.

It helped when friends who visited shared their memories of Stephen and then let me talk and talk about him. It helped when they openly discussed how he died, asked questions and didn't act embarrassed. It made me angry when someone who had treated us badly wrote and bragged that they had made a contribution to their favorite charity in Stephen's name. I was very touched when a big company we were associated with sent a gift to Children's Hospital in his name.

• • •

I hope that during these days I comforted the children and saw that their needs were met. I can't remember. The morning after we learned of Stephen's death, we had to drive to Bob's and tell him in person. On top of everything else Bob was going through, he would have to deal with the death of his brother. He had spent the weekend at home the day before Stephen died. They had gone to the movies and seemed to have a good time. It was the first time they had acted like buddies in a long while. They seemed like loving brothers and friends again, really enjoying themselves. The next day Stephen had killed himself. How would Bob handle it with everything else?

When we arrived at Bob's, I hugged him and told him his brother was dead. He cried and cried and cried. I held him, tried to talk to him, and to comfort him. With my limited knowledge at that time, I even said some stupid things about it being Stephen's right to kill himself and we had to understand. Later I learned that, of course it *had* been his right, it was his life, but perhaps we could have done something to stop him until he was thinking more clearly and could make a more rational decision. It was especially difficult for Bob during the next weeks; the rest of the family had each other, but he was by himself. I had always loved him. Now he was the only son I had left, and I wanted to do anything, *anything* to make things better for him.

On Saturday afternoon, March 23, we began Stephen's memorial service with the help of Diane and Henry, both ministers. The four of us conducting the memorial were in chairs up front. Our friends who gathered with us were sitting on borrowed folding chairs that filled the living room, entry, and hall.

I turned and looked out the window. Such crazy thoughts ran through my head.

I remembered that as I was packing decorations after last Christmas and putting the children's special candles in a box, I had accidently dropped and broken one. One child would be without a candle. I had looked for matching holders since but could find none. I should have seen that as a sign. Only seven candles. One child would die. One child died.

In order to be able to conduct the service and not cry, I programmed myself to believe that, in a short time, Stephen and I would be conversing daily. I forced any doubts I had about that communication out of my mind. I intended to show by my strength, courage, and belief that anyone who died continued on and lived fully aware in another dimension. If I could be this confident, when my beloved Stephen had killed himself, had hung himself in a tree just across the street, then surely this would comfort people who had lost loved ones themselves.

As we waited for everyone to be seated so that we could begin, I heard a voice inside my head. The voice said, "Go into your bedroom. In the seventh pile from the bathroom door, against the wall with the window, pick the seventeenth book from the top and open it."

How did that voice get inside my head? It wasn't Stephen. In fact, I couldn't tell if it was a man or a woman. It wasn't any of my three guides. I had forgotten all about them for days. I whispered to Tom what I had heard, excused myself, and went down the hall into the bedroom to do as instructed.

Books were piled along every wall, some stacked half way to the ceiling. I counted across and down. I pulled out the seventeenth book. It was *The Wisdom Of Gibran,* by Kahlil Gibran, author of *The Prophet.* I had read *The Prophet*, but this book was one I didn't remember ever seeing. It looked new and was stiff like it had never been opened.

I opened it at random to a page marked "D . . . Death" and began to read:

Man is like the foam of the sea, that floats upon the surface of the water. When the wind blows, it vanishes, as if it had never been. Thus are our lives blown away by Death.

The Reality of Life is Life itself, whose beginning is not in the womb, and whose ending is not in the grave. For the years that pass are naught but a moment in eternal life; and the world of matter and all in it is but a dream compared to the awakening which we call the terror of Death.

The soul is an embryo in the body of
Man, and the day of death is the
Day of awakening, for it is the
Great era of labour and the rich
Hour of creation.

> *Death is an ending to the son of*
> *The earth, but to the soul it is*
> *The start, the triumph of life.*

Death removes but the
Touch, and not the awareness of
All good. And he who has lived
One spring or more possesses the
Spiritual life of one who has
Lived a score of springs.

A child in the womb, no sooner born than returned to the
earth—such is the fate of man, the fate of nations and of the sun,
the moon, and the stars.

I couldn't believe it! My heart beat so loudly I could hear it in my head.
Goose bumps were all over my body, tears flooded my eyes. I turned the
page down, and held the book against my heart, crying. I was deeply
moved and grateful.

Again, I felt impressed to open the book, and this time I turned to
"Immortality:"

> *Death on earth, to the son of earth*
> > *Is final, but to him who is*
> *Ethereal, it is but the start*
> > *Of triumph certain to be his.*

> *If one embraces dawn in dreams,*
> > *He is immortal! Should he sleep*
> *His long night through, he surely fades*
> > *Into a sea of slumber deep.*

> *For he who closely hugs the ground*
> > *When wide awake will crawl 'til end.*
> *And death, like sea, who braves it light*
> > *Will cross it. Weighted will descend.*

If I did not covet immortality, I would never have learned the song which has been sung through all time.

Rather, I would have been a suicide, nothing remaining of me except my ashes hidden within the tomb.

Life is a darkness which ends as in the sunburst of the day.

The yearning of my heart tells me there is peace in the grave.

If some fool tells you the soul perishes like the body and that which dies never returns, tell him the flower perishes but the seed remains and lies before us as the secret of life everlasting.

With tears running down my cheeks, I marked the page and closed the book. But I again felt impressed to open it, and this time I came to "Spirits:"

Between the people of eternity and people of the earth there is constant communication, and all comply with the will of that unseen power. Oftentimes an individual will perform an act, believing that it is born of his own free will, accord, and command, but in fact he is being guided and impelled with precision to do it. Many great men attained their glory by surrendering themselves in complete submission to the will of the spirit, employing no reluctance or resistance to its demands, as a violin surrenders itself to the complete will of a fine musician.

Between the spiritual world and the world of substance there is a path upon which we walk in a swoon of slumber. It reaches us and we are unaware of its strength, and when we return to ourselves we find that we are carrying with our real hands the seeds to be planted carefully in the good earth of our daily lives, bringing forth good deeds and words of beauty. Were it not for that path between our lives and the departed lives, no prophet or poet or learned man would have appeared among the people.

I was stunned. I knew I had never read this book before, certainly I had never heard these passages. How beautiful. Someone *was* up there helping me. It was true, then—Stephen lives! Soon he would be talking to me, just like the voice I heard that led me to these comforting words.

I dried my eyes, and went back and sat down, holding the book. The service began. Tom and I each shared things about Stephen. He read things we found in Stephen's room among his writings. Although the following seems mature beyond his years, it was apparently his own composition. His own editing work was apparent from the words crossed out and corrections made. It began:

It was whispered in the wind, it was screamed across the plains, it fell in hushed silence on the tops of great mountains, even the deep vastness of the ocean seemed to know this dreaded message, and as the mighty waves crashed in the foaming surf, they fell with a scream of terror for the prophets spoke of the deaths of the fiery sun and the gentle moon.

And this time, as in no other time since the dawn of man, peace was restored to this lowly planet called Earth. As each man paused to observe his fate, another hand reached out for the comfort that is only found in the solace of being not alone. Whether black or white, rich or poor, all men were joined in mourning for the sun and grieving for the moon.

And in the courtyard of the fire temple, standing shrouded in black with hands upraised, chanting a fearful song to a god who was hidden far away, stood a feeble, graying, religious man who lived in time when religion was non-existent and God was thought dead. And when this man's mission was completed, he smiled, lowered his arms and departed. And as he paused at the gates, a faint sunrise could be seen beginning over the horizon.

When my turn came, I told everyone about the voice and read the passages from the book I had been instructed to find. People gasped in amazement and many eyes filled with tears. When I finished, a friend of ours—another Steve—stood up and asked if *he* could speak. He said that someone had called to tell him Stephen had killed himself and nothing more. He knew Stephen and with two children of his own, his heart ached for us. He got in his car, drove out of the city and parked. He sat for hours sharing our pain, crying and thinking. He explained that he was an agnostic but had heard the words to the poem that he now wanted to read to all of us, as it was given to him.

Stephen

Some will say you flamed a brilliant day
and died just once forever;
But we will say your flame is brighter now
than all the stars,
for how you went
and what you left.

Some will say your life was cut far short
and should have blossomed longer;

But we will say your life is fuller now
than all the fields,
for what you sowed
that now we reap.

And some will say that place is haunted now,
haunted by a tragic death;
But we will say that once upon a wooded choir,
a young man took his soul in hand,
and raising eyes to all unknown,
he took a step we all must take,
but took it bravely,
took it gladly,
and thus gave strength to every step
we ever take,
with courage, peace and love.

We all cried. It was a most beautiful gift to me, with my understanding at that time. Cathie and others stood up and read what they had felt impressed to write or to share and the service ended.

Good night sweet prince, may bands of angels sing thee to thy rest.
                    – From Shakespeare's *Hamlet*

Everyone stayed afterward to join us for cookies and coffee. I felt it had been a happy memorial for a child in pain, who had taken matters into his own hands, and left earlier than we had hoped, in a way we had not expected. Everyone said they felt hopeful and comforted.

I could hardly eat, losing over ten pounds during those first days. Having fought a weight problem off and on during my marriage to Richard, I commented that I would never be overweight again. My appetite was gone. I didn't even eat a cookie—unheard of for me with my love of sweets.

How wrong I was. Within two months, I had gained twenty pounds from the pain and sadness, and began a real battle of the bulge. Not that I hadn't understood before, but now I understood Stephen's worry about his weight a hundred times over.

My mother cried during the service, during the socializing afterward, and most of her visit. She took his death very hard and all my upbeat statements about our beliefs in life after death didn't console her one bit. I wished she wouldn't cry. Stephen wouldn't want her to be sad. The fact that I was crying myself to sleep each night and every time the bedroom door closed didn't seem the same. As long as everyone else was happy, I could pretend that I was.

Mother's coming was a godsend for the children and for me, with her love and caring. When she left to go back home, it was much worse for all of us. The real grief set in then. I was a walking zombie.

Nothing had any joy, nothing would ever be the same again. How could I go on?

CHAPTER SIX

Grief—
The Constant Companion

*On hearing of the death of his son, King David, wept and cried out,
"O my son Absalom! My son, my son Absalom! If only I had died
instead of you—O Absalom, my son, my son!"*

– 2 Samuel 18:33

*Grief fills the room with my absent child, lies in his bed, walks up
and down with me. Puts on his pretty looks, repeats his words,
remembers me of all his gracious parts. Stuffs out his vacant
garment with his form.*

– From Shakespeare's *King John*

Night after night I went up to Stephen's room. I would begin to cry
on the way up the stairs. I needed to be in his room by myself, alone. I
wanted to sit on his bed and cry where no one could hear me. Each time
I opened his door, his smell filled my nostrils. Everyone has a unique
scent; each room has the smell of the person inhabiting it. Stephen's
room was filled with his special smell.

Sometimes I screamed into his pillow, Oh, God, no! No, no, no! He
can't be dead. Stephen, speak to me, talk to me! Where are you? Oh, God,
bring him back, bring him back! Stephen, Stephen! My son, my son!
Please, God, don't let him be dead! Take me, God! Please, please bring
Stephen back!"

I would cry harder as I would recall moving scenes such as in
Shakespeare's *Romeo and Juliet*, and think of Juliet's words for
Romeo:

> *. . . when he shall die,*
> *Take him and cut him out in little stars,*
> *And he will make the face of heaven so fine*
> *That all the world will be in love with night*
> *And pay no worship to the garish sun.*

His bed was against the eaves, still unmade as he had left it, sheets and blankets in a lump on the middle. I laid on his bed and held the bedding to my nose and smelled again his smell, my tears soaking the sheets and spilling over onto the mattress. I moaned and rocked back and forth, screaming into the pillow, "Stephen! Stephen! My baby! My baby!" Dirty clothes lay around the room—pants, shirts, underwear. I held his shirts to my nose and inhaled his faint scent, then inhaled deeply at the underarms where his odor was stronger. I pleaded with God to bring him back. I even held his underwear to my face and inhaled the soiled smell.

After a few days, I sealed the underwear and clothing that still had any slight odor in plastic bags so the smell wouldn't be lost. I opened the bags daily to keep his essence in my memory. It was like a part of him was still there for those brief moments. I didn't judge anything I did. I didn't hold back in my grief. I couldn't.

I went over his room, section by section, day after day. His maple chest was filled with clothes, papers and an assortment of his things. I opened and searched each item of clothing. I turned each paper over, searching for something he had written—anything. I felt for impressions on blank paper. His room was filled with books, some from the library, some ours, some his. I went through each book thinking perhaps there was some note or something underlined to give me a fuller answer as to why he had killed himself. Perhaps some message might be found, something that would be another piece to the puzzle and a part of him. I found poems he had written and little index cards with sayings he had copied. I searched with the intensity of a cat burglar hurriedly hunting for jewels.

On his calendar he had made a concerned notation for Sunday, February 24: "Weighed 186 today. Got to start cracking down on myself! Keep Kool! " I also discovered a list of his goals that read: "1) Lose all excess fat. 2) To be very well built. 3) To be very strong. 4) To run fast without tiring. 5) To have fast reflexes. 6) To be very good at karate. 7) Have conditioned hands."

Each paper with his name or even the tiniest drawing or mark, I put in a pile. His wastebasket was filled with paper, wrappers, trash. I went through every piece. I found treasures: a picture he had done on the typewriter, a half finished school assignment, the wrapper to a beef jerky stick that he had eaten, gum he had chewed that still had his teeth prints. Diamonds or rubies paled in value to these few crumbs of him that remained.

In typewritten pages that spoke eloquently of his loving and gentle spirit, and how he felt for the girl to whom he could not express these words, Stephen had written:

> *In the silence of dreams I have felt your tears and seen a gentle beauty in your eyes. I have reached to touch your hand and feel you near, and tell you of the secrets that I feel in the wind and the majesty that I find on a starlit night. I have seen the wind playing through your hair and the sparkle that is found deep within your eyes. I have seen you move with the grace of a panther and the sleekness of a tiger and I imagine you floating high above the world, mystic and lovely, carried by the wind that swirls about your beauty. And as I observe you there, I feel a closeness that radiates from your soul and I try to speak, for I want to tell you that I know of life and love and living. But most important, I know what it means to love you. You listen quietly and speak softly, reminding that love is not promises that are soon passed by, but a remembered kiss or a touch or sigh that is shared in a time of happiness between two people. I look at you silently. You smile and then my dream begins to fade and you turn to leave. I want to follow to call your name but all that I could say was, "Take care, my love."*

I searched through each drawer of his desk, finding pencils, sketches, little bits of his life. How glad I was that he was so messy, that he hadn't emptied his trash, that he was a pack rat. I pulled up the corners of the rug, searching as far back as I could lift it, disappointed by finding nothing but paper clips and coins.

I searched every pocket of every item of clothing. My eyes raced from one thing to another. I was like a squirrel, scurrying from place to place, reaching, grabbing, hoarding anything I saw. In between searching, I would lie on his bed and hug his pillow and cry. I cried until there were no more tears, my eyes bloodshot and swollen shut. I screamed with pain into the pillow until my ears rang and my throat was raw. I felt no physical pain. The pain in my mind and heart were so severe that I felt neither thirst nor hunger for days.

In his tape recorder on the desk, I found two tapes he had made. One dated April 10, 1973 concerned his insecurities and the things that he was feeling. It was about how he didn't like to be fat and was self-conscious around girls. The other contained songs he listened to on the radio, and part of a "Kung Fu" movie we had watched together. I played them over and over to catch the sound of his voice. One word, one phrase, was like a gift.

Surely no one in the world had ever felt like this. I felt totally alone in my sorrow and agony. People would say they knew how I felt. They had no idea. Had any of them had a *child* die? I had forgotten about the grieving woman with whom I worked whose daughter had been murdered a few months before. I had forgotten that Richard's mother had lost twins at eight and twelve months of age. I had forgotten that children were killed in accidents, murdered, raped, and kidnapped. I was so consumed by my own pain and grief, I completely forgot that other people had lost their own children and loved ones. I bit my index finger until the teeth made a permanent purple bite mark on the top and bottom. The pain would stop my mental misery for a few seconds. I dug my nails deeply into my arm or thigh, anything to make physical pain greater than my heartache, even for a moment.

I read that many parents put all the pictures away when a child died. I did not. I could not! I searched for every picture ever taken of Stephen. I looked at them over and over again. I tried to find all the old negatives in the house. With a magnifying glass, I went through them, putting aside any of Stephen, even if there was just a partial side view of him, or if only his arm or leg showed. I had them developed, copied, enlarged. Some rolls from Christmas hadn't been developed. I put them in the camera shop on a rush order. Since I left Richard, I had taken so few photos. The only ones of Stephen were almost two years old. The Christmas rolls were current ones. I couldn't wait till they came back.

When I picked up the developed film, I ripped the packages open. There were only two side view photos of Stephen. At Christmas, he had asked me not to take any pictures of him until he got cleaned up. He assured me he would dress up for better pictures after we opened the gifts. Since he was sitting beside me, he had successfully avoided being photographed. I wept, inconsolable. God, couldn't you make some current photos of Stephen appear on the film? I've tried to have faith. Couldn't you do this for me? I asked everyone for pictures they had of Stephen—there were hardly any. I was heartbroken. I remembered Billie's intuitive message for me: "Be sure and take plenty of pictures this Christmas, things will never be the same. . . ."

I was in such pain, I began to blame others. Tom's son, Chris, had kept us from getting a recent picture of Stephen. I began to hate him for it. Just before we had moved into the new house, in late November, we had all eight of the children dress up and we took them to a portrait studio for group as well as individual pictures. Chris complained from the beginning. He didn't want his picture taken. I considered him the most lovable of Tom's three boys but he was nine, spoiled, and insistent upon getting his own way. No matter what he wanted, his dad was unable to refuse him.

He complained loudly and strongly. The other children, knowing how much we wanted pictures for Christmas, told him to stop complaining and get in the car. They handled it without us having to interfere. When we got to the studio, Chris kept complaining. He sulked and whined as he laid across the plastic chairs in the waiting room until the photographer was ready. When we ignored his complaints, he began to say he was sick. It was obvious he wasn't sick and we half kidded him, half scolded him. His complaints got worse. He moaned and groaned. Seeing we weren't going to bend, and afraid he was going to miss a favorite television show, his complaining intensified.

We ignored him and he began to grab his side and moan louder. He looked at his dad and said there was a horrible pain in his side. He insisted he was dying. He begged to go home. Tom was getting concerned by then. I knew there was nothing wrong with him and voiced that strongly. So did the other children. Tom was beginning to wonder. Chris began to cry and carry on. It was obvious he was doing a very good acting job, but Tom was now worried. This was his favorite child.

Tom suggested we cancel the appointment, make another one later and take him to the emergency room. He felt sure Chris had appendicitis. I told him that was ridiculous, that he was fine. I could not get Tom to bend. I decided to stay and have pictures taken of just my children and to get his four photographed later. Chris, realizing it would take some time and would miss his show, turned on the act even stronger. Tom insisted on all of us rushing him to the hospital immediately because we were in one car.

Some of the kids made sarcastic remarks to Chris as we drove to the hospital. They knew he was acting just to get his way. Chris laid in the far back of the station wagon, everyone else scrunched in the second seat and in front. He continued to moan. His dad told him to hold on, that we were almost at the emergency room. His moaning got quieter and quieter as we neared the hospital.

"I don't want to go. I'm OK now," Chris began to say. I insisted he be checked over anyway. He had ruined the photo session, and we couldn't return that night. Maybe I wasn't being fair; maybe he really *was* sick. But now he turned on the charm to his father and said he was okay and to please not make him go in. Tom wouldn't force him to be examined. All of us were quite aware by then of what he had done. Tom assured me the attacks would recur.

When we arrived home, Chris played and roughhoused the rest of the evening, watched his television show and never had another "attack." There was never a time when we could get the children all together again for an appointment. Now there would never be another time.

I reminded myself that Chris was just a child, that I shouldn't blame him that I didn't have any current pictures of Stephen. But sometimes I was so angry with him I couldn't stand to be around him. It would have meant so much to me to have a photo of what Stephen had looked like at fifteen.

No one could console me. My friends tried. They hugged me, talked with me, brought me messages of cheer, fed the family, did everything and more than anyone could expect, to be of help. The smiles, conversations, assurances that Stephen was fine that came from their lips helped for the moments they were there. When they left I went into Stephen's room again and again. I stopped my pretenses, and let down my guard. I screamed and cried into his pillow. I had killed my youngest, my baby. I hadn't known his pain, I hadn't taken time to listen to him. I had been so busy, thinking he would adjust and that things would get better, that I had killed him. How could I admit to everyone that it was I—I had killed him.

After I had berated and blamed myself enough, I began again with blaming everyone else. Richard had done *more* than his part. He had driven Stephen crazy with his faultfinding and criticisms. Stephen was never able to get his love and approval. I wished Richard would die some painful and agonizing death.

I loved Bob so much, but he had made Stephen's life so difficult because of his own pain. Now it was too late to make it up to him. Then I would realize that the miracle was that Bob had not killed *himself* with all he had been put through. I wondered how Bob had had the strength to survive. I thanked God that he had.

My hatred of Tom's ex-wife intensified. There was no doubt in my mind that her sick lies, her undermining of Tom's children, and the constant attention they always needed to stay emotionally balanced, had taken its toll on us and on Stephen. I hoped someday she would suffer as she had made us all suffer. I hoped one of her children would die tragically, that she grieve and hurt as I did. Then I felt so guilty, I prayed, "No, God. Forgive me. Don't let one of her children die. I don't really mean that."

I hated Stephen's uncaring teachers and his principal—not one of them had even called to express their sorrow at his death. They had had no time for him at school and were blind to his needs when they were trained to know better. They hadn't cared when he was alive. Why did it surprise me that they didn't at his death? When his school principal died unexpectedly some months later, I hoped he saw Stephen on the other side and was remorseful.

I hated the old church to which we had once belonged. Their rules and judgment and dogma had made Stephen fearful, doubtful, and unhappy.

I hated Tom for his lack of compassion and caring. I remembered that Stephen had said Tom always made him feel no good and always "had a better way." It had hurt him that Tom seemed to be unconcerned about his feelings. What had Tom said to him that morning before he died to push him to a point of no return? Damn Tom! As quickly as I thought that about him, I would remember how he held me night after night as I talked and talked about Stephen. How he comforted me as I cried myself to sleep. I then denied that he had played any role at all.

How could Debbie have hurt Stephen by calling him "fat?" Why hadn't Andrea stopped him from going into the woods? Why hadn't his real father, Bill, kept in contact with him and loved him? Why didn't the girls he had a crush on love him back? Why hadn't Norris finished his room long ago instead of letting him suffer and freeze in that unfinished mess upstairs?

When I ran out of scapegoats, I began to blame myself again. The real truth must be that I had killed him. I had driven him to his death. I had insisted he go to school that last day. I had instructed Tom to tell him to leave his gym bag and that we knew he was shoplifting. I insisted on finishing my education and had little time left over for his needs. I had foolishly thought things would get better at his school instead of going there and getting him some kind of help. I was the one who would often rather read than play games with him.

I had left his real dad. I had married a man who had almost destroyed the whole family and ultimately Stephen, and I couldn't find the courage to leave until it was too late. I was the weak one that couldn't stay with Richard even if it meant that Stephen might still be alive. I too often let him cook his own meals instead of seeing that he ate regularly and well. I foolishly gave him a couple of diet pills. I was the one who spent so much time trying to make things better for Tom's children, getting things for Tom's children, doing everything for Tom's children, that my own children were neglected, especially my sensitive Stephen. I was the guilty one. No one else. Sure the others had been responsible too, but I was number one on the list of his killers. I had killed him with neglect, with what I had said and done, and what I had failed to say and do. All my life I would know, everyone would know, what a failure I was as a mother, as a person. I had killed my own son. I said I loved him, then I had driven him to kill himself.

When I tried to tell this to close friends and family, they interrupted me and assured me I wasn't responsible. Stephen had made that decision himself and I needed to stop blaming myself, they said. That was not what I needed to hear. I needed to express my guilt, to own it and to talk about it. No one would let me. I carried the guilt hourly in my heart and mind. Stephen would still be alive if it weren't for me. Richard, still self-righteous, confirmed that on several visits. "If you hadn't left me . . . ," he would start in.

Sometimes I thought of turning back the clock and going back with Richard if Stephen could still be alive. I fantasized about it many times. Other times, when thinking about the hell of our lives those years, I couldn't bear the thought of living like that again, even to keep Stephen alive. That caused me more guilt. What kind of mother was I that I couldn't have sacrificed my feelings and live in that hell to save him? In rational moments, I knew that I could not have stayed in the marriage any longer, nor would it necessarily have spared Stephen if I had.

I thought about Stephen all the time. He was so good, so loving, so tender. It hadn't been *that* bad for him. He rarely complained. He was so well adjusted, so normal, so OK—so able to cope no matter how bad things were. How ridiculous. He *wasn't* OK. He had been stretched and pushed beyond any reasonable limits. He was dead by his own hand. It must have been a living hell for him. We had all killed him.

My dreams added to my guilt. One morning I awakened dreaming that three FBI men had come to the house and were sitting in my living room accusing me of a crime. I told them I hadn't done it. They all insisted I had. I pleaded with them to believe that I hadn't. They didn't budge an inch in their accusations. The whole dream continued with them accusing me, me denying it. I should have seen the dream as vindicating me from Stephen's death, because in the dream I *knew* I wasn't guilty. I just let it convince me further of the wrong I felt I had done.

There were many dreams about Stephen the first months. Stephen going north. Stephen talking with us. Stephen still alive. Stephen dead. In most of the dreams, Stephen was about twelve or thirteen; in some he was much younger. Each dream was like a gift, no matter what the content, because I *saw* him, I talked to him, sometimes I embraced him. For that moment he was *alive*. When I woke up, filled with joy at our encounters, I remembered he was *dead*, and I began those mornings by crying into my pillow.

Then came a horrible dream that caused me a year of total anguish. I dreamed that someone came to tell me that Debbie was dead. My youngest child had died, they said. The person in the dream told me when it occurred, though I didn't remember the date. I said, "Oh no, God, not two in the same year!" I woke up frightened and determined to do anything to keep her alive. I prayed, I pleaded with God, I promised him

I would try to stop grieving about Stephen. I went into her room, held and loved her. She was so full of life, so much her own person, so precious, adorable, and loving. "Not her too, God. Please, not her too. God, you can't do this to me. I can't handle any more pain. You think I can, but I can't. Please, God, please don't let Debbie die."

For one full year from the day of the dream, I watched, prayed, and bargained with God. When the anniversary came and went, I thought God in His infinite mercy had heard my plea. Later, I came to realize that the dream was not precognitive, but instead dealt with my fears and worries.

Someday when I meet God face-to-face, I'd sometimes think to myself, He will probably tell me that He can't believe the way I carried on while I was on earth. "A simple request would have sufficed," He will probably say with some exasperation. Or, He may say, "Why do you always think you must bargain and make deals with me?"

Looking through my favorite book of poetry one night during that time, I came across "The Dark Candle," by Strickland Gillilan.

A man had a little daughter—an only and much-beloved child. He lived for her—she was his life. So when she became ill and her illness resisted the efforts of the best obtainable physicians, he became like a man possessed, moving heaven and earth to bring about her restoration to health.

His best efforts proved unavailing and the child died. The father was totally inconsolable. He became a bitter recluse, shutting himself away from his many friends and refusing every activity that might restore his poise and bring him back to his normal self.

But one night he had a dream. He was in Heaven, and was witnessing a grand pageant of all the little child angels. They were marching in an apparently endless line past the Great White Throne. Every white-robed angelic tot carried a candle. He noticed that one child's candle was not lighted. Then he saw that the child with the dark candle was his own little girl. Rushing to her, while the pageant faltered, he seized her in his arms, caressed her tenderly, and then asked:

"How is it, darling, that your candle alone is unlighted?"

"Father, they often relight it, but your tears always put it out."

Just then he awoke from his dream. The lesson was crystal clear, and its effects were immediate. From that hour on he was not a recluse, but mingled freely and cheerfully with his former friends and associates. No longer would his darling's candle be extinguished by his useless tears!

I was so ashamed of my crying and grief after reading it. I tried as hard as I could to stop, but I couldn't.

The remaining three children became even more precious to me after Stephen died. It had never entered my mind that any of my children would die before I did. They somehow seemed invulnerable. We seemed invulnerable. Death, accidents, suicide only happened to *other* people. Never again would Tom's children demand and get all the attention; I would see that my children's rights were attended to. I'd like to think this was accomplished from then on, but, actually, things didn't change much.

Stephen had a bank account with several hundred dollars in it, due in part to his grandparents' insistence on his saving their gifts, and his dad's forcing him to save part of his allowance. It represented, to me, all the control and hell Stephen had endured. I donated it to my school and church for a scholarship in his name so that some young person could benefit from what we were learning. It appeared in the school catalog for the semester with his name misspelled, and his middle name not even included. Little things like that hurt more than usual.

Debbie became frightened to stay home alone for the half-hour after we left for work and before she went to school. She was equally afraid to be by herself the few minutes after school, before Andrea got home. I understood. It must have been scary to be alone in a house where your brother lived before committing suicide. Suicide was a difficult thing to be exposed to and to understand, especially for one so young.

We enrolled Debbie in a day care center for the short time before and after school. A school van picked her up and delivered her home daily when someone was in the house. Before Stephen's death, she had readily stayed with Andrea in the evenings, but it became traumatic now. I did all I could to comfort her and see that she wasn't fearful. I talked with her, made arrangements to have adult supervision or took her with us. I assured her constantly that she was safe and there was nothing to fear. Andrea seemed to handle it better; yet, her pain must have been deeper. She and Stephen were so close and loved each other so much. I had called her school and Debbie's to tell them about his death and both schools were caring and considerate, making this period somewhat easier for the girls. We couldn't help but see the difference in caring between their schools and Largo High School where Stephen had attended.

Sometimes I wanted to die too. I thought of killing myself to stop the pain, but I was responsible for three other children. No matter how much I might want to join Stephen, I could not and would not ever take my own life. But there were those awful times of such sadness that I begged God to let me die as I lay crying in Stephen's room. Then I quickly prayed and said that I didn't really want to die, to please not let me die and have the children be raised by Richard. Each month that I stayed alive, I believed it was only through the grace of God.

I read everything I could find about death. Two poems in particular devastated me; I could feel the pain in my soul. For the first time, I could truly thank God that Stephen was with us even if only for fifteen years. I hadn't thought anyone could feel the pain I felt until I realized that the pain and the loss of the parents of a very young child must be beyond anything I was going through.

God, God, be lenient her first night there.
The crib she slept in was so near my bed;
Her blue-and-white wool blanket was so soft,
Her pillow hollowed so to fit her head.

Teach me that she'll not want small rooms or me
When she has You and Heaven's immensity!

I always left a light out in the hall.
I hoped to make her fearless in the dark;
And yet, she was so small—only a little light,
Not in the room, it scarcely mattered. Hark!

No, no; she seldom cried! God, not too far
For her to see, this first night, light a star!

And in the morning, when she first woke up,
I always kissed her on her left cheek where
The dimple was. And oh, I wet the brush.
It made it easier to curl her hair.

Just, just tomorrow morning, God, I pray,
When she wakes up, do things for her my way!
         – "Prayer For A Very New Angel,"
                              Violet Alleyn Storey

Happy Birthday, Baby,
Today you would be three.
I've made a cake and bought some toys
They're here for you to see.

I hear the laughter of your friends
They're all outside at play,

We would have had a party
If you were here today.

I'd light up all the candles,
We'd count them, "One, two, three,"
You'd laugh and clap and blow them out
And hug me lovingly.

But, there really are no candles,
And there really is no cake,
And there will not be a party
For you will never wake.

Oh God, how could You do this?
Why did this have to be?
I'm slowly going crazy
With this pain inside of me.

I know if I just listen
And become so still inside,
I can hear my baby laughing
As he's walking by Your side.

I know he had a purpose
And he finished it so fast,
That he didn't have to wait so long
To join You there at last.

But, You see, I loved him dearly,
That I panic and I fear —
This pain I feel inside of me
Since he's not with me here.

So as You walk beside him
Would You gently touch his hair,
And tell him that I love him so
And just how much I care.

And then, God, while You're at it,
Would You tell him that he's three,
And wish him "Happy Birthday"
With lots of love from me.

And then, if You still have some time
Send me a ray of light,
To ease my anguished, aching heart
At least, just for tonight.
— "Happy Birthday, Baby," Carol Lavoir-Nichols

A couple of weeks after Stephen's death, I remembered Bishop Pike's book and how Pike had put out the safety pins and his discarnate son would move them. He would close and open them as a sign that he continued on the other side. If *his* son, who had also killed himself, could give him signs, make things happen from the spirit plane, then surely Stephen could. He was as good a candidate to create the same phenomena as Pike's son, I rationalized.

With this assuredness, I took five large safety pins and placed them in a certain pattern, open, on top of the high armoire in our bedroom, and noted it in my journal. I wanted to place them on an end table or somewhere easier to reach and to see, but with all the children touching them, I wouldn't know for sure whether Stephen moved them.

I could just barely reach and see the pins where I placed them, by standing on the bed. I didn't tell anyone except Tom, just in case the children investigated. Day after day I checked the pins, but they stayed the same. They never moved. I closed the pins and rearranged them and noted that in my journal. Nothing happened. I was getting discouraged. So much I had read made communicating with the dead and getting paranormal signs from them sound so easy. I wasn't finding it to be easy at all.

Ready to give up, but still checking each day, I stepped upon the bed one evening to look at the pins. This time, the pins were all moved around. They were still closed but they had been moved. I was so excited. Then my rational mind took over. Something didn't feel right. Maybe there was some logical explanation. I asked each child if they had touched them. Each one said they hadn't. Bob was visiting that weekend and I asked him. He said, "Oh yeah, Mom, I was looking for something and found all those pins on top and picked them up to look at them." Disappointed, I rearranged them. They were never moved, all the weeks I left them there, despite my pleas to Stephen or my guides to do so.

Since I had heard the voice at Stephen's service, I expected to hear it again or talk to Stephen or to receive some sign from him. There had been nothing. I hadn't even sat and listened to my guides for weeks. With every room occupied with adults or children, the move into the new house, Stephen's death and the aftermath, I was either in too much pain or just never had the time.

Since the pins were not getting moved, I had to do something. I had to know how Stephen really was, what he was doing, if he was okay. I could ask my guides these questions. I should have asked them weeks ago. Why hadn't I followed through on that before?

They had always given me correct guidance, always answered my questions or searched for the answers elsewhere to help me. They were "dead" just like Stephen. They had no bodies either but talked to me as if they still did. *They* could help me locate Stephen. They could show me how to talk to him and to find out what had happened to him. I could hardly wait to sit and listen and to make contact with them.

Stephen, 4 months old, April 1959

Stephen (5 months) and Bobby (3-1/2), 1959

Stephen (18 months) and Bobby (almost 5), summer of 1960

**Stephen (18 months) trying to kiss the bunny
in Tennessee, 1960**

**Bobby (5-1/2) and Stephen (2) in December, 1960—
before my marriage to Richard**

Stephen (2) home from the hospital after his fall, 1961

**Stephen (3) at Richard's parents' in Missouri,
Summer 1961**

**In one of his many
attires, Stephen (3-1/2)
in 1962**

Easter 1962, age 3-1/2

Stephen's first fish, age 4

Stephen (6) wearing his gladiator helmet and cape

Stephen (6) with
his sister Andrea
(3) in 1964

Playing trumpet
solo at church in
Washington,
D.C., age 10

Stephen winning his Junior High basketball trophy, 1968

Eleven years old, 1969

Stephen (11) asleep with "Pudgie," his Pekingese

Bob (14), Debbie (3), Stephen (11), Andrea (8) in 1969

Debbie (4) with Stephen (12) in Rockville, Maryland

Nearly 13, Stephen on the first day of school

Stephen at 13

The children in 1971

Stephen with Debbie's cat, 1971

Stephen's last school picture, almost 14 years old

Stephen at 15

Our family today, 1990

I Like School
I like every thing about
School. It is a wouderful
place. Im glad I can go
to School. I like my techer
veary much. Sudjehs in shhol
are interesting to me. Work
is hard that is true but
it is good you have work to
do I like home work.
I like reading and math
and spelling and the other
Subjehs in stholl. Reses is
fun that is true. We play
all sorts of games at school
Add that all together I dont
think you can add all the things
you do at shool together,
but add as much as you can
and you will find a good
School I think

Steve D

Written about his love of school
when Stephen was 8

IM NOT
GOING IN
TODAY ! I
WILL NOT BE
MISSING ANYTHING
IMPORTANT AND I
JUST CANT GET
IT TOGETHER TODAY

**The note Stephen left on
my bedroom door
in early 1974**

DEAR KATHRINE E███████

IN THE YEAR 1974, ON THE 26TH
DAY, SECOND MONTH, THERE SAT
IN A CERTAIN KINGDOM KNOWN
AS SIXTH PERIOD ALGEBRA CLASS
A CERTAIN REAL LIVE PERSON
NAMELY SIR STEVEN, A NOBLE
YET ACUTELY INSANE KNIGHT.
UPON BECOMEING HIGHLY BORED
THIS PARTICULAR KNIGHT TOOK
PEN IN HAND, AND THINKING
HIGHLY SEX ORIENTED THOUGHTS
HE DID DICTATE A LETTER OF
PARCHMENT TO THE MOST LOVELY
AND KIND PRINCESS IN THE ENTIRE
KINGDOM. THIS LETTER DID CONTAIN
UTTER GIBBERISH AND THUS
BEING COULD ONLY BE DECIPHERED
BY A SPEAKER OF FLUENT CHIPMUNK.
UPON BEING TRANSLATED THE
LETTER PRECEDED AS THUS: ⟶

§* TURN UNTO SECOND PAGE
   OF PARCHMENT

*& NOT BEING ABLE TO CALL,
I MISS YOU VERY MUCH AND
I WOULD LIKE TO SAY A
FEW THINGS THAT I PROBABLY
COULDNT TELL YOU ON THE
PHONE, TO ME YOU ARE THE
MOST BUITIFUL PERSON I KNOW
AND ALTHOUGH YOU DENY IT YOU
ARE VERY KIND AND SENSITIVE

**Stephen's unfinished letter to a young girl,
written on February 26, 1974 . . .
just twenty days before he died**

CHAPTER SEVEN

Voices From Beyond

Death—as commonly spoken of—is only passing through God's other door. That there is continued consciousness is evidenced, ever, by ... the ability of entities to project or to make impressions upon the consciousness of sensitives or the like.
— Edgar Cayce, Reading 1472-2

Do not clutch at pain and it will not linger.
— Found among Stephen's writings

While everyone else was watching TV, I climbed the stairs to Stephen's room, closed his door, and sat at his typewriter. His room was still filled with his smell, and for a moment each time I walked in, it was if he were still there. I glanced at his treasures that he would never touch again. Usually it made me cry, but I felt strangely comforted and at peace. This was such a rare state for me anymore. I looked at his calendar. It had been three weeks since Stephen had died.

I began to feel a sense of excitement and anticipation. Soon I would be able to hear him and talk to him. Beginning as I had always done in the months before, I prayed, "God, I ask for the highest spiritual guidance. . . ." After my prayer for help and protection and specifically requesting to speak with Stephen, I placed my fingers on the keyboard to type what I heard. I became very still and quiet, and listened. Why hadn't I done this sooner? My guides were on the other side too, and I could hear them—it would be easy for them to help me talk to Stephen.

I waited. Nothing happened. I prayed and waited again. Nothing. I thought I heard a few words, then absolutely nothing. I couldn't keep my thoughts still. My mind darted everywhere and gathered each memory,

201

each thought of Stephen, and raced them through my brain. I placed my fingers on the typewriter keys again and again, pleading with my guides to speak to me, to tell me about Stephen, to bring him there to talk to me.

I couldn't hear anything. I couldn't sense any presence. I couldn't feel or identify anything out of the ordinary. What was wrong with me? Where had my guides gone? Where was everyone? Where was Stephen? I felt absolutely deserted. It was bad enough that Stephen was gone. Now my helpers had left too. I waited a while and tried again. Still nothing. Then I cried.

I told my teachers and classmates about this void when I went to school and church in the next days. I expressed my worries about my inability to hear anything or to communicate with anyone. They assured me that Stephen would talk to me when he was able, that I was still just too emotionally raw to tune in yet. They would say that Stephen was fine and continued to live in spirit, that I just needed to be patient. That didn't help.

What about all the wonderful experiences I had the last two years? I had lost all my friends in the old church by following this pathway they couldn't accept. It had previously filled me with such joy. It had seemed more than worth it with all the good that had happened. I loved what I was learning. It had always brought such comfort to me. Maybe I had been wrong. Maybe the church was right and all this was of the work of the devil and God was punishing me. I could find no peace at school or church, at home or at work. Only my children kept me hanging on. I felt dead inside. I appreciated Tom's help, but he couldn't make me forget Stephen was gone. Now my guides had deserted me.

In my anguish one night, praying for help, I came upon a lovely poem, "Consolation," by Robert Louis Stevenson. I should have found comfort in his words, but I didn't.

> *He is not dead, this friend;*
> *   not dead,*
> *But, in the path we mortals*
> *   tread,*
> *Gone some few, trifling steps*
> *   ahead,*
> *And nearer to the end;*
> *   So that you, too, once past*
> *   the bend,*
> *Shall meet again, as face to*
> *   face, this friend*
> *   You fancy dead.*

Stephen had been dead exactly one month to the day now. It was a horrible anniversary and my grief was worse than ever. It was early in the evening and dark outside. Everyone was gone somewhere—Tom with his children, the girls with Richard. I wanted to stay home. I went into the family room and sat in the blue chair where Stephen had loved to watch TV. I had rearranged the room, just as I had rearranged almost every other room in the house, except Stephen's. The memories seemed easier to bear when things weren't exactly where they had been when Stephen was alive. I turned the table lamp low, leaned my head against the back of the chair and began to pray and meditate.

I prayed for Stephen, asking God to take care of him since I hadn't done a very good job of it. I asked Him to tell Stephen how much I loved him. As an afterthought, I asked for a sign that Stephen was okay, that death wasn't really the end and that Stephen really *did* continue in spirit. "Please, God, give me a sign that Stephen is okay, and that only his body is dead." A few seconds after I finished my plea, the light bulb in the lamp next to my chair exploded with a loud crack. The room went black.

I jumped up, ran down the hall, dove into bed, and pulled the covers over my head. I was terrified. I had asked for a sign, but I was scared out of my wits. With no one in the house but me, I didn't come out from under the covers until I heard a car pulling in the driveway. Then I got the courage to go back into the room. I found the broken glass from the bulb in an orderly pattern on the table around the lamp, not scattered on the floor. Tom and the friends I told about it suggested that I had received my sign. I wasn't sure. It was probably a coincidence. But I have never, before or since, prayed so sincerely for a sign. Nor have I, before or since, experienced an exploding light bulb. I didn't meditate again for days.

Finally, almost a week later, I again sat alone in the family room. This time I left *two* lights on. I rationalized that the bulb just happened to explode, and I had become unnecessarily frightened. But just in case, I didn't ask for a sign. This time I just prayed, meditated, and thanked God for the years Stephen had lived, for his life, for my other children. I felt more peaceful than I had in awhile. No one ever told me that what I was experiencing was a normal part of the grieving process. Books I read later helped me to understand that. At that time I only knew I was irritated and disappointed with myself for being unable to stop crying, and for all the other feelings I had. I treasured these rare moments of peace with no tears.

About ten minutes passed as I sat there quietly. I felt someone place a hand on my right shoulder, from behind the chair. One finger after another, then the impress of the full palm as someone gently laid a hand on my shoulder. I turned to see who it was. No one was there. I felt no fear. I just closed my eyes and the hand stayed on my shoulder. I felt comforted. I didn't cry. Perhaps it was Stephen, perhaps not. I had no idea whose hand it was, and that did not frighten me either. Soon the pressure of the hand stopped. I turned again to look. No one was there. I went to bed and slept soundly, without waking up in the middle of the night, for the first time since Stephen's death. I finally felt there might be some truth in a verse Helen Steiner Rice had written:

> *So death is not sad ... it's a*
> *time for elation,*
> *A joyous transition ... the*
> *soul's emigration*
> *Into a place where the soul's*
> *safe and free*
> *To live with God through*
> *eternity!*

A few evenings later, lying on my bed, I heard my guides speak for the first time since Stephen's death. Their voices came into my head from three directions and overshadowed my own thoughts. They told me Stephen was fine but that it wouldn't be that easy to talk with him yet until he learned how to communicate better from that dimension. They said he was being taught by helpers and reviewing his life. He was fine and sleeping and resting. He had been at his memorial service. They promised they would talk to me again soon and let me know what was happening with him and help me understand things better. I was so thankful, so relieved, that I began to cry. I asked them why I hadn't been able to hear them. They said my emotions were so intense they were unable to get through to me.

As I continued to speak to my guides, I asked why they didn't warn me that Stephen was going to kill himself. They explained that because of my intense involvement with daily activities and all the stress, I was simply not listening to them or even recording my dreams during that period of time. They tried to get through to me in my thoughts, and even in dreams, but they could not gain my attention sufficiently. My guides also said that it would have been difficult to change the course of events since this dire pattern was firmly set in place by Stephen.

When the voices stopped, I began to doubt. What if I were imagining their voices because I wanted to hear something? What if Stephen was suffering the hell and damnation that so many churches said was the consequence of suicide? After all, even the metaphysical literature I was reading differed from book to book about the afterlife of a suicide. In some books, like Dante's *Inferno,* the dead agonized in a fiery hell. In others, suicides watched the suffering of their loved ones still living, and that became their hell. Other writers said suicides slept, awoke, and slept until they could understand their horrible deed and prepare to incarnate in another body to make up for their error. Some wrote that "self murderers" could make no spiritual progress in the spirit realm until the years of their normal earthly span were over.

This drove me crazy. Many of the beautiful things in metaphysics gave me such hope and were consistent book to book, but I wasn't finding that same comfort and understanding about suicide. Nothing was written about *children* killing themselves. What happened to them? I read everything I could find. There was no source of hope or comfort. There was *nothing.*

One of the few hopeful books—*Heal Yourself* by Carl Horton Pierce—gave me a bit of encouragement with his explanation of the experience of death even though not death by suicide. He had written: "What is death? It's God's method of laying aside an overcoat of flesh and graduating man into a higher state of consciousness. Instead of being a blight and a curse, it should be recognized as a graduation. It should be a matter of rejoicing instead of grief, of recognition of God's call to higher and broader enfoldment instead of an affliction of evil."

As days then weeks went by, the fog in my mind cleared somewhat, and I began to hear my guides more frequently. Norris, Cathie, and Joanne had brought me messages about Stephen, which I had somewhat discounted, but my guides assured me that their guidance was correct. Stephen was fine. He was still being worked with and reviewing his life. He would speak to me when he could. He had not suffered, and he was not being punished or tortured in hell. He was often brought to us to visit, they told me, but we were seldom aware he was there.

I prayed that what I was hearing was true. Why hadn't one of my guides *told* me when Stephen was in the room so I could have felt him, talked to him? It didn't seem fair. I asked them why. They said they often tried to let me know they had brought Stephen to me. When he was brought into the room, I would start thinking about him and begin crying. Even though I didn't know it, I began to cry because he was there. I had thought those were times I just missed him and was remembering him. I was totally unaware that some of my tears were an intuitive response to his presence. My grief had pushed away any communication from my guides. They told me Stephen *had* been able to let me know he was in the room once and spoke out loud to me and called my name.

Suddenly I remembered! There was an incident two weeks before. I was sitting in the middle of my king-sized bed one night, feeling awful.

I was alone, crying, praying, confused, and in such emotional pain, I could hardly function. I spoke out loud to Stephen, as I often did. I called him to come to me. I begged him to be there. Nothing happened, as usual.

Then from the left side of the bedroom, from what seemed to be near the top of the ceiling, I heard a distinct voice call, "Mom!" I turned in the direction of the voice and no one was there. I said out loud, "Stephen, is that you? Is that *you* ?"

The voice didn't answer, and I kept looking at the place where it seemed to come from, then all around the room. I kept trying to talk to him, to hear him. Then I realized it hadn't sounded exactly like his voice. Maybe somehow Bob had called out to me telepathically. It hadn't sounded like his voice either, actually. I sat there for a long time, believing, doubting, and unconvinced of *who* it was. I was too wrapped up in myself and my thoughts to try to attune to my guides. I never doubted what I had heard. That was simply a fact. If it had been Stephen, I reasoned, it would have *sounded* like him. I replayed the experience over and over in my mind, but it wasn't evidential enough to give me real hope. Now my guides were telling me it *was* Stephen. I felt a rush of renewed hope.

A number of things happened during the months right after Stephen's death that should have convinced me, given me faith. But nothing was *absolutely* beyond doubt, including the guidance I was getting from my guides who directed me to books, which I would open at random and discover such gems as these:

For life and death are one, even as the river and the sea are one.
— Kahlil Gibran

Now if death is like this, I say that to die is gain. For eternity is then only a single night. But if death is the journey to another place and there, as men say, all the dead are, what good, my friends, can be greater than this? Nay, if this be true, let me die again and again.
— Socrates

When you were born you cried
And the whole world rejoiced.
Live such a life that when you die
The whole world cries and you rejoice.
— Traditional Indian saying

Death is but a door which opens into a new and more perfect existence. It is a triumphal arch through which man's immortal

spirit passes at the moment of leaving the outer world to depart for
a higher, sublimer, and more magnificent country.
    Death is but a birth of the spirit from a lower into a higher state.
The death of the body to a majority of earth inhabitants is
equivalent to annihilation of the personality of individuals.
         – From *The Philosophy of Death* by A. J. Davis

Such words helped comfort me for awhile, then doubt would set in and I would start all over again searching for "proof." I needed to believe Stephen really was okay, and more alive, as my guides said, than when he had a physical body. But my doubt was stronger than my faith.

As part of that searching, something I had forgotten came into my thoughts. I remembered reading and hearing that some psychics, like Cayce, could contact the dead. I had never met one who worked in that special way. Maybe I could find one who purported to do so and make this kind of contact with Stephen. I planned not to give them any information about Stephen or why I was there. I would see what happened. When I asked around, several sensitives or psychics were recommended by classmates.

I made an appointment with one at her home. She was a rather normal looking lady. Since I was lacking experience with this kind of thing, I expected that people who contacted the dead were unusual looking, and maybe wore a turban or dressed strangely. Sitting in front of me, the woman explained that she listened to the "spirits," as she called them.

She began, "You've lost someone you loved." I excitedly answered, "Yes." "Your father died?" she continued. "No," I said. "Oh, it's your mother." "No." "Your grandmother, or is it your grandfather?" she went on. "No." "Oh yes, I see now, it's a child. You've lost a child." "Yes," I acknowledged expectantly.

She continued, "I can see now—a little one." She indicated someone three feet tall with a wave of her hand. "No," I told her. Stephen was no baby and certainly taller than three feet. I left as soon as I could without being too rude, for there was nothing else she was accurate about. However, I continued searching, even though I had been greatly disappointed with this first attempt.

I went to a half dozen other psychics. No one brought Stephen through. I didn't doubt that there were people who really could contact the dead. I just didn't know who to see or where to look further.

Then someone gave me a book, *Always, Karen*, by Jeanne Walker. It was the story of a couple who had lost their beloved only daughter, Karen, to cancer, and in their sorrow wanted to end their own lives. They had, through a series of experiences, come in contact with Reverend

George Daisley, a minister and sensitive who lived in Santa Barbara, California. The book reported that hundreds of evidential pieces of information came through Reverend Daisley's readings, or sessions, for these parents. He could not have known this information unless Karen, from spirit, had actually been there to tell him. Karen's mother Jeanne had written the book and brought through information denying reincarnation. I did not believe that but I did believe that Reverend Daisley had actually made such a contact with someone in the spirit plane.

I was filled with hope again. Now to locate George Daisley. I wrote to Jeanne Walker and told her about my son. She answered. Thank God for people who *answer* letters. She sent me Reverend Daisley's address and phone number.

I called him. He did not give readings at a distance, but assured me that if I ever came to California he would be happy to see me. I didn't tell him why I wanted a session but assured him I would be out one day. It gave me something to hold on to. Despite living 3,000 miles away, I vowed one day to find a way to have a session with him. In the meantime, Stephen was fine, I was being assured by my guides. He would talk to me very soon. Things were looking up.

Then why couldn't I stop grieving and crying? Why did I miss him so much? It was like he had gone to camp, had stayed too long, and I was ready for him to come home. And he wasn't coming home. Ever. I couldn't stand not seeing him, not holding him, not talking to him. Sometimes it seemed it would be easier if I could just believe as most churches taught: he was dead, in the ground, sleeping, and would rise again on judgment day.

I knew that wasn't true, or anyway, not *my* truth. I had read too much, had too many experiences to believe that anymore. I knew that only Stephen's body had died. I knew his soul was somewhere else. What I didn't know yet was *where* and how to find him. It was almost like he had been kidnapped, and I didn't know where he was being kept. I could be almost positive he was "alive," but my mind, like the minds of parents whose children are abducted, would play hundreds of scenarios of his fate. Where was he? Who was he with? Was he happy, sad, hurting, safe? It was tormenting, but in the torment was the hope that one day I would find him and know how he was.

Unaware of the psychological dynamics, I tended to make Stephen somewhat of a hero during those months. As I have researched suicide and death and had training in counseling the years since, I have learned that temporarily sainting a dead child is a fairly normal occurrence. I was probably trying to make of his suicide something special and not like that of the hundreds of other kids who took their lives. It was my way of coping, of stopping some of the pain. It kept me from understanding and from healing for a long time.

Things had been so gloomy for so long that Tom decided to plan a month-long trip across country in July. We would take the children, see all the western states, visit Tom's mother in California, and, if we could get an appointment, see George Daisley. I did not feel like taking a long trip with a car full of children. I wasn't in a sightseeing mood. But I very much wanted to see Reverend Daisley, so I was willing to endure almost anything to get to him. I called and scheduled an appointment with him for when we planned to be there. Again, I only told him my name, nothing else. If he could really contact the dead, he would have to prove it, with no help from me.

In the meantime, our ministerial classes continued. When I wasn't studying our class assignments, I read every book I could find about life after death. I still couldn't find much about suicide. The libraries around us had nothing on teenage suicide. I did not even know there were teenage suicide statistics. Metaphysical books contained almost nothing. No one I knew had a child who had committed suicide— or an adult family member or friend either. I knew of no organizations to seek out. No one I asked knew either. There was no one we knew to talk to that had been through what we were experiencing. This added to my guilt, because I began to think that nobody but me had been such a failure as a mother that it had caused her child to kill himself.

In 1974, few newspapers even published accounts of teenage suicide. There was such a negative stigma associated with this type of death. Things were beginning to change, but slowly. Since that time, I have discovered groups like Compassionate Friends, Survivors of Suicide, and other helpful organizations. Many books have been written. Many studies have been conducted but back then there was almost nothing except for a few scientific books on the theory of adult suicide.

Without books there were few places to turn. There was little use in my going to psychic after psychic, since the disappointments were worse than the anticipation. Some brought through excellent information about me and about us, but their expertise was not in communicating with the dead. I was seeking only for word about Stephen and none was given. Many psychics were sincere and genuine and very clairvoyant but were unable to bring any word, any message from Stephen. All I had were the few messages from my guides and the promise of future communications from Stephen. Sometimes I doubted the guidance because it came through *me*.

The other children needed my care. They seemed to be adjusting fairly well, but I would never again be so sure and confident about the state of their lives. We talked about Stephen but it was difficult for them. They still couldn't understand why he killed himself. I tried to explain, but it was mostly words. I didn't understand either.

I found a heartbreaking note in Andrea's room one day when I was vacuuming. On a small crumpled sheet of lined paper, stained with tears, she had written, "March 20, 1974. Stephen, I will always love you. Please try to tell me why. I don't understand. It may be dumb, but I don't. Loving Always, Andrea."

Tom's children, with their various needs, continued to be with us twice a week and most weekends. Tom spent most of his time outside with them playing sports or inside watching sports on the television. Sometimes I longed for the television to be shut off for just awhile. He and the children had always watched from early morning through evening, since I had met them. They sat glued to the TV through every sports event, from football to fly-casting. Their noise, cheering and addiction to the television was nerve-wracking. I spent time watching with them when it was something I could tolerate. Most of the time, I visited with the girls or stayed in the bedroom by myself.

Tom's main mission in life seemed to serve as his children's playmate. He had a genuine love for them which I thought was wonderful, but he didn't communicate with them much. He played sports and watched TV and did whatever they asked, but they did not talk about anything but sports. It was discouraging because they went from football season to baseball season to basketball season with little break. It was loud and boring. We ate all our meals while watching their favorite teams try to knock each other down, with whistles being blown frantically by referees stopping a play. To me it seemed such wasted time and so without purpose. Often I wanted just to talk to him. Not about Stephen or my grief, but about life and spiritual things. Tom would listen but be on the edge of his seat because some play-off was coming on TV in a few minutes.

Except for the first week after Stephen's death, we worked from nine till five each day, so the days were mercifully filled. I could keep smiling and accomplish my duties at work. When I came home, the tears would flow, off and on, most evenings. I would sit in Stephen's room, lie on his bed, touch his things, try to imagine when he used to be there. I listened to the two tapes he had made, again and again. I would strain to hear his solemn voice, giving himself positive affirmations about exercising, weight loss and building his strength.

As I listened to one of them, I could feel his pain, his dreams, his fears. This was at our home in Alexandria, Virginia ,and Stephen was fourteen at the ime. His voice slow and measured, spoke as I remembered it, "April 4, 1973. I decided to start, every day, if possible, talking into the tape recorder and writing down my thoughts. I know I'm not perfect right now, but I am going to start right now trying to be better. No one is ever perfect, people always make mistakes. I hope this talking will help, maybe. Sure can't hurt.

"Most of my problems right now center around my losing weight. But I haven't been doing too hot on it, that's the cruddy part. Like today. I didn't eat anything all day except sunflower seeds, except when I got home. Then I had three eggs, four pieces of toast—which is very bad right there— plus I had some cereal and a peanut butter and jelly sandwich and a Pop-Tart and I had two pieces of bread with peanut butter on them today, and milk and . . . it's not doing much good, but it's got to come from me, from inside.

"Some of the things I've been doing are, I take karate, I try to learn other things—judo, aikido. I'm sort of upset because of my weight. It sort of throws everything out of proportion. I mean it doesn't work good. And I don't do my karate as good, I don't feel I'm in as good a shape. I feel very self-conscious, around girls especially. I like girls, I think they're cool and all, but I sorta get all tightened up when I even think about 'em. Or swimming, cause I should lose about thirty pounds. Now, I'm going to try to plan a program where I can exercise and learn to just generally improve myself. I'm going to practice karate, because I want to be very good at karate when I grow up. I've been reading the book, *Billy Jack,* and that's who I'd like to be: Billy Jack. And live on the reservation or something, or start a school of my own, and help kids who have problems. There are so many stupid people in this world, I've been drawn in with them. And some of the guys think I'm stupid too, so that's part of it. . . ."

His voice did not come on again but was followed by his recording of songs he was listening to, "I believe, I believe, I believe, I believe, I'm falling in love. It's too late to turn back now . . . ." Then, "I can't get you out of my mind . . . ." "There's something wrong with me, something in your face that keeps me hanging around, something wrong . . . I want to live, I want to give. . . ."

On one side of the other cassette, he had made himself a self-help, suggestion tape: "Concentrate, clear your mind of everything else and concentrate. Clear your mind and breathe deep, very deep. Breathe deeper, breathe from the lowest point you can and force the air up and out. Breathe in and down, breathe in and out. Breathe and use your life force. Breathe deeply, have a clear mind and concentrate on what I'm about to say.

"You have the chance to become the greatest person of all your dreams and hopes. It's going to take work and you're going to have to do this work. Now concentrate and listen to what you should do. You should stop eating. You don't want to eat. Eating is bad for you. You don't want to eat. You don't need to eat for a couple of days at a time. You don't want to eat, you don't want food at all. Food tastes bad. It slows you down. You want to exercise. You want to be moving. Moving, building your body up until (you have) the proportions of Conan the Barbarian. You want to move and not eat. You don't want food. Food is bad for you. It makes you fat and ugly. It makes you ugly and fat. Feed your body so that you are built like Spiderman and Conan the Barbarian, because when you don't eat you lose weight and when you exercise you build your body to become fast and powerful. So powerful that you will fear no one. People will fear you terribly. You'll be all power. You'll be good-looking, girls will be attracted to you. Just think of Barbara and Kathy, and how the girls will feel if you're good-looking. They'll be attracted to you, you'll be happier. You don't want food, food is *bad* for you. It tastes terrible now. When you wake up in the morning you will not want food. Through the afternoon and the morning, you will not be hungry. You will be itching to exercise. You'll want to exercise and move and build your body. Every morning for the next three weeks when you get up, you will not want food. The only food that you will want to eat is grapefruit and apples and fruits and juices. No fattening food. You'll be ugly if you eat fattening food, you'll be ugly and fat. You'll be just hanging all over and people will turn away from you. You don't want to eat, you want to be good-looking and handsome. You will not even think of food when you wake up in the morning. You will want to exercise. Exercise will be good for you.

"Concentrate and think of all the benefits. A strong, powerful body, fast speed, girls attracted to you, being good-looking, being happy. Concentrate. You have concentrated in thought of your new body and of the girls being attracted to you and of the exercise and then you will come out of it slowly, you will feel refreshed, and you will want to exercise and move. You'll be free to move and you will not be hungry."

How he suffered inside without any of us being aware. Mealtimes had been such hell for him. He had been reminded so many times that he was fat, or would get fat, and chastised for eating. His self-confidence slowly eroded away. So much emphasis was put on the outside looks by Richard as he grew up, that he had lost touch with the greater importance of the inner Stephen. Richard and I had destroyed this sensitive child. He through humiliation and emotional abuse; I through my neglect and lack of awareness of Stephen's sensitivity and needs.

Memories came flooding back as I heard his familiar voice. I wanted to see him just one more time. He had me look under his arms just before he died. He had little white bumps in several places. They didn't look serious and I told him so. Could they have been a disease I didn't recognize that affected him? He had gone to the doctor in February, just weeks before he died. They had diagnosed him as having bronchitis and given him medicine. Maybe he was sick with some worse disease and no one knew.

Had his fall when he was two done damage to his brain that was never diagnosed? Was he mentally ill as Richard said and as others hinted? "All suicides are mentally ill," I heard more than once. He didn't act mentally ill—depressed somewhat, but not mentally ill in my estimation. I couldn't be one hundred percent sure, so that tormented me. He was so loved. Didn't he know that? Hadn't I told him every day of his life how much I loved him? Was he really going to dictate some books from the other side as he said? I didn't know and my brain was mush trying to analyze and re-analyze it all.

A statue of a little boy holding his arms out with "I love you THIS much" printed on the base sat on my desk. Stephen had given it to me, but I couldn't remember when or for what occasion. I held it to me often and said back to him, "Stephen, I love you THIS much too."

It's been said in current literature that a suicide dies only once, but the survivors have him die a thousand times in their minds. I didn't know that then. When I thought of him, I saw him hanging, dangling, eyes out, tongue out, neck broken, suffocating, twisting in agony, or dying quickly. Pictures came into my mind of him suffering for hours, over and over and over again.

It is also written that suicides leave open the door to the closet of their lives with the skeletons of the family showing for everyone to see. How true. Every negative, bad, evil or uncaring deed was taken from the closet into the bright light of day for scrutiny. Every childhood action, interaction, every word remembered, every activity in which I participated was taken apart, put back and taken apart again. Each time I saw him killing himself, I experienced the same agony again in full measure. I couldn't stop thinking about it and torturing myself. I tried to put it out of my mind, to pray, to heal. The memories wouldn't stop. Sometimes it felt like they were searing my brain. On the rare times I could get them to stop, it was as if there was *nothing* left of Stephen. Memories—any memories—were better than nothing. Memories were all I had left.

All of us who loved him searched our hearts to see what we had done to push him over the brink. Then we searched some more. It was easy to find guilt. It was harder to remember anything positive we had ever done. Especially for me. I had given him birth. He had chosen to end his life at fifteen. I had failed as a mother, as a parent, as a human being. I should be dead, he should be alive. I offered an exchange with God for the miracle of his return. He had everything to live for, my life was over. No matter how I rationalized everything, the fact was: Stephen killed himself rather than be with us, with me. I must have made life totally unbearable for him, I reasoned.

How I longed to answer the phone at work and hear, "Hi, Mom, it's me." I looked for him in every crowd. I never saw anyone who looked like him. A former employee stopped by to see us a couple of months after Stephen's death. This was the first time I had seen anyone who even vaguely reminded me of him. There were some haunting similarities. I realized, with a start, that his name was Steve too. They didn't look that much alike, but whenever I saw him for months afterward I couldn't stop looking at him.

One day in May, while at work, I answered the phone and Debbie was almost screaming on the other end. "Come home quick! Come home quick, Mom!" I told her I would leave right then and asked what had happened. She said, "Mom, Stephen was here. I saw him. He had on his karate gi, standing behind the stove, cooking. He looked at me and I looked at him. He didn't say anything. Then he disappeared. Come home quick!"

I got in the car and raced home. She met me at the door where I then held her. She was talking so fast I could barely understand her. She told me she was sitting in the family room and looked up and saw Stephen standing behind the stove in the kitchen, dressed in his white karate gi. He looked like he did when he used to cook his eggs, she said. He looked at her and smiled and while she stared, he disappeared. I would question her and she told the story again and again in the same detail. She was frightened, but she was also sure now that Stephen was OK, that he was alive. She was sad, but never so worried about his death after that. She would tell the story often. There was a definite healing and change in her. She stopped being frightened to be in the house alone.

Why hadn't he appeared to me, too, God? I was thankful he appeared to her. Very, very thankful—she so needed that healing. But in my grief, I still longed for an experience with Stephen, a chance to see him once more.

The girls had begged for cats for months. Andrea's had been killed years before and Debbie's had run off when we moved. Tom didn't like cats. I thought, if they ever needed something to bring comfort to them, it was now. Tom and I agreed to let them get kittens. Debbie found the ugliest, scrawniest gray cat, out of a litter of lovely kittens, that she insisted was to be hers. We brought "Katrina K. Katt," as she was soon named, home. She grew to be a lovely and extremely well-behaved, silky grey companion to Debbie, often sleeping across her neck at night.

Andrea wanted her own cat. Before we could make arrangements, a very enterprising lady knocked at the door with a box of kittens. She said that any not given away that day would be taken to the pound to be put to sleep. I laughed and told her it was a rotten thing to do, to knock on doors to get rid of them this way. She knew no one could resist her spiel. She was right! Andrea, determined to save one from the pound, reached in the box and adopted "Dusty," who became affectionately known as "Bumper." This name was given to her because she began immediately to bump against all female breasts within reach. She had the biggest and prettiest eyes of any cat we had ever seen.

The kittens gave the girls some small comfort in the midst of the grief for their missing brother. The kittens gave them something to care for, to be responsible for, and to love. It was one of the most healing of all things for them as the cats never ceased to bring them joy. In turn, the kittens adored each other and slept nestled in each others paws. They raced through the house chasing each other up and down the stairs and under beds. We found them everywhere, from resting on the ironing board to nestling on the staircase, licking and cleaning each other. It became healing for all of us, because their antics could quickly change our tears to laughter. It was difficult to stay sad with two wildcats running relay races over and under your chair.

July came and we packed the station wagon for the trip across country. The journey would end with a visit to Tom's mother in California and the eagerly anticipated session with the psychic, George Daisley. Then we would drive back. All the children came with us except Bob. He was working and had a place of his own. There were six children and two adults in a station wagon for three weeks. I fixed lunches on the tailgate, and we drove at least eight hours or longer each day. We shared one motel room every evening on beds and sleeping bags. It was not my idea of fun. I was exhausted.

Stephen had been dead only four months. I was still in the throes of grieving. Tom's children were as demanding of him as ever. Their mother had made them fearful of me so they never warmed up to me fully, no matter how much I played with them or cared for them. My only real comfort and joy on the trip were Andrea and Debbie. Everyone seemed to be having a good time except me. I tried to act happy so they wouldn't know, but all I could do at each beautiful vista was think how much Stephen would have loved the trip. It wasn't fair, God. It wasn't fair that he wasn't with us. Why were Tom's children alive and he wasn't? Stephen was more kind, more caring than any of them. Why Stephen? I knew my reasoning was wrong, and I didn't think that way often, but I was hurting so badly. Every little thing would remind me of him. I knew I should snap out of it, but I couldn't. It was four months now he had been gone. It seemed like forever.

My spirit was broken. I had failed as a mother, as a person. I had lost my enthusiasm for life and living. I didn't want to die and leave my other children, but living hurt too much. I felt such guilt that I couldn't stop grieving. I tried but I couldn't get the pain to stop.

I had always wanted to see the western United States. It was beautiful beyond description, but it was no fun without Stephen. Nothing was the same without him. We finally got to California and spent several days with Tom's mother before driving to Santa Barbara to see George Daisley. I had even lost my enthusiasm about seeing him. No psychic had brought Stephen through yet and probably none ever would. Even when my guides told me how Stephen was doing and encouraged me that he was trying to communicate with me, I didn't believe it. I couldn't always hear them, and what I did hear, because of my skepticism, didn't always comfort me. I couldn't be sure I really heard Stephen either. The things I thought were from him were probably my imagination or what I *wanted* to hear.

My guides kept telling me he had so much to tell me himself. He would help write some books with me, through me, but I had to get rid of my doubts and learn to listen and trust what I heard. I didn't know how to do that.

Maybe people just died and that ended it all. Maybe the churches were right. Maybe this whole esoteric, metaphysical field was garbage. I was almost finished with my ministerial program. I would graduate soon, and I wasn't even sure I believed what I had been studying. Why did I think Stephen, who had killed himself intentionally, would be allowed to help from the other side. Maybe he was suffering hell and damnation and I just didn't want to believe it. Maybe I was trying to make all this into something it wasn't. Maybe I was not facing it as it really was. I felt like I was going crazy. What was true? What wasn't?

We drove from Los Angeles, to Daisley's home in Santa Barbara. It was a lovely day and a beautiful drive, and we talked about the trees. I discussed becoming a vegetarian. We had the children with us and we stopped to take pictures. I took hundred of photos of the children during the trip and after Stephen died to make up for all I had neglected taking of him. The children were to wait in the car while we had our session with Daisley, then we would leave for the trip back home.

The address we were given took us to a tree-lined street, where large homes were built back from the road on grassy lawns, surrounded by large trees and lovely flowers. Reverend Daisley's home was well-kept and felt very peaceful even before we stepped out of the car.

A well-groomed, white-haired man with a youthful walk and manner and a golden tan came to greet us. He introduced himself as George Daisley. He appeared to be in his sixties and spoke with a delightful British accent. His friendliness made us feel very relaxed. He told the children they could play in the yard until we were through. We followed him to a small guest house down the hill from his home. He would do the reading there.

We sat on a couch opposite him. He sat on a metal folding chair in the center of the room. He explained how he was able to be an alert, conscious channel and to report on what he saw and heard from the spirit realm. He asked us to confirm things immediately that were correct and to tell him if any of his messages weren't correct. He asked us no questions and suggested we take notes as he did not allow tape recording. Tom offered to be the scribe.

Reverend Daisley began with a prayer and invited those in spirit to be with us. We had not told him that I hoped for a communication from anyone who had died, though he could have assumed this. Bishop Pike himself had come to Daisley to communicate with his son, and had done so successfully according to what we had read. Nevertheless, I had been disappointed so many times that I wasn't expecting very much.

In addition, I had done something that I knew was unfair, but I still did it. I had taken a picture of Stephen out of my billfold and placed it in my flowered makeup case. "OK, Stephen," I said as I sat and prayed alone before we drove to Santa Barbara, "if you are there and you can come through and it's really you, then tell Reverend Daisley about this test I'm doing and get him to mention where I've put your picture."

Reverend Daisley began to turn his head and look around, eyes fully open. "Steve. Who is Steve? Steve is here." Hearing his name surprised me. I answered that it was my son, Stephen. He said, "He wants you to know he's fine. You're such a worrier. He thinks you're the world's worst worrier. He wants to thank you for talking out loud to him when you sit on the bed in your room. He likes it when you talk to him out loud. But he wants you to open the drawer in the bottom of the bedside stand and get rid of all the things of his you have stored there. He doesn't need those things anymore and neither do you. Give them away."

I began to sob out loud. Besides the evidential information, I began to feel Stephen's presence in the room. He would, of course, call himself Steve, not Stephen, as I always did. I *did* talk out loud to him almost every night. I *had* put all his precious treasurers in the bottom drawer of the nightstand, just as he said.

He continued, "Stephen says you have eight bicycles in the garage and he watched Tom fixing the lock on the garage door the other day."

Controlling my tears, I turned to Tom and said, "Is that right? Was the lock broken?" He said, "Yes." Still a little skeptical, I acknowledged that we did have eight bicycles, and I thought to myself that it could be a lucky guess. Though, I reasoned, how many people have eight bicycles?

"Stephen said he's glad Tom can wear some of his clothes." So many psychics had described Stephen as a little child, I assumed they didn't think I looked old enough to have a child his size. Reverend Daisley was correct; Tom could wear many of Stephen's clothes. "Steve says he was with you in the car on your drive here and loved the trees too. He says to tell Mike hello." Mike was Tom's oldest son and Stephen had been fond of him.

I cannot explain it. A part of me questioned each piece of information he brought through, yet there was in the room the presence of Stephen— his soul or his spirit or something. I could feel him. I realized I had sometimes felt this same thing in the room at home since he died, but didn't trust that it was him. Now I couldn't deny it. I couldn't stop crying. I was so thankful, so touched by the spiritual feeling in the room and Stephen's presence and the information that was so evidential.

Stephen continued to speak through the Reverend, "You know, I always wanted a motorcycle, and I have one here now when I want to use it." I said, "I don't think he ever mentioned wanting a motorcycle." Tom interrupted, "Oh, yes, he did—we talked about it several times." Then Stephen said, "Thank you for the roses at my service."

Oh no, this simply wasn't accurate. "We didn't have flowers at his service, we just had a memorial service and no flowers," I told Reverend Daisley.

"Stephen," Daisley questioned, turning and directing his voice to his right, "your mother says there were no flowers."

Reverend Daisley paused and began again, "He is telling me to tell you, 'Remember the pink roses on the mantel, Mom?'"

The pink roses! The ones I had bought in the grocery and put on the mantel. I had forgotten. He couldn't be reading my mind—I had forgotten. I sobbed uncontrollably.

"Please try not to be too emotional, it makes it harder for me to keep the contact," Reverend Daisley requested.

I tried. I really tried. But the feeling of Stephen's presence and his love and at last a communication with him that left no doubt made it difficult. Then he continued, "Stephen says open your purse and pull out the flowered container and show me the picture you put there." The flowered what? What picture? For a moment I had forgotten the "test." I then opened my purse to confirm the information. I laughed for the first time. Bless you, Stephen. You *are* here—you heard me!

Stephen continued with information about people we knew, about the family, about himself and the work ahead. "I told you, Mom, that I was going to help you write some books. Keep the channel open. Stop doubting so much."

Reverend Daisley spoke to me, "You know, my dear, *you* can do what I'm doing and many *other* things. Stephen will help you. You have a strong work ahead and a lot of helpers to work with you. Edgar Cayce is even here. He tells me he is going to work with you."

Oh, no! Not *Edgar Cayce!* Why did he have to say that? Lots of psychics thought they had to bring through some well known person like Cayce, I thought to myself. "Cayce has a message for you, but first he wants to prove to you it's him," he continued. A message from Stephen was one thing, but from Cayce, that was something different. I became doubtful again.

"Edgar says, I know you don't think it's me, but listen . . . " and he repeated the conversation we had in the car about me becoming a vegetarian, but he added, "That didn't usually come out in my readings, but in some cases, such as yours, it may be helpful for awhile, so try it."

A lucky guess or Daisley was reading my mind. Then Cayce, through Daisley, continued, telling us about five books we had in our library, giving us their titles and then saying that I had read a certain one, Tom another, neither of us a third and both of us the last two. He was correct on every count. Two of the books were not well known, one being *How to Develop your ESP* by Suzy Smith, who had personally autographed our copy recently.

Cayce added, "You have three cameras on the trip with you. Neither of you is a particularly good photographer, like I was." He laughed. "Now that you think it *might* be me, I have a message for you." Edgar Cayce paused, then through Daisley spoke loudly and firmly, "I will work with you, and I have a work for you to do in my work." He ended by saying he would keep in touch with me and help me.

I was amazed. What in the world did that mean, a work to do in his work? Certainly I did not have a warm spot in my heart for the A.R.E. since they weren't there when I needed them most. I had grown to love the Cayce information I had read. I dismissed the message with, "Well, we'll see what that means." I felt certain it really had been Cayce, because I could immediately sense a different energy in the room when he made his presence known, and the information about the books was undeniable.

Later, my guides directed me to a reading (number 294-74) in *God's Other Door*, the 1958 edition, by Hugh Lynn Cayce, regarding the interpretation of a dream of Edgar Cayce's own death. After reading it, I understood that Cayce really was working with others from the spirit realm.

Even though the physical body [Edgar Cayce's] *may be laid aside, the operation of the work, as seen and carried on in this physical state, will be going on just the same; the impressions, the lessons, the guiding forces, the directing, help and assistance to many will continue— especially to those for whom the entity* [Cayce] *feels a close relationship, and close connections in the physical.*

For, as is seen, there are peace and communion between loved ones, in and from the earth's plane, in that realm of the spiritual world. Chaos does not rule; rather that state of oneness in purpose and truth.

As George Daisley continued, my mother's mother came through with a message, and there were many other evidential things given which we could confirm. Stephen explained that I needed to bring information and truth to people who had lost hope, regarding life after death and suicide. He assured me that he would be allowed to help me. He said he was sorry for how he left and how much he hurt me, that he had no idea he would cause such pain. He said he was happy and was in school and learning every day. He confirmed that he came to visit us frequently.

The session ended. My heart overflowed with thanks for this wonderful man who had such a helpful gift which he used so lovingly and spiritually. There *was* a bridge between earth and spirit that could be traveled upon. There was! There was true hope in my heart for the first time since black Monday, March 18.

The trip back home was much better. It was time to get about my work, our work—Stephen's and mine. Stephen no longer had an earthly body, there was no longer a physical Stephen Christopher, my beloved son. I would have to learn to accept that and live without the touch of his body. I could never again embrace him and feel his warmth and tenderness. Stephen now wore a spiritual form which I couldn't see. Nevertheless, I could sense his presence and hear and feel him in a different way. Now we could begin our two-way conversations. It would not be the same, but it would have to be enough. I began to sense that something really helpful and hopeful to others could come from Stephen's and my painful experiences.

꧁꧂

CHAPTER EIGHT

Conversations With Stephen

Our birth is but a sleep and a forgetting. The soul that rises with us, our life's star, hath had elsewhere its setting and cometh from afar. Not in entire forgetfulness and not in utter nakedness, but trailing clouds of glory do we come from God who is our home.
                                                    – Wordsworth

He who knows how to live does not fear death.
          – Ancient Shaolin saying, found among Stephen's writings

A few months after Stephen died, a scientist with several advanced degrees came to one of our weekly meetings at the house. He was working with Paranormal Voice Recording, later called Electronic Voice Phenomena, and suggested we work together as part of a research project.

He further suggested that I read the book, *Breakthrough*, by Konstantin Raudive, a Latvian scientist who had done an amazing experiment in electronic communication with the dead. He told me to listen to some of the actual voices of the dead on the record, included with Raudive's book. Raudive, a Swedish citizen, had documented recordings of 50,000 of these voices, speaking in many languages.

The voices had been captured on his tape recorder in answer to questions Raudive had asked. The voices registered at about twice the normal rate of speaking and were sometimes difficult to understand. But the more they were listened to and worked with, the easier it became. One voice said words to the effect, "We are not dead where we are. We are more alive than you."

He told us of other books about this technique as well, including *Voices From The Tapes: Recordings From The Other World* by Peter

221

Bander, and of the writings of Suzy Smith and others who had reported similar phenomena. He said that Edison had been working on a device to communicate with the dead when he himself died.

We read in *Strange Facts about Death* the following which confirmed what he had told us:

> Thomas Alva Edison . . . the world's greatest inventor, had a long-time interest in matters few biographers so much as mention: the spirit world. He had built and was in the process of refining a unique valve-operated receiving set whose purpose was to capture and magnify messages from the spirit world. *Scientific American Magazine* said: "When a man of the standing and personality of Edison carried on experiments looking toward communication with the dead, our readers are interested in what he is doing and what he has to say about his theories and his work."
>
> Edison confided his belief that "all the old and accepted theories about the unit of human life are wrong. When we find the ultimate unit of life, we shall learn that the journey through far space never could harm it. Personalities embodied in such ultimate units, will be able to affect matter when life in the body has ceased."

Having read all the books and hearing the tape, we became believers in the technique and validity of the voices. These were voices of people who had died. They were not random radio waves. The voices answered from their dimension in response to questions asked. You could not hear the voices until you played the tapes back. The research provided proof that the dead continued and communication with them was possible.

We began two years of varied experiments to establish these electronic communications with the spirit plane. We recorded a number of voices and had some incredible experiences. The books being written and the work being done with this research throughout the world gave hope of a way to contact the dead "scientifically."

One evening, as a group of ten of us meditated together with the tape recorder on, asking those in spirit to speak with us, a most unusual event occurred. We heard no message, but when we played the tape back, a voice called out each of our names clearly, one by one.

We were encouraged. However, the work was long and tedious. Tapes had to be played dozens of times, over and over again, to enable us to clearly discern the voices. Despite our efforts, we were not getting the consistent results that others in the country were reporting. With all of us working full time jobs and our family responsibilities, we simply could not devote the time needed to get those results.

I longed to hear Stephen's voice. I became discouraged when, week after week, I was unable to hear him. With the pain I was already experiencing from his loss, I would sometimes feel like giving up entirely.

All of us in the house took our turn using the recorder each night from 2:00 until 5:00 a.m., the time current researchers found reception was better. One evening at 2:30 a.m., as I took my turn, I sat with my head in my hands, exhausted. I thought to myself, "If this doesn't work soon, I'm going to quit." When I played the tape back, I heard, "Mom," with a long pause followed by, "Don't quit, don't quit." I couldn't be sure it was Stephen's voice with those few words, but it renewed my efforts for months afterwards to communicate with him in this way.

Yet months and months went by, with only a few words appearing on the tapes. Not having the scientific bent for long-term research, we all became tired and discouraged—and very sleep deprived—from "listening" night after night. Conditions in the family demanded my attention, and despite several articles and a mention in a book about the work we were doing, we reluctantly quit. My heart longed to see this work continue, but I personally just felt unable to do it justice.

We dropped the ball on this, and I have always regretted it. Someday, I believe that the research will be sophisticated enough that we can go to special places, pick up a phone or other instrument, and talk to our loved ones who have journeyed on before us.

Even so, I was now beginning to really use and appreciate the spiritual opening and psychic gifts accompanying it that had occurred for me two years before. I had worked on refining and attuning these gifts during my years in the Spiritual Science school. It was now paying off in a most wonderful way.

Stephen and I began to talk frequently. He said it *was* his voice on the tape we recorded, and that groups worked from the spirit plane side trying to make a bridge for that communication. While he was allowed to bring that one message, his assignment was not to work in this way. He encouraged me to continue taping if I wanted to, but said that it would be much easier for me to talk with him telepathically as I did with my guides. Others could do the paranormal voice research more fully.

Sometimes the experiences with Stephen were so evidential my faith was strengthened, and I believed totally and completely. Other times I floundered in doubt, thinking I might be losing my mind. I sat at my typewriter whenever I could. I prayed and asked that Stephen be allowed to communicate with me. Then I got quiet, meditated, and listened. Most of the time I felt his presence within a few moments. I spoke to him out loud, "Oh, Stephen. I can feel you. I love you. I love you. I'm so sorry for all I did to hurt you. I love you so."

He would often say, "I love you too, Mom," just as he always had. Only I would hear his voice inside of my head, "overshadowing my thoughts," as he put it. The communications were much like telepathy. I could hear the words inside my head—words I wasn't forming or thinking, that moved my own thoughts aside. He said that those like himself in spirit, or on the other side, whatever we wanted to call it, vibrated at a different, faster rate than when in an earthly body. Therefore, it was very difficult to see them with our physical eyes. Not impossible, but very difficult. He explained that at times when we raised our own energy vibrations with prayer, meditation, or other means, we could see and hear that dimension as well as other dimensions.

Those in that spiritual dimension, who worked with us in this dimension, could speak to us telepathically without a voice. We could learn to hear them if we practiced listening. He explained that they were able to project thoughts to our minds that could overshadow our own thoughts or be pushed away by our thoughts. That is why, he said, we needed to learn how to put our thoughts aside for a time to hear what they had to share with us. Meditation was the way to begin.

I had been listening to my guides for several years. They spoke to me in the way he explained. The information he shared was similar to what they had also told me. However, when Stephen spoke, I had no trouble recognizing it was him. He was delighted that I was ready to make a clearer contact and promised to help me more and more as he himself learned. Sometimes the sheer emotion of being able to talk to him would cause me to cry and lose contact. Other times I couldn't quiet my mind enough to hear anything.

When I was able to hear clearly and fully, the information he shared was always interesting and helpful. Many times it was very evidential. On the occasions when I wanted him to give me something to "prove" our communications were valid and true, it seemed as if nothing came through. Only when I let go of the need to "prove" anything, would a series of things be given that were verified beyond doubt.

I have tried and tested the guidance he has shared with me in every conceivable way. Doubt and skepticism have battled within me against hope and trust, each claiming a victory at times.

What I share in this chapter and throughout the rest of this book, comes not from me, but through me, from Stephen. It strikes a chord of truth within my own heart and soul. This information has helped me understand life more fully by understanding that transition called death.

I have extensively researched suicide. I have studied why adults and young people kill themselves and I have asked Stephen to share his insights from that dimension. Through this, I have been able to see and understand much more. I know he lives, yet I will not pretend for a moment that I wouldn't prefer to have Stephen sitting across from me with his "old" body, talking and sharing as we once did.

At first, this form of communication with the mind is much harder and takes far more time and effort than talking out loud as we're all used to doing. But I believe it's more than worth the effort to learn how. And once learned, it becomes easier and easier.

Stephen and my guides say this way of communicating is the bridge between our dimensions, to which we all have access. It is that same bridge that connects us as we sleep at night, then often disappears from our consciousness as we awaken, the same bridge that connects us with all other souls, living and dead. They say we can become fully awake in our sleep and in our conscious states. We can experience not only communication with loved ones who no longer have physical bodies, but we can also remember and use that awareness to access the untapped powers of our minds.

Stephen and my guides directed me to numerous books and to certain Edgar Cayce readings which confirmed this. In the Cayce readings I found these insights:

> . . . *with error entered that which is called* death, *which is only a transition—or through God's other door. . . . Death in the material plane is the passing through the outer door into a broader consciousness of material activities.*
>
> – Reading 5749-3

> *Be sincere with yourself and other outside influences, even discarnate entities with and through whom you may obtain much, will be sincere with you. Sincerity will drive away those that might hinder, but do not use them, do not abuse them. . . . Aid them!*
>
> – Reading 3657-1

> . . . *the desire must be attuned to the same vibration of the one in the other plane, as a radio; . . . .*
>
> – Reading 5756-8

> . . . *and these* [the spirit plane entities] *sought . . . to communicate of themselves that there might be known not only their continued existence . . . in a world of matter but of finer matter. . . . although the various communications given at the time were from those thought to be dead or in other realms, yet their souls, their personalities, their individualities, live on; . . . All could hear, if they*

would attune themselves to the realm of the activity during such an
experience.

– Reading 5756-14

In a lecture in 1934, Edgar Cayce said, "The soul of man is individual and lives on! . . . we may become conscious of our continued existence, whether in the physical realm, the spiritual realm. . . . When we pass into another plane, our development *begins* right there in that plane. Just as our birth into the physical brings a gradual unfoldment and development in the physical. . . . It once bothered me a great deal as a child that God spoke to the people in the Bible and did not speak to us. Now I believe that he does and will speak to us if we will only listen . . . we build barriers between ourselves and God."

Many of the readings indicate that Edgar Cayce talked frequently with those in dimensions other than the earth plane.

In this state the conscious mind becomes subjugated to the
subconscious, superconscious, or soul mind; and may and does
communicate with like minds. . . . information may be obtained,
either from this plane or from impressions as left by the individuals
who have gone on before. . . .

– Reading 3744-2-A-11

With these readings and numerous spiritual experiences that occurred, I grew daily to trust more and more as Stephen spoke. The following are some of his communications:

"Mom, I can't say enough times—I'm here! I am not dead. I'm alive! More free and alive than when I had a body. Only my physical body is gone. I want you to bring to people a greater knowing of the state and dimension they call death. Death is not the end, it is simply walking out of the physical form and into the spirit realm, which is our true home. It's going back home. For awhile, all of us share a temporary home on the earth dimension with each other, learning and growing together. When it's time, we go back to our real home. We unzip the body, so to speak, let it fall to the ground and walk through the next door clothed in our spiritual form, which was always there inside the physical body.

"Let me digress here a little bit and tell you what led up to my death and explain to you what happened when I died. I know you want to know, even though you are fearful about hearing. You see, the missing link for most parents is that they find their child dead and they don't get to say good-bye. There is no farewell hug. They do not know why the child killed himself. Many kids don't leave notes, or if they do leave them, they're angry and want to strike out or blame someone, so the notes reflect that. The parents are in anguish. None of their questions can be answered. Their plea, sometimes for years is: 'Why? Why? Why did he do it? Why didn't I stop him? Why did I drive him to his death?' Since all the notes are written in the young person's moments of anguish and lack of hope, the very information in the notes can be misleading and cause the parents untold guilt all their lives. After all, many of the notes left either imply or clearly state, that they, the parents or family or friends, were to blame.

"What I want to explain to you is why I did it—why I took my own life. I can give you a perspective about my suicide and the suicide of other young people too. Along with the hundreds of books you have now read, it will enable you to see an added dimension and have a fuller understanding of suicide and of death in general. Hopefully, all our communications and your research will enable us—that's right, Mom, you and me, together—to help other parents as well as children who feel killing themselves is the only solution to their problems.

"I feel you bracing yourself, Mom, tightening up your stomach because you don't know if you can handle what I'm going to say. Some of what I have to tell you is not going to be easy to hear. Some of it has to do with mistakes that you've made. Some of it has to do with a lot of other things. You're not to blame for the choice I exercised in taking my life. It was my decision, right or wrong. I know it was a totally wrong decision. I have to accept the responsibility for what I did.

"You often said that there were no clues or indications that I was unhappy or suicidal, and you know that's not true now, as you have looked back. You see things a lot differently than you did. At the time I died, you didn't see any clues. You could find nothing to read. There were almost no books out about adolescent suicide and the signs to look for. I think that if you could have located and read the little that was written, you would have gone through the grieving process sooner and understood better. On the other hand, you might not have communicated with me and thought I was just another statistic. You could easily have wanted to put it all behind you. In some ways you were kept from reading things that would do that to you. Your guides tried to keep some books— ones that would discourage you too much—away from you. Others, we tried to help you find. We sometimes were able to and sometimes not.

"My decision was incorrect, but out of that wrong choice, I have been blessed here with a chance to work with you and others. And we have a chance to help others together. You from your side, me from mine. We're not that far apart, actually.

"Let me tell you some of the things I have come to a greater understanding of here. When you left Dad, I hated what all happened. Dad always made me feel bad about myself. He was so critical that sometimes I hurt so much I would go in my room and crawl under the covers and cry. Sometimes I wished he was dead, then felt horrible guilt about my thoughts. But at least I knew what to expect. When you left him, I understood how miserable you were, but my world crumbled. I didn't mind Dad moving out, but we had to move away from my friends and out of our home. None of us wanted to leave the house. You knew you should have fought harder to keep us there, but you didn't and that began the difficulties.

"Remember how the church people condemned you for all the things you were reading and studying? Then when you and Tom got together, it got worse. I didn't like him and I hoped you two would break up and we could move back in the house without Dad. I didn't trust Tom from the beginning. After I was dead and you stayed with him because of how good he treated you, I wanted to barf, because he didn't treat me very well when I lived. And I knew you couldn't trust him.

"As long as I can remember, Bobby used to hurt and torment me. I wanted him to love me because I really loved him. I remember when I killed his hamsters. I felt awful, but he had pushed me and pushed me for so many days that I was in a rage. I couldn't stand up to him, so I killed something of his that would hurt him. I felt sick afterwards because I loved those little animals. It wasn't that there was anything wrong with me mentally as much as I was under such incredible pressure from Bob.

"You see, Mom, Dad was so fault-finding, overbearing, and cruel to all of us and especially Bob, that Bob struck out at me to stop some of his own pain. You even knew that and went out of your way to help Bob and me, but you were in pain too. You hurt and you would sometimes take your pain and anger out on us too. I can see it all more clearly from here and can explain it to you better. Dad was the victim of victims. His parents, bruised emotionally by their parents, took their anger and frustration out on him. He took it out on you and all of us. Sins of the parents visited upon the children . . . right? Some of this you understood back then, but you were helpless to change it."

While I was listening to Stephen on a particular day, he called my attention to *The Promise Of A New Day* by Karen Casey and Martha Vanceburg. In it I read: "Words are more powerful than perhaps anyone suspects and once deeply engraved in a child's mind they are not easily eradicated. Some of our greatest adult sufferings are owed to the many innocent abuses inflicted upon us as children. Harsh words, demeaning punishments, too many silent treatments taught us who we were. Many of us remained disheartened even diminished because of these powerful memories. When we accept criticism as accurate and deserved, it molds our characters and eventually we live up to these assessments."

Stephen and my guides also directed me to a particular page in another book, *Each Day A New Beginning*, put out by the Hazelden Foundation, that read: "The need for love is universal. Each of us longs for the affirmation that assures us we are needed, appreciated, desired. We are strengthened by the strokes others give us and when no strokes are forthcoming, we sometimes falter. With emotional and spiritual maturity comes the understanding that we are loved unconditionally by God and the awareness of that love, the realization of its abiding presence will buoy us up when no other love signals to us. Most of us still lose our connection to the omnipresent God, however, thus our buoyancy is tentative."

In addition, a piece I found in the *Self Realization* magazine said: "Bringing children into the world—through whom parents can extend their love and understanding—is not only a nature-given right, but also carries with it a God-given responsibility. Society demands training if one is to be a lawyer, accountant, or mechanic. But how few are preparing for parenting—the most demanding of occupations! The best chance for success in raising children is if the parents themselves set the right standards by their own example. Children need to see that the results of those standards imposed on them are beneficial. When guidance is given by example, and with love and understanding, it will enhance the karmic good already present in the child from his past lives and provide opportunity for further growth. To thus nurture inherent good tendencies and to plant seeds of new ones in young lives given into their care is the God-given duty of parents—a skilled profession indeed."

Stephen went on to say, "I want to tell you how I felt about my childhood and then what I have seen as I have reviewed my records in this dimension. I'll share with you what I went through on the day I killed myself. I want to be able to do this honestly, even if it hurts you. My hope is that this information will help kids like me, so they will not kill themselves. Maybe it can help parents to understand their children better, and keep them from killing themselves. If only one person reads this book and pauses to think things through and doesn't kill himself, or if only one person starts listening to and understands their child better and the child doesn't kill himself, or herself, then my foolish act and our work on the book will not have been in vain.

"If someone says a person killed himself because of this book, don't believe it for a second, because some people would use anything as an excuse for doing the act rather than getting help. This will not be a catalyst for people taking their own lives. So you must have no guilt nor pride because this book comes not from you but from my soul to yours. It is not of us but through us and our pain. It is also being directed by a group here with me. Some of the helpers you know, others you haven't become acquainted with yet.

"You did not cause my death. What happened the morning of the day I decided to take my life contributed somewhat to my decision, but by no means was it the only factor. Nor was it Dad's fault or Tom's or my teachers' who ignored me. It was not your sister's fault or anyone else's. Each of you played a role in my life and in my death, but it was my choice and mine alone. That is always true no matter what notes are left blaming others. It is always the soul's responsibility, their choice, no matter what age, for even a young child is an old soul. Blaming oneself adds to the pain and guilt that the individual or family feels they deserve for what they did or did not do that caused the death.

"Mom, as I looked back over the records, there was a terrible time getting me in to be born to you. You didn't want another child, and you were extremely careful not to get pregnant. Yet, we had set up the possibility of this work before you incarnated. By we, I mean a group of us souls that had a work to do together. First Bob would probably come in, then me. We all had lessons to learn with each other—karma it's sometimes called. What people forget is that karma isn't some bad thing. We reap what we sow, both the positive and the negative. So we had some good karma and some not so good karma to deal with. As a soul without a body yet, waiting to enter through you, I could only use thought to impress information to you. When you did get pregnant it was because we worked hard on that one to see that you slipped up.

"Remember, we all meet when we sleep and dream, whether we are incarnate in bodies or not and we see certain patterns unfold, choices we may make. We always have the free will to choose differently, and that's why we have certain feelings to do or not do things. We don't quite know why we feel this way or that, but it's the intuition, carried over from our higher mind or residue from our dream states. Because of your sensitivity, you knew that I might not stay with you long. You were shown that I had some lessons that I might not meet well and might choose not to reach adulthood. You also knew that you and Bill would not stay together and you were shown possibilities of other things which would not be easy.

"You created all kinds of ailments during your pregnancy with me, even armoring yourself with weight to try and stop the pain you were feeling both physically and emotionally from this unconscious awareness. Your guides and I worked diligently with you to have you listen to us, but you were far less aware then and would not, so I watched you suffer and struggle and was unable to help. While you were pregnant with me, you were taught and instructed, both during sleep and while conscious, on other levels, about my life and our potential future.

"Your subconscious memory was so strong that when you awoke, you would get very ill, sick at your stomach. We worked hard to influence you to counteract the medication you were taking so that neither you nor I would be damaged because of it. Not long after I was born came the Thalidomide problems. It could have been me, because for a time you had several different drugs a week prescribed to you to stop the nausea. We worked on impressing Dr. W. to use certain drugs that would be less harmful. Even the doctor who examined you so roughly was worked with by us afterward to see the harm he almost caused you and others. We were able to get through to him, it worked— he was more gentle with his patients from then on, but you had no idea of that.

"If you but knew the help everyone gets from other dimensions without being consciously aware of it most of the time, and how the smallest things can change others' lives. Everyone has spirit plane helpers, everyone has angels helping them, and everyone can talk to and hear God if they will listen.

"We thought it funny that you thought you would die giving birth to me. It was just your fear because you loved Bobby so much and were so uninformed about pregnancy. You would not have fared well in natural childbirth at that time, with your fear of pain and death. We were all there during the labor and delivery, and you were out of your body a lot, talking with us.

"I had some mixed feelings about coming back in a little body again as a baby and having to grow up. Before I entered, I reviewed my past lives and lessons I hadn't learned and would have to meet in this experience. I also reviewed my gifts and strengths and saw that I was to have a good brain and a strong body, that my nature would be kind and loving. I saw that people would like me but I would not like myself. Issues of self-esteem and loving myself needed to be dealt with. Hard lessons of discipline and the need to learn joy, had to be learned. I saw that I might turn to food as a crutch, under stress, and have a battle with my weight if I weren't careful. Worries and fears about what others thought about me were strong lessons to learn, not to mention lessons with Bob and Dad. It may help you to know, Mom, that most of the karma you and I had was good.

"When I was born there was a beautiful bond between Bobby and me. I talked to him with my mind and he heard and talked back to me the same way. Babies are almost always totally aware, or most of them are. That may surprise you, but it's true. They hear and experience everything going on around them, whether it's said aloud or just thought. If parents were aware that every argument, every word said *and* thought is heard and deeply impressed upon the subconscious mind, they would guard their words and thoughts carefully.

"Actually, all of us hear each other's thoughts all the time, and it's why you have certain feelings, for instance, that someone says one thing and means another. You hear and you know, but you deny it. You are far more than just physical bodies. Newborn babies, being totally aware from birth, are just more susceptible and sensitive to the positive and negative thoughts and energies from everyone.

"Those parents who begin to work with the soul of the child before conception, during pregnancy, and in the very early years can truly help direct the new age soul. It enables that soul to be of greater spiritual service and mental awareness to help change the world. Or at least their corner of the world. Ideally, a parent should not leave the child with someone else and be away often until the child is at least five years old. This will not be liked nor accepted by the modern parents, but for the best sake of the child, it's true. This is not to say that the mother or father should give up all their interests, but that the responsibility of bringing in a new soul is of such importance that it should be a high priority. If parents truly knew and believed how critical the first five years were for the right foundation, they would sacrifice and devote those years to full parenting, whenever possible. Or if unable to spend this time so dedicated, opt not to bring in a soul until they could. You were unable to do this with Bob or me and it weakened our foundation.

"You're going to read more and more about this in these years ahead. Many new age souls have difficulty finding parents through whom to enter. They can see that they will not be given the guidance and tools needed at this early stage in their development, to help them be of an awareness and mentally or emotionally strong enough to do the work they came to do. Many either wait or come in under less than desirable circumstances. They often fail to do what they contracted to do, because of the lack of a strong and secure root system in the early years.

"There is also a powerful link between the diet of the young and their conduct. The correct diet will help with juvenile delinquency, lethargy, hyperactivity, and disease. By training the parents to greater awareness in helping their children eat correctly, be fed correctly, the entire planet can be helped! Those who say correct diet is *the* way, *the* answer to everything are incorrect. It is a big piece of the puzzle, but not the whole puzzle."

Stephen suggested that books by Lendon Smith, M.D., "The Children's Doctor" were ones that would help many parents set a better foundation for children. Later, I looked for books by Dr. Smith and discovered *Feed Your Kids Right, Improving Your Child's Behavior Chemistry, and Food for Healthy Kids*. I read them and felt great sadness at all I hadn't known about feeding my children correctly in their formative years. I knew as soon as I read them that the program Dr. Smith suggests would have given Stephen a greater handle on his life and added strength. Stephen confirmed this.

"If enough parents banded together, as has been done in some places, the horrendous diets in the school cafeterias and day care centers could be changed," he pointed out. "Children are being fed the equivalent of poison with sugared cereals, soft drinks, white flour, and processed foods. What is taken into the body is very, very important, for the soul can have a great purpose and be mired down by the lack of energy and vitality to do the work. I was one of these.

"In my case, I was hypoglycemic. My blood sugar was low and erratic, from my faulty diet. The first couple of years of my life, you gave me exactly what the doctor ordered. Unfortunately, it was food without any life in it. Jars of baby food, white bread, sugar and bottled milk were not healthy choices. Breast milk is so important the first three years. If I had been a car needing leaded gas, what you gave me was equivalent to filling the car with kerosene and expecting it to run.

"Even when you cooked everything from scratch as I was older, there was too much sugar and wheat and not enough raw fresh vegetables and fruits. You didn't know that then and didn't understand. It is foolish to say if the diet is right there would be no suicides. Of course, this isn't true. However, a better national diet would drop the percentages considerably. There are many other factors, even if the diet is ideal, but a proper diet helps you think more clearly, have more energy and stay well and feel better about yourself. It helps your brain chemistry to function better. These things could be the difference many times between choosing death and choosing to live.

"The same diet isn't right for everyone, as you have found out. The book we led you to on body types, *Dr. Abravanel's Body Type Program,* where you test to see what body type you are and eat for your body type for proper weight and emotional stability is as near to the *truth* as you can find. It would have helped me. It provides a way of helping many who are tormented about weight and diets.

"The book by Dr. Marshall Mandell, *Dr. Mandell's Five Day Allergy Relief System*, is another perspective in understanding how foods you are allergic to create disease and keep you from losing weight. Also, the *Carbohydrate Addict's Diet* book explains about insulin release from excess carbohydrates and snacking all the time, which makes for excessive cravings. *Food Combining for Health* is another book to read to become aware of how certain foods shouldn't be eaten together, for better health and balance. All of these, and many more, including Richard Simmon's concept in 'Deal A Meal' dieting, learning to control foods and portions, can be used separately or in combination. None of these were available when I was alive but could help lots of kids and adults now. I wish that I had known about these things.

"Meal time was my personal hell for as long as I can remember. Dad was always on us about eating and meals were awful. That's where my problems with digestion and assimilation began. My stomach churned during his lengthy lectures almost every meal. None of us knew then how bad it was to eat under those circumstances. I would be forced to clean my plate. Lots of times I was stuffed and didn't want any more food. Other times I wasn't hungry to begin with. There were times when certain foods were so repulsive to me, I would gag. I knew, and children know, sometimes intuitively, food they shouldn't be eating at the time. I was given no choice, except by you when Dad wasn't around. I was often hungry after I left the table because of the stress or inadequate diet. I wanted to eat all the time because I was actually not getting enough vitamins and minerals. The ones in my food weren't being assimilated correctly. You had a sweet tooth and made too many baked goodies and homemade bread. We drank diet cola which made it worse.

"You always said I didn't need to lose weight, and I always thought I did. Dad had this thing about us all keeping slim, and you and I just ate more when he nagged. There was stress and tension all the time. I didn't even know why I was always hungry and couldn't stop eating. I thought I had no will power. It made me feel awful about myself.

"Bob would have been helped a lot during all his difficult times by changing his diet and adding vitamin therapy. He was under stress ten times more than I was with Dad and everything else; and, it wrecked him for a while they tell me here. He's really the strong one, Mom. You should be proud of him. His life was a living hell and he hung in there. He had it so much worse than I did, and he didn't cop out. He got tougher to survive. I got weaker.

"Think about what will probably happen when Dad dies. He will have to come back in another lifetime and experience as a child all he did to us unless he has a complete healing and change of heart, and he hasn't yet. The reason he was born sterile is that he mistreated children in the past and didn't learn his lesson this time around either. He is repeating old patterns again and again.

"Reincarnation is true. Think about it. It's the only thing that makes sense and shows how just and fair God is. People do not come back in the bodies of animals—that's called transmigration and simply is not true, nor do they become rocks or trees. All these have a vibration or lower form of consciousness. Anyone who thinks they remember being an animal or plant has simply attuned themselves to that kingdom and become in such rapport as to identify with it this way. Some can take their consciousness into plants and animals for brief periods of time. People come back as people. The bodies change but the soul returns again and again to learn and grow. I've loved looking at past lives here, both mine and others. Sometime I'll talk to you about that in greater depth and we'll write about it.

"There would be no fairness or justice in the world if a baby entered and was killed or died at three years old, and a Mafia leader who kills and has people killed, lived to be ninety, and seemingly gets by with it. The child will have other opportunities to reincarnate in other bodies, and the criminal will some day, some life, be made accountable for what he has done. It is not God measuring out punishment—it is the law of cause and effect. Humankind is given free will. Choices made create growth and strength, or lessons to be met and relationships to be resolved.

"Your guides and I live in this dimension close to the earth, actually existing in your exact space but at a different vibratory speed. Some call it the astral plane, but it's known by many names. Within this dimension are many levels; plus there are higher planes with many levels, and other even higher planes.

"In this plane we create the reality we desire. That is why so many books, written by those who have been here, or brought through from those who are here, describe things so differently. If we want a beach and sunshine, warmth and lots of food around, then we will see and experience that as long as its needed. If we want clothes, a home, furniture, just like we had on the earth plane, we can learn to manifest that with thought, or our helpers can do it for us when we arrive. If you have a negative thought, that will manifest as well, if you allow it. As you grow in awareness, what you desire and what you create changes.

"Some of those entering here have places prepared for them by others already here for their own good while they learn. They do not understand their ability to create all that they desire at any time. Some would create things to hinder their progress. Some do not know they are dead. Others will not accept that they are dead for a long time. Many, who were so dogmatically positive their religion was correct, flounder when "heaven" isn't what they expected.

"Sometime after we arrive and are ready, we begin to review the lifetime we have just experienced. We do this in stages for no one could handle it all at once. We begin to look at specific things honestly and clearly, not fogged over as we often did in physical bodies; and we see what we did correctly and incorrectly. No one sits in judgment on us. Though we judge ourselves very harshly at first, we soon begin to ease up and see what we can learn from reviewing our mistakes and our strengths. There are those who piously felt they had done such good, they expected their rewards at God's throne the moment they arrived. Boy, are they disappointed when they review their life. All the judgment and deceit they've hidden is fully revealed.

"At first, it is very emotional because you see all the people you have interacted with, helped, hurt, and forgotten. You see clearly all the things you so carefully hid from others. Unfortunately, everyone around you sees them too. Soon, what others see about you is unimportant. What you see about yourself, how far you fell short, and what golden opportunities you failed to use, is heartbreaking. You feel such shame, other times anger. Later, there is a little more detachment, almost like studying a subject in school—but that subject is you. All of it is something you know must be worked with and understood before you can advance further. Or before you can again claim a physical body to return and get about what you have left undone.

"Depending upon the consciousness of the person arriving here, the degree of enlightenment, choices made and the work accomplished, some souls can quickly claim a body and return for the next experience. Others may have to wait years and years to reincarnate for a variety of reasons, such as needing longer to learn and grow in preparation for returning, or to be taught and helped to correct serious character flaws that have slowed the soul's progress. There are lots of reasons.

"The more aware soul selects the parents and circumstances for the next incarnation carefully, for he knows that if too many obstacles are put in the way it may be difficult to accomplish all he came in to do. On the other hand, some souls choose extremely difficult situations for just that reason. If those opportunities can be handled right, great and rapid soul growth can be made in that one incarnation.

"Some souls select parents where there will be damage to the chromosomes of the fetus, knowing in advance that there will be grave physical or mental difficulties. In such adverse circumstances there is possible rapid and great growth for the soul, and perhaps a wonderful opportunity to help teach the parents and family. However, there are souls sent into those circumstances because of a need to learn lessons they have ignored.

"Others seeing in advance a pattern where their parents may divorce, need to experience that particular set of circumstances. Many choose vehicles knowing they will be given up for adoption, so they can get with the correct parents for their soul growth. Others choose parents to enter, knowing they will be left for years in difficult foster homes or orphanages or neglected, for particular lessons. I could go on and on but there are so many varieties of experiences that one might choose, that I just want to give you a brief picture about such choices.

"The soul choosing, either knows beforehand the patterns that will happen, or that the possibility of those happening is very high. They need these particular experiences for growth, not having learned them correctly before. Or being the perpetrator of these very things, need to experience them and make amends. There are other souls who do not have difficult karma to work with but choose a family or situation to be teachers, to give those around them a chance to choose better.

"A case to illustrate the point: the three children you worked with who were sadistically, sexually molested and almost murdered by the husband of their baby-sitter. At first glance it would seem, by those who believe in 'an eye for an eye,' that these young children must have done the same thing to someone in another life, perhaps to the man who did this to them. Not so. They came in as teachers to their family to help raise their vibrations with love. They knew they were apt to be put in a circumstance such as this, to give the man an opportunity to choose differently, more correctly, more lovingly. He did not. Had he listened to the inner guidance coming to him from his guides and the angels of the children and followed that, he would not have molested them, and made strides in soul growth. In jail now, with no help or counsel, he will likely again and again choose incorrectly when he is released because he has set a pattern through wrong choice. Many children will continue to suffer because of his misdirected choices.

"A soul of promise became a soul lost and off the spiritual pathway. When he dies, he will be taken to a special place where he will be worked with. There will be healing done with him, but depending on his choices here, it will take many, many years until he is ready to incarnate again. When he returns, he will again have opportunities to choose more correctly. This has happened twice before with him; each time he has fallen short. One day he will have to choose to break the pattern. We do not know how long it will take for him to let the Spirit well up within him in righteous action. His choices, thus far, have delayed his soul growth for lifetimes.

"I was a soul preparing to enter, choosing you as a parent, seeing the roadway ahead with all its boulders, feeling I was strong enough to climb over them or find a way around them. After I was born and grew older, I chose incorrectly many times because of my sensitivity. My last choice, in taking my own life, ended my opportunity for growth. There was also part of the teacher in me for Dad, that was to show him love. I did that to the best of my ability. I gave him my devoted love and adoration. It may look like it didn't help at all, but as I reviewed our records, I saw that it did.

"The love I gave and the little he let himself receive, caused him to be gentler than in his last lifetime. In his last incarnation, he physically and emotionally abused his six children, even causing brain damage in two of them. His records show he disfigured his wife with his fist. He callously starved and tortured his horses. No one called him friend and no one grieved when he died. It may seem hard to believe, but I have seen these records. I was one of the children. I learned much tolerance and unconditional love for him this lifetime. My karma with him is finished, especially as I have understood and forgiven him since I have been here. His karma continues."

I asked, "Stephen, is that why he had such violent streaks and such a cruel way with all of us, breaking the coffee table, driving holes in the walls with his fist, and forcing Andrea to sit on the toilet for hours?"

"Yes, Mom, but not nearly as bad as in his last life. So some good was done.

"Let's talk about you a minute, Mom. The reason you chose your parents was to get a strong physical body from your Dad, because your mother had weak lungs and tuberculosis, which would be inherited. This was eliminated by the strength of his genes. You chose your mother because you would be loved so totally and taught sensitivity and empathy to prepare you for your work. You also would meet some other lessons, which you can see more clearly now. You saw the pattern where you might choose to get pregnant too early. Always you had free will and choice, though. Bob and I would have been born to you with another father, later, had you chosen differently. So few things are 'destined.' There is so much free will and it is not always exercised in the wisest or best way. When you made choices that set up the patterns you experienced, we reviewed things, learned all we could to prepare and did all we could to enter, even though circumstances were less than ideal. We could have chosen other parents, but all things considered, wanted to be with you. You would be our strength and stability, we felt, as we grew.

"Want to know why *I* chose you? Well, we go way back. I have been your brother, father, mother, aunt, uncle, husband, and on and on. We had some great experiences, and we had some less than great ones. Overall, you had encouraged me, supported me, and inspired me. Most of all, you had loved me even during lifetimes when I wasn't so lovable. I knew I could count on you."

"Oh Stephen, you couldn't count on me. I let you down."

"You did and you didn't. You got so caught up in all the emotions and stress that you weren't sensitive to my needs. You always made me feel loved, but you weren't always strong enough to help me when I most needed it. You would try to please everyone around you and forget about us sometimes."

"I'm so sorry, honey. Forgive me."

"Mom, I'm not telling you this to make you feel bad or to blame you. I want you to see the bigger picture, the pieces to the puzzle that make a whole. Not only about us, but about our connected dimensions.

"And, no, I did not have to die. I did not have to take my own life. While the scales were tilted somewhat in the direction of the possibility of such a choice, when I incarnated, it did not have to occur. But so many things had weakened my spirit that eventually the scales tipped, and I made an unnecessary and incorrect choice. I considered creating what would have seemed to be an accident instead of hanging myself. With all the stigma associated with suicide, I started to think that perhaps you and I could bring it out of the closet and into the light of day, and help more people this way. My hope and prayer is that we can.

"There are so many things I want to share with you that aren't for this book. That will come in our next book. This one is somewhat of an overview and about suicide and my death. The next will be in greater detail about this dimension and life here and other lives.

"What you need to hear next is about suicide and what happens to those who kill themselves. You have worried for years that this book and the information I have given you could cause someone to take their life because it sounds so good over here. What will actually happen is that it will cause people to treasure their lives more, take better care of themselves, do all they can to make the best of this life. It will bring hope to people who have had a loved one die at their own hand. It will bring reassurance knowing that these souls who leave in such a way are not suffering the hell and damnation that many churches preach, but that they continue. They are learning, being taught, being helped and they themselves, helping others.

"What happens to the suicide is not much different from what happens to someone who dies of old age or in an accident. Your guides and angels are with you at the moment of death, usually helping your soul release from the body, just before you die. Usually you can see your body when you leave it but don't always know it's you for a few moments, then reactions differ. Some cry, some get frightened, some turn away; everyone reacts in their own way. Your helpers move you to another place and you are met by friends and loved ones who have preceded you—a kind of welcoming party. You see hazy forms around you that become clearer. You find it hard to believe you're dead because you feel so alive, so free, so light, and aware. There is no feeling of weight because you have shed your physical form, and that feels wonderful once you become aware of it fully. You have a body but it is weightless and finer, lighter. It may look the same for awhile until you discard that form for another, even lighter and finer one.

"You may want to have explained to you what has happened, or you may yourself try to explain to whoever is near you. It can be overwhelming or it can be joyful, depending upon the circumstances of your death and your consciousness and awareness while you were in a physical body. Often you want to sit down and rest or sleep. When you are ready, your helpers discuss this new dimension with you, your death, and how you planned this trip. There are rarely ever any real 'accidents.' Whether suicide or a natural death, you have helped in the planning of it for some time, and you become conscious of that after you arrive in this dimension.

"Your consciousness, your state of mind, determines the course the next days and weeks take. Most souls want to see loved ones left behind to see how they are, to see how they are taking the death and to tell their families and friends they are OK. You feel the same emotions you always did; things don't change much for quite awhile. You may cry or laugh, be fearful or sad, be playful or shy. Your personality continues pretty much the same.

"Many souls are encouraged to attend their funerals or memorial services, if there is one. Most want to. It can be a very difficult time emotionally, or a very healing time. Sometimes the number of people who come to the service to pay their respects, and what you can hear them thinking and saying aloud about you, makes you feel great. You know how much you were cared for. It works the other way also. You may not have treated others very well during your life, and few people may care that you're gone. Or those who do attend may not be thinking wonderful things about you. There are these experiences at both ends and many in between.

"Almost everyone without exception wants to tell someone remaining behind that they aren't dead and that dead doesn't mean what they think. They want to talk to their loved ones or friends, to give them a message. They want to let them know that they are really alive—more alive than ever.

"With this request, a helper takes you to visit. Somehow you are able to see and hear your families almost in the moment of asking. Other times, preparation is needed before you are taken. When you see your family, you begin to talk to them, but they act like they don't hear you. You raise your voice, you can't help yourself, or you touch their shoulder or embrace them so they will know you're there. In your frustration, you may shake your hand in front of their face and yell at them. They totally ignore you for the most part. Occasionally, someone will seem to hear or look up and you renew your efforts. They usually go back to whatever they were doing. Occasionally a young person or one of your pets or some very sensitive person in the family may hear you or sense your presence. When that happens you are overjoyed and begin to frantically try and communicate with them. Most often, they lose interest shortly, thinking it to be their imagination. Sometimes the dog will bark or growl, or the cat will pace back and forth and turn its head toward where you are.

"Your helper then explains that they can't see or hear you at your current vibratory level and you will need to learn how to lower your vibrations, directing the message from the center of your forehead to theirs and think hard about what you want to say. You try. It doesn't work. You're told it will take training and time. You are impatient and you want to talk to them *now*. You feel such a sense of urgency to let them know you are OK. And you can't. It makes you crazy to be unable to be heard.

"You become aware that you don't need to talk with your mouth; you are hearing your helpers and everyone you meet with your mind. Their mind talks to your mind without words. You try it and your helpers hear and congratulate you. You try to talk to your earthly family that way and they still don't hear, but you realize you can usually read their thoughts. This can be a good experience or very, very painful. People can have some very ugly and negative thoughts. The ones who love you can also have such pain that their thoughts cause you anguish. Nothing is hidden when you can hear their thoughts, so you sometimes hear things you never knew, which astound you. You can become irritated and judgmental about the very family members you have always been so fond of. You have to work on staying loving and not getting frustrated and angry.

"Hundreds of souls here simply never get through to anyone they know, because so many people don't realize that it's really possible to talk to us in this dimension. It can be a very frustrating time. Many on this side work diligently to learn to work with their energies and minds to set up communication, then become quite good at it, and still no one will listen.

"There are astral places or houses here specifically to act as communication stations between dimensions. We can go to these places for help when we are unable to make the link by ourselves. Despite this, and all the efforts made in these places, consistent and clear communications are difficult. It's akin to trying to locate a station on a radio and then losing it, or having static disrupt the reception.

"You can perhaps understand two things now. One, how fortunate I am to have you listen, and, two, how important it is despite your worries and doubts that you get the message out to others. What I have given you is very simple, truly just an overview of what one may experience no matter what type of death.

"Now that you've had time to process this, Mom, let me finish explaining about *my* death."

CHAPTER NINE

Stephen Reviews
His Life and Death

Men often mask themselves and that which is simple is rarely understood.
—Ancient Shaolin saying, found among Stephen's writings

And God shall wipe away all tears from their eyes and there shall be no more death, neither sorrow nor crying. Neither shall there be any pain.
— Revelations 21:4

"I thought about killing myself when I ran away the first time, when we lived in Virginia," Stephen went on to explain. "Things had been real bad for me for months. You could tell from the note I left for you which said, among other things, 'I don't feel like going on, life's not worth living.' I just didn't have the courage to do it then. I had been reading a lot of literature on different oriental philosophies, and suicide was considered an honorable death in many cultures. Perhaps in certain cases it is, but I need to tell you this and hope you believe it. **Suicide is never, *ever*, the correct decision for a young person.** It wasn't for me, it isn't for any child. It's understandable in many cases, but it's never correct. Let me explain some general things before I continue with perspectives of my life and death.

"Since I've been on this side, I've been taught and instructed about suicide and my own choices. My helpers have shown me why suicide is never correct for young people. The reason I say 'young' is because they have shown me, also, that suicide is sometimes a correct decision, under certain circumstances, for some adults. For instance: if the thinking is truly clear and things have been planned out and thought through; if the

243

person has accomplished their soul purpose; if it's not a cop-out to keep from doing what they came in to do; if their own inner guidance is that suicide is the correct spiritual way for them to release; if there is no doubt that it is for the very highest good for themselves or another; if it's done with much thought and prayer and not done in anger and vengeance. Lots of *ifs*.

"You may wonder what such circumstances could be. An elderly couple in failing health that simply cannot accomplish any more in their frail bodies, can take direct control of their lives and leave through their own choice if they are sure, beyond doubt, that they have done all they can, learned all they need to learn. Every case is different, and no one can judge the correctness or incorrectness of it, for that falls upon the shoulders of the person making such a decision and their spiritual attunement.

"Perhaps a soldier, finding himself captured or being tortured and knowing he was unable to hold out much longer, might take his life rather than reveal information that could destroy his regiment and many lives.

"A terminally ill person, in great pain, having exhausted all means of being healed might choose to take control of his life rather than continue to endure suffering, or for reasons of wanting to end astronomical medical bills, for his family, simply to prolong his life for a short period. There are other instances where taking one's life might be spiritually correct, if done with the right intent or to help others. These are just a few examples. Also taking their lives under these spiritually correct conditions can free the soul from a body where they are not making any growth. This enables them to get to the spirit plane where they can learn and grow, which often prepares them for a future reincarnation more rapidly.

"The truth is, most deaths are some form of suicide, either conscious or subconscious. It's really is true, my helpers tell me. For instance, cancer is an acceptable form of death, whereas oftentimes it has been created or activated by the individual as a way to get out of circumstances they cannot tolerate, or because they have lost hope. This is not true for every case of cancer, of course, but for a great many. This is also often true for those with the major terminal diseases. The diseases are not visited upon people by some unloving god. They enter bodies where choices are being made many times as to whether to live or die. The person would never overtly take his own life, and an incurable disease is an acceptable way to release. How can anyone blame someone for dying of a disease they aren't responsible for? But they *are* responsible. Emotions and stress left unattended, unhealed, open the door to disease entering and viruses being activated, when the door could be shut.

"Books like *You Can Heal Your Life* by Louise Hay, *Who's The Matter With Me?* by Alice Steadman and Catherine Ponder's *Dynamic Laws of Healing* shed light on this for those interested in further understanding of themselves. Hundreds of 'miraculous' healings occur when people change their thinking—choosing life instead of death. This very knowledge is the bridge in understanding suicides. The person who kills himself has taken a deliberate action to release from his body. Those who die from disease, or even from many accidents, have done exactly the same, but do it in a more subtle or covert way. Some are aware they want to die and leave signs, hints and messages.

"Some of the death wishes are more subconscious, but even then there is an awareness somewhere on the conscious level. Thoughts may have come to the persons to change or do something differently, and they didn't heed them. Other thoughts, perhaps, had come from time to time about the foolishness of what was being eaten, smoked, or done incorrectly. Many fool themselves into thinking their diseases have come to destroy them against their will. Others who die 'accidentally,' whether through car wrecks, drug overdose, or some 'freak' accident that is unexplainable, nevertheless have been instrumental in creating their own death. When they reach this side, they are able to view the whole experience and cannot then deny their own active role.

"Many young children who drown or have accidents, voluntarily release from the body, subconsciously, or even consciously at times, for a higher purpose. They see and are instructed on the spiritual level, usually when asleep, that they cannot accomplish what they came in to do because of the situations around them. They become aware that they will be unable to change these situations. They see that, even when older, they will be unable to fulfill their life's purpose because of the patterns being built in their childhood. Other souls enter knowing that they will only be in physical bodies for a period of time, because their early death can teach valuable lessons to the parents or those who remain. Others, experiencing diseases that will be fatal, know that their death may serve to save scores of other lives. Some children who are killed in various ways, come in knowing that their deaths may even affect public consciousness for the better. What is amazing, I have discovered, is that the parents, in their higher consciousness while asleep and in other states of awareness, are also aware that the child will release long before their own death and are preparing for it—not consciously, though the rare parent is sometimes aware, but subconsciously.

"Many researchers feel there is a gift in the death of each child if the survivors will look for it. It will not ease the pain totally, but can bring understanding and comfort. Parents whose children drown, for instance, could spare themselves much guilt by knowing they did not cause the accident by looking away for a few moments. This is where there will always be confusion and controversy, for parents should always be watchful of their children so that they are protected in every possible way. But if the child is part of a work or a plan to teach, some accidents cannot be prevented no matter how careful the parents are. Almost all deaths of children under twelve, and some even years older, are a part of the soul plan of the incarnating soul. They enter, most often, as teachers, to teach the adults around them, then release in various ways when they are finished. Crib deaths are not 'accidents' as such but should be looked at for the lessons to be learned by the adults and families remaining alive. Oft times these very souls that leave at such a young age, reincarnate into the same family with the same parents at the next pregnancy.

"Now, these deaths are not suicides. They are planned, on the bridge between earth and spirit, as part of a greater work, either before entering, or as conditions change, by the souls of the child, family members, and others associated with the child. This is different from young people who have a mission to fulfill in a physical body, and a full life to lead, who overtly take their lives and 'check out' prematurely. Suicide of children is not part of a spiritual plan. This is taking the gift of life and destroying a great soul opportunity. There is a big difference. Whether the young person is 'terminally' ill, depressed, or overloaded with burdens, there is always a better way than 'self murder.' There is such a life force in a young person, that with visualization, holistic healing, changed diet, or whatever is best for their own particular healing, they can often get well, mentally and physically.

"If they do die, it is almost always a part of their karmic, spiritual plan, and many beautiful lessons can be learned by them and their families. While this may be somewhat difficult to fully comprehend, it is true. Most young children who commit suicide take their lives in a moment of anger, depression, lack of hope, or very unclear thinking, or combinations of these. Intervention through counseling, or genuine caring by an older person or a concerned adult, can save a precious young life of promise. Such help can actually save and strengthen a whole incarnation for that soul. And taken a step further, can help that soul continue in growth and awareness until they are able to be of help to others as adults.

"Young children are old souls. They are growing in small bodies, but they are, in consciousness, every bit as mature as, or more mature than, the adults around them. This is not to say treat the children like adults, for they need to be nurtured as children as they grow, but realize there is the soul part of them that is mature, that is not a child.

"When children die very young, their helpers and others on our side, work with them until they manifest that old soul quality, that maturity in spirit. To be more easily recognized, they may appear to those left behind as the young child they were, but they actually reach their soul maturity rather quickly. Parents grieving for the young babies they held, that seemed to be snatched from them by death, should know three things— first, that they were only babies in that particular incarnation and are old souls, and secondly, that they are being cared for in spirit with every bit as much love and caring as the parent gave them. But also that, at night or when the parent sleeps, they connect with that child all during the sleep state. There is no feeling by the child of being deserted, nor a feeling of the loss of the child in that state by the parent. It's the very reason that a person very close to that child, mothers in particular, may desire to sleep a great deal after the death of a child, for she is nurturing, holding, and being with that one she loves and misses during the time she sleeps. What is even more interesting, is that even when the parent isn't sleeping, the higher self, let's call it, or another level of the mind is in constant connection with the higher self of the child at *all* times. There is absolutely no feeling of separation in that state. The more aware individuals become of themselves as multi-dimensional, the more conscious memory they can have of that state. With this awareness, the pain of death and separation would be greatly eased.

"A parent may feel the presence of the child or imagine they heard them, after they die. It is not imagination. There are often frequent dreams of the loved one which indicate the connection in the dream state. Not that the events in the dream happen as they are remembered always, but rather are filtered from the experience and are a sure sign of a connection. The dreams of the meetings may not be remembered, but there is still the coming together. Children are often brought to see the remaining family, especially until the parents are more aware of how to commune with them with the higher mind. They may speak to someone in the family, and the person may feel their presence and actually hear their voice. Usually the family member thinks its their imagination, but sometimes they *know* they are not hallucinating.

"In other words, there is no separation, no feeling of loss in the higher realms. The awareness of that coming together and what is shared at those times is only lost when you awaken, because you have forgotten how to remember fully. So never say I *lost* a child, or *lost* a loved one. No one is ever lost to anyone they love.

"Mom, don't be concerned about how some will react when they read this. To those who will not open their minds to truth, nothing can be written or said to pry that closed mind ajar. But many who read what we are sharing with you will resonate to the truth in their hearts and it will bring them peace and understanding about their children who have died such as nothing else has. This guidance then is the healing balm for those ready to hear.

"Sorry I digressed. Let me continue. I almost let myself die when I was two when I fell down the stairs at church. I could see some of my life pathway ahead, and I didn't want to go on. When I was asleep, my spiritual helpers would assure me I could make it. I wasn't so sure. I didn't try to kill myself, but a part of my life force was ebbing away. I was unlinking from my physical body a little when I slipped on the stairs. My helpers and your prayers and the prayers of all those people at church tilted the scales. I reviewed my options and with help, I chose to stay. You almost checked out at two, also, when you had diphtheria and nearly died. Same thing happened; your mother literally prayed you back. That, with the awareness of your work ahead, did the trick. So everything isn't predestined at all. You have a great deal of choice and free will, even at two years old.

"The day I died, here's what was happening. Remember, I see it now from a clearer perspective than when it happened. It was Monday and I hated Mondays. The weekends were all that kept me alive for weeks. Mondays were when I had to go back to school and try to hide my fat body under my raincoat. Mondays were when I was back in prison after a furlough. I was with you recently when you read that more people commit suicide on Mondays and in March than in any other time. Also, that more young males are successful at suicide than females because of the methods they use, such as guns and ropes. As you read, age fifteen begins a high risk time for teens. Sorry that I am so statistically average. [Laughter]

"I hardly knew anybody. Largo High School was so big that it took weeks to learn where everything was. There was nobody to help me, and I would stumble into classes late. Kids would look at me and not speak to me, even when I would say hi to them.

"The teachers would sometimes answer my questions but be in a rush to leave the room after class, or tell me that I could make an appointment with them later. I could sense they really didn't want to be bothered. And don't think that was my imagination; far more is perceived with 'feeling' than intellect. I knew I was a new student and they didn't know me, but I wished just one of them had cared a little. I went all day without anyone to talk to or anyone to eat with. I stopped eating at the cafeteria, it felt so awful to sit by myself. If I sat with other kids, they kept talking among themselves, and the few times I would try to get into the conversation, they would ask, *'What?'* like they were irritated at me for interrupting them. Sometimes they said things behind my back and laughed. I went in the library or sat outside or wandered around. I felt too fat anyway and rationalized I didn't need to eat, but it just made me feel worse.

"I was so lonely I wanted to die. I hated school then, really hated it. At least I had had a few friends back in Alexandria. Not like I had in Rockville all those years, but a few. Here it was a hundred times worse. When school was out every day, I couldn't wait to get home. I wanted to forget everything about school.

" I loved my room despite the mess and Norris and Diane and the baby up there. It was my sanctuary. I could stand the loneliness at school then because it wasn't lonely at the house. You and Andrea and Debbie and Tom's kids were downstairs or around. I felt good at home. I didn't want to leave. Some days, I would sneak back from school without ever going in, and then I watched TV and hid away in the house until you got home.

"I would also eat everything not nailed down. I had low blood sugar, food allergies, and was under such stress that food made me feel better for awhile. Then, afterward, I felt worse and fat—really fat.

"I was actually depressed, though I didn't know it and you didn't know it. I was in a depressed state from the wrong diet, loneliness, and being uprooted from my schools and friends. I was depressed because I didn't feel I was worth much. No matter what I did all my life, I could never please Dad. I felt guilty for skipping school. You know how much I had always loved school and the teachers and my friends. Now I hated it every day.

"You were busy a lot, even though you would always listen and talk to me when I needed you. I hated to bother you. I knew how hard it was with Tom's kids and all that was going on. I was proud of you for studying for the ministry. A lot of things you were learning I liked a lot and believed. I didn't like some of the weird things at your church. You have to admit some of it was strange. [Laughter]

"I hated visiting Dad, but felt guilty when I didn't. I felt sorry for him, but he made me feel like shit. Leave that in—'like shit.' He found fault with everything I did. I know he loved me in his way, but being around him was crazy-making. Every time I let down my guard and felt sorry for him or was caring, he shoved the knife in when I was least expecting it. His girlfriends were nice and he was nicer around them, just like you were sometimes nicer around Tom. I just wanted him to like me and tell me he was proud of me. I felt like a fat pig around him and food was an obsession with him, 'Don't eat that, don't eat this . . . you've had enough to eat . . . .' I was fifteen and he treated me like I was five. After a visit with him I felt like I had been beaten with a broom. I really did.

"Tom made me sick. He was Mr. Macho all the time. He wasn't much fun to play sports with. You always thought how great he was, playing sports with us kids, but he was mean. He would do anything to win. He didn't exactly cheat, but he stretched everything to the limit of cheating. He was so determined to win whatever we played, that it was never any fun. I didn't like him. I didn't trust him. I watched how he looked at girls and women, and I thought he was a lech. He treated his kids like little kings and us like peasants. I liked his kids, I really did. They were sneaky little rascals, always doing things that were just on the edge of trouble, but we had lots of fun. I liked them better when they weren't around their dad. Around him they were whiny, demanding, and acted like babies.

"Andrea was my good friend. I liked her a lot, and I loved her. Things were rough on her too. She never did complain much, and she and I did lots of things together. Debbie was a brat sometimes, but I couldn't help loving her. We all spoiled her when she was little, she was so cute. She could really be mouthy when she wanted something. You let her get by with a lot, but mostly none of us minded too much. Most of the things she did were so funny. I think we all understood she was the baby and her ways made Dad laugh, which was cool. So weekends were my salvation. I loved Friday nights and Saturdays. I started feeling stressed by Sunday afternoons because Monday was coming.

"The last weekend was not all that different from most except Bob was home. He wanted everything done his way. It really worried me, all that he was going through. We went to the movies that Sunday, and he wanted to go to one and I wanted to go to the other, and we went to the one he wanted, but that was OK. I wanted us to be friends. I still loved him, but I irritated him so much. I wanted him to like me, like he used to.

"Sunday night I felt fat—really fat. I had eaten all weekend and my stomach was sticking out and my pants were tight. I felt awful. I still kept snacking, I couldn't stop. I was getting hot in school wearing my raincoat every day. Soon I would have to take it off or die. Pardon the pun, Mom. It was my security blanket, without it everyone would see how fat, fat, fat I really was.

"Now, reviewing all that happened from here, I see things differently. It is not easy having a physical body. It weighs you down. You get obsessed about it. Particularly if you have low blood sugar and vitamin deficiencies, and excessive insulin release, which I didn't know I had and you didn't know I had. You know how it was, Mom. The mealtimes with Dad were torture and everything you ate was commented on or you were always told *not* to eat things when you were hungry or thirsty, and to eat them when you were full. It also creates a lot of stress and strain and some real bad thinking.

"I look at my records here whenever I want. You can see them just like watching movies, except you can become part of the experience when you want to get into the feelings more. I see now, I wasn't that fat. In my head I was fat. I did need to lose about twenty pounds, but I didn't look like I thought I looked. I didn't see all the good things about myself. All I saw was fat.

"Somewhere in my warped thinking, I thought that if I got slim everything would get better. Everyone would speak to me, girls would like me more and all that. So my way of getting slim was to stop eating. That was great for one meal, but by the time I got home from school, I was so hungry I ate three times as much. Then I hated myself and ate more.

"About this time, Kathy told me she might be pregnant. I had such a crush on her. I was crazy about her, but I handled it real well on the phone with her when she told me. Afterwards, I felt like someone had kicked me. I would never have touched her if I'd been her boyfriend and here some jerk had taken advantage of her. I was hurt and jealous and protective. I didn't have a car and couldn't get to her, and our phone conversations left me very frustrated. I was the only one she could talk to, so she told me every detail, which hurt me even more.

"Lynn was so cute, and I liked her a lot, but I only saw her when she and her mom were with Dad. She was nice enough, but I called her and she would be busy or have to get off the phone. So it felt like I didn't have anybody. No car, no friends, nobody. Just a fat ugly body."

"You had me, Stephen. I loved you."

"Mom, you just weren't enough then. You were busy. You were my mother. Part of being my age and growing up was to pull away a little anyway, to become a little independent. Kids do that in preparation for leaving home in the years ahead. I know that now, I didn't then. I just knew that how much you loved me and how good-looking you thought I was didn't mean much. I actually thought that you loved me no matter how fat I was and wouldn't tell me how awful I really looked.

"I went to bed that night wishing I were dead. I was not going to school ever again and be embarrassed and lonesome and ignored. I had decided to stay home Monday. When I told you, you insisted I go in, but I went back to bed. Tom came to my room to tell me you said I had to go to school. He said you all knew I had shoplifted some things. He told me not to take my gym bag to school or anywhere and you would both talk to me that night when you got home.

"I didn't know why I took things occasionally. Many of the kids did, and I guess it seemed like I was more part of things with them. We'd all sneak things out of the store. We'd all laugh and grin at each other. We only took little things, not expensive things, but for that little while, I felt like one of them, like everybody else. They'd leave the store and go off with their friends, and I'd come home and here would be this stuff in my gym bag and I felt awful. I'd try to enjoy whatever it was, but it made me feel worse. I didn't even need the stuff. That's no excuse. I'm not trying to excuse what I did.

"Well, anyway, that did it! I thought, that son of a bitch, Tom, had no right to make me feel bad. Who was he? Nothing but a creep. I was humiliated. Nothing I ever did was OK with him and now he rubbed it in by telling me I had shoplifted. I *had* to have my bag. It went everywhere with me. I was sick about getting caught. I had only lifted a few things from the drug store, some tanning stuff to make me look darker and a few things. I knew I shouldn't have, but I did and now I was caught. I would probably be made to take them back and feel like a fool. I felt like a fool now. A fool. A fat fool. I wanted to die from embarrassment.

"I couldn't tell you I wasn't going to school now. You would both make me go or make me feel worse. I would *have* to go. I would show you both, I would pretend to go and stay home. But you messed that up, Mom. You wouldn't let me walk and you wouldn't leave before I left, so I was stuck with getting in the car with you. I had decided I wouldn't stay, no matter what. You said, 'Stephen you just can't take things from the store. We can pay for them. It's not right. We'll talk tonight. I love you, honey. We have to get these things straightened out.' Right in front of Tom. I was hurt and angry. I would show you both. I turned right around and didn't go to school when you let me off. I sneaked back home. I ate and watched TV and felt worse and worse. I decided not to be humiliated more. I would be gone when you got home. I decided to go to the woods and spend the night where you couldn't talk to me. I might even kill myself.

"I gathered together some of my things. I packed enough food to last a few meals. So, you could see how ambivalent I was. I found my little hideaway in the woods, sat down, and began to think about killing myself. My thinking was muddled. I could hang myself and then you'd all be sorry. I would never again have to go to school and be humiliated there. Nobody cared anyway. You had Tom. He didn't care about any of us. The girls didn't care. Dad didn't care, for sure. I was just an embarrassment to him. Maybe I could help more from the other side. For sure I couldn't do anything here.

"My thinking changed from wanting to show you and hurt you, to how free I would be dead, and how much I could do and help from the other side. I had been reading things about life after death, and we had talked about it. It would be better than what I was going through. I honestly didn't even consider the finality of it all. In my mind it was like—I'd show all of you. I wouldn't be a bother anymore, and maybe I could help. You had said that people don't die, they continued on the other side. I could do something there. I couldn't do anything alive. As I thought further I imagined you'd all regret what you did, and I'd come back and you'd appreciate me more. After all, in the movies and on TV, people got killed one night and were on another program the next. I didn't specifically think that, but my consciousness was like that. Death and its real meaning were somewhat cloudy then. I didn't think how absolutely irreversible and final it would be.

"My plan caused me to feel better, almost excited, with something to plan for. Something I could do, something I had some control over. The more I thought about it, the better it seemed. I began to write notes to everyone. As I wrote them I had some funny feelings. I felt important, but I felt sad. I felt people would sit up and listen, but I felt a pain in the pit of my stomach. I felt like crying, and I felt sorry for myself; then I changed and felt strong and brave. My feelings were like a merry-go-round—up and down and around and around.

"I had brought a rope along, not to hang myself especially, but I always brought a rope camping. Remember, Dad taught us that. So I began to plan and practice certain knots with it. Then I wrote a few things, then I would think. I climbed up the tree. It was getting late in the afternoon, dusk, almost time to start getting dark. I sat on the limb and let the rope down to touch the ground, then shortened it so that my body wouldn't touch the ground when I jumped. I might jump and hit the ground if it weren't just right. So I climbed up on a higher limb. That ought to work for sure. I knotted the rope around the tree limb, so it wouldn't come undone. Then I put the other end around my neck with a perfect slip knot.

"I stood up on the tree. I had on my navy blue shirt, and I was writing the notes in my little spiral book. I put it in my pocket before I jumped so that someone would find it. I had been indecisive about whether I'd do it or not. I'd been thinking about it for a long time now, it seemed. So I wrote more notes and went into a state of elation almost, of real high-pitched, false, and intense joy.

"Now that's the real danger stage, I've learned. If someone had been there to help me through that stage, I would not have killed myself. But there was nobody there, and I had made some pretty final choices. There I was, writing the last notes and I was feeling so high about it, like maybe I could really help from the other side. I felt impotent about helping as a fifteen-year-old with my ugly, overweight body. So I began to feel sure I could help from the other side. There was a sense of excitement, of going on a journey. There was also that fear in the pit of my stomach that moved like an electric basketball.

"I didn't sense any presences around me. As you read the one note you thought that a guide or being was there telling me the things I wrote. [Stephen had written in a booklet separate from his notes: "Getting scared will syke you out and may make you lose. Avoid confrontation during this time breath deeply and clear mind of thought of losing then practice to overcome fear."] Actually, I was just giving myself a suggestion so I wouldn't back out. I had written that much earlier.

"Later, I discovered that even before I left my body, there were all kinds of beings around me—angels and guides—and they all helped me. At that time I couldn't see any. I had some moments of real doubt and fear. And then I had some moments of real courage. And my courage fought with my fear. There was a war on that tree. What I thought was that my courage won. What I see now is that my fear won.

"I was writing the notes before I got up on the tree, and then up on the tree I took the pad and pen with me. It was exactly like you thought— I flipped to the back of the book, and I started writing. I was scared then and started to cry; you can see the change in my handwriting. I'm sitting there with the rope around my neck, wanting to be stopped, and yet not wanting to be a coward by backing out. I don't think at that time I had any thought that someone might come and find me. There were other times I did, but I didn't at that time. I was pretty far back in the woods and nothing could have stopped me then.

"So I finished the notes, and I asked *God* to stop me. It was the final thing. I asked God to stop me if I shouldn't kill myself. That was probably the hardest note for you, Mom. You had some anger toward God at times for not doing what I asked. You were mad at yourself for not teaching me that God would not step in and stop me if I did something foolish. I finished the last note and was shaking and crying. I kind of expected God to step out of the woods and stop me, and I waited but He didn't. I waited a few minutes more. I even said out loud, 'Now, God, it's up to you. Stop me if I shouldn't do this.' Then I put the notebook in my shirt pocket. I was shaking so bad that I dropped the pen and it fell on the ground. I started to go down and get it but I didn't.

"First I was going to jump. I stood up. It looked so far down, it scared me. I started crying. So I sat down. I kept trying to make myself do it and couldn't. Then I forced myself and jumped. Not a real jump, just a kind of slide and easing-myself-over-the-limb-jump. I died instantly. I did feel a moment of pain. I'm not going to tell you I didn't. There was a moment of blinding pain. The pain only lasted for a little bit and it stopped.

"I felt like I was floating up. I was like an air bubble under the water. It felt like I had dived into deep water and was coming up, but I could breathe in the water. I floated up out of my body and it felt like there was somebody at each elbow, but I couldn't see anybody. And I looked around and there were kind of misty-like forms, but I couldn't see them very clearly. I floated above my body. I looked down. I could see the top of a head, and then I kind of floated away and I could see this body hanging there by the neck. For a moment I couldn't figure out who it was. It didn't look familiar.

"When I realized it was me, panic took over. I mean *panic*. Instead of being excited that I was out of my body and was still alive and could see and think, I suddenly realized how mad you and Tom were going to be. I had this moment of feeling like a kid that had done some bad thing and was going to be caught and punished for it. I didn't realize that there was no way you could punish me for this. I had created my own punishment. I started to really cry; tears filled my eyes and I sobbed. I hurt so bad, and my heart was pounding—I felt like I still had a body. I felt just like I always did, except that I wasn't touching the ground. I was suspended in the air somehow, without falling.

"And as I looked around, the forms around me began to become clearer. I saw Grandfather H. I didn't even remember him except from his pictures, and there he was. I saw your grandfathers. I saw a lot of people that I'd only seen pictures of in the albums. I saw a couple of friends of mine—not real friends, but acquaintances that I had known, and I remembered that they were dead. I saw a whole lot of people I didn't know, but I felt like I knew them from somewhere. I was confused and didn't know what to think. I was sad, but I was also surprised, and I was kind of excited. I guess I stopped crying. Some of them came up to me and hugged me. Others said, 'Hi, Steve.' All I could see were the people. I felt so much better. Then when I looked, I could see the body hanging there. It gave me a terrible feeling each time I saw it. It grossed me out. I didn't want to look at it. It was strange. I knew it was my body, but it didn't look like my body. I had my body, it seemed. It was confusing.

"Panic set in again. Then this cold feeling all over. Maybe I was going to throw up. Then I began to feel I was going to sleep. I just felt myself kind of moving upward and away. Kind of a swishing sound. I just moved upward and away and I fell asleep. There was a lady there helping me, a sweet and kind lady dressed in white, who held my hand.

"The next thing I knew, I woke up and it was daylight, and I felt so good. I just felt wonderful. I looked around and there was kind of a misty look everywhere, then it got clearer. I looked closer. I was lying down on my bed, and there was a window. I could see the sun outside. And I tried to remember where I was. You know how you wake up in a strange room or someplace and you don't know where you are? I couldn't remember where I was. I had some vague thought come to me that I had seen somebody hanging on a tree, and I fell back asleep.

"They tell me that you woke up in the middle of the night after I had hanged myself, crying and very sad. It was raining outside and you were concerned that I was getting wet. I wasn't consciously there, and I didn't know that. I think you've always thought that I came to your bed after I did it and tried to tell you, but I really didn't. That's not what happened. What you felt was the bond between us severed. Your intuition being so strong, you sensed something had happened. But you didn't consciously know what, only that it made you cry. Later, I was taken to you by some helpers and we were together a little while, but neither of us remembered. It was just to prepare you until you were informed the next day about me.

"I kept waking up and getting afraid and then very gently going back to sleep. Someone came and sat by me. I could hear them talking to me, then I'd go back to sleep. I didn't really want to hear what they were saying to me. You know how sometimes you wake up for school and you don't really want to go, so you go back to sleep, but you're aware of what's going on even though you're still not ready to get up. It was that kind of a feeling.

"Mom, I know this isn't easy. I know how it hurts and how sad it makes you. Just kind of breathe deeply and relax. I remember waking up again and this really nice lady was sitting beside me. I thought at first she was a nurse. She had on a white dress. Just a sweet, nice lady. She didn't say her name, but she talked to me quite awhile. It felt like I knew her. She said, 'Would you like to go for a few minutes and see your mother? She has just been told what happened to you. She's hurting a lot.' And I said, 'Yeah, how do we get there?' She said 'Just come with me,' and she took my hand and it seemed like the next minute I was in the living room standing beside her as you sat on the couch, and two men sat across from you.

"I was so shocked, I didn't say anything for a second, and then I said, 'Mom, Mom! It's me, Steve. Mom! You won't believe what happened!' You didn't answer me. You didn't even look over. I thought you were too busy talking to them to see me. I didn't want to interrupt you, so I saw Tom and said, 'What's wrong, Tom? Tom, what's wrong?' He didn't look at me or answer either. I looked around. There were Andrea and Debbie, and Tom's kids. I turned to Andrea and said, 'What's wrong, Andrea?' She was crying and she didn't answer me either. The woman very gently put her arm around me and said, 'They can't see you. They can't hear you. But we brought you here to see your mother and be with her.'

"I said, 'Am I dead? I *am* dead, aren't I?' And she said, 'That's what they would say.' I said, 'Oh, NO!' Suddenly I felt so embarrassed to be there, because I felt like you and Tom could see me, and how irritated and angry you must be. Then somehow, even though you weren't crying, I could feel your hurting inside, your heart inside my heart. I had never hurt so bad, *ever*. Not even when I jumped from the tree.

"Then I remembered again the pain and jumping off the tree. It had been like standing by a cold pool and dreading jumping in the cold water. Thinking I *had* to, then doing it and feeling the shock of the cold water when I hit. Then the pain stops and you get used to the water. Only this pain wasn't stopping. I wished I could go back and not jump. I must have been crazy.

"I felt sick. I wished I could kill myself to stop hurting. Funny statement, huh? Here I am 'dead' and wishing I could kill myself. Not so funny in this dimension, by the way. No matter how much you hurt or how bad you feel, you can't kill yourself here. I hated what I had done to you. I never realized how much I loved you and you loved me. I never realized how much I loved my home and the girls and Bob. I wanted to be back. I screamed at you, 'Mom! Mom! I'm here! I'm here, Mom! Look! I'm not dead! I'm *here*!' You turned as if you heard me and looked away. I went over and grabbed your shoulder, then hugged you and hugged you, but you didn't even know I was there. It was strange, you didn't feel the same. In fact I could hardly feel your body.

"I began to cry. I couldn't stop. I hated to cry in front of anyone. Here I was blubbering in front of the men and Tom and you and all the kids, and the woman with me. I still couldn't stop. I cried and cried. It hurt so bad. I forgot that no one could even hear me. The lady could, though, and said, 'Steve, let's go now.' I said, 'No! I want to stay.'

"I remembered when I was born, for some reason. I was scared and wanted to cry then too. It felt like I was in a tight box being held against my will when I entered into my body as it was being born. I couldn't stop crying, and I wanted out of there, but no one heard me. Then some angels came and sang to me and held me and rocked me back and forth, and I was better. They stayed with me until I was taken to you, then stood around, and I watched them while you held me. Then when the nurse took me back to the nursery, I was scared again and started to cry. They sang to me and made nice sounds and held me.

"The lady with me was like the angels, I thought. She was the only one who seemed to hear me, to know I needed something, that I was alive.

She didn't look exactly the same as the angels I had seen. I would have to ask her if she was an angel. While I was crying and standing in the room and listening to all of you talking and ignoring me, I remembered also when I fell at church. You had told me about it many times, but I never remembered. Now I could remember. I had almost let myself have that accident. I could see what was going to happen if you married Richard, and I decided I didn't want any part of it. I was not going to go through that for anything.

"It really hurt when I fell. I was never unconscious, but it hurt so much I couldn't even cry. I couldn't get my breath. I didn't know how to tell you how much I hurt and how scared I was. Angels sat by me then and held me until I got to the hospital. There were a lot of others around too, my guides and lots of people who gathered around, that you and the people at church couldn't see. That time, Jesus came to me and talked to me and stayed with me too. I used to visit with him and with angels when I was asleep. Remember I used to tell you about it when I woke up? His visits with children in their dreams is a fairly frequent occurrence, I've been told, and is not their imagination, nor just a 'dream' but an actual experience with him. He looked a lot like the paintings we had of him, not exactly, but quite a bit. I recognized him.

"He talked to me about being with him or staying with you and said I would have to choose. He talked to me just like an adult, and I talked back to him the same. He said he would help me make the best of the situation if I stayed and that I could help a lot because it was going to be very, very rough on you, Mom, and on Bob and on me. He didn't mention Andrea and Debbie. They weren't even born then, were they? I guess I thought that if I was hurt and died, you wouldn't have a wedding and marry Richard. They showed me that my death wouldn't stop it, and they showed me how things were going to unfold, and I didn't like it one bit.

"Then I was allowed to watch what it would be like for you without me. I could feel your pain and how much you loved me and how much you hurt. I saw the church people praying and even Bobby praying for me to live. I didn't want to, but said I'd stay. You know the rest. I never was quite the same after that experience. There was no brain damage, but I was more subdued if you think back. What I saw coming put a damper on my spirit. It's funny how I could see the whole thing so clearly now, right there in the room with you, and had never remembered it until then.

"Remembering convinced me even more that I had to let you know I was OK. I tried again, 'Mom! Mom, listen! I'm here. I'm sorry! I'm sorry! I didn't mean to do this! I'm really sorry.' I went to Andrea and begged her to tell you. She was still crying and didn't hear me either. I tried all Tom's kids, then Debbie as a last resort. Debbie heard me! She didn't know what to say. You've forgotten this, but she came over to you and sat in your lap and hugged you and said, 'Mom, don't be sad, Stephen's OK. He's not dead. He's here with us.' You hugged her and said, 'I know, honey, don't you be sad either.' You thought she was just being sweet and trying to make you feel better. She could hear me! My little eight-year-old sister could hear me. I tried to get through to her again, but it was no use.

"I was standing there crying like a baby, but so many things became clearer. I discovered that I could read all your minds. At first I didn't know that. I thought you were all saying the things I heard. I began to realize that I could hear what you were saying *and* what you were thinking.

"Tom's kids were wondering about getting some of my things—my weight bench and stuff. I told them they could have the stuff, but they didn't hear. Andrea was blaming herself for me being dead. She was thinking how she could have stopped me from going to the woods and that she hadn't been a good sister to me. Your mind was racing like a roller coaster. You covered everything from calling people, to thinking about my body, to doubting I was dead, to wondering why the pain in your stomach wouldn't stop, and even to what the neighbors would think. Debbie was actually wondering why everyone was so sad. She knew I was alive. Later she doubted that, but not then.

"The lady asked me again if I was ready to leave. I didn't want to go. I said, 'Where is my body? I want to see my body.' She nodded and I followed her. There was something on a stretcher. Tom came out and they pulled the cover down and there I was. Yuk. It grossed me out. I looked awful. My hair was all messed up and my skin was strange looking. It didn't look like me at all. I didn't want anyone to see me looking like that. Suddenly I had a thought! What if I jumped back into my body and then I couldn't be dead? I would just sit up and walk in the house and say, 'Fooled you, I'm alive.'

"I tried it. I went over and tried to squeeze into my body, but I kept slipping out. I finally made it but nothing happened. I could see and hear just like I was in it, and I could sit up, but the body didn't move. I tried and tried. I tried pulling my hand up, getting under my shoulders and pushing myself up. I couldn't budge my body. I couldn't even lift the sheet covering my body. I thought I was so weak that I couldn't even lift my own hand.

"I turned around and said, 'Help me.' The men in the ambulance didn't hear me but the lady did. 'Please help me get back in my body,' I begged her. 'I can't do that,' she said. 'You can't stay in your body anymore. You will have to stay here with me. Let's go and we'll talk about it some more.

They can't hear you right now. There'll be a time when they *can* hear you, but they just can't right now. Let's go, dear, and . . . '

"I tried not to be impolite but said firmly, 'I don't want to go. I want to stay here where I belong. I am not *dead*. I did a dumb, stupid thing jumping off the tree with the rope around my neck. I'm really sorry. I want another chance. Just help me get in my body and make it move, and I *promise* you, I won't do anything dumb like that again. Please! Please! I promise if you'll help me, I'll do anything you want.'

"'Steve, you can't undo what you've done. You can't use this body anymore. There is nothing I can do. There is nothing *you* can do here. Come with me and we'll get you settled and talk about all this.'

"'I am not leaving here!' Mom, you know how polite I always tried to be, but I just knew if we left I wouldn't be able to find my body and have another chance. So I refused to leave. She said OK and stayed with me. I went back inside to try and talk to all of you again. It was getting more and more frustrating. I felt like crying, then I felt like yelling. I thought if I could just sit by you and have you hug me and tell me everything was going to be OK, it would be. So I sat down by you and snuggled against you, but I realized again that I couldn't exactly feel you, even though I was sitting right there touching you. I guessed you couldn't feel me either. You ignored me.

"'Oh God, NO! What have I done? I *am* dead. God, please give me another chance. I don't want to be dead. I'm sorry! I made a mistake. Help me stay here.' I started to cry like I never cried in all my life.

"I woke up later in the same room I had been in before and looked around. It wasn't a strange room after all; it was like my room at home. Only as I looked, it was different. I looked out the window and it wasn't my back yard. The lady was sitting in the chair near my bed. 'What's going on? Tell me what's going on.'

"'Steve, you aren't using your physical body anymore. You were feeling very, very badly and you ended your earthly life. Now you are going to be living here with us. I'll tell you again what it's like here. You've forgotten our conversations. I'll help you meet some of your old friends and relatives and get acquainted.'

"'But I don't want to be here. Is this heaven or hell? Are you an angel? Where is my family? Why isn't my backyard outside, and why is my room different?' I tried to be nice but I was feeling scared. Maybe this was a dream and I was going to wake up. 'Is this a dream?'

"'No, my dear, this isn't a dream. This isn't heaven or hell. This is a wonderful place where we can have one foot a little on earth and another a little in heaven, I guess you could say. It's certainly not hell—there really isn't a hell unless someone wants to create that. You don't need to create that. We thought you might enjoy a room like the one you had. Let's go outside and I'll show you around.'

"'I don't want to see anything. Can you show me where my family is and let me visit them?'

"'It would be better if you waited, Steve. Then you can see everyone if you like. There are a lot of people here who want to see you and welcome you.'

"'Why are you here? Are you an angel? If you aren't an angel, then why are you here? Are you dead?'

"'I guess people would say I'm dead,' she laughed, 'but don't I look alive? You will discover that dead doesn't mean what you have always thought. And I'm here because my job is to help young people like yourself, who come here to visit a little too early, get adjusted and acquainted. I am not an angel, but there are angels here.'

"She was trying to be so nice, and I hated to make her feel bad, so I agreed to go with her. First I asked her all kinds of questions and we talked for a long time. She took me to see Grandfather H. again. He and I talked about my real dad and lots of things. He was very nice and looked just like his pictures. I met your mother's mother and father and talked with them and we talked about the family. I met lots of your relatives that I didn't know and barely remembered from the photos you and Grandmother had of them. It felt like I knew them and they treated me like I was one of the family. I thought about some people I knew who were dead, but I didn't see them.

"I looked around and it wasn't all that different from where we lived except that it wasn't familiar. There were trees and birds and streets and houses and people everywhere. Some were friendly and happy, some spoke to us, some walked by without speaking, others waved. There were kids my age and every age, playing and running and walking with their friends. There were some old people, but not many. Later, the lady told me that people evolved toward or from their ages to an ideal age they create for awhile.

"I was miserable. I tried to act happy, but there were things I needed to take care of back home. This was not where I was supposed to be and I knew it, even if the lady didn't, and I was going to find some way to get back. This was not heaven. In heaven, angels floated around on clouds, playing harps. Here nobody had wings; nobody was on a cloud. They were just ordinary people like at home. Only this wasn't home and I didn't like it here. It was OK for someone else but not for me. I wanted to go home—*now*.

"I decided to go back to my room and lie down to think. Then I was there. I didn't know how I got there. I hadn't walked, I was sure. The lady was there too. 'Stephen, you can use your mind here because you don't have a body anymore. You actually do have a body for now, but it's a finer, etheric body, and you won't be limited like you were with a physical body.' I looked down and was shocked. I wasn't fat. I was lean, like I'd been working out on weights and not eating. I stood up. I wondered how come my clothes fit. I must have lost thirty pounds. I looked in the mirror on my wall. Neat-o! Wait till the kids saw me. Wait till Lynn and Kathy saw me.

"'Stephen, you look wonderful and you'll feel better soon. Your friends back home will not be able to see you. This is what's sometimes called your spiritual body and your thoughts create exactly what you want. We can see your body here, but your family and friends will usually not be able to.'

"I laid back down on the bed, sick at my stomach, and fell asleep. I woke up and remembered the woods and what I had done. I got sicker. I was going to throw up. Suddenly I was there in the woods. What had happened? I could see the tree where I did it, but the rope was gone. I wondered if it had left a mark. When I thought that, I kind of floated up to the branch and could see that there was bark missing from the tree. Nothing else was around. Everything else was gone. For sure I'd throw up, I thought. I was back on the bed, but I didn't throw up.

The lady said, "'They are going to have a memorial service for you. Would you like to attend? You can see everyone, and it may help you feel better.'

"'Yeah, but they can't see me, right? I don't want to go, I'll stay here.' I thought about it for awhile and decided I did want to go, so I told her I'd changed my mind. She explained that the service would be in a few days and she would help me get prepared. I asked her if I could go see my brother. She agreed, and we started walking out of the room and almost immediately we were with Bob.

"Bob was lying in his bed, smoking. I said, 'Hi, Bob.' He glanced over at me and I said, 'Hi, Bob,' again. 'It's me, Steve.' I said to the woman, 'He can see me, he heard me.' She said, 'Not really. He doesn't even know you're here with us yet.' He will be told very soon, but right now he doesn't know.' I felt lousy. I thought, he has enough problems to deal with and when he finds out what I did, he is going to feel terrible. He will hate my guts and think I'm stupid.

"I started to leave, but I went over and hugged him because I realized how much I loved him and wanted us to be friends. He didn't even know I was there. I started remembering all the good times we had had together, then some of the pain. We left.

"I thought that since we were close by, I would visit all of you at the house again. As I thought that, there we were. Right at the door. I tried the door knob to open it and found myself inside. The door didn't open, but I was inside. I realized I had gone through it.

"I walked through the house looking for all of you. No one was there. I felt so lonesome and homesick—worse than when I had been at camp and was ready to come home. I walked up to my room and everything was like I left it—a mess. But someone had gone through my things and they were piled up on my bed. Some of my clothes were in big plastic bags on the bed. All my private papers were stacked and moved around. Nobody was supposed to touch my private things. I bent to pick them up and put them back and couldn't move them. I couldn't lift a little piece of paper. This wasn't fair. These were my private things. Who had a right to mess with my things?

"I stormed down the steps to complain, but had forgotten that no one was there. Even the lady was nowhere to be seen. I went into every room, just looking, until you got back from wherever you were. I decided to lie down and watch TV and have a snack. I couldn't turn on the TV or open the refrigerator. I could lie down on my chair, but that was all.

"I heard the car pull up and looked out the window. You were home! You and Tom and Andrea and Debbie. I ran out to meet you. 'Mom, it's me, I'm back.' You looked right through me. You looked awful. No makeup, which you always said made you look sick anyway. Your eyes were swollen and your shoulders were slumped over and you started crying on the way in the door and ran up to my room and fell on my bed. I followed you. You grabbed a shirt of mine on the bed and tucked it under your face and cried and cried. I held you, but I still couldn't really feel you and you couldn't feel me, and that made me crazy. I really was dead. Dead. Dead was supposed to be *dead*. I could hear and see and do everything I had ever done. I was not really dead. I knew I wasn't, but everyone else thought I was. What could I do? This was awful. You were crying because you thought I was dead. I'm hugging you and trying to tell you I'm not, and you don't even know it.

"I am explaining all this to you, Mom, because it's important to understand the unbelievable pain and frustration I felt. Most of us, no matter how we die, go through this agony. Usually, when you have a body, if you do something you shouldn't, it's rough for awhile, but it gets better and you can make up for it. When you kill yourself, it's over. It's final. Anything you loved and enjoyed on earth is finished. No matter how hard you try to change it, there is nothing you can do.

"It was a very difficult time for me. Back in my new room, I asked to go see Dad and the lady said, 'Let's wait a bit. Let me take you somewhere.' We walked down the hall of this house where my room was until we came to a big building. We entered a large room, like a library.

There were tables and people sitting around reading and looking at things. I asked her if this was a library, and she suggested maybe I'd like to find something to read. I went over to a bunch of books on a shelf. I wasn't really interested in reading, but I didn't want to make her feel bad, so I looked at different books. I spotted a book on life after death. When I picked it up, it had a funny feeling to it, like little electrical things on my hand. I opened it, and as I looked at the words, I could read them and feel them go inside my head. It was the strangest feeling, like the words would become pictures in my head. I could read and see and hear at the same time. The book was about the changes when you die and how you need to prepare yourself for what it's like not to have a body. At the time, I thought it was a strange coincidence to find that specific book. Now I know it was part of what I had to learn if I were to grow. It was no coincidence at all.

"I became very aware of my body again. My stomach was lean and flat. I touched my body and it was firm and solid. I thought dead people had bodies like ghosts but mine was a real body or so it felt. The book said the world in this dimension was very much the same as when we had a physical body until we got acclimated to not having such a body. I read the whole book, but even in reading it, I was being prepared for other ways of learning. I realized I had read the entire book in just a few minutes, and I didn't even skim through it.

"I saw a library full of people, yet I later learned it was more a thought form created by a lot of other people. It wasn't imagination. It was actually created out of needs many of us had at the time. The same as my bedroom and chest and clothes—everything. After awhile, I didn't need to create these things anymore.

"You know how I hated to hurt anything or anyone. Yet I had done something so awful by killing myself, that it had hurt everyone I knew a hundred times more than if I had beaten them. Every time I got to visit someone, they were crying or talking about what I had done or carrying on terribly. Some of the things they said and thought were not very nice. I heard myself and my act analyzed, picked apart, judged, criticized in the worst terms, and talked about with fear and disgust. Almost no one understood except you and a few others. I got so I dreaded visiting anyone else.

"You tried to make me a saint for awhile out of your lack of understanding. I kept sending you messages about how I really was and not to do that. My friends' families tried to convince them I was mentally disturbed and very sick. Everyone became an expert on why I had done what I did. Some said they had always known I was disturbed. A few were compassionate, saying, 'It's a wonder one of our children hasn't done the same thing after all they went through. It's a rough time at that age,' or 'I wish I had known how to help him.' Some said it was the satanic things you believed, others said God was punishing the family for you leaving Dad. It was awful to hear some of it and not be able to say anything back.

"At school, rumors went around about what I had and hadn't done. I thought that was the most disgusting because *nobody* ever gave a damn. Teachers, to add to the gossip, said they had watched me and known there was a problem there. Some kids made up lies about things I had drawn or done or said, just to get attention. You know the truth—not one, not *one* even remembered me clearly.

"The substitute teacher that wrote a paper on me some months later was no better. When she came to you, she didn't really remember who I was. You sensed that from her incorrect description of my hair, but you were trying to cooperate. She, like so many, had an incorrect perspective of teenage suicide and the reasons so many kids kill themselves. Besides, she had ignored me too. She only jumped on the bandwagon because here was a real live (pardon the pun, Mom) suicide and a chance to write a first-hand paper. She didn't care about me or any of your feelings. [A substitute teacher who said she had taught Stephen, came to the house and asked to interview us. She said she was researching suicide and wanted to write about Stephen's death for a special paper she was doing. We shared our deepest feelings with her and let her read his notes. She sent us her paper. Her conclusion was that, among other things, my past marriages and our frequent moves had driven Stephen over the brink. It was not what I needed to hear in the midst of my grieving, truth or not.]

"My notes were another thing, Mom. I meant them when I wrote them, and they made sense. Then I realized I should have written other things, different things, things I really meant and felt more strongly about. Now that's pretty typical of suicide notes. You have read that same thing, and I have discovered that here. There is truth in the notes, but they were written in the emotion of the moment, and I was not in a clear state of mind. I'm working a lot now with kids who take their lives, and a lot of them leave horrible blaming notes to hurt someone, when they didn't feel that way most of the time. The people reading them are devastated, sometimes for the rest of their lives, and carry terrible guilt. Most of these notes are written in a very unclear, emotional, and fragile state of mind.

"The few books out now about adolescent suicide each have parts of the puzzle, but not the whole, clear picture. The picture is never whole without an understanding of life after death and what happens when the soul leaves the body. Without it, it's like going to a movie and the projector is shut off before the end. You have no idea what happens. You can guess, but you can't be sure what the ending was. It is never quite finished. There is always a slight questioning and wondering that is never fully resolved.

"As I got to know the lady who helped me over and took such loving care of me, I found out a lot about her. She was a mother. All her own children had been killed in a fire, and then her husband left her before she died. On this side, she was able to reconnect with her children and then, out of the agony she had experienced, volunteered to be trained to help young people like myself. Her role wasn't just to meet me when I died. As I began to make choices which could end in a suicide, she was assigned to me to try and help me choose differently. She did all she could, but I was beyond listening. She was there to help me once I made the final decision. I know you will think this strange, but I never called her by name nor asked her name. I didn't need to.

"One of the reasons I waited so long to help you get this book out was that you weren't ready to bring it through with all this information. We wanted you to feel very sure it would discourage, not encourage, anyone to take their life. Plus the world wasn't quite ready for it—it is now. I needed time to prepare. You needed time to grow and get out of the relationship with Tom. And you needed time to heal.

"Just to remind you, Mom, you had a dream when you were married to Tom that our book was in print. You held it up to look at it and were smiling. When you woke up, you realized that the book showed another name after your first name, not your married name with Tom. You couldn't remember what the name was, but it was different. It concerned you.

"It won't be easy for some parents to hear that their children will be in the watchcare of angels and guides. Or that these helpers will assist in preparing them either to return or, when the time is correct, to go to other realms. If families knew they can always contact their children and *do* when asleep, or meditating, and even when awake—in their other bodies—that knowledge could be very healing for them. Some parents will be watching for their children to come back as grandchildren or other children, and could become too possessive with them. I hope when we get through with all this information we're going to include that that won't be a problem. Many of the kids will not come back during the lifetime of their families, so there's no reason to watch for them. It usually takes longer to prepare suicides to return than that. A lot of parents and relatives will meet their children immediately after they themselves die. Together they will prepare to come back in family units to try to change and strengthen some of these patterns together.

"Lots of parents whose children die, want to die too. Some let themselves grieve so much they do get sick and die. Others create accidents to die because they don't care anymore, and others take their own lives. None of these are good or correct choices. True, they will see their child when they come here, but not as much and as fully, usually, as when they are still in their earth bodies and the child is in its spirit body. Here, they will miss the ones who remain alive, just like they missed the child who died. Their child is learning and growing, and a parent, dying in these ways must also learn and grow, and may be working on totally different issues. This means they may be about their business in different ways and in different realms much of the time. If the parents will keep themselves safe and well and remain in their bodies, they will visit these children in dreams, meditations, and in other realms of consciousness far more frequently than if they come here. Also, sometimes parents let themselves die prematurely or commit suicide, to be with the child that died, and that child has reincarnated, or is in other realms and they aren't able to be with them much at all. Better to live fully and help others as a gift to the dead child, and know with a certainty that you are meeting them, and can begin to remember those meetings."

"Stephen, people are going to think this is crazy. What do I say, 'Hey, do you know I talk to my son who died? He killed himself, but he's OK. He's not in hell. He says it's a lot different than we can imagine. He says, if your kid died, you can talk to him. . . .'"

Stephen laughed and answered, "Yeah, Mom, something like that. I know how hard it has been for you to learn to hear me well, then how hard it was to learn to trust what you received, and now I'm asking you to tell the world. I know how you feel. I have given you so much information, and the others you talk to here have brought you such proof that you can't deny it, can you? Trust that those who read what we share will sense the truth and let it transform their thinking and their lives.

"We need to build the bridge between the living and the world of spirit, between the fundamentalist thinking and new thought. The bridge has actually always been there, as written about in many religions and teachings, but has been obstructed from the view of most by dogma and fear.

"Mom, I think you ought to start from when I died and tell the rest of the story so I can comment on that and share the rest of the things I have to tell you."

CHAPTER TEN

Life Goes On . . . And On

I firmly believe in the continuation of life after what we call death takes place. I believe there are two sides to the phenomenon known as death; this side where we live, and the other side where we shall continue to live. Eternity does not start waith death. We are in eternity now. We merely change the form of the experience called life—and that change, I am persuaded, is for the better.

— Norman Vincent Peale

The evidential psychic guidance from George Daisley and the frequent communications with Stephen helped a great deal. I was healing more each month. The needs of the other children and a full time job kept me busy.

I still dealt with doubt and skepticism, but it lessened. I still grieved and sometimes it was overwhelming. The eighteenth of every month was an anniversary I dreaded. There was a popular song at the time, "Rainy Days and Mondays get me down . . . ," it went. Stephen had died on a rainy Monday, and I had to turn off the radio when the song came on.

Birthdays, monthly anniversaries of his death, holidays—all were the most difficult. The first Christmas without Stephen was awful. We spent even more than usual on the children, perhaps trying to fill in the void left by his death. I wanted to give him a gift. The feeling was overwhelming to give him something. But how? What can you give a child who no longer has a body? Loving words were not enough. I needed to give him something more.

I decided to do something for some family in need. The family didn't need to know it was my gift to Stephen. No one would know but me, and that would be my gift to him. It would be a special gift to him because

269

he had loved helping the families at the housing project those many years ago. That first Christmas I located a destitute family with several young children, in one of the pockets of poverty in our affluent Montgomery County in Maryland. With snow covering the ground, and temperatures way below freezing, they existed in a two room shack and boiled pots of water to keep warm. They had no heat, little food, and the door to the shack was propped up with no hinges. Their clothing and bedding barely kept them from freezing. They had lost everything previously in a fire.

I got the entire company we worked for behind the project and collected a truckload of furniture, food, clothing, and presents for them. In a moment of caring, I washed Stephen's raincoat, underwear, and treasured clothes and gave them to the family. A hundred times, I wanted them back to hold close to me. As we delivered the gifts and I saw the genuine thankfulness in their eyes, I offered this to Stephen as my Christmas gift to him. Every year, I did similar things wherever I was. No one but our family knew about this special gift to Stephen. I finally shared this secret years later when a woman whose child had died voiced the same need, to give a gift to her child.

Some nights I still cried myself to sleep. I put Stephen's photos all around the house. I joyed in the memories of him and any precious jewel of a memory that someone shared or I remembered as the months went by.

I told everyone for months that Stephen had a right to take his own life, whether we agreed it was right or not. Only much later did I realize I had missed the point. The suicidal state is a transient state. Had Stephen had counseling or help, his suicide might have easily been prevented. The depressed state before suicide or the euphoric state does not last much over ten to thirty minutes. Very often, a good counselor or friend can help turn that state around and see that the young person gets further counseling to make other wiser choices. Since most potential suicides are ambivalent anyway, help before and during the crisis can often prevent the final act. Help afterward can help stabilize the child, and he may never consider such an incorrect choice again. I had no awareness of that at the time.

The first anniversary of his death, I had a very difficult time. All the pain and agony were replayed again and again during the two days I associated with his death—the eighteenth, when he killed himself and the nineteenth, when his body was found. The pain and depression continued for weeks afterward. All kinds of doubts crept in. Perhaps I imagined that Stephen could sometimes talk to me. I couldn't prove it for sure, despite all the evidential things he shared. Maybe I was fooling myself in order to cope with his death, to keep from feeling more guilt. I analyzed and over-analyzed his death, life, and afterlife. Maybe

Daisley could read minds. Maybe all the books I read about life after death were just fictional. I could not keep my doubt from creeping in to torment me. It was like a mixer had been turned on, and left on, in my brain. My outer life looked as if it had returned to normal, my inner emotional life was far from healed.

My grieving was abruptly cut short by an event that created another kind of devastation. Even though it was a year since Stephen's death, I thought I was dealing with all the pain I could ever handle. There was more to come.

Tom was confronted by a neighbor about molesting a child. He admitted it, and began to confess other things to me. He had several times brought to our home a woman who worked for him, and had sex with her in our living room while I was at work. He had "messed around" (his words) with another child; and he was having relations with men.

I was stunned. There weren't enough words to describe what I felt. I was numb with pain and in complete shock. I kept asking him over and over, "Why?" and, "Why a child?" He said he didn't know, he was sorry. He said he loved me and pleaded for me to help him. He said that he didn't know what had gotten into him.

My mind began to reel. I thought about all the adult magazines and pornography he was always buying. He had wanted to let the children read them, but I wouldn't allow it. He had let his own children see them, and had "accidentally" left them laying around. I put them away whenever I found them. I had tried to be liberal and open minded about it all, but it was uncomfortable for me, and I didn't think it was appropriate around any children whatsoever. He was always introducing sexual topics into every conversation. He could not drive down the street without commenting on some woman with large breasts or tight pants. And now this.

My brain and heart went dead. I cried and cried. I asked for details. A hundred times I cried out, "Why?" All night I lay awake. God, what is this? First Stephen, then this. What have I done to deserve this hell? I must be the worst person on earth to have all this happen. I must be so awful that God hates me and wants to hurt me until I just give up and die. Crazy thoughts such as these raced through my mind until, by morning, I had convinced myself that I had driven Tom to do all of it. I had been grieving for Stephen for a year, and I must have neglected Tom to cause him to do all those things.

In that state of mind, I covered for him. I protected him. I took care of him like a mother. And he let me. He swore it would never happen again. I believed him. I promised myself I would be such a good wife. I would stop grieving about Stephen. I would do everything so I wouldn't drive him to do it again. After all, I reasoned, I was responsible for Stephen's death. I must be responsible for Tom's unfaithfulness and child molesting. As I write it now, I realize how utterly mixed up I was, and how in my grief and guilt about Stephen, and in my pain, I was willing to be the scapegoat for everything.

We had been talking about moving out West since our trip across country. After this trauma, the West began to be more and more appealing. The group of us who meditated and studied together weekly began to ask for inner direction about moving. Several of us began to have experiences and guidance to move to the Southwest. More and more, we felt led to consider Phoenix, Arizona. I wanted to get away, guidance or not.

I loved what I had seen of Phoenix except for how hot and dry it was. It seemed a good choice. It was so difficult to be in a house where the child you loved had filled each room with his laughter and was now no more. Every room still held precious and painful memories of him. Every time I stepped out of the front door of the house, the woods across the street stood as a sentinel to bear witness to the place where Stephen had walked to hang himself and die. Though I had loved the woods, I could never bring myself to go into them again after his death.

It was difficult to walk through a living room where my husband had brought another woman and had sex with her. The thoughts of that often pushed away those tender ones of the times Stephen had filled the room with his presence. I was hurt and raw from the pain. I wanted to get away. I just couldn't tolerate any more of the memories the house held.

Soon, a group of us decided together to make the move. About sixteen of us, including children, sold most of our possessions, our homes, and anything we could live without. We packed our cars, bikes, and animals and began a caravan trip across the country to Phoenix. It was late June, 1977. Tom's children and Andrea and Debbie rode with us in the station wagon. His children would fly to their home after summer was over.

Just before we left, I went up to Stephen's now vacant room and said good-bye. Soon no one would ever remember that a loving teenage boy lived and dreamed and suffered there. I took one last look from the front door of the house across the field to the woods where Stephen had breathed his last breath. I closed the door and walked to the car. I hoped that Stephen could find me in Arizona.

After a long and strenuous journey, we drove into Phoenix the evening of the Fourth of July. Heat lightning was flashing in the sky, horizon to horizon. Fireworks of all colors were going off when we caught our first glimpse of the skyline as we drove into the city. Debbie said, "God is welcoming us to Arizona." Indeed, it seemed as if He were.

We looked for land in the weeks to come where we could all live together. The money from the sale of our house would be the down payment, and we would all begin our new lives. It didn't work out that way. Several of the couples were having difficulty. One man emotionally mistreated his girlfriend's child, which made me want to strangle him. He seemed to take out all his irritations and aggressions on this young boy. This was particularly disturbing to me because, since Stephen's death, I couldn't bear to see anyone hurting a child— emotionally or physically. Another couple we cared deeply about were having great difficulty because of the heat and sporadic employment. The Arizona heat combined with job hunting was exhausting. Only the third couple and their child were adjusting fairly well.

We were all living in separate apartments until we found a place to buy. Tom and I had rented a two-bedroom unfurnished townhouse. We had one bedroom, and the six children slept in the other bedroom and in the living room, on beds and on the floor.

My son Bob was getting his life together and had married a friend with whom we had gone through ministerial school. They had decided to move to Arizona with us. They had come a few weeks earlier, and now they too moved in with us. Four adults, six children, a dog and cat resided together in these close quarters in the sweltering Arizona summer. Without air conditioning, we would have melted together in a lump.

As crowded as it was, it was nonetheless refreshingly new and different. It was just fun enough to keep our minds occupied. Within a few months, all the couples but one besides ourselves moved back to Maryland.

We bought a house with a pool where we planned to live temporarily until we decided in what part of town we wanted to reside, what we wanted to do, and where we would be working. In Maryland we had a church and center plus our jobs. Here we would have to begin again to rebuild all of those things. There was no time to spend trying to contact Stephen. Besides, I didn't want to do anything to make Tom do what he had done before, so I tried to keep my loneliness and my grief about Stephen to myself. Sometimes I just could not. I tried to cry only when no one was around.

One Sunday afternoon in August, I opened the newspaper to look at the ads. As I was turning the pages, I saw an ad that was glowing with light. It literally looked as if a spotlight framed the inch square ad. I turned around to see if there was a light shining from behind me on the paper, but there wasn't. My heart began to beat rapidly. Something strange was going on.

The ad was for a secretary to the director of a holistic medical clinic. I had worked as a secretary before, but I was a minister now. I had been doing counseling and lecturing, and I had also developed some reputation on the East Coast where we lived, as a psychic. I could do life readings—"tune in" to someone and tell them things that I "saw" and knew intuitively. This was the work I was to do. Being a secretary again was not an option.

Nevertheless, there was something paranormal about the light illuminating just that one ad. I got quiet and began to meditate. Immediately my guides began to speak to me. I didn't even know what holistic meant, and they explained that it had to do with healing the body, mind, and spirit. They told me that this clinic believed in the Edgar Cayce work and patients came there from around the city, and from afar for treatment according to the medical information Edgar Cayce had given psychically in his sleep state. I was to go to work for the director, they said. They even told me his name. I hadn't previously known there was such a clinic, nor had I ever heard of the doctor.

My guides instructed me to call for an appointment. They said that I would be called back before 2:00 p.m. and would go in for an interview and be hired. They instructed me not to tell my employer-to-be about my psychic abilities. They would tell me when it was the correct time to tell him. Until then I was to do whatever secretarial work he needed and to help in whatever way I could. They said this was a part of the next step toward what I had incarnated to do. They also told me this was part of what Edgar Cayce meant when he said, "I have a work for you to do in my work," but that this was only one further step. "His" work was far more than just through this organization, but that would come later, they assured me.

If I called the number and this were true, I would never doubt their guidance again. This was my usual vow, which I always broke. However, this guidance was so far-fetched, that I fully expected the voice at the other end of the phone to say, "Are you kidding? Dr. who?" Instead, the voice confirmed what I had been given and said someone would call me back to schedule an interview. The phone rang just before 2:00 p.m. The manager was on the other end. He set up the initial interview, and I went to meet with the doctor.

As instructed, I did not tell him what I did, just of my genuine interest in Edgar Cayce and his work. Nor did I tell him that soon after the session with Reverend Daisley, Edgar Cayce had begun to speak to me directly a number of times, sharing many things with me, and that he continued to do so. The doctor and I talked for an hour. He hired me on the spot, and I began work with him the next week.

How about that! My guides had been right! I began my secretarial job. Transcribing dictation from the Dictaphone, filing, and being Girl

Friday was boring after the work I had been doing the last years, although I liked the organization and the people. I kept asking my guides if I couldn't tell the doctor what I *really* did—give readings to people, in an altered state, sharing what was in their auras, helping in this way, instead of typing letters. They told me to be patient, that everything would soon unfold.

We sold our house and bought another one, also with a pool, in Tempe, to be closer to the university. Andrea, who would graduate from high school in a couple of years, could attend close to home. We lived there four years, enduring the long daily drive because of the eventual benefits to the children and their education. None of them, however, attended that university when they graduated from high school.

Within a few months at the clinic, we began to plan a seventeen-day holistic medical program. About fifteen patients were to participate in each of the intensive residential healing programs. It was suggested that one component of the program should be for each patient to receive a psychic reading something like the readings Edgar Cayce did, even though the headquarters in Virginia Beach didn't recommend or approve of psychics. The doctors believed it could be very helpful to people. One woman on staff could see auras and they thought perhaps they could work that in too.

Here was my chance at last, to tell them I could see auras too and knew what the colors meant. I could tell them I saw other things as well. My guides cautioned me to wait until the time was right. I finally got the okay, met with the doctor, and told him about myself at last. By then, he trusted me; we were friends and he never questioned that I was telling the truth. Little by little, he worked me into the program, and I began to give life readings for every patient who came through that program and also for those in another seven day program that was developed.

The readings were tape recorded. I would alter my consciousness; I called it "clicking down." I didn't quite know *how* I could do what I did, except that since my experiences in 1972, I could see things I couldn't see before. I worked with the other doctors also, and even had a series of Kirlian photographs taken of my hands when I was in those altered states. The photographs showed remarkable changes from one state to another. Months later, I learned to work in an EEG delta wave or sleep state—a state very similar to the working state of Edgar Cayce. In those states, I could access information of which I usually wasn't consciously aware. A friend had worked with me for months helping me learn to work in this deeper state of consciousness. It was exciting though sometimes unpredictable. It was surprising to me that I was able to do this. I felt I was a most unlikely candidate to work in this way.

My work at the clinic was to extend over four years. These years were good for me for the greater part. We traveled overseas, and we met hundreds of fine people, many of whom still remain friends. People who had readings referred their friends. I did counseling and readings five days a week. I also worked in the special programs on weekends when those were scheduled. I taught meditation, visualization, and psychic development to the groups and classes.

In the work I did, I found comfort and a lessening of my grief as we saw patients change their thinking and their lives and get well. Out of my pain and healing, I saw how I could help others. I found this most appropriate and true verse:

> *God does not comfort us only to make us more comfortable. He*
> *comforts us so that we may also become comforters.*
> – Helen Steiner Rice

On the side, I was studying Gestalt counseling with a fine trainer who also counseled with patients in the programs. We became friends; he helped me, perhaps more than anyone up to that time, to get to know myself, to take back my power, and to become more whole. I had been carrying a lot of excess emotional baggage for a lot of years.

The counseling and training with this instructor was timely because another crisis occurred. Tom had also been hired by the clinic as Director of Patient Care. He had gone to Virginia Beach with the doctors in the summer of 1979. He came back acting very differently. He said he had met a woman who was willing to have an open marriage. He said he was in love with her. I was broken-hearted, but Tom wasn't finished. With that revelation, he also let forth others, like a dam bursting. Not only did he and the other woman want to get married, he wanted an immediate divorce. He bragged about how he had slept with someone else we both knew, how he was having an affair with one of the therapists at the clinic, and how he had been having sex with a woman who worked with the patients in the programs.

I collapsed from his revelations. I had not even suspected anything since there was never a let up in his constant affirmations of his undying love or his desire for me. The revelations didn't end there—he had also had an affair with a male attorney friend while visiting in Washington, D.C., and he had been visiting gay baths and bars on his lunch hours and in the evenings. It was hard to believe he could squeeze all that in; but, he convinced me it was so, and later, I found it was all true—and more.

The pain and despair I felt were overwhelming. I counseled with my Gestalt instructor who helped me get stronger and stop putting up with what was going on. After much soul-searching and prayer, I decided I would give Tom his freedom. I was tired of wondering who he was having sex with every time he went out the door.

I could see no hope that the marriage could continue. What he had done hurt, really badly, and I realized I loved myself too much to put up with it any longer. We had gone for counseling, yet his behavior continued. After some extensive counseling on my own, I finally realized that the problem might be him and the way *he* was, instead of me and my grief over Stephen. Maybe I would never be enough for him. I needed to begin being enough for myself.

On the night when I finally decided I would give him a divorce, I put on my sweats and sneakers and went to jog around the block before bed to pray and to release him and to get on with my life. I was forty-one and healthy and strong. I could survive. As I was running, I prayed and asked God to help me. I told God I was ready to release Tom to do whatever he needed, and I asked God, please, to give me a sign that it was right. I expected maybe an inner knowing, some feeling of confirmation.

As I continued my thoughts and jogging, and was slowing down my pace in the final blocks toward home, a man jumped from the shadows of the alley. He grabbed me from behind and held my throat with one hand and my mouth with the other. Without thinking, some powerful force of energy welled up in me enabling me to break free. I screamed at the top of my lungs. I was already tired from jogging, but ran faster than I had ever run in my life. I never turned around or looked back. I screamed all the way home, quickly grabbed the door handle, and stumbled inside.

Tom called the police. I was shaking all over. I could hardly speak. The police were there in minutes. They put me in the squad car, Tom by my side, and we cruised the neighborhood looking for the man. Someone had been raping women in Tempe in recent weeks, they told us. We had not heard or read about it. I certainly would not have been out at night running alone if I had known that. The rapist was beginning to cut his victims with a knife when he was finished with them. They told me I had been very lucky.

We didn't find the attacker so we went home. The police took my statement and told me how well I was handling everything. I wasn't at all. I was shaking all over and was in shock, and I told them so. They assured me that many women who had been attacked became so hysterical they were unable even to answer any questions. I had been lucky, *very* lucky, they kept telling me.

My warped thinking saw this attack as an answer to my prayer for a sign and that God wanted me to stay with Tom and work things out. The fact that I came to that conclusion is a reflection of my muddled and heartbroken thinking at the time. Years later, I realized that if it were a sign at all, it could better have been interpreted as showing I could handle anything, and by breaking free, would not be hurt. Whichever, deep inside, I wanted to stay. I wanted our marriage to work.

I called the woman for whom Tom wanted to leave me. She had no idea of the things Tom had done, and she assured me she did not want an open marriage. She immediately broke up with him. Tom asked me for forgiveness, promised undying faithfulness, and we resumed where we left off. The doctor and his wife, the people for whom we were working, had been helpful during Tom's affair. The doctor's wife, also a physician, counseled me to save the marriage at any cost. It seemed saved.

Any opportunity for communication with Stephen was lost in the turmoil of trying to keep the marriage together. For months, I never tried to talk with him, although I still missed him and grieved for him.

Tom and I were still working together. At the end of a particularly busy seventeen-day in-patient program, we had taken the patients to their farewell dinner at a restaurant. We would bid them good-bye the next morning. Tom and I came home and sat down in the living room to read the paper. Debbie was doing homework on the floor near us. It was ten days until Christmas, 1979, and the house was already decorated with some of our holiday treasures.

Across the room, on a table, there was a ceramic Christmas tree with a music box that played "Silent Night." A neighbor in Maryland had made it for me twelve years before. Suddenly it began to play on its own. It had never once done that in all the years before. It played and played and played, as if someone had wound it to its limit. We all looked up and listened, somewhat surprised. The energy in the room became very electrically charged. I could feel a presence—Stephen's presence.

Before I could speak, Debbie said, "Mom, Stephen's here." Immediately the music box stopped. Stephen? Stephen! I too knew he was there. I could feel him, even Debbie could feel his presence. Tom went back to reading. I said, "I can hear him speak. Can you hear him?" They couldn't, but Debbie asked me to see what Stephen had to say. I got a steno pad and pen and began to listen. His message, as usual, overshadowed my own thoughts.

Stephen said he and I needed to start writing a book together. It was to be the first of many we would work on together. He said he was working in that dimension with Edgar Cayce and Arthur Ford and others; and, they wanted me to start sitting and listening to them soon. Arthur Ford? The one Ruth Montgomery spoke with? I knew Edgar Cayce spoke to me upon occasion, but why would the others want to speak to me?

As his communication drew to a close, Stephen added, "Mom, I know how hard it is for you to believe that we can talk to you like we do and to know you're not fooling yourself. I know how you don't want to mislead anyone, and I know what a doubter you are. So here's something you can *prove*. At the medical program today, you were listening to the girl play the piano and wishing you had a piano to learn to play. We're going to work on some people to impress them to give you a piano; you'll get it just before Christmas. That should prove to you we're real and you're not crazy."

I read Stephen's words to Tom and Debbie. Debbie squealed, "Yea! We're going to get a piano. If Stephen says we are, we are."

I said, "If we get a piano, I will *never* doubt again." Famous last words, as usual.

The experience with Stephen had been so overpowering, yet I didn't want to get my hopes up watching for a sign. A piano? We had wanted a piano for a long time; but, they were expensive and with our low salaries at the clinic, having to use our savings to survive, it was way down on our list of priorities. I thanked Stephen for talking to me, no matter what happened and I went to bed.

The next morning, Tom and I dressed and went to say good-bye to the patients as they were preparing to leave and return to their homes. After being together for seventeen days, it was always sad to see the program end. One of the couples, a businessman who had sold his company back East, and his wife, who were retiring to Arizona, handed me an envelope. Inside was a note telling me they wanted me to get a piano and were impressed to give me enough money to buy one. Enough $100 bills were folded in the envelope to purchase a piano.

It was difficult to talk, to even thank them. I protested, saying that I couldn't accept the money. They would not hear of me not accepting it. So I told them the story about Stephen and what had happened the night before. They made me promise never to reveal who they were, that it would remain our secret—theirs, mine and Stephen's. We went out the next day and bought a marvelous piano. It was delivered just before Christmas.

Still fearful of driving Tom into some other woman's arms, I was reluctant to communicate with Stephen too much. I still missed him greatly. Time just did not heal the longing to see him and the terrible void in my life. Once, in the early months of 1980, I was lying on my bed when a movement at the ceiling caught my eye. A Jonathan Livingston Seagull sculpture suspended from the ceiling by nylon string was spinning slowly around. How unusual! It had never done that before. It was too heavy for a breeze to stir it, but it was moving as if a wind were taking it round and round. As I watched, that electrical feeling came again into the room. I could feel Stephen's presence. Perhaps he had caused it to move.

Out loud I asked, "Stephen is that you?" No answer, so I added, "If it's you moving the seagull, make it turn right three times." That would tell me for sure. Since it was turning to the left, he would have to change its direction.

The seagull stopped and turned to the right exactly three times and then began to slowly spin the other way. Wait a minute, this can't be. The air conditioning or heat must be on, causing this to happen, I thought. I put my hand up by the vent, but no air was coming out of it. I went to the window to see if it was open or if a draft was coming in. I stood on the bed to see if there was an air current at the ceiling that I couldn't feel on the floor. Nothing. Maybe Stephen was moving it after all.

"OK, Stephen, if it's really you, make the seagull turn to the left once, to the right once, and then to the left again." I watched. The seagull stopped, turned left, then right, then left. I tried to think of some rational explanation for this. Each time I asked Stephen to move it one way then another, it moved exactly as I asked. I gave even more complicated instructions and they were precisely followed. Well, I thought, if it is him, maybe I can ask questions and he can move it in answer. We'll see. Three times to the right would be yes, once to the left no. For a half hour I asked him every question I could think of. Each question was answered by the movement I had requested, and the answers made sense.

When I was communicating with Stephen later, he said that he was getting stronger and able to do things such as making the ceramic Christmas tree come on and the seagull move. It was what he could do to help confirm to me it was him and to strengthen my faith, in preparation of the work we were going to do together. He said he wished my doubt wasn't so strong. Then he wouldn't need to do all this. He complained that it took a lot of work and effort. Then he laughed. His laughter was always uplifting, and not long after I found this poem:

> *Though I am dead, grieve not for me with tears,*
> *Think not of death with sorrowing and fears,*
> *I am so near that every tear you shed*
> *Touches and tortures me, though you think me*
> *dead . . .*
> *But when you laugh and sing in glad delight,*
> *My soul is lifted upward to the light;*

Laugh and be glad for all that Life is giving,
And I though dead will share your joy in
LIVING.

– Author unknown

On March 3, 1980 at 10:00 a.m., I was scheduled to conduct a funeral service. The wife of an employee at the clinic had died of cancer. She was only in her thirties and had left behind a grieving husband. The night before, I was having a very difficult time pulling the service together. Her parents and family were very orthodox in their beliefs, yet many of her friends and associates believed in metaphysical teachings and life after death. How could I do a service that would be helpful and uplifting for both groups and not offend anyone? I had no idea.

I was sitting on the floor in the living room. The rest of the family were in other rooms, involved in their own activities. My notebook was blank. I could not pull things together. What was I going to do? The service was tomorrow. "God, if you want me to do this, you're going to have to help me. I don't know what you would have me do," I closed my eyes and prayed. Then I got quiet to listen. When I opened my eyes, I found myself reaching toward the bottom shelf of a bookcase in the corner. The books were crammed together so tightly that I had to pry out the book that I was reaching for. As I looked at the title I thought, "How can I possibly use anything out of this book?" It was *Psychic Exploration* by the astronaut, Edgar Mitchell. Having read some of it, I felt it was simply not appropriate for use in a funeral, if I remembered correctly.

What the heck. I opened it to see if there was something I could use. I was sitting cross-legged on the floor, and when I opened it, a gold ring fell into my lap and against my leg. I had a funny reaction, my heart beat accelerated and goose bumps chilled all over my body. I picked up the ring and looked at it—it was a plain gold band, like a wedding ring. It looked brand new.

"Ah ha! Someone in spirit is trying to give me a message of something to use out of this book after all. I'll turn through the book until I find the impression the ring made on the page and see what it says," I thought to myself. The book was about two inches thick, and since it was crammed as it was in the bookcase and the ring was more than one eighth of an inch wide, there would be a strong impression on the pages where it had been. The ring seemed to have fallen out of the middle, I thought. So I began to look, page by page. I couldn't find an imprint of the ring on any page. I took the book under a brighter light and, again, turned page by page, from beginning to end and back again. No imprint. This was very strange.

I called for the children to come in and asked if they had put the ring in the book or had ever seen it. No one had. We discussed the fact that those books had been in that shelf, untouched, for almost two years. We had not loaned any out. In fact, they may not have been more than dusted since we moved into the house. I had read the book while in Washington, D.C. This was puzzling.

I climbed up on the couch, holding the ring, and lay there wondering. I prayed and asked for guidance about where the ring came from and what it meant. Without being aware of it, I fell asleep. When I awoke fifteen minutes later, I had no answers, but the entire funeral service came to me. I knew what to say, what Scriptures to use and how to conduct the entire service. No guidance was given about the ring. I put it on my right finger without thinking, and it *fit perfectly.* That *was* a strange coincidence!

At the grave site the next morning, standing under the awning placed over the casket and flowers, with a large crowd in attendance, I shared what had come to me, not mentioning the ring. As I closed the service, I saw a light at the far end of the casket, like white, shimmering heat waves in the form of a body. I knew it was the spirit essence of the woman who died. She was there. I didn't tell anyone what I had seen. Then the Gestalt therapist who was my trainer came over and said to me, "Did you see that shimmering light at the end of the casket? She's here!" I told him I had seen it and that I too sensed her presence. We were interrupted by the family and friends who came to share their appreciation for a "most wonderful and inspiring service," as I heard again and again. I thanked God; I knew I hadn't done this myself.

I shared the story of the ring with this friend and with the two doctors with whom I worked. The woman doctor said she felt it was given to me to share with the woman's husband, that the gold band symbolized the love between them which was without end, that despite her death, the bond between them would continue in love. That sounded nice, and I sought out the man and told him the story before he left. He seemed comforted by it. I sensed that it wasn't the whole story of the ring.

For days the ring haunted me. I wore it constantly and touched it repeatedly. It made me feel peaceful and comforted. It was probably my imagination. One evening, I sat to pray and talk to my guides. The three who had worked with me for so many previous years had been "promoted" to other levels. Now there were four others who were assigned to me. I asked them about the ring. They told me that the ring was from the earth plane, but that Stephen, with their help, had placed it in the book. It was an "apport," a phenomenon which they reminded me I had read about. There are many such reports of objects that have materialized seemingly out of nowhere. I was told to wear the ring, and each time I had questions or doubt, I was to touch it and ask, and I would know the answer and any doubts would be eased. It had no other magical or special powers and was of no value to anyone but me, but my guides could work with me through it. It would be a focal point of attunement, a gift from them and from Stephen, to help me keep up my ever-faltering faith.

How could this be? I tested it out. I would read something, wondering if it were true. I would ask "yes" or "no" and touch my ring and "know." Each time I needed some clarity, I just touched the ring, prayed, and an inner knowing came. Other people tried it when I told them about it, but it simply didn't work for them.

Now, the story should end here about the ring, but what happened next was equally amazing. A well-known Kirlian researcher came to visit us from England. Kirlian is a special type of photography that photographs the energy patterns coming from plants, objects, and people. These patterns are thought to be related to the aura. A finger tip or a leaf or other object, is placed on a special photographic plate which is "exposed" by an extremely high voltage rather than by light. There is much speculation about the interpretation of these photographs, but the general consensus is that there are subtle energy fields around every object which can be measured or photographed. Humans, then, are not just a physical body, but have an etheric body emanating energy of all kinds.

This Kirlian equipment did only black and white photos on glass plates, but you could see the image as it was being done. Other more sophisticated equipment now produces colored prints. We invited a group over to do some experimenting, and the researcher photographed many of us. You could see patterns, each one different, around our fingertips. He also photographed some keys and inanimate objects. The energy patterns around these were flat and very different from living things.

A thought came to me to ask him to photograph my special gold ring. He knew nothing about the strange way it had come to me. He laid it on the plate, and when he photographed it, a white bead of light appeared about three-fourths of an inch from one side. He did it again and the light remained. He apologized that the plate wasn't clean and lifted the plate and wiped it off and began again. The little bead of light remained regardless of the way he turned the ring.

Another Kirlian researcher who was there offered to help, and he too removed and cleaned the plate. The light remained. It was suggested that I touch the ring and photograph my finger and the ring. The plate was readied. As I touched it, a heart shape of energy formed around the whole ring and flowed off the plate. Everyone saw it. The researchers couldn't believe what they saw. They completely disassembled the equipment and set it up again, then photographed me touching the ring again. Another heart, with little beads of energy surrounded the whole ring. It happened a third time. I still have the black and white negatives from this experiment. Stephen was delighted to remind me the next time we talked of the "evidence" I could not deny. I always wear the ring as my link to his dimension and his ongoing love and help.

In 1978, I had gone to Egypt for the first time. The doctors were leading a tour to visit the great healing centers of Europe and the Middle East. It was exciting to visit England, France, Germany, Switzerland, Egypt, Jordan, Greece, and Israel. In Egypt, I bought, as a souvenir, a crudely made musical instrument resembling a guitar or mandolin. It had a fat wooden base and horsehair strings. The Egyptian who made and sold them played them like a fine violin and the sound was lovely. When any of us tried to play it, we could bring out only a piercing squeak. We tried everything, occasionally getting a note, but mostly heard that shrill squeak. All of us who bought one laughed because none of us could make these instruments play.

We returned home after three weeks. I propped the instrument against the fireplace in the family room as a decoration, since it could never be used as a musical instrument by any of us. Bob, a very good guitarist, was the only one who could make it sound somewhat like it had in Egypt. So there it rested with its little bow next to it, against the fireplace.

One night, while we were all sitting in the room watching TV, we heard the instrument squeak and begin to play very loudly. We looked to see who was playing it, but it was still propped there where it always was. The sound kept on and on. We went to the fireplace to see where the sound was coming from—surely not from the instrument. To our amazement, we could clearly hear the sound coming from the strings. We picked it up and the sound stopped. We laid it down and it continued. This went on for over ten minutes, all of us searching the room, trying to find some explanation. We couldn't imagine what was happening. The energy in the room changed, and you could feel a presence. The hair on my body raised, my heart beat accelerated, and goose bumps came over my body. Some of Tom's children were living with us now, and one of them said, "It's just Stephen letting us know he's here." As soon as he said that, it stopped playing.

It got to be a family joke. I would be at the clinic working and get a call from one of the children, saying, "It's happening! The instrument is playing again. Stephen's here." They would hold the phone next to the instrument to let me hear it. We even tried moving it to other places. Still, it continued to play fairly frequently. The kids accepted it after awhile as a normal activity of their friend and brother, Stephen, letting them know he was there with them. Occasionally they would get a little spooked, and then any sounds would scare them. The Egyptian instrument continued to play its little melody for more than a year. It ended abruptly when our big, white Samoyed dog, Angel, chewed it up one night as we slept.

Tom and I seemed to be doing fairly well. The work at the clinic was long and hard and any spare time was spent with the children. The television was still on most of the time, but I utilized that time to take care of the house or go back into my bedroom to meditate or work.

I was proud of how the girls were doing. Andrea was a star basketball player for her high school team, and she was becoming a really fine young woman. Debbie was growing up, maturing, and developing quite a few psychic abilities of her own. She could sometimes see auras and had a real intuitive sense about people. I shared many of Stephen's communications with her.

There remained an underlying lack of trust with Tom, but I began to think it was just in my mind. He pledged his devotion daily, and spent all his spare time with me or the children. At least we were together and, I rationalized, doing a good work.

He went to empty the trash outside at the dumpster late one morning and seemed to be gone a long time. Something felt wrong. I went to see what had happened. As I opened the gate into the alley, I saw him with his hands down a young girl's pants. I screamed, "What are you doing?" He stopped, and I ran back in the house, sick at my stomach.

He came in red-faced and upset. "What's the matter?" he snapped. I shouted, "What's the *matter*? What do you mean, what's the matter?" He tried to convince me I was imagining what I'd seen. I was hysterical. I screamed and cried. I told him I was going to leave him, I told him he would go to jail. He apologized over and over and begged me to forgive him. After days of tears and talking, I did just that. I forgave him.

Some months earlier, Stephen and my guides had lovingly tried to warn me that Tom wasn't as I thought, that he was doing things that were harmful and that could cause great trouble. I saw pictures of things in my mind that shocked me. These were the kind of visions I had that so frequently proved to be evidential. I went to Tom and told him of them. He denied that there was any truth to my impressions. He told me I was getting crazy guidance, that none of it was true. He convinced me that I was jealous, insecure, and imagining things. He was so convincing. I wanted to believe him, against my own guidance.

All my communications from Stephen and my guides were in boxes. There were hundreds of typed sheets, notebooks, and papers in which I kept the journals of my experiences. I was devastated to think that I was getting wrong guidance. Not only wrong, but really specific, negative guidance about Tom that wasn't true. What was wrong with me? Maybe the devil did have me. In a moment of despair, I emptied the boxes in a metal trash can, lit a match and slowly burned them all to ashes. I cried and cried. I told Tom what I had done. He said I shouldn't have burned it all, that some of my guidance was very good, but I had just been wrong about him.

For months, I didn't listen or get guidance for myself. I didn't talk with Stephen. I gave readings for others, wondering if I was misleading them too. Once, when I finally was so strongly impressed by the presence of Stephen and my guides, I sat at my typewriter and began again to listen. This would have to go in new directions as all my old communications were destroyed. They told me I had made an error in destroying the guidance, that several books I was to write were destroyed. They did not again mention Tom. When I asked them why they misled me about him, they only said, "We're sorry for your pain. Let's begin." Little by little, I began to trust them again because so much evidential information was coming through. Stephen shared many helpful things with me in the following months, but nothing was mentioned about Tom.

My guides had been right about Tom after all. They had not misled me. In fact, they had erred on the side of giving very little information. I had been unable and unwilling to face the truth. When I caught Tom with the young girl, I knew the pictures I had seen in my mind about him had been true. I was only deceiving myself. I forgave him but my feelings for him died.

My days at the clinic were soon to come to an end. Situations at the clinic were becoming very difficult for many of us. It was a good work, built on the readings of great psychic, but there were problems that had not been, and would not be, resolved. Many of the staff and all but two of the board members resigned at the same time for the same reasons. I resigned along with the rest.

Tom and two other partners had been running the pharmacy at the clinic and were asked to leave. We started a new organization. While Tom and several of us were working day and night to build our new organization, an amazing thing happened. I felt total and pure unconditional love for Tom. A Christ-like love welled up in my heart for him. I told him so. I also knew we would not stay married; I did not tell him that. My guides would not comment one way or another. There was some work Tom and I still needed to pursue.

Stephen encouraged me about the work and directed me often as to what to do. I still cried sometimes when I looked at his picture or thought of him, but I could function. I was not whole as I had once been, but I had become a survivor.

During that time, I renewed a friendship with a wonderful woman for whom I had done a reading at the clinic. Helen Mae would become a dear friend, one of the truly good friends I was to have in my lifetime. We shared many beautiful times together. She helped our work in every way—physically, emotionally, financially. Her father had died years before, and he would speak to her from the other side frequently, as did her mother. She helped me to raise my thinking and my consciousness considerably.

Often in my readings it was mentioned that people had guardian angels, or that angels were in the room. For Helen, a far stronger message came through. Helen was told she came in to do an "angel ministry." At first, we had no idea what that meant. As time went by, the angels themselves began to speak to her, and she brought through such uplifting messages from that realm that all of us were ministered to by them. There was no doubt that the guidance was from this higher source. As a successful businesswoman, she was taking a risk, going out on a limb so to speak, to talk about what was happening to her. She had the courage to do it, and out of that courage came a book, *The Angels Speak,* which has been read by thousands. This work with the angels added another rich dimension and awareness to so many of our lives.

Helen and I shared the things we received, and we helped each other with our doubts and fears. Other than never telling her about Tom's indiscretions, there was nothing I didn't share with her. She cared about Tom, and such knowledge would have destroyed their relationship. Besides, I didn't tell anyone those dark secrets except my counselor.

Stephen and my guides began to prepare me for major changes coming in my life. Frankly, there had been enough changes in my life for one incarnation, I told them. But they assured me that there were more to come.

CHAPTER ELEVEN

Matchmaking From the Spirit Plane

Let's praise him with shouts of joy and effervescent faith, for the Lord does not delight in our solemnity.

          — Found among Stephen's writings

When the one man loves the one woman and the one woman loves the one man, the very angels leave HEAVEN and come and sit in that house and sing for joy.

          — Found on a plaque, author unknown

My personal strength began to grow. Not only was I getting stronger, but I was also less tolerant of people who tried to take advantage of me. The term "taking your power back" was being used and tools to do this were being taught. I was learning to do just that.

Quite unexpectedly, in January of 1982, a good friend asked me for a personal favor. Would I do a reading for a friend of his and the friend's wife? His friend was one of the directors of A.R.E., the Edgar Cayce association in Virginia Beach. He had written a number of popular books about Cayce, one of which I was familiar with, *Meditation and the Mind of Man*, that I used as a textbook in the meditation classes I taught. I thought it was a good book, but I had some misgivings about the organization he worked for, for a couple of reasons. First, they were not supportive of psychics, even though their whole work was based on the readings of a psychic. Second, their president, Hugh Lynn Cayce, had wanted the doctors I worked for at the clinic that bore their name, to fire me, simply because I worked psychically in much the same way Cayce did. The doctors assured him there were no complaints about my work and refused to comply with the request. I continued giving readings at the clinic for the next four years. As a result of all these things, there was little warmth in my heart for the A.R.E., although I loved the Cayce readings. However, my friend talked me into giving both the man and his wife readings. Because of our friendship and his love and admiration for this man, I reluctantly agreed, but I was not looking forward to it at all.

I had seen the man from A.R.E. only at a distance when I was working at the clinic. He always gave the keynote address at the annual medical symposium the clinic sponsored. A year or two earlier, the doctor I worked for turned to me once after this man had spoken and said, "He's the best speaker in A.R.E.," then added, "Maybe in the country." I said, "He *is* good, but he seems rather cold." "Cold?" he responded in surprise. "He's not cold at all. He's very warm and caring. Let me introduce you." Somehow he never did, so we never met.

Now I had to give this man a reading. I didn't want to do it, and I was nervous. I didn't want to be a specimen he was examining and comparing to Edgar Cayce. He couldn't get me fired since I was now the head of my own organization, but he could add to the difficulties between our respective groups, and I was wary of all of that. I wished I hadn't promised I would do the reading. My only prayer was that the man would change his mind when he arrived.

He came to Phoenix in late January. He still wanted the reading. My friend told me that the man's wife wasn't very interested in the psychic field and was very skeptical about psychics, but she had agreed to have a reading also. Oh great, I thought, she didn't believe in all this and he was part of an organization that didn't refer people to psychics. I couldn't figure a way to get out of doing the readings and didn't want to disappoint my friend. He loved the work I did and was always bringing people around for readings, probably whether they wanted them or not.

My friend arrived at the center with the man and his wife. I went to shake hands with the man and, instead, he gave me a hug. I was surprised. I remembered how aloof he had seemed all those years. His wife was very cold and her eyes were not friendly.

I worked with his wife first. I could see from her aura that she had some healing ability and also that she carried a great deal of anger. After the reading, I asked her how she reconciled her healing work and her anger. She denied the anger. Oh well, that wasn't unusual. She said that she was a skeptic but added that the reading was interesting. That didn't bother me. What people did with the guidance was their choice.

I always prayed and asked God to speak through me to bring help and hope to people seeking spiritual guidance; the rest was up to the person.

Of the hundreds of readings I had then given, the feedback had almost always been positive. I knew it was not me but God through me. So, in that altered state, I just let go and let God. My responsibility was to stay spiritually grounded and clear.

Next was the one I most dreaded working with—the man, Dr. Herbert Bruce Puryear, psychologist, Director of Research and President of Atlantic University at A.R.E. Since I hadn't read most of his books, I realized I knew very little about him or his work. Okay, I thought, let's get it over with. I was trying not to be nervous just because of who he worked for. I bet *I* loved the Cayce work as much as he did, and probably wasn't as dogmatic about it as some A.R.E. people seemed. *Who* he was didn't intimidate me; I had worked with many well-known people. But who he worked for *did*. Edgar Cayce himself kept reminding me from the other side to remember our work and his own mission, not what the organization did. So here I was, giving a life reading to someone who might later try to discredit me.

I turned on the two tape recorders and began the reading. He had a most unusual aura with a double rainbow of light around him. The pink in his aura was all filmed over, and across his heart was a block of energy. I told him this. He said that over a half a dozen other psychics he had worked with had told him the same thing. He knew there was a blockage in his heart center and he was working on clearing it, he assured me. Well, he wasn't into denial like his wife, I thought. That was good. I went into a deeper altered state and then the reading was over.

At that time, I could not hear my voice when I was in the altered state, so afterward clients or patients would comment on what came through. On rare occasions, I would play the second tape after they were gone and listen to what they had been given. The information that came through always amazed me. For sure, I could claim no credit. It was obviously from a Source beyond myself.

Dr. Puryear and I talked about a few of the things in the reading. He gave me some feedback and was warm and friendly. Herb, as he asked me to call him, said he had been researching psychics since the '50s, and we talked about his interest in the metaphysical field.

In the last thirty years, he had received dozens of readings from psychics all over the world, he told me. He was very interesting to talk with about his research and experiences. He seemed to be a nice person after all, and not as I had judged him. He wasn't cold as I had thought, just somewhat reserved.

I wondered how he and his wife got along, since they were so totally different; he had none of the anger she manifested. I wondered what had caused him to close down emotionally with such a blocked heart center. Oh well, it was none of my business, and we didn't talk about it.

Two months later, in March, Herb sent me a series of questions in a letter, and asked me to do another reading for him at a distance. It was the first time I had heard from him. He wrote that his mother had died during that time. He called a few days after the letter to see when the reading could be done. My schedule was full for months in advance, but I promised him I would work it in just as soon as I could. A few weeks later, he called about a client of his who was having some serious emotional problems and asked if I could tune in briefly and share with him whatever I received. I did. He thanked me.

He called several other times. Each time, it was about someone with whom he was counseling. He gave me their names, asking me to share whatever I received. When I called him with the information, he thanked me, with little comment.

Many months afterward, he told me that at the same time he called me, he also called several other sensitives, asking the same questions about his clients. He used all the information he received as perspectives with his own counseling; but, he said, the information he received from my Source was always the most consistent, helpful, and verifiably correct.

I was finally able to do his second reading in April. I listened to it afterward to see what the answers had been to his questions, in case he called and wanted to discuss it. It was not particularly meaningful to me since I didn't know the people or situations about whom he asked. Later, he told me he had listened to it many times, and it gave him hope for the work he had come in to do. He said he had felt that perhaps he had failed to do what he had come to do, and each time the information gave him renewed hope. It was always nice talking with him about the Edgar Cayce work. He was very nice; I had been wrong about him.

I didn't hear from Herb for quite a while. Then he called one day in June. He was coming out to Arizona through a series of circumstances where he had gotten a free airline ticket. He and a minister friend were coming to attend a Hopi and Tibetan meeting over the July Fourth holiday. He asked me to get some guidance about whether he should come and how important it was. He said he would add whatever guidance I received with what he himself had obtained, and make a decision. He didn't tell me what his guidance was.

I told him I was so busy that I didn't know when I could get to it; but, I would try to tune in as soon as I possibly could. I also told him I was spending two weeks in Hawaii with Tom and three other people, and was leaving several days before he arrived, if he came on the dates planned.

He said he would be sorry to miss us, but asked me to see what I could find out as soon as possible about his own trip.

A week passed and I almost forgot to do what he asked. I was at home working when Stephen and my guides reminded me that he needed some guidance. The typewriter wasn't working, so I sat down with a pen and paper to listen and ask for any information that could be helpful for him. My guides said he should make the trip here—it was going to turn his life around. Afterward, he would begin to do the rest of what he came in to do with his life. They shared some other guidance for him which I wrote down, and then I went about my work. Later that day, I realized he needed to get the information soon in order to make a decision. I had better call him and read it to him over the phone, then mail him a copy. I did. He thanked me and said to have a good trip to Hawaii. I said the same regarding whatever he decided.

I didn't hear from him again. However, in two readings for our "angel friend," Helen, we were both told we would be doing some work with him. We couldn't even imagine what that might be. A few days before we were to leave for Hawaii, a chiropractor friend came by and mentioned that Herb was coming out for the meeting and was staying at his house. I said to give him my best and that we were sorry to miss him. Herb had evidently also gotten guidance to come out for the Hopi-Tibetan conference.

The next day, our travel agent called and said that we had been bumped from our Hawaii flight. The five of us traveling wouldn't be able to leave until four days later. We were so irritated. All our plans were made, clients had been canceled, and arrangements had been made for the children. As much as we traveled, we had never had a flight changed like that. Our agent apologized and said she had tried to get us on another flight so we could leave as planned. But because of the Fourth of July holiday, nothing could be done. There were not five seats available on any flight. She advised us not to try standby during a holiday. We would have to change our plans.

Since we were going to be in Phoenix over the holiday, I decided to make the best of the situation and have a party at the house. I invited lots of friends. I forgot that Herb would be in town at that time for his meeting until his friend called to talk and reminded me. I invited them to come to the party if they had time. He didn't think they would.

Despite the delay, we were going to Hawaii at last. It was my dream of a lifetime. As I planned the party, all I could think of was the trip to Hawaii. There was only one problem: my relationship with Tom was over. I was sleeping on the couch or staying in another room, meditating and working. Our lives were running parallel but not together. We didn't fight. I realized that he was always in his other world of sexual fantasies or sports. He wasn't even aware of what had happened to us or to me. If anything, I felt more compassionate and loving toward him than I ever had. I didn't know where he went or with whom—maybe no one, maybe . . . it didn't matter. I tried not think about it. Those were his choices. He now had the freedom from me he had always wanted.

I worked on plans to leave him as soon as we returned from Hawaii. It was our final trip together. There were a hundred things to do in preparation for a separation and divorce. He didn't want to be with me. He wanted to be with other women or other men. All but one of his children was living with us, and he had allowed his daughter to move her boyfriend into her room, and his son to move his girlfriend in with him. I was very uncomfortable with the whole situation. It was a zoo. It would be up to me to move out. He and his children could have the house. I planned to tell Debbie when we returned, and move us both out of the mess.

Stephen and my guides advised me almost daily during this time. I said to Stephen several times that I would never marry again. I meant it. I didn't ever want to hurt as I had with Tom. He couldn't change how he was. My counselor said he was a sociopath and that sociopaths are never sorry for what they do, only sorry they got caught. Tom's dream was of an open sexual relationship, maybe even sharing our bed with someone else, with me in it. My dream was not the same. I had learned to accept that in him, but it was still painful. I didn't want that kind of lifestyle or marriage.

On July 4th, dressed in a pair of old shorts, I played hostess to dozens of people eating outside on the patio and swimming in the pool. I was winding down a ten-day juice fast and feeling clear and strong. I was taking control of my life and I felt good. Hawaii was beckoning in a few days. I would soon be free of this emotional mess with Tom and his children. I felt at peace. I didn't know what the future held, but as the saying went, I knew Who held the future.

Half way through the party, there was a knock on the door. In came our chiropractor friend with Herb. I was surprised, but it was good to see them both. Herb and I hugged each other, and he visited with everyone and so did I. During the afternoon, we kept gravitating back together to talk.

As we were talking by the pool toward the end of the day, I got lightheaded from the fast. He brought me fruit and gave me his sunglasses. He was really nice. This was strange. What was happening? We were definitely attracted to each other. He didn't even know I was leaving Tom, and he was married. What in the world was going on?

The party broke up, and Herb told me the Tibetan-Hopi meeting had been canceled but that he had decided to come anyway and meet with some people. He asked if we could get together and talk since he would have some extra time. I agreed and said I'd call him and let him know when.

I was shaken. I had never felt like this. We could talk—really talk—about anything and everything. As much as I liked him and enjoyed being with him, I decided not to meet him, and that would end that. I went upstairs and laid down on the bed. Stephen and my guides began to speak to me. I got paper and pen and began with a prayer, then listened.

They told me that everything had been planned to cancel my trip and to bring Herb here. Herb's own guides helped to get him a free airline ticket to Phoenix, knowing the meeting would be canceled. They said neither of us were accomplishing what we had incarnated to do. They also said that he and I would be involved in a work with many others, and that work could be of help to a lot of people. Oh! It wasn't a personal thing after all. I had been reading the feelings all wrong. It was a work that had to do with our life's mission. I could handle that.

Herb and I met the next day at our center. He began by saying that for years psychics and sensitives had told him a marriage separation was in the future; he acknowledged to each of them that he knew that to be true. He said that he had been very unhappy in his marriage for years, and had known from the beginning they should not have been married. For the last fifteen years, he had known he wouldn't remain in the marriage. He had suggested a separation numerous times. His wife had threatened to leave many times. She hated living in Virginia Beach, resented the organization he worked for and his work there, and said she would not live in his shadow anymore. I knew what he said about his wife must be true because his friend had told me Herb's wife had told him those same things for many years, when they talked on the phone.

The final straw that ended the marriage had occurred a few months before, he continued. When Hugh Lynn Cayce had gotten very ill, he asked Herb to take his place and speak at the A.R.E. conference at Asilomar in California. Herb said he prayed for guidance and felt divinely directed to go. His wife was very angry and said some cruel things about his guidance. That did it!

Something of clarity and finality happened inside him, he said. He decided he was going as he felt guided, and that it was time for them to permanently separate. He reminded her that she always questioned his spiritual guidance. The heart of his life work was to live by his own spiritual guidance and to teach others how to do the same. He always cautioned people to seek guidance for themselves and not to use it to control others. The way in which she had ridiculed him for many of his other decisions, and for this final one, was the last straw. He told her with finality that he was not going to live like that.

He had also asked, before he left, for a stronger leadership role at A.R.E., feeling that they were going in directions that Edgar Cayce would not have wanted. Twenty-four people prayed with him each hour of the day for the correct outcome of this proposal.

Herb said that as he boarded the plane in June for California, he made plans for when he returned and would move out and end the marriage once and for all. At Asilomar, he told close friends of his plans and they were supportive of him. When he returned from the week in Asilomar, the trip to Arizona needed some planning. He had simply called me and asked for another perspective on what he had received in regard to the trip.

I told him about Tom and me. We talked and shared as if we had known each other for years. Something very special was happening between us. We meditated and prayed together several times. We both knew there was some work ahead for us to do together. We didn't know exactly what, but there was a peaceful feeling of "coming home," of being with your dearest friend. I told him everything I had ever done, every good and bad thing about myself. We shared for hours. He told me things he hadn't been able to talk about in years. We discovered, to our absolute amazement, that we had gone through the identical things in our marriages. He had experienced, except for a suicide of a child, everything that I had. Everything! When I told him what I'd been through, he understood—really understood. He had been through it too. We knew three days after the party, that we not only loved each other deeply, but were going to spend the rest of our lives together.

The next day, I was to leave for Hawaii and he for Virginia Beach. He might be made a leader of his organization—the decision wasn't in from the Board. I couldn't think that far. I could not and would not move to Virginia Beach. There would have to be some other way. Maybe I would live here in Arizona, and he could fly out to visit weekly. It was too complicated to reason out, but I knew Arizona was where I belonged. My work, my children, and my life were in Arizona.

The next day, I boarded the plane to Hawaii with Tom, my friend Helen, and two delightful bachelor friends of ours. Herb came to see us off. His plane left minutes before ours.

I couldn't believe how much I cared for him. It was more than being in love, more than friendship. It was like finding a long-lost family member whom you loved dearly. We had the same ideals, enjoyed the same things, were interested in the same esoteric teachings, and shared the same love for the Cayce work. I had never felt anything like this and neither had he. We hadn't even slept together. How could we possibly know how we felt? But we did.

Hawaii was all I had hoped it would be, except I wished that Herb was with me. I prayed and asked that Stephen be allowed to travel along with us from spirit, to enjoy the beauty. He was often there, and many times we talked. He delighted in the grandeur of Hawaii as did I. We discussed Herb and my feelings, and he and my guides talked and acted like they were the matchmakers.

After a week there, traveling to each island for a few days, doubt began to creep in. Herb and I had been in each other's presence only a few hours, and we were planning to spend our lives together. This was crazy. Or was it? I prayed and asked for guidance. Nothing came. We had just visited the rain forests and waterfalls on Maui when, clearly and distinctly, one of my guides said, "You will see a most unusual rainbow today and it will be a covenant to you that the Lord blesses this union and your work together ahead. Don't be fearful. Don't let doubt enter. Look for the rainbow."

It was early in the afternoon and it had been misting and raining since we woke up. No sun could get through the heavy layer of clouds. I looked up at the sky all the rest of the day. No sun, no rainbow. In fact, the clouds were darker and it was raining more than ever. My whole being filled with doubt. I was worried anyway about all that had happened. Now one of my guides had misled me. It was after 5:00 p.m. and we were ready to get in the car and head back to the hotel for dinner. Why was I getting incorrect guidance when my doubts were already so strong?

Without warning, the clouds parted and a brilliant ray of sun came through. I looked all around. There was the sun at last. But there was no rainbow to be found anywhere. The day was ending. My heart sank. As I moved to the door of the car, something caught my eye. There in front of the car, in a six-foot puddle of water mixed with oil, the one ray of sun hit the mixture and formed circle after circle of brilliant rainbows.

We all stared at it in amazement and grabbed our cameras to take pictures. Everyone commented that they had never seen such beautiful rainbows, such intense and clear colors. They didn't know what I had been told. I couldn't stop smiling. Thank you, God.

Herb and I had agreed to meditate together each evening while I was in Hawaii despite the six-hour time difference. We had some deep spiritual experiences those nights. We talked by phone frequently and shared what was happening. My doubts went away.

Herb made several major decisions in Virginia Beach. When I returned, he had decided to move to Arizona. He had talked with Charles Thomas Cayce, who did not want Herb to be in a leadership position in

A.R.E. There were three major leadership positions in A.R.E. Charles Thomas did not want Herb to be in any one of them. That being the case, Herb knew that even if the board gave him a position, it still wouldn't work. If that's the way Charles Thomas wanted it, that's the way it would be. Herb said he would not divide A.R.E. with a fight for leadership. So he handed in his resignation.

The board would misinterpret his resignation, not knowing of the conversation and of Herb's interest in what was best for the organization. One board member, not knowing what had happened, told him later that they couldn't believe he was so impatient to leave, that they might well have given him what he asked for. Another said some of the board were worried about letting him be president, fearing his wife had put him up to it and would try to run things and influence his decisions. Thus that chapter of his life was closed.

After Herb got back from his July visit to Phoenix, and I returned from Hawaii, we decided I would fly out to Washington,, D.C. to be with him for a week. He had moved into the loft of his house rather than moving into an apartment while preparing for his separation. It would take him a few weeks to pack his files at the house and his office. At the end of August, I would fly back to Washington D.C. again and meet him. We would drive across the country towing his car behind a U-Haul that was packed with all his books and files. He was leaving everything else. "Thank you, God," I said. "I could never have lived there. You must want us in Arizona." I was thankful He did.

Stephen was pleased with our union. He could now tell me again how intensely he had disliked Tom and how many things I hadn't known about him. He said that he had been shown that Herb and I had been making plans for years at the soul level during our dream states, to find each other and to be together, when the time was correct. Most people, he said, who marry or ultimately work closely together meet in this way before they actually come together physically. He said we had a work to do that was beyond what we could fully understand at that time, but that later he and my guides would elaborate. I was so in love that the work now paled in comparison to just seeing Herb again.

Herb was getting all kinds of advice and "guidance" from many sources about his decision. Scores of letters of congratulations poured in to him. Several sensitives across the country channeled almost identical information about what was happening in his life and what the future held. His own relatives said they wondered when he would finally leave the marriage and were so happy for him.

His brother, who later became a good friend and doesn't hesitate to express what he feels, affirmed our decision. He said that after he had seen Herb on the one and only visit he ever made to Herb's home during thirty years, he questioned to himself, "How much longer is he going to live like that?"

People all around the country supported him in so many ways. The majority wrote and called in support. But there were some who felt he had deserted his wife and his work. Herb's wife knew better. During that period, she had a dream in which Jesus appeared to her; He said, "If people don't stop saying Herb is simply going through a middle-age crisis, they're going to have Me to deal with." This was an extremely clear and powerful message to her and all of Herb's critics. But just like my old church when I left, there were those who accused him of everything from male menopause to being misled by some psychic in Arizona. One rumor was that he had run off with a twenty-year-old blonde. I liked that rumor.

Later, his wife denied he had ever mentioned separation, but people who knew him knew the truth, and some called to confirm his discussions about separation with them months before. Theirs had been a publicly respectable marriage, but everyone who knew them had observed the problems.

He had called me on the phone and proposed. When I arrived in Washington, he gave me a beautiful engagement ring on my birthday, with four diamonds forming a cross in the center and lapis and malachite petals, forming a flower. I had never been given diamonds before so it was amazing that two other friends gave me jewelry that birthday with four diamonds in exactly the same configuration of a cross.

The story of the ring was fascinating. He was counseling a woman months before who had no money, but had jewelry she wanted to barter with. She suggested he pick something to trade for their sessions. He chose the ring. He knew it wasn't for anyone he knew, but he said he knew it was for someone special. So he put it in his desk drawer, wrapped securely, and waited. It fit my fourth finger perfectly.

Here I was, having vowed never to marry again. I had been burned, heartbroken, and unwilling ever to let myself feel anything like love and caring again. Now I was acting like a teenager in love. But there was a difference.

This was a wonderful romantic relationship, hearts and flowers, nurtured by cards and love messages we sent each other daily with weekly phone bills in the hundreds of dollars. But there was also this incredible sense of mission. It was as strong as the romance. We didn't even know for sure what we were to do. Herb had always believed in a spiritual university. I had wanted a place where people could learn and grow and use their intuitive abilities safely and spiritually.

Stephen and my other guides would drop us little tidbits of information about what was ahead, but they wanted us to search it out ourselves, work on it ourselves. Then they would give us more.

At the end of August, I flew to Washington, D.C. and met Herb as we had planned. We traveled across country and visited some of his friends and family, driving the U-Haul and pulling his car to Arizona. We meditated and tuned in and asked for guidance all during the trip. As we drove through one lovely area of New Mexico, a huge double rainbow appeared, touching the ground from one valley to another. We stopped, took photos, and felt it was a good omen after the one in Hawaii. Rainbows became little signposts that we frequently experienced. The ten-day trip to Arizona gave us a chance to really get acquainted, to talk about all the things we had never yet had time to share.

Stephen liked Herb. His messages were encouraging. Here he was helping to match-make from spirit. It was funny. His guidance also helped me understand what was happening. Shortly after arriving in Phoenix, Herb and I rented a home. We planned to marry but hadn't set a date. We knew we would spend the rest of our lives together. There was a knowing of the depth and strength of this relationship that was like no other we had ever experienced. All lovers feel this way, I'm sure, but we also felt a deep soul commitment to a work.

Herb's chiropractor friend came to us with a vision he had. His vision was evidential because he really didn't want us together. He told us that he had been sitting on his bed, deeply troubled about us, when suddenly he had an open vision. He saw two people at an altar in a church. It was Christmas Eve, almost Christmas Day. The heavens opened and angels came down and stood around the couple, then the angels parted as Jesus descended and stood in front of them and placed his hands on their heads. He saw the face of the couple. It was Herb and I.

Later, we learned that it wasn't just his vision. It was an actual spirit plane confirmation of the blessing of our union, which he was permitted to glimpse.

He said he knew God was telling him that Jesus Himself blessed this union, and that we should be married at Christmas. We all cried as he shared his vision and agreed we would look into the possibility of a Christmas wedding. We had talked about how we loved the Christmas Eve candlelight mass. But with both of us being divorced, who would perform such a wedding?

With help from the other side, and through a friend, we found an Eastern orthodox monastery led by an abbot who was himself quite psychic. We spoke with the abbot and told him our story. He was delighted and very pleased to conduct our wedding. Their chapel was a converted stable that could seat only seventy by taking a small wall out. The abbot told us of his clairvoyant experiences. He could see spirits, and people often came to him just before death so he could help release them to the other side. His religious and metaphysical beliefs and experiences were much like ours. We freely shared with him our experiences. The wedding was planned for Christmas Eve at the stroke of midnight.

It would take a miracle for our divorces to be final in time. That miracle occurred. We were married with great joy in our stable at midnight. The sanctuary was filled with seventy of our friends. Before the service, a Pavoratti tape poured out Christmas music. Afterward, we had a reception at our home which began at 2:00 a.m. with French champagne from Helen, enough food to feed an army, and a wedding cake made from a recipe used at the Greek Olympics over 3,000 years ago.

Herb joined the organization that Tom, his partners, and I had begun, as president of one division. Tom married the pharmacist, one of his partners, a week after our wedding. We thought we could all work well together, but within a few months it became clear that Herb and I were to begin our own new work together.

Herb was given the name Logos in a meditation, and Logos Center became incorporated as a church and foundation in Arizona, on May 26, 1983. We planned three divisions for Logos: an interfaith church, a holistic center, and a university or educational outreach. We began a private practice using offices in our home. We saw clients, gave readings, and started weekly study group and meditation meetings.

We worked well together. Herb began to conduct the life readings I did. Because of his knowledge of the Cayce work, he was able to bring more information from the readings than ever before. We made lots of friends who became like family to us. We were on our way to a joyous and enduring love and work together.

Just before Christmas of 1983, Helen was visiting our home and we were catching up on all the news. The piano that Stephen had been instrumental in getting to us was behind the chair where Helen was sitting. The ceramic Christmas tree was on top of it. It had never again played since that one time, nine years ago. We were in deep conversation.

"Be quiet! Be quiet!" I broke in. "What?" "Shh . . . Listen. Listen!!" The Christmas tree had started playing again all by itself after all those years. It played "Silent Night" just as it had when Stephen had come into the room that evening. I said, "I can feel Stephen here, Helen. I can feel him." Helen confirmed, "I know. I can feel my Dad here too."

With our acknowledgment of our two visitors, the tree stopped playing. We could feel their presence in the room, but neither of us could hear them. We were so excited, we talked for hours. She had heard the "tree" story often and was thrilled to experience it herself. Later, Stephen confirmed that, yes, they were both in the room and just wanted to let us know they were there and to wish us Merry Christmas.

In 1985, we moved into an acre facility with two buildings, several blocks from the home we had bought the year before. The facility had been a Baptist church and school. We began offering Sunday services, classes for children, and educational programs.

In 1986, again just before Christmas, Helen, Herb, and I were once again sitting in the living room, talking. The doorbell rang. Herb got up to answer it. No one was there when he opened the door. He sat down to talk and it rang again. I answered it and again, no one was there. The next time it rang, I jumped up quickly and opened the door to catch whoever was playing a joke. No one was there. As we both stood at the door looking, it rang again and again. Helen said, "It's my Dad. He's here. Dad's here." You could feel his presence. I said, "Stephen's here too." We could feel them both so clearly. We were delighted. When I asked Stephen about it, he said they just wanted to let us know they were with us and wished us a Merry Christmas. The doorbell never rang like that before nor has it since.

• • •

Often now I would sit and talk to Stephen. His guidance was always uplifting and helpful. Most of all it was hopeful—sharing views of the future of our work that gave us the encouragement to take more steps. I still missed him being in the body I had loved, but now I was taking time to listen and let him help more and more. He had more to tell me about teenage suicide.

One spring afternoon, on the way back from the college where I was taking a semester class in creative writing, Stephen began speaking to me in the car, which he often did. He was telling me about my writing, how to make the best use of some money, and very lofty promises of the future. I asked him if he were positive about the things he was telling me. Immediately, a truck came up on my right side. It had "STEVE" painted on it in huge, bold letters. He said, "Is that enough proof?" and laughed.

He elaborated on the death of children. "Only rarely when children under eighteen kill themselves, either by accident or suicide, do we find that the family situation doesn't play a major role. Now this may not please a lot of psychologists and psychiatrists, but it's true. There are always those who, despite good upbringing and love, go off the deep end, of course, but many pull themselves back on track if the home environment is supportive. Of course, thousands never kill themselves under the worst of circumstances in the family. Since there is not always a consistent pattern, counselors and statisticians have overlooked many things. When this is examined more closely and differently, it will prove to be correct.

"Much also depends upon past life choices of the person, child, or adult. If they have chosen wrongly, and taken their lives in the past, they will often be in the rut of choosing wrongly in the present and future. I know the mention of past lives will turn off some people, but other seekers will be brought true hope and understanding for the first time, of this as an influence. It just makes sense, Mom. Real seekers will remember some of their own past lives and it will make sense of so many things happening in their current incarnation.

"There are a lot of good books that will help people in their understanding of life after death, past lives, and a fuller psychic awareness. Herb's *Edgar Cayce Primer* and his *Reflections on the Path* are two that can help many people begin their journeys in fuller understanding. His book on meditation, *Meditation and the Mind of Man,* is good to aid the seeker in learning to meditate, which can enable them to make contact with us better. Robert Monroe's *Journeys out of the Body*, and, of course, Ruth Montgomery's *Search for the Truth* are excellent for understanding other dimensions of reality. *There is a River* by Thomas Sugrue and *Twenty Cases Suggestive of Reincarnation* by Ian Stevenson, M.D. can help with past life awareness; and the Kenneth Ring and Raymond Moody books on near-death experiences are really great. Also, *Diary After Death* by Franklin Loehr, *The Blue Island* by W.T. Stead, and the Helen Greaves's books, *Testimony of Light* and *The Challenging Light* all contain very informative perspectives of life after death.

"Mom, maybe it will help if I paint you a picture. Let's say that I was born, or began my childhood, with a large backpack on my back filled with a few stones—stones from past life experiences and stones from genetic things, from both you and Bill. The first few years with the two of you added another stone or two to the pack. When you left Bill and got out of the marriage, a couple of stones were added because I was dealing with feeling deserted and pulled away from ones I loved. The years with uncaring baby-sitters added a few more stones. When you married Dad, well those years added a bunch of stones. Dad was not good about helping build our self-esteem.

"There was a weakness with you in not knowing how to stand up to him, so this added more stones. As Bob took out more and more of his aggression on me, even more stones were added. The situations in the schools with the kids teasing me, hurting me, and ignoring me put in additional stones. Some of my own incorrect choices and reactions threw in more stones.

"Let's call those stones emotional weights. When I chose to eat incorrectly and knew better, or experimented with different things, this too added other stones. Mom, I didn't take drugs or alcohol, though I tried each of them once, but I didn't like them. However, the guilt added another stone.

"I really let what people said hurt me too much and another stone was added. As the situation got worse with Dad, and he forced us to do things that were emotionally against the pattern of our growth and development, many stones. Then I hit adolescence and all the hormonal changes, and that added still another stone. This may surprise you, but despite the divorce from Dad, no stones were added from just that. However, when Tom came into the picture with all his kids and all the chaos, a couple of stones got placed in the pack.

"You always thought that if you had stayed with Richard, I would still be alive. I wouldn't have. The things that were created in that relationship with him from ages two to five and the years before I died, added so many stones that by then the weight was getting so heavy I wasn't able to reach around in back and remove the stones to ease the load. I seldom knew how to take off the backpack and release some weight. It was strapped so tightly, held by my feelings of inferiority.

"The people at church who came down so hard on us added stones. When I agreed with them and said things I didn't mean, I added my own stones. The mess with Tom added a lot in a short time. He didn't like me and he didn't like Deb. He liked Bob some and Andrea okay. Now this backpack thing isn't the greatest metaphor, but bear with me. The backpack became so full, so heavy, that I could hardly carry it during the week, but felt I could rest it somewhat on the weekends.

"When you sent Tom to tell me about not taking my gym bag to school and that you knew I had shoplifted, I lost face. It wasn't that he didn't say it well, but there was a smugness about it. With Kathy pregnant, no girls who liked me for a boyfriend, no friends around, ugly and overweight, the pack got so overloaded that as I sat on the tree it just weighed me down—pushed me over and down I went. I'm not trying to blame anyone, or absolve myself. I'm as much or more to blame than anyone. I had a chance to change things, to choose differently.

"If you can reach kids soon enough, get them counseling, help relieve some of the peer pressure for awhile and teach them how to cope with it, and help them develop self esteem, you can prevent ninety percent of the suicides in kids. We can easily see that from here. Some of their backpacks are getting overloaded too. Parents think that one problem or one act made the child kill himself. It didn't. It just added that extra stone that tilted the scales to overload.

"Some of the current suicide statistics say suicide is the third cause of death of kids ten to fifteen or young people fifteen to twenty-four. Some statistics say it's the second cause of death. I am going to tell you the truth. Suicide is the *number one* cause of death of young people thirteen to twenty-four. Number one. You will see new research in the future, with single person car accidents, suicides that are covered up by family and doctors, plus all the typical suicides already listed considered, and it will prove to you what I'm saying. We have known that here for a long time. Some researchers already know this to be true. It may get worse if things aren't done to help change it. The pattern we see from here looks like it will get much worse, despite incorrect statistics from some corners saying the suicide rate is dropping. It isn't true—it's rising. That will be proven too. Already, many researchers have spoken out about it, both in the United States and overseas. The knowing precedes the statistical support.

"It's not just the kids, it's people of all ages. The suicide rate of the elderly is the worst. Actually, as I've told you, some of the elderly suicides aren't always wrong. It can be a more correct decision if it's handled correctly, or at least it's an option. This is not true of adolescents.

"I can't say it strongly enough—it is never correct for a young person to commit suicide, there is always a way they can be helped, there is always someone who cares. It isn't always easy, and it will take a lot of work, but there is always a way. Help us bring this understanding and guidance we are sharing with you, to the parents and children. Just a little awareness of the many influences in a young person's life, can help remove some stones from their backpack and prevent others from being placed there. The needless deaths of thousands of precious lives can be prevented."

CHAPTER TWELVE

'Twas Heaven There
With You

*Lord, forgive me for my efforts to serve you only when convenient
to do so and only when it is safe to do so. Father, forgive me, renew
me and send me out as a usable person that I may take more
truthfully the meaning of your love.*

— Found among Stephen's writings

"Mom, this is our first book together, and I can only skim the surface
and share such a small bit of information about so many things with you.
You can't possibly put in all I have already shared, and there is so much
more. This is a start.

"I want you to leave in this book the things I've told you to write about
yourself—don't edit them out. As hard as it is for you to be that honest
and revealing, my life and death can't be understood as well without
knowing about your life. Your sense of guilt and the feelings that you
caused my death are something parents and families can relate to. Some
of your choices and actions did contribute to my overall pattern and the
action I took to end my life. How you have understood this and resolved
it, and how you have grown, can give hope to others. Most people do
sugar-coat what they write. Hardly a book tells it like it is. You have told
it like it is and you have allowed me to do the same no matter how it hurt.
You've done this even when you know the skeletons in the closet will be
revealed.

"You *know* death isn't the end and that we who die or take our own
lives really can and do communicate with those who remain, if they will
let us. When you lost the fear of death, you began truly to live. That will

307

be true for others too. That knowledge is what will help usher in a new age of hope and understanding. People used to communicate with their 'dead' and there was a lot less pain and feeling of separation. So I want you to explain in your own words how you get in touch with me, and how we talk and I'll add my two cents worth."

Stephen, Edgar, and the others taught me to do several things. I begin with a prayer. I ask God that only the very highest spiritual guidance comes through. I ask to be a clear, pure channel of truth and hope. Usually, I take my hand and make a cross from my chest to my forehead, though I know it isn't necessary to do any of this, and I make a smaller one on my head.

Many times I read *God Calling* or *Daily Word* for the specific day, or a passage from *Opening Doors Within*, or something from the Cayce readings or the Bible. I read whatever is spiritually uplifting to me. If I feel inclined, I do a few chants using a rolling "om."

I work with different breathing exercises. I usually breathe in through my right nostril very slowly and out through my mouth three times for strength, then in through my left and out through my right nostril three times to open the higher spiritual centers. Other times, I use various breathing exercises until I feel relaxed.

When I begin attuning by lying on the floor or resting my head on the back of a chair, I often do a breathing exercise I love from *The Miracle of Metaphysical Healing,* which I have adapted for myself. In my mind's eye, I watch my breath going in and out for a minute. Then I inhale deeply and extend my diaphragm or stomach, hold the breath a few seconds, then exhale through my nostrils or mouth forcefully. I do this about three to six times. Then I do the same breathing technique, but as I exhale, I visualize the breath as white light, going throughout my whole body, from toes to head. I see it ending at the center of my forehead and staying there until the next breath. After three to six times of this, I am usually relaxed and beginning to slightly alter my consciousness. I either continue to rest where I am and listen, or get up and sit at the computer or typewriter. Often I stay quiet afterward and meditate or still my mind for a few more minutes, using prayer or affirmations I have memorized. Evidently, Stephen and my guides know when I am ready to listen because I begin to hear the voices, and I type what I hear.

Most of my communication with Stephen and the guides used to be done at my typewriter. Now I sit at my computer and prepare to listen. Occasionally, I use pen and paper, but that is so slow that I can't record for as long a period. After my preparations, as I am meditating or praying, thoughts will begin to come, overshadowing my own thoughts.

Sometimes I receive very deliberate words, one at a time, then I usually start to hear sentences or phrases. I can interrupt the communication to ask questions, and it will continue where it left off. At times, Stephen or my guides tell me to wait and then another one of them continues. Sometimes, whole concepts are given which I put in my own words, though if this occurs, they correct anything that isn't exactly as they want it said.

There are times when even though I'm not thinking about Stephen, I will hear him call me. We have our car conversations and our unplanned visits in this way. I've found that if I forget to record them, I don't remember part of what is said. It's like my dreams, if I don't record them, I forget most of them. I ask questions and sometimes he answers, sometimes not. At times he doesn't know the answers but says he will try to find them.

"Is that about it, Stephen?"

"Yes, but let me explain about the levels you access. My dimension and the others are like floors in a huge skyscraper. The elevator takes you to one floor and there you find information about past lives, let's say. On another floor you can find out about or talk to people who have died. On another, records of your current life. Another, spirit plane doctors and helpers with information about health and the body. Still another, angels or the masters.

"We can call the top floor the penthouse, where you can meet God and talk to him and hear what he has to say to you. Your elevator is your higher mind—the ability to raise your consciousness. Let's call meditation and prayer the power that runs the elevator. When you step into your elevator, the type and degree of your attunement takes you up or down to certain levels. As you yourself became more clear and more aware, you knew exactly which buttons to select for which floors. Had you gone to a lower floor, you could not have made contact with me, or a higher one, the same. There is a specific floor where I have my offices, so to speak, and I can usually be found there. You have developed a good ability to find the floors you need most times. Some sensitives are so good at accessing one and only one floor that they don't even know the others exist.

"When you pray or meditate and call me to come and chat, I hear, or am brought the message by a helper, and try to come as soon as possible. Usually I can be with you in seconds or minutes. Occasionally, I am involved in a class or learning something and am delayed a few hours.

"I visit you in your dreams quite a bit. Unfortunately, you remember only about ten percent of your dreams. You can prepare with affirmations before sleep or specific suggestions to remember more, as can most people. You and I have great dream contact. As I've told you, most people have frequent dream contact with loved ones who are in this dimension. That bit of knowledge should comfort many parents. When a child dies, there is always contact between their souls in the dream state. It's a good place to communicate with them. Often their prayers and attunement to the child can be comforting and helpful for the child as well as themselves.

"There is a way you can communicate with missing children, with people at a distance from you, or with people with whom you want to resolve difficulties. It's called soul linking, or mind linking—which is not mind control. You can even do it in your dimension between two physical bodies. You first pray and ask to link mind to mind, or soul to soul with the person, according to their free will. When you do, it's like you pick up the receiver of a phone, dial their number, it rings, they answer, and you begin to talk to them. Then, with your mind, you can comfort them, send them healing, talk to them, even teach them, and they *will* hear. They will not be conscious of hearing, but they will hear more fully than if you spoke to them out loud. This attunement is *not* to be used to bend their will to yours or to influence them to think and believe as you do. It is *not* to be used in this way, though, of course, many working with mind control techniques do. Much negative karma is created if this technique is used incorrectly. The person you ask to link with may not consciously remember, but they *will* hear. Most often, you begin to see changes in your relationship for the good when you are together in person. If you are apart, a feeling of peace and serenity is felt about the relationship. It can be extremely comforting to have such a link until a missing child is returned, for example.

"You can do this also with the mind and soul of a person, even if you don't know who they are, such as one who has abducted a child. Sometimes you will hear an inner 'no' when you request to link with them, and they won't allow it. If this happens, ask to meet them instead, in your dreams with your angels and theirs, and request that the angels minister to them. Usually, however, they will let you make a contact in that higher state. You can, out loud or telepathically, commune with them. You can appeal to the goodness within them, to the higher part of themselves, to release your child and cause no harm.

"Just a brief word about angels in this regard. Instead of worrying, parents would do better to ask for angels to be with their children daily at school, at home, and as they play. Angels, except for the children's specific guardians, must be called upon to help. They will not interfere unless asked. Call on angels of love and protection to stand around your loved ones at all times. If a child has disappeared, use powerful prayer and call upon protective angels and angels of all kinds and your guides or those of us here in spirit to help. Unless separation and death are part of the karmic pattern of the young entity, miracles can and do happen, and many children are returned unharmed.

"In the same manner, someone in a physical body can also soul link, meet in the dreams and send angels to someone *without* a physical body, those you call 'the dead.' When you know you have established the soul link, talk to the person, tell them how you feel and what you are wishing to communicate. Ask questions of them and listen for the answers. Ask them to tell you how they feel, what they are doing. Listen. It really works!

"It can be done by us here also. We don't need words. We think or telepathically say whatever we want to say to each other, but we can ask for fuller communication by doing the soul linking. It's a wonderful healing tool and great comfort to all who do it whether we have bodies anymore or not. It is not the imagination, but always remember that what you think to be imagination is the foundation of intuition and other soul abilities. **Imagination is your golden key to unlocking your greater awareness.**

"Let me tell you a little more about suicide, OK? There is hardly a person who hasn't contemplated suicide at one time or another. This can even be considered temporarily normal and healthy when the mind is so overloaded that this fantasy is used as a temporary escape. It is *not* good to dwell on it nor to act it out. Many people feel out of control of their lives. Thoughts of taking their own life can, at times, be enough of a temporary release to get their thinking back on track. The great majority of souls entertaining the notion also discard it as the rational mind and the law of self-preservation take over.

"All people have a great soul need to feel some control over their lives. Most of them, if they feel they have some say about their lives, some control, are not going to kill themselves. Children at an early age need to be able to make some of their decisions, to feel some control and to exercise that control, mistakes or not. It is not helpful to do everything for them or to instruct them on how to do every single thing. They rebel from being over-controlled. They also grow up lacking strength of judgment and choice. Their character is often weakened.

"In the last decade, so many helpful books about self-esteem, co-dependency, and self love have been written—inspired is probably more correct. There are dozens that are written for kids and adults alike to read to get some help and understanding. Some of the current books are like balm to the soul. I want you to list them at the end of the book.

"So many people wonder, if death isn't the end and their loved ones continue, why it is so hard to make contact with them. They also question why God keeps humankind from knowing about life after death and reincarnation. God doesn't; we do it to ourselves. We separate ourselves and believe what we are told, rather than what we feel intuitively, what we know within. The information is widely available. There are so many good books by credible people about life after death and reincarnation. Some people are afraid to read them. Some fear being misled because all the books don't agree. What they forget is that we all have the power of discernment—not skepticism—but discernment. Don't give that power to some authority outside yourself. If you question and are unsure, ask God, ask your higher self. If you consistently seek and ask, you will know. No one will have to tell you what is truth or be able to convince you something true is false, or of the devil.

"Others are so frightened and fearful because of religious dogma that their souls shrivel. Whenever people are fearful, it shows their beliefs aren't that strong or they wouldn't be so scared. They are afraid that if they were to allow themselves to search openly and honestly, it would shake the very foundation of their beliefs. They feel safer in their limited seeking and thinking.

"There was a time on earth, they have shown me here, when the consciousness of humankind was such that all dimensions could be freely accessed. It was truly like a Garden of Eden for awhile. No wars, no fighting, no crime. Later there were times when many could walk freely between dimensions and others couldn't. Then more and more people forgot their Divine nature, their One-ness with God and all creation. Walls were placed between dimensions, not by God, but by man's incorrect thinking and choices.

"Here, in this dimension, we can access your dimension freely. You can't visit ours as easily because you have forgotten how. Most people don't trust anything they can't touch or see with their eyes. Our vibratory rate here is higher and faster, and you can't ordinarily see it with your eyes, but you can with your inner vision. You can hear it with your inner hearing. People don't trust that. They don't think it's real, because it's not what they have been taught to believe. They forget that they once knew how to use the sixth sense, the higher mind, at will.

"Meditation is the gateway to the bridge between our dimensions. When you meditate regularly, the gate stands open most of the time, giving you free access. When you meditate sporadically, the gate must be opened each time. This makes more work for you and discourages you because it takes up most of your scheduled meditation time to reopen the gate. Your impatience often makes you stop when the gate doesn't budge easily.

"Prayer is the road that leads to the gateway, across the bridge, and beyond. Many people pray and pray for help and then get up and run about their business. They never stop to listen and to hear the answer to their prayer. They wonder why no one hears and nothing changes in their lives. When you pray, take equal time to listen. If you hear nothing at first, keep listening. Pray five minutes and listen fifteen is good advice. Edison didn't get voices with *his* first efforts—inventing the telephone took 700 experiments before he was able to transmit voices. If you *persevere,* you will learn to hear us. That's why meditation could be called the space in which prayer is answered. Meditation is listening to God speak, answer, comfort, and love you. Meditation strengthens your faith, prepares you to hear not only God but those He sends in his stead as messengers—angels, guides, helpers.

"Angels have never been people, and people do not evolve into angels. Angels are assigned to every single person born, whether they are Christian or not. I add that because, unfortunately, a well-known minister on your plane preaches that only Christians or those who believe in Jesus get a guardian angel. Of course, that isn't true. Mohammed had an angel, for instance, as does every Jewish person, every Hindu, every Buddhist. Angels do not have feathered wings. Some people who see into that dimension see energies around them, their ability to move quickly and easily and have described them as having wings. Besides, unless angels are depicted with wings in paintings and on statues, how would one distinguish them from ordinary people? Angels are higher than humankind on the hierarchical ladder. They are next to and from the throne of God we have learned, but that's just to show symbolically their position in the hierarchy. All people have guardian angels assigned to them when they are conceived. The angels stay with them the whole incarnation, trying to help them along the pathway, with protection, love, and counsel. Most people never listen. Many aren't even aware it's possible.

"Every sincere prayer is taken by an angel to the person for whom the prayer is said. The story you have heard about the man being operated on who left his body, drifted to the top of the room, and observed his surgery is true. He saw angels of all sizes. Some came and stayed for a long time, others were in and out quickly. He wondered what it meant and a Voice told him that the angels were bringing the prayers people had prayed for him. Some were long and deep prayers, and they were symbolized by larger angels who stayed for greater periods of time. Others were quick prayers or prayer-thoughts brought by small angels staying only for short periods. Some large angels also came and went quickly—powerful prayers of less length, the story goes. In essence, this is absolutely true. I'll tell you much more about angels in our next book.

"This dimension isn't some heaven with angels floating around with wings and golden streets and clouds where you don't do anything but play your harp and wander around. How boring that would be, don't you think? It's much harder in school here. When you're on earth you have a body, and you're very conscious of having a mind when you have to concentrate. Everything shifts one level here because you don't have a physical body—the mind becomes the body. The subconscious then becomes like the mind. The superconscious and the subconscious then have to be trained or worked with in a different way.

"We have more access to what you would call the superconscious, though certainly that's a limiting term, and to the subconscious mind. I'm trying to think of words to explain this better. We have to exert and develop more control. We have to discipline ourselves more because we go where our thoughts go.

"When you have a physical body, only your thoughts go and your body stays, unless you have an out-of-body experience. In this dimension, if you think, if you let your mind wander, you're off with your mind. You go with your thoughts. You can even create things with those thoughts. It makes it very difficult to accomplish things for a long time because you're at the mercy of your thoughts. You may think that's wonderful, but it's really not, especially at first. It means you have to learn to discipline yourself like a person who does gymnastics, or you'll fall off the bar. So it's not that easy. However, once you learn, it's great. You can create almost anything you want. Only you don't do that, because you soon realize how foolish and useless it is when you can be learning and advancing, unencumbered by 'things.'

"I want to tell you how it really is here emotionally. You know how bad your grief was when I died? My grief was like the combination of the grief of everybody in the family. I felt it all. I hadn't meant to hurt anyone. My thinking and planning were faulty; but, it wasn't my intent to hurt anyone. When I felt and saw each of you grieving, it was as if I were a sponge—I soaked it all up. I wanted to console each of you, but there was absolutely nothing I could do. Your grief and lack of attunement kept you from hearing me.

"You know how it was when Debbie was little, crying and hurting, and you went to her and hugged her and it helped a little? Or you fixed her something to eat or brought her a toy to cheer her up? There were all kinds of little things you did to help her feel better. We can't even do that after we learn a lot of techniques here, because the person on earth has to be willing to let that happen within their mind. We can scream and yell and offer help, and some of us do to get your attention, but you usually can't hear us, especially at first; even later, very few people hear or listen.

There is nothing we can do. Nothing! It's the most awful feeling because you would give *anything* if you could go back and undo your death and you can't, ever. There is no place which is hell as such, but the pain we feel creates our own hell emotionally, for a long time.

"After a short while, most of your friends who still have bodies forget about you. They don't even talk about you. It hurts too much, and they don't understand why you killed yourself. They may even be mad at you for doing it. It's easier for them to forget it all happened. When you try to impress on them you're still alive, they don't even hear, or they ignore you. You feel crazy, tormented, wasted. That's when the helpers on this plane take over and you start getting on with your life here, if you will allow it. Some won't.

"You've read and I've told you that there is a gift that each child who commits suicide leaves. There is a gift to be found in *every* death if you'll look for it. This is too difficult to hear when a young person first dies, but it is true and should be sought later. They didn't take their lives to leave this gift, but out of their death and your struggle, a gift can be discovered. This applies to the death of all children. Mom, think about it. How would you describe the gift you found in my death?"

"Stephen, when I first read that, it was annoying to me, and it took a long time to find a gift even years later. I guess the gift you left me has a lot of parts. You gave me a gift of trying to understand suicide and to be open and to talk about yours and not hide it. It made me read all the information and research about suicide and add to it the esoteric or metaphysical truths I discovered. My own grief gave me opportunities to counsel others about suicide and death. Later, I lectured and wrote about it. You have given me the gift of this information from you. You have given me a gift of how to work with my doubt and to trust things beyond my five senses. You have actually given me a basket of gifts and I thank you. But I would rather you were here with me and I could have watched you grow up, get married, and have children."

"Mom, I'm sorry too. There were some little souls that would have come through me if I'd held on. I've met them here, and they are still waiting to be born through other parents. There aren't suitable ones available yet because of my choices. My incorrect choice slowed down their progress considerably. I've seen the girl I would have married. She is married to someone else and is not very happy. I see how I could have been a good husband to her. You would have liked her, Mom. She's cute as all [a term Stephen used for many years, and one which I had forgotten until he used it here] and kind as can be. Her husband is a lot like Dad was. They can't have children. Sometimes it has made me cry to visit her. I've tried to comfort her, but she doesn't hear me. My wrong choice impacted on so many lives in a bad way.

"Here's another truth, just as it's true that out of everything a lesson can be learned: it is *not* true that everything that happens is a sign or for the best. It's craziness to look for signs every time something happens. Mom, remember when you saw the raven on your car and thought it was a sign that the car was going to die on you? It was still running, years later. The bird simply landed on your car. You can learn a lesson from it, though. It made you take better care of the car, and it made you see how most things are *not* signs. So it was a good lesson, huh? Use good common sense and discernment, and you don't get fooled as often.

"Also, everything does *not* happen for the best or everyone would be a puppet without free will. Everyone is not exactly where they should be, either. Wrong choices, and there *are* wrong choices, create incorrect outcomes and unnecessary learning experiences. You can *make* the best out of them, but they did not happen for the best. There's a big difference.

"Mom, you can teach others all these things I'm telling you. Your honesty about suicide, for instance, can help others to clean the skeletons out of their closets. Suicide is still a taboo subject to talk about and people are ashamed to admit that one of their family members has taken his or her own life. Mostly, they just don't understand why, so they don't talk about it, as if that would make it go away. And there is such guilt carried on the shoulders of those left behind. There is still such stigma about suicide.

"Everyone feels partly to blame in some way. Or they get angry and try to blame the dead person, when inside they carry the secret guilt that maybe they did drive the person to their death. It is true that almost every person that knew the one who killed himself has contributed to the pattern of the soul who made that choice, but that soul is ultimately responsible for his or her choice. There are other and better ways to stop pain and to handle stress than to kill yourself and destroy your opportunity to fulfill your soul purpose. When you end your life, you destroy a most precious gift from God.

"Many people have an inner feeling that there is more to afterlife than the heaven and hell they've been taught. Their souls still remember their real home. What I am sharing is information to reawaken those memories. Each time you are born, you come into this existence with precious gifts—your body, mind, and soul. You come in to do something that no one else can do quite as well.

"Do you remember that quote from Norman Vincent Peale? I love his philosophy. So add it in."

"OK, Stephen, here it is:"

There's something you can do better than anybody in the world. You just have to find your niche. You've got a life to live. It's short, at best. It's a wonderful privilege and a terrific opportunity—and you've been equipped for it. Use your equipment. Give it all you've got. Love your neighbor—he's having just as much trouble as you are. Be nice to him; be kind to him. Trust God and work hard.

"It doesn't matter if it's being a teacher, cleaning streets or being president. Your obligation is to use your gift in the very best way, to help you become the very best whole person you can and to help others at every opportunity. All work, all vocations, all jobs are completely equal in God's sight and that is soon discovered over here. Your soul awareness is to acknowledge a higher power, God, as the One-force within you and in all things. You need to learn to see God in everything and to manifest that Godness in all you do and say. You are to be a light, a bearer of light, and to see and know of the light within yourself and all others.

"To destroy that gift before you finish your assignment is a total waste. If you're very old, that's one thing. Though I must tell you that the yogis are right; you can have a conscious death, which is not suicide, when you are finished living, which is a better way.

"When you are a tree in full bloom, or your blossoms haven't even set on yet, or your growth has just begun, and if you cut down that tree before it can bear fruit and reach full maturity, you have destroyed that gift. What a waste. That tree will never grow again. The forest is the less because of the loss of its beauty and majesty. Only the stump remains to remind the other trees that there in the woods once stood what could have become a magnificent sentinel. Another seed will have to be planted. You will have to go through conception, birth, and growth again and again and again. Perhaps the new tree will not be as strong as the one you destroyed. Perhaps the new tree's growth will be stunted with the memory that it too could be cut down in its prime, and pulls its branches and buds in, in fear. And on it goes.

"Another thing, when I told you I would give you evidence through the moving of the second hand of my watch, that I was with you as you wrote this book, I don't think you realized what fun we would have, did you?"

Stephen had told me to take the watch that he had always worn out of my jewelry box and place it near where I sat to write this book or listen to him. He said to watch it and write down where the hands were and the exact time it marked. This was the watch that had been on his body when he died. When I took it to be repaired, they said it couldn't be fixed.

About two years after Stephen died, Uri Geller, a well-known psychic, was on television and a group of us were watching at the house. Geller suggested everyone get broken watches and spoons and forks. He demonstrated how to hold the watches to see if we could create enough energy to make them run. Or enough power to bend the spoons and forks. I ran to get Stephen's watch. We were eager to see what would happen. Nothing we touched, started working or bent during the whole program. I had really hoped that I could make Stephen's watch run. I believed energy could be directed that way, but I was unable to do it.

Debbie came into the room just before the program ended. We told her what was happening. She watched Geller, picked up Stephen's watch, held it with her eyes closed and calmly said, "It's running." We grabbed it from her, and sure enough, it *was* running. We tried to shake it to see if it would stop. It wouldn't. This was amazing. It did work. The watch ran about twenty-four hours and stopped, never to run again. No matter what incantations we did over it, we couldn't even get the second hand to move one space.

Stephen asked me to take the watch to Hawaii when Herb and I went there in August of 1987. I was instructed to note the placement on the hands, write it down, and he would make them move every time he came into the room to dictate to me. Our dear friend, Virginia Ryder, had loaned us her condo on Oahu near Waianae for a month each year, to get away from everything and to write. Located on the twelfth floor, from every room we could see mountains and ocean on each side as we sat at our computers to write. Herb wrote in one room, I in the other. The watch rested on my typing stand. I noted the placement of the hands in my journal.

Deep into my writing, I didn't even think about Stephen's instructions but, as promised, he interrupted me and told me to look at the watch. It had moved twenty seconds. Ever doubtful, I shook it, but the second hand had stopped, and I couldn't make it run. The next time Stephen called my attention to it, it had moved four seconds, the next two, the next fifteen, the next ten. He was excited. "See Mom, I can do it with help. Whenever I'm in the room, I'll try to make it move. Sometimes I can, sometimes I can't, but I will try and you'll know I'm here."

Sure enough, the entire month I was writing, the second hand moved again and again when Stephen entered the room, until it had moved more than two hours ahead before we came back to Arizona. I kept it by my computer at my office at home and it moved almost every time Stephen and I communicated. If I didn't have time to write for several days or weeks, it didn't move. It truly was fun to work with him in this way, and it made my doubts go away.

In August of 1988, I forgot to pack it when we flew to Hawaii. We called our secretary to send it along with some computer things we had also forgotten. The computer information arrived, but the watch has never been found. Our secretary packed and mailed it, yet it was not in the box. I questioned Stephen. He said he will return it to me. He hasn't yet.

"Mom, I *will* get it to you. Just wait.

"Now, let me finish by telling you how much I have grown. I sometimes feel like you're the child and I'm the parent. We have a wonderful staircase and bridge that God has given us to keep in touch with each other when one of us dies. It's so simple. People have so complicated communication between dimensions. We have to teach them how to get up the staircase and across the bridge.

"Remember when I told you that I couldn't communicate with you for awhile? I was being taught in other dimensions that you can't access yet. I can tell you some things about them later, but I will mainly be working with you from here in this dimension with which you are familiar. My assignment for now is to help you get this book out, then several more. I'm working for credits toward graduation to other work here, and depending upon how well we do, I'll get my degree. Or I will have to repeat some things. [Laughter]

"I had an IQ of 158. You thought it was 157. You're off by a point. Give me that point. [He laughed again. I checked the paperwork the school had given me when Stephen died, and sure enough, I was wrong. It was 158.] A lot of good it did me. But that's pretty special in a physical body—a gift. I could have helped so many people. I had lots of abilities. I had a good mind and a strong body. I genuinely wanted to help others. I blew it. I let my backpack get too heavy. I didn't choose correctly, and I hurt a lot of people. I hurt many more than my family and friends. All the souls I could have touched and aided that hadn't even met me, that were waiting for the help I could have offered.

"I did something final, in a moment of darkness, that I can't ever undo. I will never have an opportunity to be in exactly those circumstances again with so much going for me. I live with that knowledge and regret and sadness always. I wish I hadn't hurt so many people. I wish I hadn't hurt myself. I wish I could stop time and have another chance to use the Stephen life the right way. I never will.

"There are hundreds of kids here in my group that died as I did, by taking their own lives. Many of them work and pray daily to contact their loved ones who remain behind. They just want to let them know they are

OK and are learning and growing. They want to tell them they love them and that they're sorry. Very rarely does anyone hear. Some of their families are so ashamed of this act of their children that they refuse to think or talk about the child. Some are so hurt and angry that they never recover. Others still pray for these loved ones but feel they sleep, unaware, in their graves. Still others feel that to think of an afterlife or the possibility of contacting a loved one is to deny the death and may be psychologically damaging.

"Whatever their reasons, their hearts are seldom truly healed, and their loss affects them the rest of their lives. It is never truly resolved except by a very few. Even those few lose the golden opportunity of continued communion with the one they love. For death need not separate. Death is simply exchanging one suit of clothing for another, and learning how to establish a different way of communicating. There is a two-way phone line we can use as you now know.

"Our hope and prayer from our dimension is that together we can be aware of the bridge between us, or the phone line, if you will, so that all who so desire may freely walk back and forth upon the bridge at will or pick up the 'phone' and chat. We hope we can help those who remain behind to lose the fear of death, so they will live their lives more fully and accomplish their soul missions. We hope that with the help of those such as yourself, we can bring to the survivors of suicide, the walking wounded as they are often referred to, the knowing that their loved ones are not suffering hell and damnation, but are functioning, learning, and growing in spirit.

"Our choices were wrong in cutting our lives short, but we are making amends and seeing more clearly here. We would love nothing better than to make a contact with those we love. Even if it is a brief contact to let them know we're OK, that we continue, that we love them and are very sorry for the pain we've caused. We would like to tell them of our lives here. If we were away at a university, wouldn't they like us to call and let them know how we're doing? Well, we're at the Great University that all will one day attend. We're doing very well in some classes, poorly in others, but we miss our families and want to share what's happening to us. We want our loved ones to know we need their prayers. Don't forget us. But don't stop living because of what we did and because of the guilt and shame we left you with. Love us as you did when we were there and if it feels right, pick up the 'phone' and let's talk for a brief moment. It would make us so happy. We think it would make some of you happy too and help you heal a little more.

"If we could write a poem from here, to our loved ones, it would be much like the one you came across, Mom:

If I should ever leave you
whom I love
To go along the Silent Way,
grieve not,
Nor speak of me with tears,
but laugh and talk
Of me as if I were
beside you there.
(I'd come—I'd come,
could I but find a way!
But would not tears and grief
be barriers?)
And when you hear a song
or see a bird
I loved, please do not let
the thought of me
Be sad . . . For I am
loving you just as
I always have . . .
You were so good to me!
There are so many things
I wanted still
To do—so many things
to say to you . . .
Remember that I
did not fear . . . It was
Just leaving you
that was so hard to face . . .
. . . .
But this I know:
I loved you so—'twas heaven
there with you!

– "To Those I Love," Isla Paschal Richardson

"I love you, Mom. Thanks for listening. I am so sorry for what I did. There is nothing I'd like to do more than give you a big hug, one that you could feel. I'm so glad you kept trying and didn't give up. Keep the lines open. I'm not finished."

EPILOGUE

There Is No Death

*To live in
hearts
we leave
behind
is not
to die.*

– Campbell

I asked Stephen's two sisters and his brother to write a few words about their brother before they read the manuscript. After I read the letters, I asked them if I could include them in the book.

Here is Debbie's letter:

> *Being the youngest in the family, I really didn't comprehend death. I did know it was a sad thing, and I would never see my brother again.*
>
> *I was the last member in the family that saw him. I do clearly recall the day before his death. Stephen had packed a duffel bag and also a sleeping bag. As he left the house, I opened the door and asked him where he was going. He said, "I'm going to build a fort." My reaction was why do you need a sleeping bag. I watched him walk away. I was a bit confused about the bag. And that was the last time I saw him . . . for now.*
>
> *I was afraid to be alone or go up to his room. I really don't know why.*
>
> *One Christmas Stephen got me a mouse. He carried it in his pocket, trying to hide it from me so it would be a surprise. When it died, he and I put it in a small box with a poem on it and buried it.*

When it snowed, Stephen and all of us kids had great fun. Steve would pull us up a hill like we were mountain climbing. He used to make me go home because my mittens got too wet.

I remember he liked karate. He had a robe he always wore. He liked cooking eggs and eating breakfast. I remember that most— him in the kitchen.

Not long after his death, he appeared to me in the kitchen, cooking. It was only a few seconds but as clear and lifelike as a "live person" standing there. I was very stunned and scared.

I was convinced many years later that there really was life after death. This was only one sign at the time, but there were many later to follow. A Christmas tree music box started by itself and knowing in our hearts that somehow he had started it—a door bell ringing by itself, musical instrument playing alone, etc.

Stephen just has a way of letting his family know he is just fine.

I'll always wonder why he took his life, but someday we'll all know the answer.

If it wasn't for him appearing to me, I might be very sad about his death.

[Debbie was eight when Stephen died]

Andrea's letter follows:

The first thing that comes to mind, I suppose, is "blame"—who or what circumstances would cause someone to take their own life. The next thing that comes to mind is why should anyone be "to blame."

I can remember the day the police knocked on the door like it was yesterday. Other things have faded with the passage of time, and that makes me sad. Someone who is as important as a brother or sister should stand out in your memory, but when they aren't around to remind you, it becomes more difficult to remember.

Steve was the most gentle of all of us, more introspective, I suppose. It took a lot to make him angry. Not to say that Stephen didn't have his moments, they just seemed less frequent than mine, Bob's or Deb's.

I can remember having him teach me how to mow the lawn, ride a skateboard, "throw like a boy, girls can't throw right," how to ride a two-wheeler, build a fort in the woods. Once he even tried to teach me how to play the trumpet. At that time his favorite musician was Herb Alpert. He wanted to be able to play like that some day.

For some time the martial arts were a pastime. "Kung Fu" was a favorite TV show, and karate was the focus. When he got his gi and first belt, I think it was a highlight. For days he wore the gi and practiced throwing punches "the right way." Breaking boards with his hands and feet became a goal.

Camping was special. It was special for all of us. Both Stephen and Bob liked to help build the fire and keep it going. Going for hikes to look for wood and anything else we could find. I think it gave him a chance to feel close to Dad. Something that wasn't easy for him all the time. I think he really wanted Dad to be proud of him and like him. Sometimes he didn't think Dad did or was.

I also remember times at the beach, teaching me how to body surf, looking for shark's teeth, fishing for crab with chicken legs, walking along the shore in the morning, finding the horseshoe crabs that had washed up on the shore during the night.

Some things are harder to define, just vague or slight: Deer Park Retreats, visiting Nanny and Poppy and going to Miller Lake. BB gun fights in back of Uncle Dean's house with Sheri, Sandi and Tiger. Hide and seek with Ralph, Mary and Joanne P. at night in the summer. Making homemade ice cream—I'd sit on the top and he'd turn the crank. Painting the house on Heathfield—we painted the house, the back porch, the scooter, and each other. Boy, Dad was pissed!

His favorite color was a deep blue, favorite song for a time was "Er Es Tu" (It Is You), favorite musicians were Herb Alpert and another trumpet player who died of cancer at the highlight of his career.

The day the police knocked I remember very well. Actually, I should go backward here to the day he left home.

I walked into the master bedroom to ask a question, and he was in the bathroom. His green and black checkered bag was sitting on the bed. I asked him what he was doing. After a few moments, he said I had to promise not to tell Mom. He said he was going away for a couple of days to think. He'd be fine, not to worry and not to tell Mom. Being a typical little sister, I asked if he wanted me to go along. I just didn't think about how worried you'd be about him.

The next day, Chris and I were out for a walk, and I looked over to the other side of the street where an ambulance and police cars were parked. From the trees, a guy in a suit carried a bag that looked like Stephen's. I made a comment to Chris that Stephen had a bag that looked kinda like that, and thought nothing more about it.

All the kids were in the house and Tom was making popcorn. I answered the door and two guys ID'd themselves and asked to speak with my mom.

I got Mom and was asked to go into the other room. Curiosity got the best of me, and I listened at the edge of the door. It felt like my stomach dropped to the floor. After that I was kinda numb. Part of me decided that there was a mistake and he was fine. The other part knew there was no mistake.

After that, I suppose, was getting used to not seeing him anymore. And waiting for him to come to me in a dream or spirit and explain why he chose to leave that way. The next was anger for him leaving and wondering if I could have done something to prevent him from dying. There was a time I felt like he "copped out," afraid to face whatever his fears were.

As for now, I wonder where he would be in his life—college grad, married, children? How would my life be different if he were still alive? Even then and still now, I have a respect for his quiet strength.

I guess that's all for now, except I miss him.

[Andrea was almost thirteen when Stephen died]

A letter from his brother, Bob:

What can I say about a brother who we lost before he ever became a man? I could tell you how much I wish he was here now with his family. I could also tell you that if I had the ability to travel physically back through time, the first stop would be one of intervention, to keep my younger brother from doing that act which would this life keep us ever apart.

I could tell you how my heart and soul aches and how many times I've needed a brother to lean on and talk to. I could further expound on the guilt over not caring and treating him as well as I should have while he was alive.

The thing that is the most distressing to me is the fact that none of us saw it coming. Looking back it's easy to say, "We all saw the patterns," but during the time preceding his death, I would have never believed any member of our family capable of taking their own life, except for myself. You see, I failed in something that Stephen did not. I remember standing in front of the bathroom mirror and taking an entire large bottle of aspirin. I remember the total hopeless feeling that life was not worth going on living. I remember laying down in bed and waiting to die. And I remember coming to the next day, vomiting blood. I also remember that my little brother took care of me that day, thinking that I had the flu. I remember that he made me bologna and cheese sandwiches and a cold glass of milk.

I also think back on the times he would just sit and watch TV alone, and I would come home and not even bother to say hello. I remember his favorite TV show was "Kung Fu" with David Carradine and how he would get up during the commercials and imitate the moves he would see on the show.

I remember he would read books on the art of being a "ninja," but, most of all, I remember him not having any friends and spending most of his time by himself. I guess if I could look back and point to any one thing that was an obvious danger signal, it was him spending too much time alone.

I feel intense guilt for not having been any kind of decent brother to him. The plain fact of the matter is, I constantly picked on him. You see, shit rolls downhill, and our stepfather, Richard, was constantly on my case either physically or mentally. So I learned how to transfer some of that onto Steve.

When I would do something wrong, instead of admitting it and incurring the wrath of my stepfather, I would usually try to blame it on my little brother. I remember one instance in which Steve and I got into a fight while the folks were gone. I threw a crayon at him and he ducked and it hit the wall, leaving a purple mark. Well, it was just our luck that he noticed the mark the instant he came home. We both were so used to getting spanked with a belt, that neither one of us was about to admit it. So Richard got us up every thirty minutes throughout the night until around 3:00 a.m. when Steve couldn't take it anymore and confessed to my "crime."

Another instance that comes to mind is that one day when I was about 14, I decided that I couldn't take any more of Richard and decided to run away. As young as I was, I realized that I would need something to eat, so I took a huge roast out of the freezer and hid it in the bushes. Somehow, later I changed my mind and forgot about the roast outside. About a week later, Richard found the roast covered with maggots and went crazy. I knew that if he found out that I had done it, there would be hell to pay. So I denied it. But, as usual, both of us were punished until one of us broke down— Steve. Thank you, baby brother, for saving my hide all of those times.

I remember when Steve was younger that when he got spanked by Richard, he would wet himself and in return for that "crime" he would get beaten even more. I could go on and on and on and on and on, but it wouldn't bring him back, and it wouldn't change Richard from the asshole he is even still today.

Steve killed himself when I was eighteen, and my initial reaction was to cry for all of thirty minutes. Then I started to get angry and told myself over and over again that it was a chicken-shit thing to do. At the time of his death, Mom had recently and finally gotten divorced from Richard and found what we all considered at the time, an easy-going, relaxed new partner. During this period in my life, I was totally uncontrollable.

The week before Steve died, he and I went to see "Enter the Dragon" starring Bruce Lee. I remember that it was at a movie theatre in the mall and that it was one of those where they have several different choices. The one next to the movie we were watching was rated "X" and I felt that it was time my little brother broadened his horizons.

We snuck into the movie—more or less I dragged him into it. Well, we were only there about fifteen minutes before an usher started walking down the aisle and checking people's tickets. So we returned to the karate movie.

Afterwards, we hung around the mall, and I remember daring him to dump his popcorn down onto a man that was sitting on a bench on the lower level. When he did, we ran laughing. That was the last time I ever laughed with my little brother. That was also one of the few times that I remember us being really happy together and being crazy as a team.

Steve, I really need you now and wish you were here so we could do all the things that we never got a chance to do when you were alive. There's something missing in my life that only you can supply, and that something is the total love that a brother can give. I look around me and I see other people who have brothers and take them for granted, and I want to go up and shake them and say that they better pray to God that they never lose them.

I often wonder what it would be like if you were alive still. Would you be married? Would you have kids? What would you be doing for a job? But there is one thing that I know that no matter how much distance would be between us, I would still have a baby brother to call my own, and he would have a big brother, who though he may be one of the world's most screwed up people, he would always be there in a moment of need.

Steve, you know, there are three nieces and a nephew that would love you, and the sad thing is, they never knew their Uncle Steve.

God, I never knew how much I missed you until I wrote all this down. I always was angry and considered you a coward and now . . . well, now all I can do is cry and tell you how sorry I am that I wasn't there for you when you needed me. Steve, things change. When you get older you develop a better sense of family. I wish you could have grown old with the rest of us. There are so many things we could do together and it tears my heart in two knowing that this life we never will.

I wish I had Mom's gift and could communicate with you— maybe that would make things easier. But I haven't been able to. I want to say something to you that I could never say to you in life: I love you and miss you and hope the best for you in all you do.

All I ask of you is forever to remember me as loving you. . . . Your brother, Bob.

[Bob was eighteen-and-a-half when Stephen died]

• • •

Stephen and I were talking recently and he asked me to add this:

"Mom, I cry every time I read what Andrea, Debbie, and Bob wrote. I miss being with all of you. No matter how much I join you from time to time, it's not the same. I miss my family.

"We finally did it—you and I, Mom. We're finally finished. Sometimes I thought we'd never get the book done and I got as discouraged as you did. But we did it! You learned to listen, and I found a way to speak to you in a different way.

"I have some messages for my family. Tell Bob how proud I am of him and all he's doing, and not to be discouraged—ever—the best is still ahead. Tell him I think his three children are great and a lot like the four of us used to be when we were little. Tell Andrea she did a great job at the university and I'm proud of her, and I like her partner. Tell my little sister she turned out real well and that Krystalyn [Debbie's daughter] is exactly like she was.

"Tell them all that I love them and visit them often. I wish they could see me and hear me. How I wish I could give them a hug and spend time together and celebrate holidays with them. I think I would have been a good ' Uncle Steve.' I miss all of you so much—far more than you will ever know. I wish I could turn back time and undo what I did and be with all of you like I used to be. But wishing won't make it so.

"Tell my bigger family this: If a child has died, or killed himself or herself, don't forget them. Pray for them, listen for them. Get on with your own life, but keep the connection open with their dimension. It won't slow their progress or yours if you let yourself ' visit ' with them from time to time, just like when they were still alive. Some of them may even help you write a book about your experiences, and that's not a joke. Out of your pain, you might help comfort another. Don't grieve and mourn and stop living. Do all you can to help everyone around you. Your loved one in spirit will know your good works, and it will be like a gift to them and make them very happy. One day you'll be together again, even more so than when they were alive.

"Most of all, to any of you, no matter what your ages—especially those of you who are young people—who read this and are thinking about taking your own life, please listen to me for a moment. Don't do it. Please, don't do it. There are other options. Talk to your parents if you possibly can. Let them know how you're feeling, let them get you help. Don't underplay how unhappy and discouraged you are. Tell them just how badly you feel. Don't tell them that everything is OK just to make them feel better when it isn't. This is your *life*. Ask them to help you. Maybe you think they will yell at you and not understand. Well, try to make them understand. Maybe you think it will hurt them too much. If you kill yourself, it will hurt them a hundred times more.

"If you can't talk to your parents, call your minister or a hot line or a counselor or older friend. Sometimes kids your own age are too frightened of their own feelings. They have no idea what to do so they aren't much help to you, either. Find someone, *anyone,* who will first listen, then get help and counsel for you and keep in touch with you until you are thinking more clearly.

"I'm having my mother put some resources in this book. Use them. Or call her and the organization she and Herb are directors of—The Logos Center—at 602-483-8777. They care and will either help you or direct you to someone who will. But don't try to handle it by yourself. Sometimes you can't. I couldn't. It's nothing to be ashamed of. We all need help. If you get yourself help, then you will stay alive to help someone else later in your life. You don't want to hear that so many kids are worse off than you are, but it's true. They need your help. A lot of you needed the help I could have given, and I can see that clearly now, but I screwed that up.

"Suicide is so final. Once you do it, that's it. You can't change your mind. Remember how hard I tried to undo what I did? Trying to climb back in my body? The depression and agony I suffered when I realized I was dead? There was no going back and it was a hundred times worse than what I was feeling that made me kill myself. Besides, once you are out of your body and in this dimension, everything doesn't change. You don't suddenly feel perfect and excited about this new adventure. Not at all. You really want to kill yourself then, but that's impossible here. It takes months to get to feeling OK and you never get over longing for your family or those you leave behind. Especially because *you* can see and hear *them*, but rarely can they see and hear *you*.

"Don't do it. Please, don't do it. Pray and ask your guides and angels to help you through the crisis. You will be throwing away God's gift to you—your life. This life is your chance to *do* something, to grow and become the best you can, to help someone who is hurting worse than you are. When it's not your time to be here yet, it is *not* better than where you are right now. It's much, much harder.

"There are groups of us here that hear your cry. We are assigned to help you if you ask us, and we will try to help you through the bad times. Sometimes we will comfort you, sometimes we will send a thought of someone you should contact, sometimes we will tell you of foods that are literally ' driving you crazy.' If you don't think you can hear us, it's not because we're not there. You have to keep trying, and learn to listen in a different way. Other times we will try to impress upon you that there are disruptive energies coming from people around you, as well as from other levels here, that try to discourage you with their thoughts and actions. So, there are times that some thoughts you have are ' sent ' to you and not your own at all. If you think there is the slightest possibility that is true, then ask God and your angels to stand between you and those thoughts, and they will lessen.

"But, again, there are also agencies and hot lines staffed by people specifically trained to help you through these difficult times. I felt so alone. I didn't know where to turn for help and I felt without hope. There weren't many places to turn when I was in such pain, but there are now.

"I have asked my mom to include an article written by a psychiatric nurse [see Appendix] that shows you how it really is after you kill yourself. I hope it helps you make a different choice.

"Don't do it! Maybe the worst is true, that no one in your family loves you and you don't have any friends. Maybe. But God loves you. And you must learn to love yourself. You're OK. God doesn't make *junk*. And he loves you enough to give you the greatest gift he can give—*life*. Treasure it. He loves you as if you were His only child. When you go to sleep, ask God to send his angels to heal you and to help you see things differently. He *does* and *will* answer your prayers. He won't stop you from a wrong act once you set it in motion. He will try in a hundred ways to help you choose correctly and never to take those first steps toward taking your own life. He will send guides and angels and all the forces for good in heaven to try to direct you in a different and better way than suicide. Ultimately, only *you* can make the final decision. To take your life is never correct. To live life fully, to love yourself like God loves you, to become the best you can be, filled with joy and happiness, finding the good in life, and helping others is His plan for you. He created you to succeed, to be triumphant—not to fail. He created you to know that He loves you. That there is nothing you and He can't do together.

"So, *please* . . . DON'T KILL YOURSELF!

Steve"

• • •

Let us not be afraid to love our dear ones, foolishly fearing to lose them in the midst of death. Love them so dearly, so truly, so purely and forever unlamentingly, even in temporary love kindling separation that you find in them the everlasting true love of God. Finding divine love you will find beneath its canopy all your loved ones of all incarnations. . . .

– Paramahansa Yogananda

The over-long pregnancy has ended, and Stephen's book has been birthed. Stephen tells me that he and I have other books to write in the next years. We still continue to meet frequently on the bridge between our dimensions.

Stephen has now been in the spirit plane longer than he was here, this time, in a physical body. I am thankful that we can talk often together, but I would prefer to hear the voice I remember and to hold him close to me. There is no longer a physical body, Stephen Christopher. He has returned to his real home and uses only the spiritual body that he has always had and will always have. That body continued when he discarded his physical form through his own choice.

I am thankful he lives, even if it's not in this realm, here with me. I am grateful to God who loaned him to me for a while. I know of His watchcare over Stephen and our loved ones who die. I am comforted that He has provided for those of us who remain behind a way to communicate with our loved ones and friends in spirit. When that way of communication is difficult, I also know it is not He who has made it so, but my own doubt and blindness and fear.

I may always be among the "walking wounded" as family survivors of suicide are sometimes called. But I am blessed with children, grandchildren, family, and friends who walk beside me to share the pain, and as the years have passed, the more frequent joy. I am blessed with a wonderful husband who loves me deeply and faithfully and with whom

I can share my spiritual ideals and work. I am doubly blessed that Stephen can join our daily walks from time to time.

Susan White-Bowden ended her book, *Everything to Live For*, the story of her son's suicide, with the following statement: "I truly believe that if I had known then what I know now, my son would still be alive today. I pray that this book makes others stop and think about their lives and relationships with their children, and teens with their parents. My insight comes too late to save my son, but not, I hope, too late to save other kids. That is why I have spent the hours and emotions writing this book."

I also believe that had I known what I now know, Stephen would be alive and I would be entertaining his children, my grandchildren, instead of writing this book. When Stephen and Bob were born, there were no books written on co-dependence, such as Melody Beattie's *Codependent No More, Beyond Codependence* and *The Language of Letting Go,* and Pia Mellody's *Facing Codependence* and *Facing Love Addiction* to help me understand how to free myself from the toxic relationships that did irreparable damage to me and to my children. There were no books on sexual addiction, such as Richard and Elizabeth Brzeczek's, *Addicted to Adultery,* Jennifer P. Schneider, M.D.'s *Back from Betrayal: Recovering from His Affairs* and Patrick Carnes's *Out of the Shadows: Understanding Sexual Addiction* and *Don't Call it Love: Recovery from Sexual Addiction*. There were no books such as these to help me understand that the constant affairs and molesting of children by my partner had nothing to do with me, but were a dangerous addiction. There were no books to help me know how to recover emotionally from those affairs. Nothing was yet written on victims, offenders, and Messiahs, such as *When Helping You is Hurting Me: Escaping the Messiah Trap*, to help me better understand myself and everyone around me.

John Bradshaw had not yet written his incredibly helpful books nor had he appeared on television to change all our lives as we learned about family dynamics and the wounded child within. Tony Robbins was a child himself, and the world had not been blessed by his powerful Personal Power audio tapes and his best-selling books, *Unlimited Power* and *Awaken the Giant Within.* His work helped me reclaim my own personal power and gave me powerful tools to use the rest of my life, but it wasn't available then.

M. Scott Peck, M.D. had yet to write *The Road Less Traveled* and *People of the Lie* to show me and my children pathways for healthy emotional growth and an understanding of human evil. Louise Hay's *You Can Heal Your Life* was not yet published to offer us new information about loving ourselves and how to make wiser choices and create a better life. Karen Blaker's *Born to Please: Compliant Women/Controlling Men* hadn't yet been written to help me understand how to escape from being an emotionally battered woman. *Women Who Love Too Much* and *Letters from Women Who Love Too Much: A Closer Look at Relationship Addiction and Recovery* by Robin Norwood could have helped me understand that I was not alone and that other women struggled as I did with relationship addiction. Dr. George R. Bach's book, *Stop You're Driving Me Crazy: How to Keep the People In Your Life from Driving You Up the Wall,* was not yet written either, and thus I did not know how to identify and stop the crazy-making techniques of the people in my life. *The Screwtape Letters* was in print, but I had not heard of C.S. Lewis or read any of his popular books. I was unaware of his insights about the subtle manipulation that occurs from discarnates who want to get humankind off track, or that some disruptive souls in physical bodies try to do the same.

There have been dozens of books in the years since Stephen's death that have helped me carve out a more wholesome and emotionally healthy life. I have attended university classes, workshops, self-help groups, lectures, and sermons with topics on everything from relationships, philosophy, addictions, and self-esteem, to meditation, visualization, psychic development, and more, that have strengthened every step that I've taken. In the libraries and bookstores I have borrowed and bought, then read every book I could find about suicide, death, and life after death.

None of these were available in 1958 when Stephen was born to prepare me to be the best mother for him. None of these were available in the 1960s to enable me to cope with or leave Richard. None of these were available on March 18, 1974 and for years afterward to enable me better to cope with such an overwhelming challenge as the suicide of a child.

For the last sixteen years, I have led tours and traveled around much of the world, collecting books from every country, seeking out people to hear their stories and benefit from their expertise, and then sharing my own experiences.

Herb and I know ourselves better than we ever have. We are no longer victims, and we are recovering from our own addictions and co-dependency issues. We enjoy loving, healthy relationships with our friends and most of the toxic people are out of our lives. We are mending the bridges and healing our relationships with the association where Herb worked and with the clinic where I worked. As they, like ourselves, have changed and grown, we have lectured and done workshops for them, referred many people to their work, and resumed old friendships.

All of us who are committed to learn and grow are not the same people we were a decade or two ago. There can be no growth if there is no forgiveness, and, after all, as someone humorously observed, "The best way to get even is to forgive and to forget."

I understand children much better now, and I am more aware of what they need spiritually, mentally, and physically, what hurts them, and, hopefully, how to help them more fully. This knowledge is wonderful and I pray that I may use it in the best possible way.

I learned it all too late to save Stephen's life.

There is no excuse for any of us to be so psychologically and spiritually illiterate anymore. We have all the tools we need in this day and age to become emotionally healthy adults. We can learn to apply what we know and to teach it to our families and others as we have the opportunity. We must learn to raise emotionally healthy children, filled with zest and joy for life. To raise children who have strength of character and coping skills taught to them from birth, through the love and understanding of their parents or caretakers. It is the only hope we have for saving the lives of the children we love.

Thousands of children took their lives last year. They shot themselves, hanged themselves, overdosed with drugs, drove their cars into lamp posts, and slit their wrists. Even more will kill themselves each coming year. Only we, as more caring, less self-centered, better informed parents and teachers, can prevent the loss of these precious young lives.

My prayer is that those of you whose children have already committed this irreversible and heart-breaking act called suicide will find some comfort and peace in knowing that your loved one still continues, fully aware in spirit. Don't stop talking about them. Don't try to forget them because of the pain or shame you feel. They need your prayers and love as always.

If you want to try to communicate with them, don't be discouraged if it is sometimes difficult. Persevere and trust. Accept the truth of the confirmatory experiences you have had with them. You are re-learning telepathy, which you will use when you are together again. It is a soul-to-soul way of even clearer communication than words. It won't end the pain or loneliness you feel for your child. It is nothing like having them with you to hold and to love, but it will be another step in your healing, so that you too can begin to live again.

I am thankful that God loves us and has prepared a way for us to grow and heal and communicate with our loved ones who die. I am deeply thankful that He also sent His angels and guides and Jesus to show us the way.

And, especially, I am forever thankful that my beloved son, Stephen, LIVES!

> *There is no death! Our stars go down*
> *To rise upon some fairer shore;*
> *And bright in heaven's jewelled crown*
> *They shine for evermore.*
>
> *There is no death! The dust we tread*
> *Shall change beneath the summer showers*
> *To golden grain or mellow fruit,*
> *Or rainbow-tinted flowers.*
>
> *There is no death! The leaves may fall,*
> *The flowers may fade and pass away;*
> *They only wait through wintry hours*
> *The coming of the May.*
>
> *And, ever near us, though unseen,*
> *The fair immortal spirits tread;*
> *For all the boundless universe*
> *Is life; **there are no dead!***
>
>   – "Resergam," Attributed to Bulwer-Lytton

Not the end . . .

APPENDIX

Helpful Information and Resources

I. ARTICLES OF SPECIAL INTEREST REGARDING SUICIDE

"Before You Kill Yourself . . . Read These Brutal Facts
About Suicide," Renee T. Lucero:

You've decided to do it. Life is impossible. Suicide is your way out.
Fine—but before you kill yourself, there are some things you should know.
I am a psychiatric nurse, and I see the results of suicide—when it works
and, more often, when it doesn't. Consider, before you act, these facts:

Suicide is usually not successful. You think you know a way to
guarantee it? Ask the 25-year-old who tried to electrocute himself. He
lived. But both his arms are gone.

What about jumping? Ask John. He used to be intelligent, with an
engaging sense of humor. That was before he leaped from a building.
Now he's brain damaged and will always need care. He staggers and has
seizures. He lives in a fog. But worst of all, he *knows* he used to be
normal.

Even less violent methods can leave you crippled. What about pills?
Ask the 12-year-old with extensive liver damage from an overdose.
Have you seen anyone die of liver damage? It takes awhile. You turn
yellow. It's a hard way to go.

No method is foolproof. What about a gun? Ask the 24-year-old who
shot himself in the head. Now he drags one leg, has a useless arm, and

no vision or hearing on one side. He lived through his "foolproof" suicide. You might too.

Suicide is not glamorous. You may picture a movie star in a slinky negligee drifing off to eternal sleep from an overdose of pills. But your picture omits a likely sickening reality; as she dies, her sphincter muscles relax, and that beautiful gown is soiled with her excrement.

Who will clean your blood off the carpet, or scrape you brains from the ceiling? Commercial cleaning crews may refuse that job—but *someone* has to do it. Who will have to cut you down from where you hanged yourself, or identify your bloated body after you've drowned? Your mother? Your wife? Your son?

The carefully worded "loving" suicide note is no help. Those who loved you will *never* completely recover. They'll feel regret, and an unending pain. And rage, because at that moment, you cared only about yourself.

Suicide is contagious. Look around at your family: sons, daughters, brothers, sisters, husband, wife. Look closely at the four-year-old playing with his cars on the rug. Kill yourself tonight, and he may do it ten years from now. It's a fact that suicide often follows suicide in families, and kids are especially vulnerable.

You do have other choices. There are people who can help you through crisis. Call a hot line. Call a friend. Call your minister or priest. Call a doctor or hospital. Call the police.

They will tell you that there's hope. Maybe you'll find it in the mail tomorrow. Or in a phone call this weekend. Or when you meet someone shopping. You don't know—no one does. But what you're seeking could be just a minute, a day or a month away.

You say you don't want to be stopped? Still want to do it? Well, then, I may see you in the psychiatric ward later. And we'll work with whatever you have left.

• • •

"Please, God, I'm Only Seventeen"

As seen in a DEAR ABBY column by Abigail Van Buren.
Dist. by UNIVERSAL PRESS SYNDICATE. Reprinted
with permission. All rights reserved.:

Suddenly I wakened. My body was mangled. I was saturated with blood. Pieces of jagged glass were sticking out all over. Strange that I couldn't feel anything.

Hey! Don't pull that sheet over my head. I can't be dead. I'm only 17. I've got a date tonight. I'm supposed to grow up and have a wonderful life. I haven't lived yet. I can't be dead.

Later, I was placed in a drawer. My folks had to identify me. Why did they have to see me like this? Why did I have to look at Mom's eyes when she had to face the most terrible ordeal of her life? Dad suddenly looked like an old man. He told the man in charge, "Yes, he's my son."

The funeral was a wierd experience. I saw all my relatives and friends walk toward the casket. They passed by one by one and looked at me with the saddest eyes I've ever seen. Some of my buddies were crying. A few of the girls touched my hand and sobbed as they walked away.

Please, somebody wake me up. Get me out of here. I can't bear to see my mom and dad so broken up. My grandparents are so wracked with grief that they can hardly walk. My brother and sisters are like zombies, in a daze. Everybody. No one can believe this and I can't believe it either.

Please don't bury me. I'm not dead. I have a lot of living to do. I want to laugh and run again. I promise, if you give me just one more chance, God, I'll be the most careful driver in the whole world. All I want is one more chance. Please, God. I'm only 17.

II. INFORMATION REGARDING GRIEF

How To Help When A Child Dies:

For an excellent brochure, "How Can I Help?" order from The Compassionate Friends, P.O. Box 3696, Oak Brook, IL 60522-3696 or call 708-990-0010. In addition, Compassionate Friends offers a variety of helpful resource materials.

Among the suggestions and insights in this brochure: Grief lasts far longer than anyone expects; don't expect your friends to be unchanged by this experience. Stay in touch with the family, and mention the child in conversations. Don't be afraid to cry with the parents. Don't say "I know how you feel." Avoid using "it was God's will" or "at least you have other children." Listen; understand that the parents have a need to talk about their child. Don't presume to offer answers about serious questions the parent may have about God's role in the child's death. Be aware of what needs to be done and offer to do specific tasks. Give special attention to surviving children who are often hurt and ignored. Don't assume the surviving children aren't hurting because they don't express their feelings. Share a fond memory of the child. Remember the family on the child's birthday and death anniversary. Take the initiative to suggest lunch or movie as relief from the isolation of grief when appropriate. (Reprinted by permission of The Compassionate Friends.)

• • •

Suggestions For Friends and Relatives of the Grieving Survivor:

1. *Get in touch.* Telephone. Speak either to the mourner or to someone close and ask when you can visit and how you might help. Even if much time has passed, it's never too late to express concern.

2. *Say little on an early visit.* In the initial period (before burial), your brief embrace, your press of the hand, your few words of affection and feeling may be all that is needed.

3. *Avoid cliches and easy answers.* "He had a good life," "He is out of pain," and "Aren't you lucky that . . .," are not likely to help. A simple "I'm sorry" is better. Likewise, spiritual sayings can even provoke anger unless the mourner shares the faith that is implied. In genreal, *do not attempt to minimize the loss.*

4. *Be yourself.* Show your own natural concern and sorrow in your own way and in your own words.

5. *Keep in touch.* Be available. Be there. If you are a close friend or relative, your presence might be needed from the beginning. Later, when close family may be less available, anyone's visit and phone call can be very helpful.

6. *Attend to practical matters.* Discover if you might be needed to answer the phone, usher in callers, prepare meals, clean the house, care for the children, etc. This kind of help lifts burdens and creates a bond. It might be needed well beyond the initial period, especially for the widowed.

7. *Encourage others to visit or help.* Usually one visit will overcome a friend's discomfort and allow him or her to contribute further support. You might even be able to *schedule* some visitors, so that everyone does not come at once in the beginning or fails to come at all later on.

8. *Accept silence.* If the mourner doesn't feel like talking, don't force conversation. Silence is better than aimless chatter. The mourner should be allowed to lead.

9. *Be a good listener.* When suffering spills over in words, you can do the one thing the bereaved needs above all else at that time—*you can*

listen. Is he emotional? Accept that. Does he cry? Accept that too. Is he angry at God? God will manage without your defending him. Accept whatever feelings are expressed. Do not rebuke. Do not change the subject. Be as understanding as you can be.

10. *Do not attempt to tell the bereaved how he feels.* You can ask (without probing), but you cannot *know*, except as he tells you. Everyone, bereaved or not, resents an attempt to describe his feelings. To say, for example, "You must feel relieved now that he is out of pain," is presumptuous. Even to say, "I know just how you feel," is questionable. *Learn* from the mourner; do not *instruct* him.

11. *Do not probe for details about the death.* If the survivor offers information, listen with understanding.

12. *Comfort children in the family.* Do not assume that a seemingly calm child is not sorrowing. If you can, be a friend to whom feelings can be confided and with whom tears can be shed. In most cases, incidentally, children should be left in the home and not shielded from the grieving of others.

13. *Avoid talking to others about trivia in the presence of the recently bereaved.* Prolonged discussion of sports, weather, or stock market, for example, is resented, even if done purposely to distract the mourner.

14. *Allow the "working through of grief."* Do not whisk away clothing or hide pictures. Do not criticize seemingly morbid behavior. Young people may repeatedly visit the site of the fatal accident. A widow may sleep with her husband's pajamas as a pillow. A young child may wear his dead sibling's clothing.

15. *Write a letter.* A sympathy card is a poor substitute for your own expression. If you take time to write of your love for and memories of the one who died, your letter might be read many times and cherished, possibly into the next generation.

16. *Encourage the postponement of major decisions until after the period of intense grief.* Whatever can wait should wait.

17. *In time, gently draw the mourner into quiet, outside activity.* He may not have the initiative to go out on his own.

18. *When the mourner returns to social activity, treat him as a normal person.* Avoid pity—it destroys self respect. Simple understanding is enough. Acknowledge the loss, the change in his life, but don't dwell on it.

19. *Be aware of needed progress through grief.* If the mourner seems unable to resolve anger or guilt, for example, you might suggest a consultation with a clergyman or other trained counselor.

•

A final thought: Helping must be more than following a few rules. Especially if the bereavement is devastating and you are close to the bereaved, you may have to give more time, more care, *more of yourself* than you imagined. And you will have to perceive the *special needs* of your friend and creatively attempt to meet those needs. Such commitment and effort may even save a life. At the least, you will know the satisfaction of being truly and deeply helpful.

From the folder "Is There Anything I Can Do to Help?" by Amy Hillyard Jensen, copyright © 1985, Medic Publishing Co., P.O. Box 89, Redmond, WA 98073. Reprinted by permission.

III. SUICIDE PREVENTION INFORMATION

Warning Signs and Behaviors of High Risk Individuals Contemplating Suicide:

• Major loss (of loved person, home, possessions, or status), especially if preceded by other losses. A suicide in the family.
• Neglect of appearance.
• Withdrawal from people, especially close friends or family.
• Putting oneself down. Continued lack of self esteem.
• Unusual or extreme change in school performance or attendance.
• Change in sleep patterns—insomnia or oversleeping.
• Weight loss or gain.
• Self-injury.
• Staying away or running away from home.
• Irritability and restlessness.
• Angry outbursts at home or school.
• Use of alcohol or drugs as an escape from pain.
• Sudden beginning of self-destructive or risk-taking behavior, like fast driving.
• Intense feelings of being trapped and helpless, without any hope of changing the situation.
• Specific threats of suicide (verbal or written).
• Prior suicide attempts.
• Giving away prized possessions.
• Preoccupation with death or suicide.
• Walks slowly, talks slowly with difficulty, slumps rather than sits.
• Personality changes—nervousness, anger, apathy or cries frequently.
• Extremes sadness or hopelessness.
• Says he's hurting his loved ones by staying alive, or is a burden to them.
• Makes vague statements couched in deep misery, or prompted by guilt.

Your child or loved one may have some, and in extreme cases, all of these signs and behaviors. Some of these feelings and behaviors may be an indication of depression and suicide is not being considered. However, they are warning signs and a call for help.

Stephen manifested a number of these signs, and I believe that had I recognized them for what they were—that he was seriously contemplating suicide—he would still be alive today. Most suicides are ambivilent, and by becoming aware of these warning signs, you may be able to intervene and save a life.

• • •

The following is excerpted from an article written by John Hudson, an Assistant Principal of Paradise Valley High School District in Arizona, regarding his establishment of a suicide prevention program in his school and other schools:

The Paradise Valley School District is meeting the problem of adolescent suicide head on through the establishment of a suicide prevention program. . . . All too often we hear "If only I had known," "I wish there was something I could have done," in response to suicide. The truth is that, more often than not, something could have been done. Individuals in crisis do give off many signs and signals. We are capable of "reading" these, and providing support which might help to bring someone through their crisis.

The program . . . consists of a two fold training experience. The first part involves instruction dealing with classic examples of and traditional approaches to suicide. The second facet deals with an innovative approach which involves the use of intuition.

For years we have been taught to disregard the information our intuition provides us with and to opt instead for what is logical and safe. For example, when encountering a friend or acquaintance who we feel is "not himself," we often ask, "Are you OK today?" The automatic response is "Yes, I'm fine." Many times we "know" (intuitively) this person is not OK, but by accepting this response, we are "off the hook." The training participants receive in this program, sensitizes them and helps to bring these intuitive messages into focus. We are conditioned to pay attention to what these messages tell us.

In addition to the effectiveness of the intuitive training, the other major strength of this program, is its team approach. Adults and students participate in the training sessions and form a Suicide Prevention Team as *equal* partners. This provides all involved with valuable insights.

Behaviors often times indicative of individuals contemplating suicide:

• A sudden change in attitude from deep depression to a calm, determined or even cheerful outlook. This can indicate a decision to solve problems through suicide.

• Ending of a relationship (boyfriend-girlfriend) particularly if this is the only supportive relationship an individual experiences.

• A sudden significant drop in grades.

• Multiple pressures: home, grades, behavior.

• Suddenly becoming accident prone.

• An inability to fit in or belong to any group, possibly leading to ridicule.

• Lethargy, lack of interest in surroundings, perhaps accompanied by excessive periods of sleep.

• A perceived inability to live up to parents/friends/personal expectations.

• Feelings of shame or guilt for having brought dishonor upon family or friends.

• Loss of supportive relationships due to family relocation.

• • •

Steps You Can Take To Help An Individual in a Suicidal Crisis:

• Listen and show that you care.

• Stay with the person if you feel there is any danger.

• Ask the person to express his or her feelings. Letting out pent-up emotions is essential in resolving the stressful situation. Let the person speak about his troubles at his own speed.

• Ask open-ended questions (what, how, tell me more about).

• Paraphrase and reflect thoughts and feelings.

• Don't argue or preach.

• Determine if the person has a plan. Assume a fact-finding, problem-solving attitude. The fewer supports and the more specific the plan, the greater the suicidal risk. (Talking openly about it will not cause more trouble or give the person ideas.)

• Assess suicidal potential: ask about frequency and intensity of self-destructive thoughts and feelings; ask about stressors (recent events, circumstances, losses); ask about actual plans and means of suicide; check the person's own estimate of his/her self control.

• Assist the person in defining alternatives and other options.

• Keep calm—at least act calm (but concerned).

• Try to detect what the person is trying to communicate, and to whom.

- Don't try to "cure" the person.
- Don't rush the person to the hospital.
- Talk to the significant other or family member of person, in the presence of the suicidal person if possible. Do not agree to keep a secret of the suicidal intent.
- Take a break to consult with others. Facilitate getting professional help for the person (accompany if necessary).
- Call a suicide prevention hotline.

REMEMBER: NO MATTER HOW MUCH THE PERSON MAY SEEM TO WANT TO DIE, ON SOME LEVEL HE ALSO WANTS DESPERATELY TO LIVE.

Twelve-Step Principles To Aid with Personal Dependencies:

This is the basic Twelve Step Program, modified to be more personal. Contact Twelve Step groups in your area depending upon the particular addiction or concern you need help with.

1. I, _____ (name), admit I am powerless over alcohol/drugs/food/emotions/gambling/sex/other and that my life has become unmanageable.

2. I believe that a power greater than myself can restore me to sanity.

3. I will turn my will and my life over to the care of God as I understand God.

4. I will make a searching and fearless moral inventory of myself.

5. I admit to God, to myself, and to another human being the exact nature of my wrongs.

6. I am entirely ready to have God remove all of these defects of character.

7. I humbly ask God to remove my shortcomings.

8. I will make a list of all persons I have harmed and become willing to make amends to them all.

9. I will make direct amends to such people wherever possible, except when to do so would injure them or others.

10. I will always continue to take personal inventory, and when I am wrong, I will promptly admit it.

11. I seek through prayer and meditation to improve my conscious contact with God as I understand God, praying only for knowledge of God's will for me and the power to carry that out.

12. Having had a spiritual awakening as the result of these steps, I try to carry this message to others and to practice these principles in all my affairs.

Often by acknowledging the first step, affirming a belief in a power greater than ourselves, turning our lives over to God, then continuing working on the other steps, a crisis can be avoided and a life saved.

• • •

Perhaps when wondering how to deal with your children, these words can help to provide a perspective from a child's point of view:

• DON'T spoil me. I know quite well I shouldn't have all I ask for. I'm only testing you.
• DON'T be afraid to be firm with me. I prefer it—it makes me feel secure.
• DON'T let me form bad habits. I have to rely on you to detect them in the early stages.
• DON'T make me feel smaller than I am. It only makes me behave stupidly "big."
• DON'T correct me in front of other people if you can help it. I'll take much more notice if you talk to me quietly in private.
• DON'T protect me from consequences. I need to learn the painful way sometimes.
• DON'T make me feel my mistakes are sins. It upsets my sense of values.
• DON'T be too upset if I say "I hate you." It isn't you I hate, but your power to thwart me.
• DON'T take too much notice of my small ailments. Sometimes they get me the attention I need.
• DON'T nag. If you do, I'll have to protect myself by appearing deaf.
• DON'T make rash promises. I feel badly let down when promises are broken.
• DON'T forget that I can't explain myself as well as I'd like. This is why I'm not always accurate.
• DON'T tax my honesty too much. I'm easily frightened into telling lies.
• DON'T be inconsistent. It completely confuses me and makes me lose my faith in you.
• DON'T put me off when I ask questions. If you do, you'll find I stop asking and seek information elsewhere.
• DON'T tell me my fears are silly. They're terribly real.
• DON'T suggest that you are perfect or infallible. It gives me too great a shock when I find out you're neither.
• DON'T ever think it is beneath your dignity to apologize to me. An honest apology makes me surprisingly warm toward you.
• DON'T forget I love experimenting. I can't get on without it, so please put up with it.

• DON'T forget how quickly I'm growing up. It must be hard to keep pace with me, but please try.

IV. WHERE TO FIND HELP

Assistance and/or referrals are often available from such organizations and listings as: Suicide Prevention Centers; Crisis Intervention Centers or Crisis Centers; Mental Health Clinics; Hospitals; Family Physicians or Holistic Practitioners; Ministers, clergy, churches; New Age Churches; Metaphysical Centers; Health Food Stores (don't laugh—they often have great networking links); County Mental Health Department; U.S.Government Printing Offices for a variety of information and pamphlets.

Specialized self-help groups are often listed in the *Yellow Pages* or through telephone information under: Survivors of Suicide; Alcoholics Anonymous (AA); Al-Anon: Families Anonymous; Gamblers Anonymous; Narcotics Anonymous; Overeaters Anonymous (OA); Parents Anonymous; Sex Addicts Anonymous; Sexaholics Anonymous.

If a number listed below does not work in your area, telephone 1-800-555-1212, the directory assistance number for toll-free listings. Numbers change often, and some "800" numbers are unavailable in particular areas. If you are unable to locate help, dial "911" for emergencies.

The following resources are listed in alphabetical order:

• Adcare Referral, (800) 252-6465. For drug and alcohol problems.

• Adults Molested as Children, (408) 280-5055.

• Alcoholics Anonymous (AA), General Service Headquarters, 475 Riverside Drive, New York, NY 10015, (212) 870-3400. Literature. Phone 212-683-3900 for referral to someone in your area.

• Al-Anon Family Group Headquarters, P.O. Box 862, Midtown Station, New York, NY 10018-0862, (212) 302-7240. For the families of alcoholics or substance abusers.

• American Association of Suicidology, 2459 S. Ash Street, Denver, CO 80222, (303) 692-0985. For suicide or other crisis. List of survivor groups, publications, books, films, newsletters focusing on survivors.

Goal is to understand and prevent suicide. Promotes research, public awareness programs, training for professionals, volunteers, and other programs for the understanding and prevention of suicide. National clearinghouse for information on suicide. Annual conference on suicide.

• American Psychiatric Association, (202) 682-6000. Provides referral to psychiatrists in your area working with suicidal teens or others.

• American Psychological Association, (202) 336-5500. Will provide a list of psychologists in your area working with suicidal teens, or others.

• Anorexia Nervosa and Related Eating Disorders Information Line. P.O. Box 5102, Eugene, OR 97405, (503) 344-1144, or (503) 686-7372. Information and referral service for questions regarding eating disorders and their treatment.

• Childhelp USA, Child Abuse Hotline, (800) 422-4453. If you are being sexually abused and need help, or if you want to report abuse, you will be directed to the appropriate counselors. Literature available also.

• Cocaine Hotline, 1-800-COCAINE. Referral service for drug treatment. Information.

• Co-Dependents of Sexual Addicts (CoSA), P.O. Box 14537, Minneapolis, MN 55414, (612) 537-6904. Support groups for families of sexual addicts.

• The Compassionate Friends National Headquarters, P.O. Box 3696, Oak Brook, IL 60522-3696, (708) 990-0010. Local chapters offering healing and hope for bereaved parents. Newsletter by subscription.

• Concern for Dying, 250 W. 57th Street, New York, NY 10107. Conferences on death and dying. Distributes the Living Will. Newsletter and other material. Annual convention.

• Contact USA, Pouch A, Harrisburg, PA 17105-1300, (717) 232-3501 for Helpline Telephone Numbers in your area and information. Over 73 centers. Affiliated with LifeLine International with groups in ten countries.

• Covenant House, East Coast, (800) 999-9999. Help and referrals.

• Emotional Health Anonymous, 2420 San Gabriel Blvd. Rosemead, CA 91770, (213) 283-3574.

• Families Anonymous, P.O. Box 528, Van Nuys, CA 91408, (800) 736-9805 and (818) 989-7841. Support program for drug, alcohol, and behavior problems in children. Assists parents in developing a better understanding of the problems. 500 groups worldwide. Literature.

• Grief Recovery Institute, 8306 Wilshire Blvd., Suite 21A, Beverly Hills, CA 90211. To talk with someone, no message service, Monday through Friday,. 9 a.m.-5 p.m. PST: (800) 445-4808. To talk with someone during business hours or to leave a message 24 hours a day: (213) 650-1234. They believe grief is a natural reaction to loss and will try to lead people in directions of healing. Seminars, certification programs for grief counselors. They use the *Grief Recovery Handbook* by John James.

• Hemlock Society, P.O. Box 66218, Los Angeles, CA 90066. Supports voluntary euthanasia for the advanced terminally ill and the seriously incurably ill. Publications.

• Incest Survivors Resource Network, 15 Rutherford Place, New York, NY 10003, (505) 521-4260. Support groups for incest victims.

• Life Resource Center, One Eliot Place, Fairfield, CT 06430, (203) 259-8804. Dr. Marcia Harrison, Director. Counseling Center for those in the Northeast area. Dr. Harrison, a psychologist and minister, is affiliated with Logos Center in Scottsdale, Arizona.

• Link Counseling Center, 348 Mount Vernon Highway NE, Atlanta, GA 30328, (404) 256-9797. Director: Iris Bolton, author of *My Son, My Son*, about the suicide death of her son. Counseling and referrals

• Logos Center, P.O. Box 12880, Scottsdale, AZ 85267-2880, (602) 483-8777. Rev. Anne Puryear and Herbert B. Puryear, Ph.D., Co-Directors. Counseling and referral.

• McGirr, Marilyn, Ph.D., Psychologist. Phone (201) 567-3816, Monday/Wednesday/Friday, Englewood, New Jersey. Phone (908) 654-8074, Tuesday/Thursday, Westfield, NJ. Counseling adults and teens. Associated with Logos Center in New York/Connecticut.

• Mothers Against Drunk Drivers (MADD) Headquarters, 511 E. John Carpenter Freeway, #700, Irving, TX 75062. Victims Hotline: (800) 438-6233. Literature: (214) 744-6233. Referrals to groups in your state. Acts as the voice of the victim of drunk driving accidents. Information for victims and their families on bereavement groups. Newsletter and brochure.

• NAR-ANON, P.O. Box 2562, San Pedro, CA 90731, (310) 547-5800. For families and friends of recovering addicts.

• Narcotics Anonymous (NA), P.O. Box 9999, Van Nuys, CA 91409, (818) 780-3951. Referrals throughout the worlds for addicts and recovering addicts.

• National AIDS Information Clearninghouse, (800) 458-5231, also in Spanish.

• National Committe for Youth Suicide Prevention, (415) 877-5604.

• National Council on Sexual Addiction, NCSA, P.O. Box 20249, Wickenburg, AZ, 85354, (800) 321-2066. Send self-addressed stamped envelope for information.

• National HIV and AIDS, P.O. Box 6003, Rockville, MD 20849. Information Service Hotline: (800) 342-AIDS. General publications, AIDS packet.

• National Institute of Mental Health, (301) 443-4536. Literature on mental illness, depression.

• National Mental Health Association, (703) 684-7722, for community mental health clinics in your area.

• National Runaway Switchboard, (800) 621-4000. Crisis hotline. Counselors trained in crisis intervention. Referrals.

• National Self-Help Clearinghouse, (212) 642-2944. Send stamped self-addressed envelope to: 25 W. 43rd Street, New York, NY 10036 for information and literature.

• National Youth Crisis Hotline, (800) 448-4663.

• Nationally Sexually Transmitted Disease Hotline, (800) 227-8922.

• 1-800-ALCOHOL. Phone (800) 252-6465 for 24-hour help and referral regarding alcohol and drug abuse.

• Overeaters Anonymous (OA), (602) 831-6849. Doris, World Chairman for young people. Meetings, literature, youth newspaper, and pen pals all over the world. Help for young people with eating disorders and weight problems. Referrals to groups in your area for adults and young people.

• Parents Anonymous, 6733 South Sepulveda Boulevard, Suite 270, Los Angeles, CA 90045,(800) 352-0386 in California, (800) 421-0353 outside California. Also: (800) 775-1134. Self-help organization that provides safe, supportive weekly meetings where parents can discuss their problems with their peers and with trained volunteer professionals. Free and open to all parents who are overwhelmed, isolated, or afraid of their anger toward their children. Referrals.

• Parents of Murdered Children, 100 E. 8th Street, B-41, Cincinnati, OH 45202, (513) 721-5683. Physical and emotional support. Information about the criminal justice system as it pertains to survivors of a homicide victim. Newsletter.

• Parents United, P.O. Box 952, San Jose, CA 95108, (408) 453-7616. For those who have experienced sexual molestation. Provides assistance to families affected by incest and other types of child sexual abuse. Crisis and long-term support. Training of professionals. Literature. 24-hour coverage.

• Sex and Love Addicts Anonymous, P.O. Box 119, Boston, MA 02258, (617) 332-1845.

• Sex Addicts Anonymous (SAA), P.O. Box 3038, Minneapolis, MN 55403, (612) 339-0217. Support groups for sexual addicts that follow a program adapted from Twelve-Step program of AA, in dealing with sexual behavior. (Sexual addicts are people who compulsively repeat sexual behavior that is often abusive, exploitive, and damaging to their lives at home and at work.)

• Sexaholics Anonymous (SA), P.O. Box 300, Simi Valley, CA 93062, (803) 581-3343. Groups for individuals wanting to stop sexually self-destructive thinking and behavior such as fantasy, pornography, incest, or criminal sexual activity. The group believes that the sexaholic is addicted to lust and sex as others are to alcohol and drugs. This behavior is often followed by guilt, remorse, and depression, and may do serious damage to relationships.

• Sexual Compulsives Anonymous, P.O. Box 1585, New York, NY 10113-0935, (212) 439-1123.

• Society for the Right to Die, 250 W. 57th Street, New York, NY 10107, (212) 366-5540. Publications, convention. Protects the rights of dying patients.

• Suicide Prevention Hotline, Humanistics Foundations Hot line, (800) 333-4444, or call 310-983-8383. Can help you or refer you for help in your area.

• WESOM, Inc., P.O. Box 46312, Chicago, IL 60646, (312) 792-7034. Computerized service, leave a message and telephone number and your call will be returned. This is the "We Saved Our Marriage" organization founded by Richard and Elizabeth Brzeczek, authors of *Addicted to Adultery*. Groups throughout the country, based on 12-Step program, for addiction to adultery and for wives or husbands whose spouses are unfaithful.

• • •

Whenever Richard Cory
        went downtown,
We people on the pavement
        looked at him.
He was a gentleman
        from sole to crown,
Clean favored, and
        imperially slim.
And he always was
        quietly arrayed,
And he was always human
        when he talked;
But still he fluttered
        pulses when he said
"Good morning," and he
        glittered when he walked
And he was rich—yes,
        richer than a king.
And admirably schooled
        in every grace;
In fine, we thought that

he was everything
To make us wish that we
        were in his place.
So on we worked, and
        waited for the light,
And went without the meat,
        and cursed the bread;
And Richard Cory, one
        calm summer night,
Went home and put a bullet
        through his head.

– Edward Arlington Robinson

References
and Related Reading

As I researched suicide, explored Stephen's death, delved into our family dynamics, and tried to understand myself, I personally read every book listed here, as well as dozens of others I have not included. I have selected some of the books and publications that gave me special insights, broadened my understanding, and helped me to heal. Since I read these books over a period of years, I am putting an asterisk (*) beside those books that I would consider "read first" or "recommended reading." Then, as time permits, read the others that sound helpful to you.

Following these books, you will find additional resources including recommended movies, and audio and video tapes of special interest.

– Anne Puryear

Abravanel, Elliot D., M.D. and Elizabeth King. *Dr. Abravanel's Body Type Diet and Lifetime Nutrition Plan.* New York: Bantam, 1983.

*———. *Dr. Abravanel's Body Type Program for Health, Fitness and Nutrition.* New York: Bantam, 1985.

———. *Dr. Abravanel's Anti-Craving Weight Loss Diet.* New York: Bantam, 1990.

Al-Anon's Twelve Steps and Twelve Traditions. New York: Al-Anon Family Group Headquarters, Inc., 1981.

Alexander, Helen Mae. *The Angels Speak.* Denver: State of the Art, Ltd., 1984.

———. *Angels Can Light Up Your Life.* New York: Vantage Press, 1993.

*Alvarez, A. *The Savage God: A Study of Suicide*. New York: Random House, 1972.

American Psychologist Special Issue: Adolescence. Vol. 48, Number 2 (February 1993). American Psychological Association.

Anderson, Dorothy, B. and Lenora J. McClean. *Identifying Suicide Potential*. New York: Behavioral Publications, 1969.

Atkinson, J. Maxwell. *Discovering Suicide: Studies in the Social Organization of Sudden Death*. Pittsburgh: University of Pittsburgh Press, 1978.

Bach, George R. and Ronald M. Deutsch. *Stop! You're Driving Me Crazy: How to Keep the People in Your Life From Driving You Up the Wall*. New York: Berkley Books, 1979.

Bach, Richard. *The Bridge Across Forever*. New York: Dell Book, 1984.

_____. *Jonathan Livingston Seagull*. New York: MacMillan Co., 1970.

Bander, Peter. *Voices From the Tapes: Recordings From the Other World*. New York: Drake Publishers, 1973.

Barbanell, Sylvia. *When a Child Dies*. London: Pilgrims Book Services, 1984.

Batzler, Louis Richard. *Some Paranormal Perspectives on Suicide, From the Rising Tide of Suicide; A Guide to Prevention, Intervention and Postvention*. Spiritual Frontiers Quarterly, Summer 1988, Volume XX, Number 3. Philadelphia: Spiritual Frontiers Fellowship, Inc.

Beard, Paul. *Living On: How Consciousness Continues and Evolves After Death*. New York: Continuum Publishing Corp., 1981.

*Beattie, Melody. *Codependent No More: How to Stop Controlling Others and Start Caring for Yourself*. San Francisco: Harper & Row, 1987.

————. *Beyond Codependencey: And Getting Better All the Time*. New York: Harper/Hazelden, 1989.

*————. *A Reason to Live*. Wheaton, IL: Tyndale House Publishers, 1991.

*————. *The Language of Letting Go*. New York: Hazelden, Harper Collins, 1990.

Bender, David L. and Bruno Leone. *Death and Dying: Opposing Viewpoints*. St. Paul: Greenhaven Press, 1987.

Berent, Irving, M.D. *The Algebra of Suicide*. New York: Human Sciences Press, 1981.

Berkus, Rusty. *To Heal Again*. Encino, CA: Red Rose Press, 1986.

*Berry, Carmen Renee. *When Helping You is Hurting Me: Escaping the Messiah Trap*. San Francisco: Harper & Row, 1988.

*Bethards, Betty. *There Is No Death*. Novato, CA: Inner Light Foundation, 1985.

Blaker, Karen, Ph.D. *Born to Please: Compliant Women/Controlling Men*. New York: St. Martin's Press, 1988.

*Bolton, Iris with Curtis Mitchell. *My Son, My Son: A Guide To Healing After a Suicide in the Family*. Atlanta, GA: Bolton Press, 1983. (1325 Belmore Way N.E., Atlanta, GA 30350)

Boss, Judy. *In Silence They Return*. New York: Manor Books, 1972.

————. *A Garden of Joy*. St. Paul, MN: Llewellyn Publications, 1974.

Bozarth-Campbell, Alla, Ph.D. *Life is Goodbye, Life is Hello: Grieving Well Through All Kinds of Loss*. Minneapolis: CompCare Publications, 1983.

Bradshaw, John. *Homecoming: Reclaiming & Championing Your Inner Child*. New York: Bantam, 1990.

————. *Bradshaw On: The Family: A Revolutionary Way of Self Discovery*. Deerfield Beach, FL: Health Communications, Inc., 1988.

————. *Healing the Shame that Binds You*. Deerfield Beach, FL: Health Communications, Inc., 1988.

*Brown, Les. *Live Your Dreams*. New York: William Morrow and Co., 1992.

Browne, Joy, Dr. *Nobody's Perfect: How to Stop Blaming and Start Living*. New York: Simon & Schuster, 1988.

*Brzeczek, Richard and Elizabeth Brzeczek, with Sharon DeVita. *Addicted to Adultry*. New York: Bantam, 1989.

Budge, E. A. Wallis. *The Book of the Dead*. New York: Bell Publishing Co., University Books, 1960.

Bundesen, Lynne. *GodDependency*. New York: Crossroad Publishing Co., 1989.

Burnham, Sophy. *Angel Letters*. New York: Ballantine, Random House, 1991.

————. *A Book of Angels*. New York: Ballantine, Random House, 1991.

*Caddy, Eileen. *Opening Doors Within*. Scotland: Findhorn Press, 1988.

*Carnes, Patrick. *Out of the Shadows: Understanding Sexual Addiction.* Minneapolis: CompCare Publishers, 1983.

―――. *Don't Call it Love: Recovering from Sexual Addiction.* New York: Bantam, 1991.

Casey, Karen and Martha Vanceburg. *The Promise of a New Day.* Minneapolis: Winston Press, 1983.

Cayce, Hugh Lynn. *God's Other Door and The Continuity of Life.* Virginia Beach, VA: A.R.E. Press, 1958.

Chaney, Earlyne. *The Mystery and Meaning of Death and Dying.* York Beach, ME: Samuel Weiser, Inc., 1988.

―――. *The Book of Beginning Again.* Upland, CA: Astara, Inc., 1981.

―――. *Remembering: A Story Of Life After Death.* Upland, CA: Astara's Library of Mystical Classics, 1974.

Choron, Jacques. *Suicide.* New York: Charles Scribner's Sons, 1972.

Coca, Arthur R., M.D. *The Pulse Test: Easy Allergy Detection.* New York: Arco Publishing, Inc., 1982.

Constas, Robert M.D. *Death Does Not Exist and the Psychology of Becoming Oneself.* Sedona, AZ: Aquarian Educational Group, 1979.

Cornish, John. *About Death and After.* England: New Knowledge Books, 1975.

Course In Miracles. Foundation For Inner Peace, 1975.

Cramer, Kathryn D., Ph.D. *Staying on Top When Your World Turns Upside Down: Turn Your Stress into Strength.* New York: Viking Penguin, 1990.

Currie, Ian. *You Cannot Die: The Incredible Findings of a Century of Research on Death.* New York: Playboy Paperbacks, 1978.

Danto, Bruce L. and Austin H. Kutscher. *Suicide and Bereavement.* New York: ARNO Press, 1977.

Davis, Dorothy W. *Robin's Return and Ray.* New York: Vantage Press, 1986.

*DeAngelis, Barbara, Ph.D. *Secrets About Men Every Woman Should Know.* New York: Dell, Bantam, 1990.

Deats, Sara Munson, Ph.D. and Lagretta Tallent Lenker, M.S. *Youth Suicide Prevention: Lessons From Literature.* New York: Plenum Publishing Corporation, 1989.

Delacour, Jean-Baptiste. *Glimpses of the Beyond.* Delacourte, NY: 1973.

Dempsey, David K. *The Way We Die: An Investigation of Death and Dying in America Today.* New York: MacMillan, 1975.

Dobson, James C., Dr. *Love Must Be Tough: New Hope for Families in Crisis.* Dallas: Word Publishing Inc., 1983.

Dorff, Francis. *The Art of Passing Over.* New York: Paulist Press, 1988.

Doss, Richard W. *The Last Enemy: A Christian Understanding of Death.* New York: Harper & Row, 1974.

Dublin, Louis I. *Suicide: A Sociological and Statistical Study.* New York: Ronald Press, 1963.

Dunne, J.W. *Nothing Dies.* London: Faber and Faber, 1951.

Durkheim, Emile. *Suicide: A Study in Sociology.* New York: Free Press Paperback, MacMillan, 1951.

Each Day A New Beginning. New York: Harper & Row, 1982.

Easwaran, Eknath. *Dialogue with Death: The Spiritual Psychology of the Katha Upanishad.* Petaluma, CA: Nilgiri Press, 1981.

Evans-Wentz, W.Y. *The Tibetan Book of the Dead.* London: Oxford University Press, 1957.

Exupery, Antoine de Saint. *The Little Prince.* New York: Harcourt, Brace & World, 1971.

Farnese, A. and Franchezzo. *A Wanderer in the Spirit Lands.* California: Health Research, 1965.

Farthing, Geoffrey. *When We Die.* London: Theosophical Publishing House, 1968.

*Finch, Stuart M., M.D., Elva O. Poznanski, M.D. *Adolescent Suicide.* Springfield, IL: Charles C. Thomas, 1971.

Foos-Graber, Anya. *Deathing: An Intelligent Alternative for the Final Moments of Life.* Reading, MA: Addison-Wesley Publishing Co., 1984.

Ford, Arthur. *The Life Beyond Death.* New York: Berkley, 1971.

Fox, Emmet. *Life after Death.* California: DeVorss & Co., 1966.

Fremou, William J., Maria de Perczel, and Thomas Ellis. *Suicide Risk, Assessment and Response Guidelines.* New York: Pergamon Press, 1990.

Fromm, Erich. *The Anatomy of Human Destructiveness.* Greenwich, CT: Fawcett Crest, 1973.

Fulghum, Robert. *All I Really Need to Know I Learned In Kindergarten.* New York: Ivy Books, Published by Ballantine Books, 1986.

Gerber, Richard, M.D. *Vibrational Medicine: New Choices for Healing Ourselves.* Santa Fe, NM: Bear and Company, 1988.

Gernsbacher, Larry Morton, Ph.D. *The Suicide Syndrome.* New York: Human Sciences Press, 1985.

Gibran, Kahlil. *The Prophet.* New York: Alfred A. Knopp, Inc., 1951.

*Giffin, Mary, M.D. and Carol Felsenthal. *A Cry For Help.* Garden City, New York: Doubleday, 1983.

*Giovacchini, Peter, M.D. *The Urge to Die: Why Young People Commit Suicide.* New York: MacMillan Pub., 1981.

*Greaves, Helen. *Testimony of Light.* Suffolk, England: Hillman Printers, 1980.

―――. *The Challenging Light.* Suffolk, England: Neville Spearman Ltd., 1984.

Grollman, Earl A. *Suicide: Prevention, Intervention, Postvention.* Boston: Beacon Press, 1988.

Hafen, Brent Q., Ph.D. and Kathryn J. Frandsen. *Youth, Suicide, Depression and Loneliness.* Evergreen, CO: Cordillera Press, Inc., 1986.

Hampton, Charles. *The Transition Called Death.* Wheaton, IL: Theosophical Publishing House, 1943.

*Hay, Louise L. *You Can Heal Your Life.* New York: Coleman Publishing, 1984.

―――. *Heal Your Body.* Santa Monica, California: Hay House, 1984.

―――. *I Love My Body.* New York: Coleman Publishing, 1985.

Hayes, Patricia and Marshall Smith. *Extension of Life: Arthur Ford Speaks.* Roswell, GA: Dimensional Brotherhood Publishing House, 1986.

*Heller, Rachel F., Dr., and Heller, Richard F., Dr. *Carbohydrate Addicts Diet.* New York: A. Dutton, 1991.

Hendin, Herbert M.D. *Suicide in America.* New York: W. W. Norton & Co., 1982.

Hewett, John H. *After Suicide.* Philadelphia: Westminister Press, 1980.
Holzer, Hans. *Life After Death: The Challenge and the Evidence.* Indianapolis: Bobbs-Merrill Co., 1969.

Hyde, Margaret O. *Suicide: The Hidden Epidemic.* New York: F. Watts, 1986.

James, John W. and Frank Cherry. *The Grief Recovery Handbook: A Step by Step Program for Moving Beyond Loss.* New York: Harper & Row, 1988.

Jampolsky, Gerald G., M.D. *Goodbye To Guilt.* New York: Bantam, 1985.

————. *Love Is Letting Go Of Fear.* Millbrae, CA: Celestial Arts, 1979.

*Janda, Louis H., Dr. and Ellen MacCormack. *The Second Time Around: Why Some Second Marriages Fail While Others Succeed.* New York: Lyle Stuart Books, Published by Carol Publishing Group, 1991.

Joan, Polly. *Preventing Teenage Suicide: The Living Alternative Handbook.* New York: Human Sciences Press, Inc., 1986.

Johnson, Christopher J., Ph.D., and Marsha G. McGee, Ph.D. *Encounters With Eternity: Religious Views of Death and Life After Death.* New York: Philosophical Library, 1986.

Johnson, Debbie. *How to Love Yourself.* Portland: Deborah Johnson Publishing, 1988.

————. *How to Make Your Dreams Come True.* Portland: Deborah Johnson Publishing, 1989.

*Johnson, Robert. *We: Understanding the Psychology of Romantic Love.* San Francisco: Harper & Row, 1983.

*Johnston, Jerry. *Why Suicide? What Parents and Teachers Must Know to Save Our Kids.* Nashville: Oliver-Nelson Books, 1987.

Kastenbaum, Robert. *Is There Life After Death?* New York: Prentice Hall, 1984.

Kelsey, Morton T. *Afterlife: The Other Side of Dying.* New York: Paulist Press, 1979.

*Klagsbrun, Francine. *Too Young to Die, Youth and Suicide.* New York: Pocket Books, 1976.

Kramer, Kenneth. *The Sacred Art of Dying: How World Religions Understand Death.* New York: Paulist Press, 1988.

*Kubler-Ross, Elisabeth. *On Death and Dying.* New York: Macmillan, 1969.

*————. *On Children and Death.* New York: MacMillan, 1983.

————. *Death: The Final Stage of Growth.* Englewood Cliffs, NJ: Prentice Hall, Inc. 1975.

————. *Questions and Answers On Death and Dying.* New York: MacMillan, 1974.

Kung, Hans. *Eternal Life After Death as a Medical, Philosophical and Theological Problem.* New York: Doubleday, 1984.

Kushner, Harold S. *When Bad Things Happen to Good People.* New York: Avon Books, 1981.

Laddon, Judy. *Beyond the Veil.* California: ACS Publications, 1987.

Lake, Dr. Tony. *Living with Grief.* London: Sheldon Press, 1989.

Leder, Jane Mersky. *Dead Serious.* New York: Atheneum, 1987.

Leogrande, Ernest. *Second Chance to Live: The Suicide Syndrome.* New York: DaCapo Press, 1975.

Lester, David, Ph.D. *Why People Kill Themselves: A 1980s Summary of Research Findings on Suicidal Behavior.* Springfield, IL: Charles C. Thomas Publishers.

Lester, Gene and David Lester. *Suicide: The Gamble with Death.* New Jersey: Prentice-Hall, 1971.

Leszcynski, Janna. *A Time To Grieve, A Time To Dance.* Evergreen and Janet A. Leszcynski, Publishers, 1983.

Levine, Stephen. *Meetings at the Edge.* New York: Anchor Press, Doubleday, 1984.

Lewis, C.S. *The Screwtape Letters.* New York: MacMillan, 1961.

*Loehr, Franklin. *Diary After Death.* New York: Pillar Books, 1976.

Lorimer, David. *Survival?* London: Routledge and Kegan, 1984.

Lubetkin, Barry and Elena Oumano. *Bailing Out: The Healthy Way to Get Out of A Bad Relationship and Survive.* New York: Prentice Hall, 1991.

Lukas, Christopher and Henry M. Seiden, Ph.D. *Silent Grief: Living in the Wake of Suicide.* New York: MacMillan, 1987.

Lum, Doman. *Responding to Suicidal Crisis: For Church and Community.* Grand Rapids, MI: William B. Eerdmans Publishing Co., 1974.

Lund, David H. *Death and Consciousness: The Case for Life After Death.* New York: Ballantine Books, 1985.

Lundberg, Jean Pancer and Derek Lloyd Lundberg. *Teenage Suicide In America: A Handbook For Understanding.* Dayton, OH: P.P.I. Publishing, 1985.

*McCoy, Kathleen. *Coping with Teenage Depression*. New York: NAL Penguin Books, 1982.

McCulloch, J. Wallace and Alistair E. Philip. *Suicidal Behaviour*. New York: Pergamon Press, 1972.

McIntosh, John L. *Research on Suicide: A Bibliography*. Westport, CT: Greenwood Press, 1985.

————, ed. *Suicide and Its Aftermath: Understanding and Counseling the Survivors*. New York: Norton, 1987.

Mack, John E, and Holly Hickler. *Vivienne: The Life and Suicide of an Adolescent Girl*. Boston: Little, Brown & Co., 1981.

MacLaine, Shirley. *Out On A Limb*. New York: Bantam, 1983.

Madison, Arnold. *Suicide and Young People*. New York: Clarion Books, 1978.

Mandell, Marshall, M.D. *5-Day Allergy Relief System*. New York: Pocket Books, 1979.

Mandell, Marshall, M.D. and Fran Gare Mandell, M.S. *The Mandells' It's Not Your Fault You're Fat Diet*. New York: Signet Books, 1983.

Mandino, Og. *The Greatest Secret In The World*. New York: Bantam, 1972.

Mannes, Mary. *Last Rights*. New York: William Morrow and Co., 1974.

Maris, Ronald W. *Pathways to Suicide: A Survey of Self-Destructive Behaviors*. Baltimore: Johns Hopkins University Press.

Martin, Joel, and Patricia Romanowski. *We Don't Die: George Anderson's Conversations With The Other Side*. New York: Berkley Books, 1988.

Meaker, M.J. *Sudden Endings*. New York: Doubleday, 1964.

Meek, George W. *After We Die, What Then?* Columbus, OH: Ariel Press, 1987.

*Mellody, Pia with Andrea Wells Miller, and J. Keith Miller. *Facing Codependence*. New York: Harper & Row, 1989.

————. *Facing Love Addiction: Giving Yourself the Power to Change the Way You Love*. San Francisco: Harper & Row, 1992.

————. *Breaking Free: A Recovery Workbook for Facing Codependence*. San Francisco: Harper & Row, 1989.

Mitchell, Edgar. *Psychic Exploration*. New York: G. P. Putnam's Sons, 1974.

Monahan, Evelyn. *The Miracle of Metaphysical Healing.* West Nyack, NY: Parker Publishing Co., 1975.

*Monroe, Robert A. *Journeys Out Of The Body.* New York: Anchor Books, 1977.

*Montgomery, Ruth. *A Search for the Truth.* New York: Bantam, 1967.

————. *Here and Hereafter.* New York: Fawcett Crest Books, 1968.

————. *The World Before.* New York: Fawcett Crest Books, 1976.

————. *A World Beyond.* New York: Fawcett Crest Books, 1971.

*Moody, Raymond A. Jr. M.D. *Life After Life.* New York: Bantam, 1975.

————. *Reflections on Life After Life.* New York: Bantam, 1978.

————. *The Light Beyond.* New York: Bantam, 1988.

*Morse, Melvin, M.D. *Closer to the Light: Learning from the Near-Death Experiences of Children.* New York: Villard Books, Division of Random House, 1990.

Munsch, Robert. *Love You Forever.* Canada: Firefly Books, Ltd., 1986.

Myers, John. *Voices from the Edge of Eternity.* Spire Books Pyramid Publications, 1968.

*Norwood, Robin.*Women Who Love Too Much: When you Keep Wishing and Hoping He'll Change.* New York: Pocket Books, 1985.

————. *Letters from Women Who Love Too Much: A Closer Look at Relationship Addiction and Recovery.* New York: Pocket Books, 1988.

O'Connor, Nancy, Ph.D. *Letting Go With Love: The Grieving Process.* Apache Junction, AZ: La Mariposa Press, 1984.

Osis, Karlis Ph.D. and Erlendur Haraldsson, Ph.D. *At the Hour of Death: The Results of Research On Over 1,000 Afterlife Experiences.* New York: Avon Books, 1977.

Pearson, Linnea, with Ruth Purtilo. *Separate Paths: Why People End Their Lives.* San Francisco: Harper & Row, 1977.

Peck, F. Scott. *People of the Lie: The Hope for Healing Human Evil.* New York: Simon & Schuster, 1983.

————. *The Road Less Traveled.* New York: Touchtone, 1978.

Pederson, Duane and Helen Kooiman. *Going Sideways: Hope, Love, Life versus Suicide.* New York: Hawthorn Books, 1974.

Pelgrin, Mark. *And A Time To Die.* Wheaton, IL: Theosophical Publishing House, 1962.

Pelletier, Kenneth R. *Mind As Healer, Mind As Slayer.* New York: Delta Publishing Co., 1977.

Philpott, William H., M.D. and Dwight K. Kalita, Ph.D. *Brain Allergies: The Psychonutrient Connection.* New Canaan, CT: Keats Pub., Inc., 1980.

Pike, James A. Bishop. *The Other Side.* New York: Doubleday, 1968.

Pincus, Lily. *Death and the Family: The Importance of Mourning.* New York: Pantheon Books, 1974.

Plath, Sylvia. *The Bell Jar.* New York: Bantam, 1972.

Poems That Touch The Heart. Garden City, New York: Doubleday, 1956.

Portwood, Doris. *Common Sense Suicide: The Final Right.* New York: Dodd, Mead & Co., 1978.

*Puryear, Herbert Bruce, Ph.D. *The Edgar Cayce Primer: Discovering The Path to Self-Transformation.* New York: Bantam, 1982.

———. *Sex and the Spiritual Path.* New York: Bantam, 1980.

———. *Reflections on the Path.* New York: Bantam, 1986.

———. *Meditation and the Mind of Man.* Virginia Beach, VA: A.R.E. Press, 1978.

———. *Day by Day: Steps to a New Life.* Virginia Beach, VA: A.R.E. Press, 1981.

*———. *Why Jesus Taught Reincarnation: A Better News Gospel.* Scottsdale, AZ: New Paradigm Press, 1993.

Quinnett, Paul G. *Suicide: The Forever Decision.* New York: Continuum Publishing Co., 1987.

*Rabkin, Brenda. *Growing Up Dead: A Hard Look At Why Adolescents Commit Suicide.* Nashville: Parthenon Press, 1978.

Rauscher, William V. *The Case Against Suicide.* New York: St. Martin's Press, 1981.

Raudive, Konstantin. *Breakthrough: An Amazing Experiment in Electronic Communication with the Dead.* New York: Lancer Books, Inc., 1971.

Rawlings, Maurice, M.D. *Beyond Death's Door.* Canada: Thomas Nelson, 1978.

Reynolds, David K. and Norman L. Farberow. *The Family Shadow: Sources of Suicide and Schizophrenia.* Berkeley: University of California Press, 1981.

Richelieu, Peter. *A Soul's Journey.* Wellingbrough, England: Turnstone Press Ltd., 1972.

Ridall, Kathryn, Ph.D. *Channeling: How to Reach Out to Your Spirit Guides.* New York: Bantam, 1988.

Ring, Kenneth, Ph.D. *Life at Death: A Scientific Investigation of the Near-Death Experience.* New York: Quill, 1982.

*Ritchie, George G., Jr. with Elizabeth Sherrill. *Return from Tomorrow.* New York: Fleming H. Revell Company, 1978.

*Robbins, Anthony. *Unlimited Power.* New York: Fawcett Columbine, 1986.

————. *Awaken the Giant Within.* New York: Summit Books, 1991.

Robinson, Rita. *Survivors of Suicide.* California: IBS Press, 1989.

Rosenberg, Jay F. *Thinking Clearly About Death.* New Jersey: Prentice-Hall, 1982.

Rosenfeld, Linda and Marilynne Prupas. *Left Alive: After A Suicide Death In the Family.* Springfield, IL: Charles C. Thomas, 1984.

Roy, Alec. *Suicide.* Baltimore: Williams and Wilkins, 1986.

Rudolph, Marguerita. *Should the Children Know? Encounters with Death in the Lives of Children.* New York: Schocken Books, 1978.

*Russell, A.J., ed. *God Calling.* New York: Dodd, Mead and Co., 1978.

*————. *God at Eventide.* New York: Dodd, Mead and Co., 1978.
Russell, Robert A. *Dry Those Tears.* Marina del Rey, CA: DeVorss & Co., 1951.

St. Johns, Adele Rogers. *No Goodbyes: My Research Into Life Beyond Death.* McGraw Hill, 1981.

*Sanderfur, Glenn: *Lives of the Master: The Rest of the Jesus Story.* Virginia Beach: VA: A.R.E. Press, 1988.

*Schiff, Harriet Sarnoff. *Living Through Mourning: Finding Comfort and Hope When A Loved One Has Died.* New York: Viking Penguin, 1987.

*————. *The Bereaved Parent.* New York: Crown Publishers, 1977.

*Schneider, Jennifer P., M.D. *Back from Betrayal: Recovering from His Affairs*. San Francisco: Harper/Hazelden, 1988.

Schneider, Jennifer P., M.D. and Burt Schneider. *Sex, Lies and Forgiveness: Couples Speaking Out on Healing from Sex Addiction* New York: Hazelden Book, 1990.

Scott, Donald, Dr. *Coping with Suicide*. London: Sheldon Press, 1989.

Seigel, Bernie S. *Love, Medicine and Miracles*. New York: Harper & Row, 1986.

*Shamoo, Tonia K. and Philip Patros. *I Want To Kill Myself: Helping Your Child Cope With Depression and Suicidal Thoughts*. Lexington, MA: Lexington Books, 1990.

Sheban, Joseph, (ed.). *Wisdom of Gibran*. New York: Philosophical Library, 1966.

Shneidman, Edwin S., Ph.D., Normal L. Farberow, Ph.D., Robert E. Litman, M.D. *The Psychology of Suicide*. New York: Science House, Inc., 1976.

―――――. *Essays in Self Destruction*. New York: Science House, Inc., 1967.

Sherman, Harold. *You Live After Death*. Greenwich, CT: Fawcett Gold Medal, 1972.

*―――――. *The Dead are Alive: They Can and Do Communicate With You*. Greenwich, CT: Fawcett Gold Medal, 1981.

Sikking, Robert P. *A Matter of Life and Death*. Marina del Rey, CA: DeVorss & Co., 1978.

Smith, Alson J. *Immortality: The Scientific Evidence*. New Jersey: Prentice-Hall, 1954.

*Smith, Judie. *Suicide Prevention: A Crisis Intervention Curriculum for Teenagers and Young Adults*. Holmes Beach, FL: Learning Publications, 1989.

Smith, Lendon. *Food for Healthy Kids*. New York: Berkley Books, 1984.

―――――. *Improving Your Child's Behavior Chemistry*. New York: Pocket Books, 1976.

―――――. *Feed Your Kids Right*. New York: Delta Book, 1979.

Smith, Manuel J., Ph.D. *When I Say No, I Feel Guilty*. New York: Bantam, 1975.

Smith, Susy. *Life is Forever: Evidence for Survival After Death.* New York: Putnam, 1974.

————. *How To Develop Your ESP.* New York: G.P. Putman's Sons, 1972.

————. *Voices of the Dead?* New York: Signet, 1974.

Stark, Harold Richter. *A Doctor Goes to Heaven.* Boerne, TX: Quartus Foundation For Spiritual Research, 1982.

*Stead, Estelle and W. T. Stead. *The Blue Island: Experiences of a New Arrival Beyond the Veil.* Washington, D.C.: ESPress, 1971.

Steadman, Alice. *Who's The Matter With Me?* Marina del Rey, CA: DeVorss & Co., 1981.

Stearn, Jess. *Edgar Cayce: The Sleeping Prophet.* New York: Doubleday, 1967.

Steiger, Brad. *You Will Live Again.* New York: Dell Publishing Co., 1978.

*Stevenson, Ian, M.D. *Twenty Cases Suggestive of Reincarnation.* New York: American Society for Psychical Research, 1966.

Storkey, Elaine. *Losing a Child.* Oxford, England: A Lion Book, 1989.

*Sugrue, Thomas. *There is A River.* New York: Holt, Rinehart and Winston, 1942.

Swain, Jasper. *From My World To Yours.* New York: Walker & Co., 1977.

Thurman, Chris, Dr. *The Lies We Believe: The #1 Cause of Our Unhappiness.* Nashville: Thomas Nelson, 1989.

Veninga, Robert. *A Gift of Hope: How We Survive Our Tragedies.* Boston: Little, Brown and Company, 1985.

Viorst, Judith. *Necessary Losses.* New York: Fawcett Gold Medal, Ballantine, 1986.

Waitley, Denis. *Seeds of Greatness.* New York: Pocket Books, 1984.

————. *The Psychology of Winning: Ten Qualities of a Total Winner.* New York: Berkley Books, 1979.

Walker, Jeanne. *Always Karen.* New York: Hawthorn Books, 1975.

Wambach, Helen, Ph.D. *Life Before Life.* New York: Bantam, 1981.

Weatherhead, Leslie D. *Life Begins at Death.* Nashville: Denholm House Press, Abingdon, Festival Books, 1969.

Wechsler, James A. *In A Darkness.* Miami: Pickering Press, 1988.

Weedn, Flavia. *Softly In Silver Sandals.* Carpinteria, CA: Roserich Designs, Ltd., 1985.

Wekstein, Louis. *Handbook of Suicidology.* New York: Brunner/Mazel, 1979.

Welch, Williams Addams. *Talks with the Dead.* New York: Pinnacle Books, 1975.

Wetzl, Joseph. *The Bridge Over The River.* New York: The Anthroposophic Press, 1974.

Whitaker, Terry Cole. *What You Think of Me is None of My Business.* La Jolla, CA: Oak Tree Publications, Inc., 1979.

White, John. *A Practical Guide to Death and Dying.* Wheaton, IL: Quest, Theosophical Publishing House, 1980.

*White, Stewart Edward. *The Unobstructed Universe: An Unparalleled Detailed Report of Life After Death.* New York: E.P. Dutton and Co., 1940.

————.*The Betty Book: Excursions Into the World of Other-Consciousness.* New York: Berkley Publishing Corp., 1937.

*White-Bowden, Susan. *Everything To Live For.* New York: Simon & Schuster, 1985.

*Whitton, Joel, M.D., Ph.D. *Life Between Life.* New York: Warner Books, 1986.

Wickland, Carl A., M.D. *30 Years Among the Dead.* Hollywood, CA: Newcastle Publishing Co., 1974.

Wilkerson, David R. *Suicide.* Old Tappan, New Jersey: Spire Books by World Challenge, Inc. & Fleming H. Revell, 1978.

Wood, Edward Cope. *A Personal Testimony to Life After Death.* Philadelphia: Dorrance & Co., 1963.

Wright, Theon. *The Open Door.* New York: John Day Co., 1970.

Yogananda, Paramahansa. *Autobiography of a Yogi.* Los Angeles: Self-Realization Fellowship Publishers, 1973.

*Youngs, Bettie B. *Stress in Children.* New York: Avon Books, 1985.

Zusman, Jack, M.D. and David L. Davidson, M.D. *Organizing the Community to Prevent Suicide.* Springfield, IL: Charles C. Thomas, 1971.

Recommended Audio and Video Tapes:

Puryear, Anne. *Coping with Suicide.* Audio tape. Logos Center, P.O. Box 12880, Scottsdale, AZ 85267-2880, (602) 483-8777.

Puryear, Anne and Herbert Bruce Puryear, Ph.D. *The Psychic & The Psychologist Present: The Millennium Tapes, A Series of Psychic Answers to Life's Most Often Asked Questions.* Audio tapes. Logos Center, P.O. Box 12880, Scottsdale, AZ 85267-2880, (602) 483-8777.

Robbins, Tony. *Personal Power Tapes: A 30-Day Program for Unlimited Success.* Audio and video tapes. Robbins Research International, Inc., 9191 Towne Centre Drive, Suite 600, San Diego, CA 92122, (800)445-8183.

————. *The Anthony Robbins Vital Life Series: The Body You Deserve!* Audio and video tapes. Robbins Research International, Inc., 9191 Towne Centre Drive, Suite 600, San Diego, CA 92122, (800) 445-8183.

Smalley, Gary. *Hidden Keys to Successful Parenting.* Video seminars. Relationships Today, Inc., Phoenix, AZ, (800) 232-3232.

————. *Hidden Keys to Loving Relationships.* Video seminars. Relationships Today, Inc., Phoenix, AZ, (800) 232-3232.

Recommended Movies:

"Permanent Record," "Ghost, " "Always," "Resurrection," "Ordinary People," "Flatliners," "Chances Are,""On A Clear Day You Can See Forever," "Defending Your Life," "The Butcher's Wife," "The Dead Poet's Society," "Dead Again"

Organizations To Contact for Help or Further Study:

Logos Center; Logos Interfaith Church, Meditation and Learning Center; Logos World University Foundation & Church, Inc., P.O. Box 12880, Scottsdale, AZ 85267-2880, (602) 483-8777. Classes, world tours, lectures, and workshops nationally and internationally, interfaith services, healing services, children's programs, groups in New York/Connecticut and Oahu, Hawaii.

Rosicrucians, Rosicrucian Park, San Jose, California. Publications, activities throughout the country. Correspondence study course.

Spiritual Frontiers Fellowship, Inc. 10819 Winner Road, Independence, Missouri 64052. Quarterly publication, conferences, groups throughout the country. Excellent speakers and activities.

Unity School of Christianity, Unity Village, Missouri 64065. For prayers write Silent Unity at same address, or call (816) 246-5400. For an urgent prayer need and no means of paying for the call, dial toll-free, 800-669-7729. Unity offers publications for adults and children, and a ministerial training program. Churches in many cities.

Self Realization Fellowship, 3880 San Rafael Avenue, Los Angeles, California 90065. Founded in 1925 by Paramahansa Yogananda. Literature and courses available on Yogananda's teachings. Centers in many cities.

Guideposts, P.O. Box 856, Carmel, New York 10512-9970. Magazine founded by Norman Vincent Peale, who also publishes *Plus: The Magazine of Positive Thinking*. Foundation for Christian Living, P.O. Box FCL, Pawling, New York 12654. Excellent non-denominational spiritual publications.

Science of Mind, United Church of Religious Science, P.O. Box 75127, Los Angeles, California 90075. Ministerial training, publications, and churches in many cities.

Astara, founded by Robert and Earlyne Chaney, 800 West Arrow Highway, Upland, California 91786. Excellent correspondence study course in the esoteric teachings. Seminars, world tours, on-campus activities. Well worth a visit.

A.R.E., P.O. Box 595, Virginia Beach, Virginia 23451. Membership which enables borrowing of the Edgar Cayce readings called "Circulating Files." Lectures and workshops throughout the country, mail order bookstore, Search for God study groups.

Iands: International Association for Near-Death Studies, Inc., 638 Prospect Avenue, Hartford, CT 06105, (203) 232-4825. Kenneth Ring, Ph.D., Co-Founder.

Kubler-Ross Center, South Route 616, Head Waters, Virginia 24442, 703-396-3444. Expert on death and dying. Author of many books on the subject. Retreat center, classes, newspaper.

Monroe Institute of Applied Science, Rt. 1, Box 175, Faber, VA, 22938, (804) 361-1500. Robert Monroe, Founder. Classes, training and workshops in altered states of consciousness. Video tapes, literature.

Twelve-Step Programs. Alcoholics Anonymous begun by Bill W. Groups and meetings in most cities. Dozens of 12-Step programs for drug addictions, food addictions, relationship addiction, adultery addictions. The phone directory or operators in most cities have a listing under Twelve-Step, Alcoholics Anonymous, or Self Help groups.

ABOUT THE AUTHOR

Anne Puryear is an author, lecturer, minister, and vice-president and co-founder of the Logos Center in Phoenix, Arizona. Her psychic work has earned her international recognition as one of the most helpful, hopeful, motivating, and life-changing spiritual counselors in the country.

Her life readings have been a source of help and hope for thousands of people over the last twenty years. Her work in an altered state is very much like that of Edgar Cayce. Anne's ability to see auras and to discern energy blockages in the subtle bodies brings an extraordinarily helpful dimension to her counseling and diagnostic work.

Her husband, Herbert Bruce Puryear, Ph.D., who conducts all of her readings, is a psychologist, minister, and author. He is also a Bible scholar and an expert on the Edgar Cayce readings. Dr. Puryear is President and co-director of Logos Center, which is comprised of an Interfaith Church, an Educational Division, and a Holistic Healing Division. They share the pulpit each Sunday at Logos Center and co-host the televised series, "The Psychic and the Psychologist."

Anne spent four years as Director of the Department of Spiritual Healing at the A.R.E. Medical Clinic, The Medical Research Division of the Edgar Cayce Foundation. There she taught classes and gave life readings for patients in special medical programs. After that, she became a co-founder of the Center for Life Guidance in Phoenix.

She wrote a newspaper column for five years, and her articles have appeared in numerous publications. Her psychic work and research with children has appeared in national publications, books, videos, and movies. She has worked with doctors, educators, and health care professionals around the world, and has appeared frequently on radio and television.

Her spiritual journey of psychic work and amazing experiences began in 1972. After reading Ruth Montgomery's book, "Search for the Truth," Anne had a series of illuminating experiences. After two open vision encounters with Jesus one evening, she was able to use her intuition in profoundly helpful and healing ways, and to develop her strong empathic abilities.

Anne has talked to God since she was a child. But she has also *listened* to God speak to her. She can often see angels and commune with them, and in her meditations, has daily conversations with her spirit plane helpers.

Anne is deeply committed to bringing to the world a greater understanding of teenage suicide and life after death. After the death of her son Stephen in 1974, she began a search to understand his suicide. She has become an expert on the subject through her studies of both the scientific and esoteric research on suicide and life after death.

Her humorous, deeply personal, and challenging presentations have captivated audiences throughout the world. Her writing reflects the same humor, honesty, enthusiasm, and charisma that characterize her lectures, sermons, and workshops.

Anne is also an artist, a certified scuba diver, a camper and canoeist, and is an avid reader and researcher. She and her husband live in Scottsdale, Arizona and her three children and four grandchildren live close by. She is currently writing several other books, dealing with suicide, grief, psychic development, and spiritual inspiration.

• • •

Anne would love to hear from you. She invites you to write and share any of your personal experiences such as: visions; communications; how you have handled your grief; helpful insights about your children or loved ones who have died by suicide or natural causes; "near death experiences"; or, if you have considered suicide and decided to choose life instead.

If you would consider sharing these for possible inclusion in one of the books she is currently writing, with or without your name being used, please indicate this in your correspondence.

BOOKS, TAPES, VIDEOS, AND LECTURES WITH ANNE & HERB PURYEAR

Anne and Herb Puryear's books, tapes, and videos are available through the Logos Center.

Their 24-tape series, **The Psychic and the Psychologist Present The Millenium Tapes: A Series of Psychic Answers to Life's Most Often Asked Questions**, is available from the Bookstore at Logos.

If you wish to be notified when Anne and Herb Puryear are **lecturing or presenting workshops in your area**, or to schedule them for speaking engagements for your organization, please call or write:

Logos Center
P.O. Box 12880
Scottsdale, Arizona 85267-2880

Telephone: 602-483-8777
Fax Number: 602-483-8494

ORDER FORM

To : NEW PARADIGM PRESS,
P.O. BOX 12880, SCOTTSDALE, AZ 85267
Or call 602-483-8777

Please send _____ copies of *Stephen Lives!*
I am enclosing $14.95 plus $2.00 postage & handling
for each copy.

Subtotal ($14.95 x no. of copies)   _____
Arizona residents add 6.7% sales tax   _____
Handling and postage not to exceed
   $8.00 if all copies are to same address _____
Add $ .50 each for air mail   _____

Total amount   _____

❑ Check   ❑ Money Order
❑ VISA   ❑ MasterCard   ❑ American Express
Card Number _____ Expiration Date _____
Signature _____

Send _____ copy(ies) to:
NAME _____
ADDRESS _____
CITY, STATE , ZIP_____
NOTE:

Send gift copy(ies) to:
NAME _____
ADDRESS _____
CITY, STATE , ZIP_____
NOTE:

NAME _____
ADDRESS _____
CITY, STATE, ZIP _____
NOTE:

ORDER FORM

To : NEW PARADIGM PRESS,
P.O. BOX 12880, SCOTTSDALE, AZ 85267
Or call 602-483-8777

Please send _____ copies of *Stephen Lives!*
I am enclosing $14.95 plus $2.00 postage & handling
for each copy.

Subtotal ($14.95 x no. of copies)   _____
Arizona residents add 6.7% sales tax   _____
Handling and postage not to exceed
   $8.00 if all copies are to same address   _____
Add $ .50 each for air mail   _____

Total amount   _____

❑ Check   ❑ Money Order
❑ VISA   ❑ MasterCard   ❑ American Express
Card Number _____   Expiration Date _____
Signature _____

Send _____ copy(ies) to:
NAME _____
ADDRESS _____
CITY, STATE , ZIP_____
NOTE:

Send gift copy(ies) to:
NAME _____
ADDRESS _____
CITY, STATE , ZIP_____
NOTE:

NAME _____
ADDRESS _____
CITY, STATE, ZIP _____
NOTE: